National Hockey League
75th Anniversary
Commemorative Book

THE OFFICIAL

National Hockey League
75th Anniversary
Commemorative Book

Edited by
Dan Diamond

FIREFLY BOOKS

A FIREFLY BOOK

Copyright © 1991 The National Hockey League and Dan Diamond and Associates, Inc.

Cataloguing in Publication Data
Main entry under title:
The Official National Hockey League 75th anniversary commemorative book
Includes index
ISBN 0-7710-6727-5 (bound)
1. National Hockey League – History.   I. Diamond, Dan.
GV847.8 N3044 1991   796.962'64   C91-095081-4

First published by McClelland & Stewart, Inc., Toronto, Canada
This edition printed 1994

Editor: Dan Diamond
Photo Editor: Ralph Dinger
Research and Captions: James Duplacey
Research: Joseph Romain
Additional Research: Pastor G. Goodhand
Main Text: Wayne Lilley, Charles Wilkins, Stu Hackel, James Duplacey, Dan Diamond
Sidebars: Gary Meagher
Index: Igor Kuperman
Photo Finishing: Doug MacLellan
Coordinating Editor: Pat Kennedy, for McClelland & Stewart
Design: Martin Gould

Printed and bound in the United States of America on acid-free paper.

Firefly Books (U.S.) Inc.
P.O. Box 1338
Ellicott Station
Buffalo, N.Y.
14205

*For players, fans, and
everyone who cares for the game*

Contents

Four league presidents have guided the National Hockey League since its inception in 1917. In this photo, Mervyn "Red" Dutton (right), president from 1943 to 1946, congratulates newly appointed president Clarence Campbell, who served in the position until 1977, when he was succeeded by John A. Ziegler, Jr. The league's founding president, Frank Calder, can be seen in the framed photograph on the wall between Dutton and Campbell. All four NHL presidents were acknowledged by the league's board of governors when, in 1985, it commissioned the Presidents' Trophy (at left), which is awarded annually to the team finishing with the greatest number of points in regular-season play.

A Message
from the President

I have a very special privilege. It is my honor to introduce this written and pictorial kaleidoscope of three-quarters of a century of the National Hockey League.

Our 75th Anniversary brings into sharp focus the extraordinary achievements of players, teams, coaches, officials, managers, and owners who have made the NHL the premier hockey league in the world. We pay tribute to them all. We are humbled and grateful for what they have done for all of us – fans of the game of hockey.

This anniversary is an occasion for appreciation and thanks, especially to our fans for their love of the game. It is our fans and our players who are the backbone of this league and will continue to be the basis of our growth in the future.

I hope you will, as I have, enjoy this book as it explores the National Hockey League's rich heritage. As we start the final lap towards a century of NHL hockey, please join with all of us in this celebration of our 75th birthday.

Sincerely,
John A. Ziegler, Jr.
President,
National Hockey League

Introduction

by Red Fisher

HOCKEY IS MAGIC TO THE EYE AND TO THE EMOTIONS. ONE MOMENT, IT is little more than ordered peace, the only sound being the gentle hissing of a puck feathering from one stick to another with lemming-like instinct. An instant later, it flares into drama.

Drama is the National Hockey League, still growing and with a bounce in its step at age seventy-five. It is, as the words and photos in these pages will show, a marriage of past and present, with the promise of a bigger and better future.

Hockey is change.

Once, it was the blinding speed and soaring talent of a Howie Morenz at center-ice, and the cold, unflinching menace of an Eddie Shore on defense. It was Joe Malone and Newsy Lalonde and the Cleghorns. And Lester Patrick, scion of the family that has earned a permanent place for itself in the game.

It was the hot, black coals of Rocket Richard's eyes as he swept in on a goaltender whenever there was a game to be won. And Gordie Howe, whose 801 goals and 1,049 assists in twenty-six seasons are the standard for everything that is good and honorable about the game wherever it is played. And why, a dozen years after his retirement at age fifty-two, Gordie remains hockey's most remarkable and illustrious role model for young and old.

Hockey is great goaltending. It is Georges Vezina and George Hainsworth. It is Frank Brimsek and Terry Sawchuk. It is Bill Durnan, Glenn Hall, and Jacques Plante. It is Ken Dryden.

Hockey is Bobby Orr. Was there ever a player like him before or since he burst on the game like a flaming, runaway comet at the age of eighteen in the 1966-67 season? With Orr, the show began the instant he hunched over and cradled the puck on the blade of his stick. A shake of his head, a jiggle of his shoulders, and he was skating at full speed. He flew past one man, then another with the swift, powerful strides of youth as the crowd roared with one voice. The stick flashed, the goalie kicked desperately at the puck – and

Opposite: Gordie Howe, shown here early in his career, would become the NHL's most durable performer and its first 800-goal scorer.

This fan's photo, taken from behind the St. Louis net on May 10, 1970, freezes the action as Bobby Orr's overtime goal hangs in the mesh and brings Boston its first Stanley Cup in twenty-nine seasons.

then there was no longer a crowd in the arena, just an explosion of noise, the same uproar that greeted most of his 270 goals.

Orr, like Howe and Morenz and Shore, set new high-water marks for the game. He was unique, just as, before him, Doug Harvey was blessed with a matchless style. Harvey didn't merely play the game: he controlled it.

Hockey is an amalgam of many things: Bobby Hull's booming shot, the electricity of a Guy Lafleur in full flight, golden mane flying. It is the purity of Mike Bossy's 573 goals in 752 games.

It is the caring, whole and constant, whether it's for a team or a teammate, or for the rich rewards set aside for champions.

It is Phil Esposito, who will be remembered forever as much for one magical series as he will be for his 717 goals in 18 seasons.

There has never been a series to match it before or since: it was 1972 and the National Hockey League's most proficient players (Team Canada) were facing the Soviet Union's best. The first four games took place in Canada, the remaining four in Moscow, in a series the NHL's stars were supposed to win easily. But Team Canada was trailing the eight-game series 1–3–1 by the beginning of the third-last game. They had also trailed 5–3 going into the third period of game eight, which wasn't decided until Paul Henderson scored his famous goal with 34 seconds remaining.

Hockey is Bobby Clarke and the Philadelphia Flyers, an expansion team which was to win the first of two consecutive Stanley Cups only seven seasons after entering the league.

It is Wayne Gretzky rewriting the record book, starting in the 1979-80 season when he led the Edmonton Oilers into the NHL. Only five years later,

he was to lead them to the first of four Stanley Cups that the Oilers were to win in the next five seasons.

Hockey is coaches such as Lester Patrick, Jack Adams, Dick Irvin, Toe Blake, Punch Imlach, and Scotty Bowman. Each had his own style, but all were dedicated to winning. Anything less was unacceptable.

Hockey is many things to many people. It is only a game, but at times it approaches life itself. Love it or hate it, the reality is that millions are touched by it.

Almost four decades have passed since I welcomed hockey into my life. Since then, much about it has changed. The NHL has expanded from the four teams that operated in its first year, 1917, to twenty-two teams in 1991-92. It will blossom to twenty-four in time for the 1992-93 season, and to twenty-eight by the turn of the century.

Rules have changed. Equipment has improved. Training methods have been tuned and honed. The players have become bigger, stronger, faster, and better. Only the love affair with hockey remains constant.

Hockey is the warmth of memories. Any fan who saw the Henderson goal in 1972 can recall the pure and soaring joy it produced.

Hockey is remembering a playoff game in Chicago in 1961. The Blackhawks (they were the Black Hawks then) were only 17 seconds away from a 1–0 victory when Montreal's Henri Richard scored from a faceoff beside the Chicago net. Another 52 minutes and 12 seconds of gut-wrenching overtime passed before Chicago scored while Canadiens' left winger Dickie Moore was serving a hooking penalty.

The Toronto Maple Leafs and Boston Bruins in Maple Leaf Gardens, circa 1941. Wooden-slatted boards, chicken-wire protective screens, and an absence of lines on the ice characterize the pre-war NHL.

Hockey is the New York Islanders and the Washington Capitals setting a modern-day record of 68:47 overtime minutes before Pat LaFontaine scored to end the game and clinch the series for the Islanders.

It is mental anguish, and the way players react to it. Moore, for example. He was a proud player, who had stoked the fire within him to two consecutive scoring titles in 1958 and 1959 – one of them even though his wrist was encased in a cast for the last half of the season. Now, though, his career was winding down and he was sitting on the bench a lot. Too much, he felt.

He knocked on my hotel door in Chicago a few days before Christmas. "Do you know what time it is?" I asked. "It's two in the morning."

"I'm going home," he said. "I can't take this any more."

"You mean you're quitting? Is that it?"

"I can't sit on the bench any more," he said. "What's wrong with me, anyway? I've stopped scoring."

"It's pretty hard to score when you're always passing off the puck. Anyway, it doesn't matter now that you've decided to quit."

"I'll go with the team to Detroit," he grunted. "If I don't play, I'll tell them I'm through."

Two nights later, Moore was in the starting line-up. Henri Richard won the opening faceoff and slid the puck back to him. One stride this side of the center-ice line, Moore lashed a shot at Terry Sawchuk. Goal! Moore skated to the boards and waved his stick at the press box. I waved back.

He finished the season with the Canadiens before announcing his retirement and later returned to play briefly with the Toronto Maple Leafs and the St. Louis Blues.

The game's great players, going back to Morenz and Malone and Lalonde, are blessed with immense skills and a deep-rooted belief in themselves. They give themselves wholly to the game in a way that has its finest flowering in the face of adversity.

"Giving Everything" is Gretzky taking charge in the playoffs. It is Bobby Baun being carried off the ice with a broken ankle and returning to score a goal. It is defenseman Harvey leading a Canadiens team shredded with injuries into New York. He was one of only three Montreal defensemen dressed for the game, which is why he played 51 minutes. The Canadiens won, 3–1.

Ten days later, the team learned that he had played all that time with a cracked ankle.

Hockey is Bruins' defenseman Gord Kluzak undergoing ten operations on his knee, yet persisting in his attempt to play and contribute to the team.

Hockey is great names and great teams – they have worked together to make the game from the NHL's baptismal year. Great names like those mentioned in these pages, and many more. Great dynasties such as the Montreal Canadiens, the Detroit Red Wings, the Toronto Maple Leafs, the New York Islanders, and the Edmonton Oilers.

The electrifying Maurice "Rocket" Richard, flanked here by Ken Reardon and Toe Blake, is the NHL's all-time leader in Stanley Cup overtime goals.

Wayne Gretzky surpassed Gordie Howe's career-scoring record of 1,850 points with this last-minute, game-tying goal against his former club, the Edmonton Oilers. Number 99's peerless skills as a point-producer enabled him to become the league's all-time point-scoring leader just six games into his eleventh NHL season.

They come and go, but the lingering dream and beauty of this game is that the years produce new and even greater stars. They are different, yet they have similarities. Gretzky, who dominated hockey in the eighties like no other player, would also have been an all-star in the six-team league. Morenz would have been one now. And what makes the years ahead of us even more exciting is that now, as the world becomes as small as a hockey puck and more open, the game truly has taken on global proportions.

Face it: a few years ago, who would have thought that Soviet players would skate into the 1990s wearing NHL sweaters? Who would have imagined that Europeans would be among the first to be drafted by NHL teams?

As these pages will show, The NHL's first seventy-five years were a celebration of excellence – for a small forest of reasons. Ownership and management have been strong. Fans have been remarkably loyal. Planning for the future has been exemplary.

The biggest reason, though, has been the players. Take away the quality of the players, and what's left? If talent doesn't count, what does?

The players have been the searing spirit and soul of this game since it began: They produce, direct, and choreograph the drama in their unswerving pursuit of hockey's summit. They are what hockey and, by extension, the NHL, is all about – from Morenz to Gretzky, from Shore to Orr, from Howe and Richard to Lafleur ... to all the nameless, faceless young bloods who will one day reach the summit.

It is to the players that this book is dedicated.

The 1931-32 Detroit Falcons finished third in the NHL's American Division. From left to right: Larry Aurie, Carson Cooper, Bert McInenly, Herbie Lewis, Danny Cox, unidentified, Johnny Sorrell, Ebbie Goodfellow.

Foundations

A
S THE NHL ENTERS ITS SEVENTY-FIFTH SEASON, AND WE LOOK BACK ON
its development and progress, it is tempting to think that the
history of professional hockey begins and ends with the National
Hockey League. But, in fact, even in the earliest days of the game,
club owners and managers, striving to ice the best possible hockey teams for
their communities, were known to line the pockets of both local boys and
"ringers" who could help their cause. The first unabashedly professional
team, the Portage Lakers of Houghton, Michigan, was organized in 1902,
fifteen years before the formation of the NHL.

Many of the game's first pros were players – often outsiders to a community – who were given jobs working for companies that sponsored the local
"amateur" teams for whom they played. These men frequently found something extra in their pay packets at the end of the week.

Most such teams were located in Canadian mining, lumbering, and farm-
ing towns, which in winter seldom lacked hockey's essential ingredient –
ice. Add to the scenario numerous and ferocious inter-community rivalries
and predominantly male populations of hard-rock miners, loggers, or farm
boys – all as tough as the land they worked – and a sense of the pedigree of
contemporary professional hockey emerges. By the turn of the century, even
so-called amateur hockey had become so hotly contested that it was not
unusual for players, who were much in demand, to earn more playing the
game than they did from their regular jobs.

Not surprisingly, top players soon became local and even national heroes.
By 1909, teams in the National Hockey Association and the short-lived
Canadian Hockey Association unabashedly employed professional players
such as Odie and Sprague Cleghorn, Art Ross, Edouard "Newsy" Lalonde,
Fred "Cyclone" Taylor, and Georges Vezina.

In December 1911 in Vancouver, two of these stars, brothers Lester and
Frank Patrick, already well-known in the NHA, shocked the eastern pro

*Above: These cigarette cards
pre-date the formation of the
NHL and depict some of the
game's greatest pioneer
players. From top to bottom:
Jack Laviolette, Cyclone
Taylor, Newsy Lalonde, Percy
LeSueur, and Art Ross. All
are members of the Hockey
Hall of Fame.*

*Opposite: Georges Vezina,
"the Chicoutimi Cucumber,"
never missed a game for the
Montreal Canadiens. Vezina,
who made his debut with Les
Habitants on December 31,
1910, appeared in 328 consecutive games before illness
forced him to leave a game on
November 28, 1925. He was
later diagnosed as having
tuberculosis, a disease that
claimed him before the end of
the following year.*

Founding Meeting

At the NHL's founding meeting in November 1917 at Montreal's Windsor Hotel, one of the first items of business was the dispersal of the players from the Quebec roster who had played the previous season in the National Hockey Association, the forerunner of the NHL. It was unanimously agreed by directors representing the Montreal Canadiens, the Montreal Wanderers, Ottawa, and Toronto that the Quebec players be taken over by the league at a cost of seven hundred dollars, of which 50 per cent would be paid to Quebec by the Stanley Cup champion, 30 per cent by the runner-up, and 20 per cent by the third-place team.

A pro-rated amount of $490 was eventually paid to the Quebec club, as only seven of the ten players on their roster reported to the four NHL clubs for the 1917-18 season.

Expenses for First Stanley Cup

At the NHL's first Stanley Cup playoff series, a two-game, total-goal affair between the Toronto Arenas and the Montreal Canadiens, rink rental cost $600 per game and traveling expenses ran to $300 per team. The gate receipts from the home-and-home series were divided equally between the NHL's three teams: Montreal, Toronto, and Ottawa. In a unique stipulation in this agreement, the Ottawa club was entitled to verify the gate receipts from the two-game series.

hockey establishment by announcing the formation of yet another professional league, the Pacific Coast Hockey Association. The PCHA routinely raided the NHA for players and, by 1914, operated franchises in both Canada and the United States. In fact, one of its franchises, the Seattle Metropolitans, became the first American team to win the Stanley Cup, defeating the Montreal Canadiens in a best-of-five final in 1917.

With World War I consuming Europe, many players went into the service, but the game had become so much a part of Canada's national fabric that several army units devoted themselves as much to hockey as to military matters. In 1916, the 228th Battalion, known as the Northern Fusiliers, deliberately recruited enough stars to enter a team in the NHA – a team that was in third place when its players were called up for service overseas. Clashes with the other five NHA teams over rights to players occasionally had to be settled by the highest military authorities, and chicanery wasn't unknown, even where the Forces were concerned. One player, released from his contract by his PCHA team so that he could enlist, turned up on the 228th Battalion roster – until it was discovered that he had never enlisted at all. Another player from Toronto admitted that he had enlisted with the 228th on condition that he be given an officer's commission.

In the fall of 1917, the strain of coping with player shortages caused by the war came to a head at the NHA's annual meeting of league executives and franchise owners in Montreal. A particular focus of contention was the owner of the Toronto franchise, Eddie Livingstone, who was so unpopular with the owners of the league's other franchises – the Quebec Bulldogs, the Ottawa Senators, and the Montreal-based Wanderers and Canadiens – that a plot was hatched to form a new league that would exclude him.

Even though Livingstone appeared to have sold his franchise to the owner of the Toronto arena where the team played its home games, the other owners went ahead with their plan to dissolve the old league and reform as the National Hockey League on November 22, 1917. Charter members of the newly formed NHL included the Toronto Arenas (now apparently without Livingstone), along with the four teams from Ottawa, Montreal, and Quebec.

As momentous as the event might now seem, it was probably not considered so at the time. The league fathers apparently viewed the name-change merely as a technicality initiated to rid themselves of Toronto's owner. But if the move accomplished that, it certainly didn't rid the owners of other difficulties. The financially troubled Quebec franchise, for example, failed to operate in the first year of the NHL. And before the new league began play in mid-December, the Montreal Wanderers faced financial problems as well as player shortages. The Cleghorn brothers, who were among the Wanderers' top stars, were both unable to play. Sprague had a broken leg and Odie risked losing his military exemption, which had been granted for health reasons, if he played hockey. The rest of the league tried to resolve the team's manpower problem by donating players, but shortly into the sched-

ule, a fire that started in the Wanderers' dressing room burned down the Montreal Arena – home to both Montreal teams – ending both the Wanderers' season and the franchise's existence.

Although strained, the NHL's first season of play, 1917-18, was not without humor. In a memorable Toronto–Ottawa game, for example, Arenas' player Ken Randall, who had been suspended until he paid thirty-five dollars in back fines for arguing with referees, paid part of his fine with a bag of pennies, which he put on the ice prior to the start of play. When an Ottawa Senator playfully whacked the bag with his stick, the crowd was treated to the spectacle of the cream of Canadian hockey talent scuttling around the ice to retrieve the coins so the game could begin.

(continued on p. 23)

The Montreal Wanderers of 1914. Nicknamed the Red-bands because of the characteristic scarlet stripe on their jerseys, they were the first team in Eastern Canada to number their sweaters. Inaugural members of the NHL, the Wanderers won four Stanley Cups between 1905 and 1910.

THE MAKING OF THE NHL

by Brian McFarlane

Professional hockey was in a sorry state when the National Hockey League was founded on a chill November day in 1917. Several crises had erupted during the National Hockey Association season of 1916-17, and the six-team circuit, which had been a major league since 1910, had barely survived. In an attempt to deal with the NHA's headaches, officials of the teams from Montreal (the Canadiens and the Wanderers), Ottawa, and Quebec City held several critical meetings at the Windsor Hotel in Montreal.

One major problem threatening the league's future, of course, was a blazing war taking place thousands of miles away. In 1916, at least two dozen of the NHA's top shooters (there were fewer than a hundred players in the entire league) had traded their hockey sticks for rifles and had enlisted in the Canadian armed forces.

Other players, perhaps hoping to avoid front-line service overseas, had joined the 228th Battalion of the Northern Fusiliers, which had a fine hockey team and, amazingly, a franchise to play in the NHA. No armed-forces team had ever before been permitted to play in a major professional league; it was comparable to witnessing a crack baseball team from the U.S. Marine Corps playing in the National or American League. The Battalion boys, with home ice in Toronto, created a hockey fashion "first" when they skated out to open the 1916-17 season wearing khaki uniforms.

Because of player shortages caused by the war,

the Ottawa Senators sought permission to withdraw from pro hockey for a year, but the NHA directors refused to grant this request. In Montreal, the Canadiens' management used the war as an excuse to cut player salaries. Sam Lichtenhein, manager of the other Montreal franchise, the Wanderers, patriotically declared that only married men and munitions workers would play for his team. Obviously he had checked the ring fingers of his players before he signed them up, because his team remained basically unchanged from the previous season. If any munitions workers sought tryouts, it was never mentioned.

In mid-season, team owners snarled their disapproval when a small core of players got together and talked of forming a players' union. The players demanded more freedom and called for a rule that would allow them to switch teams in the event of a *bona fide* residence change from city to city, with a transfer fee going to the team losing the player. One of the union advocates, Ottawa star Cy Denneny, was pacified by a deal that sent him from Toronto to Ottawa, where he could play for his hometown

Opposite: Cy Denneny was a member of five Stanley Cup-winning teams. Above: The 1917 Seattle Metropolitans, the first American-based team to win the Stanley Cup.

Senators and maintain a daytime job that appealed to him. One or two other player shuffles followed, and the union supporters were stifled.

The 1916-17 season also produced a number of on-ice *contretemps*. Howard McNamara, a rugged player with the 228th Battalion, created headlines when he became involved in a fistfight at center-ice with referee Cooper Smeaton. Then a game between Toronto and Quebec was terminated with two minutes to play when a violent brawl broke out, and officials, even with the help of police, were unable to restore order. Quebec fans tossed chairs and bottles at the Toronto players and attacked them as they ran for their waiting train after the game. Ken Randall of Toronto was suspended for a game or two for instigating a punchout with a fan during the fracas.

Difficulties persisted throughout the season. In February, the 228th Battalion was ordered overseas, forcing the hockey club to suspend operations. Attempts to revise the NHA's schedule for the remainder of the season resulted in a bitter argument, which saw Toronto's Eddie Livingstone oppose the owners of the Bulldogs, Senators, Canadiens, and Wanderers. The result of this dispute was surprising: Toronto games were canceled for the remainder of the schedule and the Blueshirts

players were assigned to the surviving teams. This decision, to no one's surprise, infuriated Livingstone. The NHA, which began the 1916-17 season with six teams, finished with four.

When Montreal and Ottawa met in a playoff for NHA honors, the Canadiens captured the two-game total-goal series 7–6. Controversy plagued the playoffs as well. Newsy Lalonde was suspended from the second game for butt-ending Ottawa star Frank Nighbor in the eye.

In the playoffs for the Stanley Cup, the Canadiens were humiliated by the Seattle Metropolitans, the Pacific Coast Hockey Association champions who had earned the right to challenge for the Cup. Montreal lost three straight games by scores of 6–1, 4–1, and 9–1. Seattle's Bernie Morris was unstoppable in this final series, scoring 14 goals.

The NHA had survived another season – but just barely. With the war effort demanding more sacrifices, and more recruits, it appeared that pro teams would be forced to suspend operations before a new season rolled around.

Meanwhile, time had failed to eliminate the

bitter feelings that existed between Toronto owner Eddie Livingstone and his NHA partners, so it was easy to deduce why Livingstone was conspicuously absent from the November 1917 hockey meetings at the Windsor Hotel in Montreal. He had not been invited. Hockey scribes of that era say it was George Kennedy, owner of the Canadiens' franchise, who persuaded the other franchise holders to dissolve the NHA and start a new league, the NHL.

The assembled franchise owners all agreed with the proposal, relieved at the prospect of putting the

Clint Benedict, who led the NHL in goals-against average on six occasions, played on four Cup-winning teams with Ottawa and Montreal.

previous year's troubles behind them. They decided to draft a constitution that was basically the same as that of the old NHA, and no changes were made to playing rules. Frank Calder was to be offered the position of president of the new league.

Kennedy, who had been feuding with Livingstone for years, was laughing up his sleeve. They hadn't turfed Eddie out of the game. They had simply started a new league – one that didn't include him. He still had his franchise in the NHA – the only problem was how would he operate in a one-team league?

Livingstone screamed loud and long about the treatment he'd received, and as predicted, he didn't give up without a battle. One day he posted a couple of retainers in the Montreal rink, home of the Canadiens. Apparently he had hopes of taking over the arena and preventing the Canadiens from playing there. But the Canadiens' owner, Kennedy, an ex-wrestler, welcomed this kind of challenge. He hired a gang of thugs and dispatched them to the arena to chase Livingstone's men off the premises. When those hired hands saw the muscular group advancing on them, they fled for their lives. Livingstone then took his case to court, but the judge sided with Kennedy, finding nothing illegal in the decision to form a new league, even if it left Livingstone on the sidelines twiddling his thumbs.

That's how the National Hockey League was born. While most historians cite November 22, 1917, as its birthdate, it wasn't until four days later, November 26, that five clubs officially joined the new circuit. The charter-member teams were the Ottawa Senators, the Quebec Bulldogs, the Montreal Canadiens, the Montreal Wanderers, and a new Toronto team to be called the Arenas.

Frank Calder, who had served as secretary-treasurer of the NHA, was elected president and secretary of the NHL, and he agreed to serve for the princely sum of $800 per season. The Quebec entry sought and was granted a place on the directorate, even though Quebec officials decided not to ice a team during the initial season. The Quebec players were drafted by the remaining clubs. If Quebec received any compensation for these players – one of whom was the legendary Joe Malone – it was a meagre amount. Quebec management had been asking $200 per player.

The Wanderers, last-place finishers in the NHA the previous season, were bolstered by Quebec players Jack McDonald, Dave Ritchie, George Carey, and John Marks. The fact that they failed to land Joe Malone, the leading scorer in the NHA with 41 goals in 19 games, is astonishing. In 1916-17, he scored more goals than all four Wanderer draftees put together. Snapped up by the Canadiens, the elegant Malone went on to enjoy a sensational first season in the NHL, scoring 44 goals in 20 games for a 2.20 goals-per-game average. It's a mark that has survived seventy-five years of NHL play.

The netminding style of Ottawa's Clint Benedict, who was a sprawler, prompted the league to make a rule change prior to the first game. In the NHA, goalies who fell to the ice to make saves were assessed minor penalties. Rather than make a farce of the game by penalizing Benedict every time he tumbled to the ice, it was decided that all goalies would be permitted to fall, sit, or even lie on the ice if they so desired, without being penalized.

The opening games of the NHL must have caused the league operators to wonder about the future of their new circuit. On December 19, 1917, only seven hundred fans turned out for the Wanderers' opening game with Toronto, even though soldiers in uniform were invited to attend free of charge. The Wanderers upset Toronto 10–9 in the opener. On the same night, the Ottawa Senators visited the Canadiens and were unable to stop Joe Malone, who scored five goals against them in a 7–4 Montreal victory.

Eddie Livingstone continued to be a nuisance to the NHL, even though Toronto was awarded a franchise with the understanding he would play no role in the affairs of the new entry. Toronto manager Charlie Querrie resigned shortly before the season began, citing interference from Livingstone as the reason for his departure. League moguls pleaded with Querrie to reconsider, and he did, returning with full power to make all management decisions.

On January 2, 1918, the new league almost came

"Phantom" Joe Malone scored seven goals in one game against the Toronto St. Pats on January 31, 1920, an NHL record that still stands.

to pieces when fire destroyed the Montreal Arena. Wanderer owner Sam Lichtenhein, who had been threatening to withdraw from the league because of the scarcity of good players, used the arena fire as an excuse to get out of hockey, even though the city of Hamilton offered to give his team a home for the rest of the season. The Canadiens, who shared the arena with the Wanderers, moved into a smaller facility, the Jubilee rink, which had a seating capacity of about three thousand. For the rest of the year, the NHL struggled along with just three teams – the Canadiens, the Senators, and the Arenas.

The Canadiens, with a 10–4 record, won the first segment of the 1917-18 schedule, and the Toronto Arenas (5–3) captured the second.

The playoff series between the Canadiens and the Arenas – a two-game, total-goals series – opened in Toronto before four thousand fans. Harry Meeking scored three times to lead the Arenas to a 7–3 triumph in a game that was marred by several fights.

The second game in Montreal was equally violent and resulted in a 4–3 win for the Canadiens. Thus, Toronto captured the first NHL championship, ten goals to seven, and won the right to meet Vancouver, the Pacific Coast Hockey Association champions, for the Stanley Cup.

The Vancouver Millionaires (9–9) had finished second to Seattle (11–7) in the three-team PCHA race (Portland finished third), but the Millionaires had upset Seattle 3–2 in the two-game, total-goals playoff series. The Millionaires, led by the legendary Fred "Cyclone" Taylor, moved east for the Cup matches, which were played alternately under eastern and western rules. Western rules allowed seven players on the ice; eastern rules, six.

Left: Cyclone Taylor established his reputation with Ontario clubs, but achieved his greatest stardom in the PCHA. Center: Reg Noble scored 28 goals in 20 games in 1917-18. Right: Jack Adams as a member of the NHL's first Stanley Cup champions, the 1918 Toronto Arenas.

Both Vancouver and Toronto had difficulty adjusting to the other side's rules in the best-of-five series, and when game five was played under eastern rules, Toronto had a slight edge and won the deciding game 2–1. Cy Denneny's brother Corbett scored the winning goal.

Five of the Toronto players – goalie Harry "Hap" Holmes, defenseman Harry Cameron, rover Jack Adams, right wing Rusty Crawford, and left wing Reg Noble – went on to become members of the Hockey Hall of Fame. Cameron and Adams were the highest-paid members of the Stanley Cup champions. Each received $900 per year.

After this near-disastrous initial season, the NHL enjoyed steady growth, and within a few years, only NHL teams would compete for hockey's most coveted award, the Stanley Cup. Until then, teams from at least fourteen leagues had fought for the famous trophy.

Long before the turn of the present century, teams in many parts of Canada played in loosely organized groups or leagues. One of the first, founded in 1885, was a league in Kingston, Ontario, which comprised four clubs. Queen's University, Royal Military College, the Athletics, and the Kingstons played a

The earliest known photo of hockey being played on an indoor rink, Quebec City, 1893.

number of games against each other, but not without difficulty. "Heads-up" play was a must: the Kingston rink of that era had a bandstand situated at center-ice.

Another league, the Amateur Hockey Association of Canada, was formed in 1886. It was a team from this organization – with boys wearing the colors of the Montreal Amateur Athletic Association – that was awarded the first Stanley Cup championship in 1893. The Cup, which had been donated in 1892 by Canada's Governor General, Lord Stanley of Preston, was a challenge trophy to be awarded to the top amateur team in Canada. By 1910, however, the changing face of the game dictated that it be contested by professional clubs.

During the last years of the nineteenth century, several leagues blossomed across Canada and the United States. When leagues folded, it was because of financial shortcomings or disputes between competitive club owners. These leagues were amateur organizations, for "play-for-pay" still evoked unsavory connotations in the late 1890s. If a player should find bills of various denominations tucked

This team from the Montreal Amateur Athletic Association was awarded the first Stanley Cup in 1893, the only time the trophy was awarded without a playoff game.

into the toe of his skate when he arrived at the arena, he quietly transferred the money to his purse or wallet. "Finders keepers" was the watchword – at least during hockey season.

Competition for talent, then as now, was fierce. Team owners and managers scurried after the best skaters and scorers. In the early 1900s, top "amateurs" could pocket up to $1,800 for a season's play.

Hockey's first professional league was organized in the United States. Dr. J. L. Gibson, a dentist in the copper-mining center of Houghton, Michigan, recruited some of Canada's best players and paid them to play for his Portage Lakes team in "exhibition" games against other mining towns. The miners bet heavily on the outcome of these contests, and Dr. Gibson's club seldom lost. In 1904, Portage Lakes

and several other mining towns formed the International Professional Hockey League, and Gibson's imports continued to shine. The record of the Portage Lakes club, in 26 league games, was 24–2.

In January 1908, the Ontario Professional League, the first fully professional league in Canada, opened for business, with member clubs in Toronto, Berlin (now Kitchener), Brantford, and Guelph. Newsy Lalonde of Toronto, the league's brightest star, scored 29 goals in nine games to win the scoring race. Eight of his 29 goals came in one game, a 12–3 win over Brantford. The league was nicknamed the "Trolley League" because the teams traveled by the electric railway that connected the four centers.

In 1909 the Canadian Hockey Association was formed, an offspring of the Eastern Canada Amateur Hockey League, which had allowed professionals to play alongside amateurs during the preceding season. After dropping the word amateur, the Eastern Canada League folded when league members were unable to get along. Franchises in the new CHA were granted to Ottawa, the Montreal Shamrocks, the Montreal Nationals, All-Montreal, and Quebec. Each club paid an initiation fee of thirty dollars, and all were fully professional. In the past, players had been required to make written declarations as to whether they were amateurs or pros.

Two teams hoping to join the CHA were rejected – one from the Ottawa Valley town of Renfrew and the Montreal Wanderers. Ambrose O'Brien, representing Renfrew at the league meetings in Montreal, resented the snub and said as much; Jimmy Gardner, who played and spoke for the Wanderers, was livid. He approached O'Brien and suggested they form a new league to include the Wanderers, a Renfrew team (eventually to be called the Creamery

Kings), and two clubs from mining towns in northern Ontario – Haileybury and Cobalt. To add interest, they would form a team of French-speaking players from Montreal and call the club *les Canadiens*. At the time, neither man had an inkling that the league they were scrambling to put together – the National Hockey Association – would one day evolve into the greatest of all hockey leagues. Nor could they know that in *les Canadiens*, they were spawning a team that would win more Stanley Cups than any other in hockey history.

Ambrose O'Brien, backed by his father, mining magnate M. J. O'Brien, paid astronomical sums to lure great players to Renfrew. Cyclone Taylor signed for a reported $5,000 annually. On a per-game basis, Taylor's salary of over $400 a game for the twelve-game schedule was almost ten times greater than that of baseball's number-one player, Ty Cobb.

The Renfrew Creamery Kings, a.k.a. the Millionaires, featured the best hockey talent that money could buy, including the Patrick brothers, Cyclone Taylor, and Newsy Lalonde. Goaltender Bert Lindsay (top row, center) is the father of Hall-of-Famer Ted Lindsay.

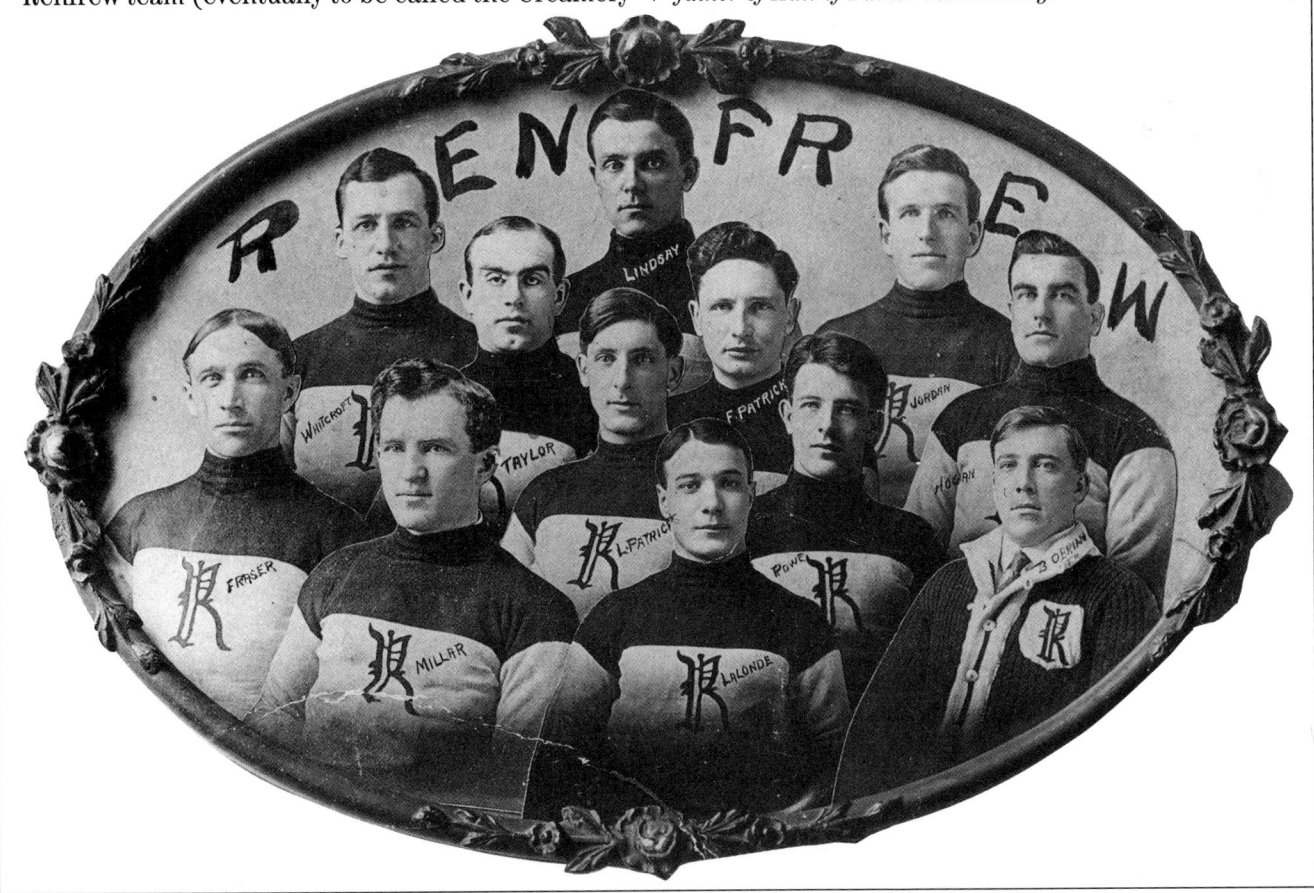

Toiling for Detroit, Cobb had to play more than a hundred games before reaching the $5,000 plateau. Former Montreal Wanderers' players Lester and Frank Patrick agreed to $3,000 contracts with the Creamery Kings.

Unfortunately Renfrew's bid to win the Stanley Cup ended in failure, even though the Creamery Kings (later called the Millionaires) acquired Newsy Lalonde midway through the season. In a close race with Ernie Russell of the Wanderers, Lalonde captured the league scoring title with 38 goals in 11 games, exploding for nine goals in Renfrew's final match against Cobalt to finish seven goals ahead of his Montreal rival. In another late-season game, Renfrew walloped Ottawa 17–2. It was in this contest that Cyclone Taylor is alleged to have scored a goal while skating backwards. Not only was Taylor fulfilling a boast he had made to Ottawa newsmen a couple of weeks earlier, he was taking revenge on the Ottawa fans who had pelted him with debris, including a whisky bottle and lemons, in a previous game.

Jimmy Gardner's Montreal Wanderers won the league championship (11–1) in the first season of NHA play and skated off with the O'Brien Trophy (pictured below), a massive bronze and silver chalice valued at $6,000. After the demise of the NHA in 1917, the O'Brien Trophy was awarded to the NHL's champion until 1923, when it was superseded by the

Prince of Wales Trophy. It was recommissioned in 1928 and presented to the champion of the NHL's Canadian Division until the league reverted to one division in 1938-39. From 1939 to 1950, it was given to the club finishing second in regular-season play. Today, the O'Brien Trophy occupies a place of honor in the Hockey Hall of Fame.

As champions of the NHA, the Wanderers also took possession of the Stanley Cup and, following the NHA season, accepted a challenge for it from Berlin, Ontario. The Wanderers won the single game 7–3.

In the spring of 1910, the talented Patrick brothers packed up and left Renfrew. They would have liked to stay around and help Ambrose O'Brien win a championship and a Stanley Cup, but they were itching to begin a mammoth project – organizing a professional hockey league of their own in western Canada.

In 1911, Renfrew, along with Cobalt and Haileybury, dropped out of major-league hockey, and the NHA recruited other clubs to replace them. Two Toronto teams were admitted, then excluded for the first season because their new arena was not ready for play. From 1911 to 1917, teams from the NHA won five of seven Stanley Cups before the league folded in order to make way for the NHL. By then, Ambrose O'Brien's interests had turned to railroad construction and Jimmy Gardner, the other principal booster of the NHA, had retired after a twelve-year career as a player and had taken up refereeing. Both are in the Hockey Hall of Fame.

Hockey's early leagues displayed all the stability of sand castles. They sprang up, encountered difficulties – most of them involving money – and folded. Fickle team owners jumped from one league to another. Players swore undying loyalty to a team and a league, only to jump at the chance to earn a few more dollars elsewhere.

One early league that made an indelible impact on the game of hockey was the Pacific Coast Hockey Association. It began in 1911 with the sale of the Patrick Lumber Company of British Columbia to a syndicate from England. As a result of the sale, hockey stars Frank and Lester Patrick became two of the wealthiest young men in Canada. At a family meeting, during which the Patrick boys won the full

support of their father, Joe, they decided to throw all of their new-found money (Joe invested a sizable amount as well) into the new hockey venture they had envisioned for western Canada. It was a league they would organize and manage themselves. They'd even be able to coach and play in the league, for Lester was only twenty-seven and Frank was twenty-five.

The family moved from Nelson, British Columbia, and settled in Victoria, the site of Lester's franchise. Frank had already asked for the Vancouver franchise and got it – no argument. A third franchise was granted to New Westminster, and invitations went out to Calgary and Edmonton to join in. Investors in the two Alberta cities thought about it, then declined. Obviously, they didn't share the Patricks' unswerving faith in hockey's future.

As for stocking the teams, the brothers went east, raided the NHA clubs, and persuaded sixteen of that league's most talented stars to move west. In most cases, a handshake was all that was needed to

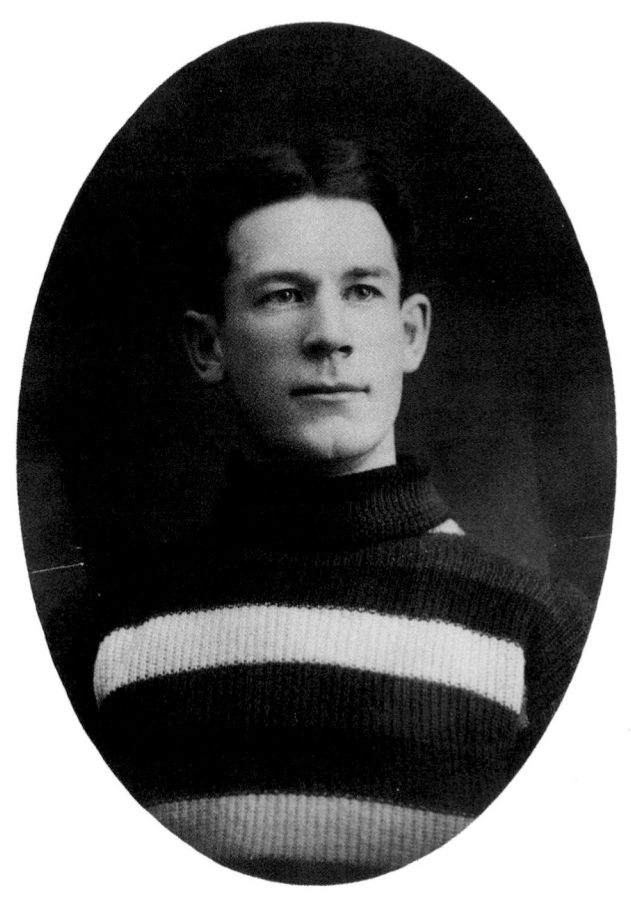

Left: Tom Phillips, captain of the Stanley Cup champion Kenora Thistles. Above: Frank Patrick, one of the game's greatest innovators, was the playing president of the PCHA.

cement a deal. One of the recruits was Jimmy Gardner, who had helped to found the NHA (and would return to it after two seasons). He jumped at the chance to serve as playing-coach of the New Westminster franchise. Others included Newsy Lalonde, Tom Phillips, Tommy Dunderdale, and goaltending stalwarts Bert Lindsay and Hughie Lehman. The Patricks didn't need an abundance of players. In fact, the three-team league, in that era of seven-man hockey and sixty-minute performers (only the NHA had thus far gone to six-man teams), got by quite nicely with only twenty-three skaters – seven or eight players per team.

The Patrick boys thought it was time to introduce

The Denman Street Arena, home of the PCHA's Vancouver Millionaires from 1911 to 1926, was the largest ice palace of its day, seating 10,500.

artificial ice to Canada, and soon two arenas housing the necessary equipment were under construction. The Victoria rink, seating 4,000, cost $110,000. The Vancouver arena, the largest in Canada, with seating for 10,500, was budgeted for $210,000 and cost close to $300,000. Ground was broken in April 1911, and the first league game was scheduled for January 3, l912. As construction moved swiftly along, people stopping by the Vancouver site marveled at the size of the ice surface. It was 220 feet long and 90 feet wide, the largest surface of its kind in the world. When completed, the arena was able to accommodate 10 per cent of the urban population of Vancouver.

All was in readiness by opening night. Lester Patrick's Victoria Senators, in their sporty red, white, and blue uniforms, lost to the New Westminster Royals 8–3, although Lester made a bit of history by scoring the league's first goal. Two nights later, Vancouver hammered New Westminster by the same score before a disappointing turnout of just over 5,000 fans.

Frank Patrick established a goal-scoring record for defensemen when he dashed up the ice and scored six times for Vancouver in a game against New Westminster late in the season. His record has never been matched, even by NHL greats such as Bobby Orr, Doug Harvey, and Paul Coffey. Ian Turnbull, a Toronto Maple Leaf defenseman in the 1970s,

came closest, scoring five goals against Detroit in a 9–1 rout on February 2, 1977.

A close race between the three PCHA clubs held the fans' interest all season, and an all-star series against eastern opponents, won by the western all-stars, helped boost the popularity of West Coast hockey. Even so, the new league's losses amounted to $9,000 by season's end.

Before the beginning of the league's second season, 1912-13, Frank Patrick lured Cyclone Taylor to Vancouver, signing him for the bargain price of $1,800 a year. Taylor's sensational rushes soon had West Coast fans in a frenzy. He attracted 10,400 fans for the second game of the new season against Victoria – the largest crowd ever to see a hockey game anywhere in the world.

By 1915, Vancouver boasted the league's best team. The Millionaires humbled mighty Ottawa in the 1915 Stanley Cup series, and the Stanley Cup came west for the first time. Every member of the Coast club was later inducted into the Hall of Fame: goalie Hughie Lehman, defensemen Si Griffis and Frank Patrick, rover Cyclone Taylor, and forwards Barney Stanley, Mickey Mackay, and Frank Nighbor. A quarter of a century later, Lester would say, "That Vancouver team my brother assembled in 1914-15

was the greatest team I ever saw."

The Patricks were renowned as the game's greatest innovators. They placed numbers on players' jerseys for easy identification. They began the evolution toward hockey's effective zone play and offside rule by painting blue lines on the ice. They introduced a rule allowing goalies to sprawl to the ice, an adaptation that would not be introduced in the east for several years yet, and they ordered the recording of assists. They invented hockey's penalty shot (borrowed from a polo match Frank witnessed in England) and were the first to devise a playoff system for their league. The playoff concept alone has made millions for franchise operators and players in other professional sports in North America.

The Patricks also brought American teams into their league. The New Westminster franchise shifted to Portland, Oregon, for the 1914-15 season and became the Portland Rosebuds. A year later, the Seattle Metropolitans joined the league and stocked its roster by recruiting practically the entire Toronto Blueshirts' line-up of the preceding season.

Stanley Cup trustee William Foran made a wise decision in that 1915-16 season. He announced that the Stanley Cup was no longer to be considered a challenge trophy, which only Canadian teams were eligible to win. He declared it a world trophy, paving the way for U.S. teams like Portland and Seattle to compete for it. Seattle took quick advantage of Foran's declaration and captured the Cup in 1917, defeating the Montreal Canadiens three games to one. In the final encounter, Seattle's Bernie Morris was sensational, scoring six goals in the Metropolitans' 9–1 triumph.

Within the next few months, the NHL had grown out of the ashes of the NHA, and for the next few years Stanley Cup clashes between NHL clubs and PCHA teams were exciting annual events.

In 1921, another league sprang up – the Western Canada Hockey League, with teams in Calgary, Saskatoon, Edmonton, and Regina – and it soon rivaled the other two major leagues in playing strength.

By 1923, declining attendance and roster raids by NHL clubs had reduced the PCHA to three clubs –

Victoria, Vancouver, and Seattle. When Seattle withdrew prior to the 1924-25 season, the PCHA was forced to close down after a thirteen-year battle for survival. Vancouver and Victoria were invited to join the WCHL, making a six-team circuit. But rumors of NHL expansion into major American markets like New York, Chicago, Detroit, and Pittsburgh (Boston and the Montreal Maroons had been admitted in 1924) made western operators edgy. Eastern salaries were escalating fast. When the NHL added the New York Americans and the Pittsburgh Pirates in 1926, the western operators knew they would no longer be able to compete for talent with the free-spending easterners.

In the spring of 1926, Frank and Lester Patrick

Left: "Bullet" Joe Simpson, wearing the uniform of the WHL's Edmonton Eskimos, was an outstanding amateur and professional rearguard. Right: Defenseman Harry Cameron scored 10 goals in 28 Stanley Cup games.

journeyed east and offered to sell to the NHL all the players from the Western League teams, with the exception of Saskatoon, for $300,000. (The Montreal Maroons had already secured the rights to Saskatoon players with a $60,000 option payment.) Even though the Patricks had no documents authorizing them to act as agents for the players involved, and even though there were no reserve clauses in any of the western stars' contracts, which meant they could easily have demanded the right to negotiate for themselves, the Patricks pulled it off.

"I've given you my word that I'll deliver these players," said Frank. "My word should be good enough." It was. He left the meeting with $300,000. Chicago paid $100,000 for the Portland Rosebuds and Detroit shelled out a similar amount for the players on the Victoria roster. Boston had already given Patrick $50,000 (with another $50,000 to come) for a package of western players, which included emerging star Eddie Shore. A few individual sales put another $17,000 in the coffers, and the money (including the $60,000 collected by Saskatoon) was split among the five western franchise

The Boston Bruins and Montreal Maroons, two of the NHL's earliest expansion teams, observe something new: the playing of the national anthem before a game.

holders. The Patricks took no commissions for orchestrating the deal.

When first approached, the New York Rangers balked at paying for Western League players. Later, they panicked and paid huge sums to acquire several ex-Saskatoon players from the Montreal Maroons. They purchased the Cook brothers – Bill and Bun – for $30,000, Frank Boucher for $15,000, and goaltender Lorne Chabot for $20,000.

With the procurement of the western stars – players like Eddie Shore, Bill and Bun Cook, Frank Boucher, Dick Irvin, and dozens more – the NHL teams, old and new, now employed the world's greatest players. Prospects for long-term success seemed all but guaranteed.

While the NHL carried on with three teams, the Patrick brothers found their Pacific Coast Hockey Association, originally a four-franchise loop, reduced to three when the Spokane Canaries dropped out, leaving the Vancouver Millionaires, the Victoria Aristocrats, and the Portland Rosebuds to finish the season.

Unlike the NHL, whose teams played six men a side, the PCHA still played seven-man hockey, employing an extra skater – the "rover" – who participated in both attack and defense. But the innovative Patricks (both of whom were serving simultaneously as players, team managers, and league executives) had introduced blue lines that defined a center-ice area. Forward passing was permitted only in the area between the blue lines. The NHL adopted this forward passing rule in 1918-19.

The Toronto Arenas, minus Eddie Livingstone, won the NHL championship and then beat Vancouver in a Stanley Cup playoff in the spring of 1918, playing the five-game series under eastern and western rules in alternating games.

The Stanley Cup had been donated by Canada's Governor General, Lord Stanley, on March 18, 1892, as a perpetual challenge trophy to be held by the

The 1915 Vancouver Millionaires, the first West Coast team to win the Stanley Cup. Front row, left to right: Frank Patrick, Si Griffis, Lloyd Cook, Hugh Lehman. Top row: Barney Stanley, Cyclone Taylor, unidentified, Mickey Mackay, Frank Nighbor.

champion hockey team in the Dominion of Canada. At first, the Cup was held by amateur teams. But with the formation of the Ontario Professional Hockey League in 1907, that league's teams began challenging for the Cup. In fact, since 1910, only professional teams have held it. (Since 1926, the Stanley Cup has been contested only by member clubs of the National Hockey League.)

Although Eddie Livingstone was officially off the scene, he continued to turn up in reports of the league's affairs, evidently determined not to be squeezed out of hockey. In September 1918, he attended a pre-season NHL owners' meeting. Livingstone, insisting that he still had rights to the Toronto franchise, raised such a fuss that the meeting was terminated with little accomplished. In the meantime, Livingstone and a new ally, Percy Quinn, talked of forming yet another league that would take advantage of the expected surplus of players as men returned from the war. To head off this undesirable development, the NHL executive urged its owners to sign exclusive agreements with the best arenas in their cities to prevent Livingstone and Quinn's new clubs from gaining access to those arenas.

When that strategy blocked Livingstone from access to Toronto's arena, he challenged the legality of the vote that created the NHL. Apparently the NHA's constitution stipulated that each team had to hold fifty shares of stock in the league in order to vote. Livingstone discovered that the Canadiens at one point had sold twelve of their shares, presumably to raise operating capital. He argued that, because they held fewer than the required fifty shares in the NHA, it had been illegal for the Canadiens to vote for the formation of the NHL. Though this argument appeared to have merit, the NHL did not respond, concentrating instead on planning for the mid-December opening of the 1918-19 season. One innovation that the league would borrow from the PCHA for its second season was the recording of assists.

In the fall of 1918, the NHL initiated a split schedule for its three teams: the Toronto Arenas, Ottawa Senators, and Montreal Canadiens. The first part (ten games) would run from December to late January, with the second portion slated to run from late January to March. The winners of each segment would then play off to determine a champion. But the Toronto franchise ran into difficulties and withdrew late in the season, reducing the NHL to just two clubs – the Canadiens and Senators – who played a best-of-seven final, which was won by the Habs. (The Canadiens' nickname was derived from *habitant*, a French-Canadian word meaning "person of the land," which was first applied to the seventeenth-century pioneer farm settlers along the St. Lawrence River.)

Meanwhile, in the PCHA, Vancouver, Seattle, and Victoria battled it out in a January-to-March schedule that eventually led to the Seattle Metropolitans beating the Vancouver Millionaires in a two-game total-goals final. In both the eastern and the western leagues, returning servicemen often found that

Local Referees in NHL's First Season

During the NHL's inaugural season of 1917-18, local referees (one per game) were employed in each of the three NHL cities at a fee of $12.50 per game.

The policy of using local referees for NHL games was discontinued in 1926 when the league appointed a full-time staff of six referees.

The 1913 Quebec Bulldogs, displaying the Stanley Cup and the O'Brien Trophy. Although the Bulldogs refused to accept a challenge from Victoria to play for the Cup, they did play an exhibition series with the West Coast's Aristocrats, which was the first meeting between the champions of the PCHA and NHA.

their war records made bigger heroes of them than their play. Still, outstanding players from before the war, like Odie and Sprague Cleghorn and Newsy Lalonde, who had not been overseas, continued to make headlines.

When the NHL and PCHA champions met in Seattle for the Stanley Cup, the western and eastern rules were again used in alternate games. (Although blue lines were now in use in both leagues, forming a center-ice area where forward passing was permitted, the PCHA still used seven players, while the NHL used only six.) At first, Montreal had difficulty adjusting to western rules and fell behind, but it eventually came back to tie the series.

Unfortunately, the local onset of a worldwide Spanish influenza epidemic forced the abandonment of the series before a winner was declared. So severely did influenza hit Montreal's Joe Hall that he never left Seattle, eventually dying in early April. Hall was one of the league's top defensemen and had played on Stanley Cup-winning teams with Quebec in 1912 and 1913.

As life settled down after the war, interest in professional hockey increased. In 1919, the Quebec Bulldogs returned to the NHL, reclaiming players who had been distributed around the league. Joe Malone, who had played with the Canadiens, returned to the Bulldogs and, on January 31, 1920, scored seven goals in a game against Toronto. This mark stands as an NHL single-game record. He finished the season as the league's top scorer with 39 goals in 24 games, but the Bulldogs finished in last place in both halves of the 1919-20 schedule, winning just four games on the season.

The Canadiens took up residence in the new Mount Royal Arena, which boasted seating for six thousand (and which had to be closed on one occasion soon after its opening when a crowd of six thousand five hundred

The Toronto St. Pats, the third Toronto-based team to win the Stanley Cup. The St. Pats entered the NHL in 1919-20, replacing the Toronto Arenas, who withdrew from the league on February 20, 1919.

Quebec's Athletic Bulldogs

The Quebec Bulldogs were two-time Stanley Cup winners as a member of the NHA, but financial difficulties postponed their entry into the NHL until 1919-20, the new league's third season of operation. The team that took to the ice in the NHL was formally named the Quebec Athletics, and numerous articles in newspapers of the day used this name. But the Bulldog name remained popular with the club's fans, and though 1919-20 proved to be the franchise's final season in Quebec — it was shifted to Hamilton, Ontario for 1920-21 — the fact that the club was called the Athletics has been almost entirely forgotten.

crammed the building, causing a balcony to give way).

Meanwhile, the PCHA under president Frank Patrick continued to poach players from the east. One who moved west from Toronto was Jack Adams; he would later return to star with Ottawa and Toronto in the NHL.

In the spring of 1920, the PCHA champion Seattle Metropolitans trekked to Ottawa to play the powerful Senators for the Stanley Cup. When the natural ice in Ottawa's Laurier Rink deteriorated part way through the series, play was shifted to the artificial ice of Toronto's Mutual Street Arena, home of the NHL's Toronto franchise, which, in 1919-20, had been renamed the St. Patricks. There, the Senators captured the Stanley Cup.

In 1920-21, the Quebec franchise, which was plagued by financial difficulties, moved to Hamilton and became the Hamilton Tigers in a four-team NHL. But the move had little effect on the club's fortunes, and the powerhouse from Ottawa again emerged as the NHL's top club. The Senators journeyed to Vancouver to face the Millionaires before a record eleven thousand fans in the opening game of a Stanley Cup series that Ottawa eventually won.

Now that the NHL had four franchises, the league, at its annual fall meeting in 1921, did away with the split schedule for the 1921-22 season. It also was decided that goaltenders would now be able to pass the puck up to the blue line, which added to the defending team's ability to move the puck out of its zone.

As the popularity of professional hockey grew, so did the value of an NHL franchise. The sale of the Montreal Canadiens, whose roster included established stars such as Newsy Lalonde, Georges Vezina, and the Cleghorns, became a benchmark for franchise transfers when Léo Dandurand, Joseph Cattarinich, and Louis Letourneau paid $11,000 for the team in November 1921. While veterans continued to shine, new stars were emerging and an influx of fresh names was turning up on team rosters.

Ottawa added Frank Boucher and Francis "King" Clancy, while Cecil "Babe" Dye, having returned to the Toronto St. Pats after a brief stint with the Hamilton Tigers, was rapidly making his mark as a scorer.

In the PCHA in 1921-22, Jack Adams, who had been scooped from Toronto, led the league in scoring, with 25 goals in 24 games. But the real news in the west was on the prairies, where a third major professional hockey league – the Western Canada Hockey League – began play. The original teams – the Calgary Tigers, the Edmonton Eskimos, the Regina Capitals, and the Saskatoon Sheiks – were staffed by local players and a smattering of ex-NHA, ex-NHL, and ex-PCHA players. The most notable of these was Regina's Dick Irvin, who had played with Portland in the PCHA before going overseas. Irvin proved that the war hadn't dimmed his talent. He led the Caps to a league title and the right to play off against the PCHA champion Vancouver Millionaires to determine the western Stanley Cup challenger.

Vancouver, under manager Lester Patrick, defeated Regina in a two-game, total-goal series and went on to Toronto to meet the St. Pats. Although the western team lost, the series went five games and showcased the talents of the St. Pats' Babe Dye and the Millionaires' Jack Adams, who finished first and second in Cup scoring, with eleven and seven goals, respectively. Adams so impressed the Toronto owners that within months they traded Corbett Denneny, one of their veteran stars, for the flashy youngster whom they had let slip west.

The new WCHL prolonged the careers of older players and opened up new opportunities for young players to turn professional. It also gave NHL owners a new trading ground and marketplace. Léo Dandurand, tired of quarreling with Newsy Lalonde (who was still a star in his mid-thirties), attempted to sell Lalonde to Saskatoon during the 1922-23 season. But the deal was nixed by NHL president Frank Calder on the grounds that Lalonde hadn't been offered on waivers to other NHL teams. Calder ruled that, instead of cash, Dandurand would get rights to a young Northern Ontario Hockey League player who was on the Saskatoon negotiating list.

Dandurand was understandably upset at the league decision. For one thing, the player he was given for Lalonde was an amateur. For another, the player was under suspension in the NOHL, which meant that he couldn't play for the Canadiens. Even when the league eventually got the suspension lifted, Dandurand remained peeved: the player he'd been given turned out to weigh 135 pounds.

Eventually, though, Dandurand would come to be pleased with his acquisition – a kid called Aurel Joliat, who would entertain fans for years and become one of the most famous stars in the Canadiens' history.

NHL hockey in the 1920s was no game for the faint of heart or body. Padding was so poor that injuries were near-constant. Stick-swinging was the order of the day and butt-ending was a high art among practitioners such

Cecil "Babe" Dye finished among the top five scorers in the NHL for five consecutive seasons, winning the scoring title in 1922, 1923, and 1925.

Frank Calder, the first president of the NHL, served as the league's top administrator from 1917 until his death in 1943.

The Ottawa Senators, Stanley Cup winners in 1923, included eight future Hall of Fame members on their roster. The Senators won the Cup five times, capturing four championships in the 1920s.

The NHL's first superstar, Howie Morenz, was best known by his geographical nickname, "The Stratford Streak." Accurate historians may prefer to label Morenz – who was born in nearby Mitchell, Ontario – "The Mitchell Meteor."

as the incorrigible Sprague and Odie Cleghorn. In 1921-22, referee Lou Marsh had called the recalcitrant brothers "a disgrace to the league and the game of hockey." During the 1922-23 playoffs, Canadiens' owner Léo Dandurand grew so disgusted at the violent play of his own Sprague Cleghorn and Billy Couture that he suspended them, doubtless contributing to the team's loss to Ottawa in the NHL final.

In 1922-23, the PCHA and WCHL played an interlocking schedule, made possible when the PCHA abandoned the rover position and went from six skaters to five and a goalie, coming into line with the other two major professional leagues. The WCHL gained some status with the addition of Newsy Lalonde as Saskatoon's playing manager. Despite Lalonde leading the league in scoring, his club – now known as the Crescents – finished in last place in the four-team circuit, far behind the Edmonton Eskimos. However, in the Stanley Cup finals neither Vancouver nor the Eskimos was much of a challenge for the Cup-winning Ottawa Senators.

Changes were occurring in professional hockey. As the popularity of the game increased, bigger and better rinks were built – among them, Ottawa's eleven-thousand-seat auditorium. Newcomers began to appear more frequently, as stars from the war years retired. The most talented of these newcomers was Howie Morenz, who had played his amateur hockey in Stratford, Ontario. Skating alongside Aurel Joliat on a line whose average weight was a mere 145 pounds, the flashy rookie helped Montreal win the 1923-24 NHL championship in a two-game series with the Ottawa Senators.

Dr. David Hart, the father of the Canadiens' former manager-coach Cecil

Hart, donated a trophy to the NHL to be awarded annually to the player judged to be most valuable to his team. The Senators' Frank Nighbor was the first recipient of the Hart Trophy.

Since Ottawa had won the Cup the previous year and Montreal was now the league champion, Canadiens' owner Léo Dandurand reasoned that the Cup belonged to Montreal. The league agreed. The "castoffs" from the western leagues, Dandurand said, would have to choose among themselves to determine a Cup challenger. To emphasize their case, the Canadiens agreed to pay for the passage of only one team to the east.

The PCHA's redoubtable Frank Patrick first insisted that the winners in the PCHA and WCHL – Vancouver and Calgary respectively – would both travel east. But he relented as far as to agree that, on the way, the western leagues would choose a champion between them. Thus the PCHA champion Vancouver Maroons (formerly the Millionaires) played a transcontinental three-game series against the WCHL's Calgary Tigers in Vancouver, Calgary, and Winnipeg.

Calgary won two of these three games, but Frank Calder, worried that the original deed that had accompanied the provision of the Stanley Cup might later be invoked (it entitled any team to challenge the Cup's holder), ordered the Canadiens to play both western teams. The Canadiens defeated Vancouver in two games in Montreal, and then Calgary in two more – the final game played on Ottawa's superior artificial ice surface – to claim the Stanley Cup.

By 1924, the NHL had made expansion plans. The league had named Thomas Duggan as its U.S. agent, and Duggan planned franchises in Boston and, later, in New York. Before the New York franchise was established, however, James Strachan and Donat Raymond paid $15,000 for a second franchise in Montreal. This new club, to be called the Maroons, would play that season in the Forum, which was then under construction. The Boston franchise, known as the Bruins, would also begin play that season under the management of Art Ross, who would eventually be one of hockey's best-known administrators.

Expansion created a scramble for players. New teams looked for a core of veterans around which to add newcomers. Established teams sought as much remuneration as they could get for aging talent, hoping to restock with young players. Not surprisingly, the PCHA and WCHL both suffered, as did amateur clubs across Canada, as the NHL went on the prowl for skaters. Players from the Toronto Granites, winners of an Olympic gold medal for Canada the previous year, were considered to be especially valuable. Ottawa snared Reg "Hooley" Smith, and the new Montreal Maroons got Duncan Munro. No one, however, was able to sign Harry Watson, perhaps the best of the Olympians, who chose to remain amateur.

To accommodate the league's expansion teams, the regular-season schedule was expanded from twenty-four to thirty games. The first-place finisher

Montreal Awarded Second Franchise

In November 1924 the Montreal Maroons joined the NHL at a cost of $15,000. Ten thousand dollars of this franchise fee was paid directly to the Canadiens as compensation for operating within their territorial limit.

Salaries Cap in 1925

In 1925 total player salaries on a given team were not to exceed $35,000. Expansion franchises in New York and Pittsburgh were given a two-year exemption from this regulation; their total payrolls could not exceed $45,000.

Jersey City Applies for Franchise

Mr. F. E. Coultry applied for a franchise for Jersey City, New Jersey, on January 8, 1926, citing plans for building the Journal Square Gardens with a seating capacity of eleven thousand.

Cleveland Bids for Franchise in 1926

Although the city of Cleveland was not granted an NHL franchise until the 1976-77 season, President Frank Calder was authorized by the NHL's Board of Governors to begin negotiations in February 1926 with representatives from the Ohio city.

The Cleveland group, led by W. T. Douglass, sent a cheque in the amount of $12,500 as a deposit on their application.

The expansion franchise fee that year was set at $50,000.

would compete for the championship against the winner of a playoff between the second- and third-place teams. But the longer schedule brought on the NHL's first labor dispute. Although Hamilton finished first, the Tigers' players contended that they had signed on to play the old twenty-four-game regular-season schedule and refused to compete in playoff games unless they were given a raise as compensation for the extra six games they played in the regular season.

Frank Calder was not prepared to have that sort of action interfere with league proceedings. In a decision that probably scuppered the best chance Hamilton ever had at a Stanley Cup, he ordered the Canadiens and Toronto, the second- and third-place teams, to play off to decide the league championship. The Habs eventually won the right to play the western victor.

Two new NHL trophies were first awarded in 1924-25. Lady Byng, the wife of Canada's Governor General, presented a new individual award in 1925. The Lady Byng Trophy was to be awarded annually to the player exhibiting the best type of sportsmanship and gentlemanly conduct, combined with a high standard of play. Again, Ottawa's Frank Nighbor was its first recipient. The Prince of Wales – later King Edward VIII – presented the trophy which bears his name, to be awarded to each season's NHL playoff champion. The Montreal Canadiens were the first winners of this award.

The West, meanwhile, had been wracked by player losses to the NHL's expansion teams. After thirteen years of keeping the PCHA alive, the Patricks had recently been forced to let the Seattle franchise fold in 1924. The league's two remaining franchises, Victoria and Vancouver, joined the WCHL, turning that league into a six-team loop that still had its share of stars. The aging Newsy Lalonde of the Saskatoon Crescents played center on a line with two brothers, Bill and Fred "Bun" Cook. Another notable, goalie George Hainsworth, was also on the team. Still, in that season of 1924-25, the Crescents lost to Lester Patrick's swift Victoria team. And in the last hurrah of the Patricks' western effort, Victoria went on to beat Calgary and then Montreal to win the Stanley Cup. The Cougars were the last non-NHL team to win a Stanley Cup championship.

The next fall, for the the first time, the NHL held a meeting in the United States. This session, which took place in New York City on September 22, was convened to discuss the formation of a new franchise to be called the New York Americans. The new club would be staffed largely with players from the Hamilton Tigers, though these players would have to apply for reinstatement because of suspensions levied the previous season when the Tigers had refused to compete in the playoffs.

The Americans and another expansion team, the Pittsburgh Pirates, would begin play that season and become the second and third American teams in the league. Managed by former Montreal Canadiens' bad boy Odie Cleghorn, the Pirates were built around a top amateur club called the

The New York Americans, whose colorful "stars and stripes" uniforms were more famous than the club itself, were the first New York-based team to join the NHL. They made the playoffs five times in their seventeen-year history, but reached the semi-finals on only two occasions.

Pittsburgh Yellow Jackets, whose on-ice leader had been Toronto-born Lionel Conacher, who had gone to Pittsburgh on a football scholarship at Duquesne University. Conacher had recruited friends from top Toronto and Ottawa amateur teams for the Yellow Jackets, and most of these players – including Roy Worters, Harold "Baldy" Cotton, and Harold Darragh – turned pro with the Pirates. As manager, Cleghorn proved to be something of an innovator; his Pirates became the first team in big-time hockey to change players while action was ongoing. He was also one of the first to use set three-man forward lines.

The league governors were quick to recognize the need to keep the lid on costs. They decided that teams could sign fourteen players and dress twelve for each game, but each franchise had to adhere to a team salary cap of $35,000.

Despite good showings by Pittsburgh and Ottawa, the Montreal Maroons proved to be the NHL's top team in 1925-26, eventually winning the playoffs following an expanded thirty-six-game schedule.

While the NHL was clearly on the move, the WCHL had not prospered by its merger with the PCHA. When fans failed to come out to watch the Regina Capitals, the franchise was moved to Portland for the 1925-26 season. Duly recognizing its U.S. entry, the league shortened its name to the Western Hockey League. The Edmonton Eskimos, led by a young Eddie Shore, won the 1925-26 league title, but were beaten in the playoffs by the Victoria Cougars, who went on to lose the Stanley Cup to the Montreal Maroons, playing on the artificial ice of the new Forum. The Maroons had become Stanley Cup champions in only their second season of play.

Although no one realized it at the time, the playoffs in 1926 marked the end of an era – the last time a team from outside the NHL would play for the Stanley Cup. Nor did anyone realize, with the possible exception of Frank and Lester Patrick, that the NHL was entering an era of explosive growth that would put it atop the hockey world for decades to come.

Player Exchanges

In 1926 the league adopted a rule that prohibited NHL teams from selling, optioning, or exchanging any of its players to any other league without first offering such players to NHL clubs at a price not exceeding $2,500.

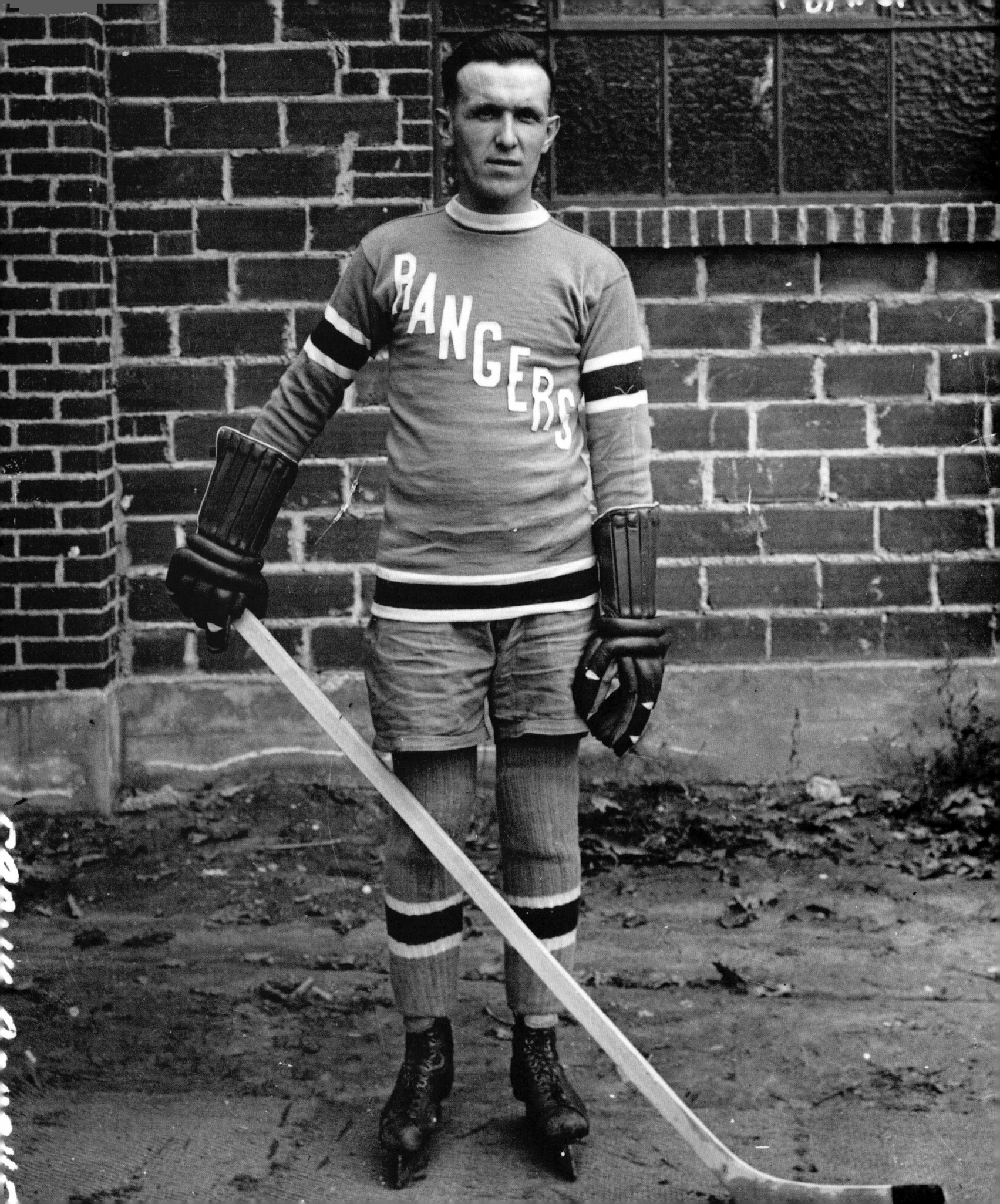

First Growth

WITH IMPROVEMENTS IN ARTIFICIAL ICE-MAKING AND THE BUILDING of rinks capable of holding large crowds, it became clear that hockey had the potential to become a much bigger attraction than it had been through the first quarter of the century. It became equally clear that the best expansion potential lay south of the border, where the Boston Bruins (formed in 1924 by Charles Adams), the Pittsburgh Pirates, and the New York Americans were already established. In the spring of 1926, representatives of Madison Square Garden met with league governors to apply for a second New York franchise, to be called the Rangers.

Applications from several groups in Detroit and Chicago were also under consideration. The awarding of franchises to interests in these two cities in May of 1926 was of particular interest to Frank Patrick, who still controlled WHL franchises in Victoria and Portland. As the NHL's expansion hastened the collapse of the WHL, he saw an opportunity to turn his interest in these teams into a money-maker. When the Chicago franchise was about to be granted, Patrick sold the owner the entire Portland Rosebuds franchise, including player contracts. He then sold the Victoria Cougars (this club was previously named the Aristocrats) to the new Detroit franchise owner. Frank and Lester Patrick also acted as agents, negotiating the sale of many other WHL player contracts to the NHL, but their efforts were far from the only wheeling and dealing going on.

With ten teams now in the NHL, both established franchises and new teams were intent on snapping up talented players – either unsigned amateurs or pros from defunct franchises. The bidding became so hot that the NHL had to step in and form a committee to apportion talent as evenly as possible. The league also had to devise a means of coping with the logistics of increased travel and more complex scheduling. The answer was two five-team divisions playing an interlocking schedule. The American Division consisted of

Opposite: Frank Boucher was the pivot of the Rangers' most famous trio, the Cook–Boucher–Cook Line. He later coached the Rangers for eleven seasons, leading the Broadway Blues to their last Stanley Cup victory in 1940.

Uniform Starting Times for Games

At its September 1926 meeting, the NHL's Board of Governors established uniform starting times for all games. It was required that all games begin no earlier than 8:15 PM and no later than 8:30 PM.

Attendance First Recorded in 1926-27

Official attendance figures were not compiled by the league until the 1926-27 season. During the 220-game regular-season schedule that year, a total of 1,119,961 fans attended NHL games for a per-game average of 5,090.

Official Scorer

The NHL began employing official scorers in each city in 1926-27. Until that time the league had relied on independent reports to compile game statistics.

Clint Benedict was the first goaltender to use face protection, fashioning a leather mask to protect a damaged proboscis. Benedict, who introduced the mask on February 20, 1930, retired permanently after the mask became dislodged in a goal-mouth scramble and his nose was broken again.

the Boston, Chicago, Detroit, the New York Rangers, and Pittsburgh. The Canadian Division was made up of the Montreal Canadiens and Maroons, Ottawa, Toronto, and – despite the apparent contradiction with the division's name – the New York Americans.

With ten teams in two divisions, an additional playoff round was added. The second- and third-place teams in each division would play each other in a two-game, total-goals series. The winners of these series would then face their division's first-place finisher in two-game, total-goals match-ups to determine division champions and Stanley Cup finalists. The Cup, now contested exclusively by NHL clubs, was awarded to the winner of a best-of-five final series.

With all the coming and going of players, as well as the appearance of the new teams, it would not have been surprising if fans had been somewhat confused as the NHL opened its 1926-27 schedule. In the Canadian Division, the Canadiens still featured players such as Morenz and Joliat. While no one could replace the incomparable goaltender Georges Vezina, who had collapsed during a game on November 28, 1925, and later died of tuberculosis, George Hainsworth, from the WHL's Saskatoon Crescents, would soon emerge as a star in goal. To honor Vezina's memory, the Canadiens' owners presented the NHL with the Vezina Trophy, to be awarded annually to the goaltender for the team allowing the fewest goals-against during the regular season. Hainsworth was its first winner.

Across town, the Montreal Maroons, winners of the Stanley Cup the previous year, had their own stars in goaltender Clint Benedict and center Nels Stewart. Up the Ottawa River, the Senators acquired Jack Adams – by now a veteran – from Toronto, to play with youngsters such as Francis "King" Clancy.

The Toronto St. Pats, who would acquire new ownership and a new name late in the season, were weakened by the loss of Adams and of Babe Dye, who had gone to Chicago. The St. Pats would rely heavily on Clarence "Hap" Day and Irvine "Ace" Bailey. Meanwhile the New York Americans' coach, retired star Newsy Lalonde, was counting on newly acquired Lionel Conacher and his defense partner, "Bullet" Joe Simpson, to keep the team competitive. But Newsy was apparently hard pressed to keep his charges out of New York's speakeasies.

In the American Division, the Chicago Black Hawks, led by star center Dick Irvin, had a distinct Portland look. During the off-season, they had strengthened their scoring with the addition of Babe Dye from Toronto.

The Pittsburgh Pirates would come to regret trading Lionel Conacher to the Americans. Manpower shortages later in the season would force them to dress manager Odie Cleghorn, who, by that time, was long past his prime. The Boston Bruins still had aging Sprague Cleghorn in the line-up, but had gone a long way to renewing themselves in "discovering" Eddie Shore, who would both anchor the defense and add to the attack.

The last Toronto St. Pats team poses in front of the Mutual Street Arena in Toronto. The St. Pats had made the playoffs only once since winning the Cup in 1922, and were sold to a group headed by Conn Smythe on February 14, 1927.

The Detroit Cougars, built around a nucleus of WHL players from Victoria, had a problem of their own: their new rink wasn't ready when the schedule opened, and games had to be played in Windsor, Ontario. The Chicago Black Hawks, too, had not quite met one entry condition: a rink capable of holding ten thousand. Theirs held just five thousand.

If there was one team that seemed to have everything going for it, it was the New York Rangers. Perhaps the best move the New York owners made was hiring Conn Smythe as manager. An engineer, veteran of the war, and successful amateur player, manager, and coach, Smythe was a hockey nonpareil. Hired by Col. John Hammond to assemble the Rangers, he had begun the job by signing goaltender Lorne Chabot, and then had built a powerhouse that featured Ivan "Ching" Johnson and American-born Clarence "Taffy" Abel on defense, as well as Saskatoon scoring stars Bill and Bun Cook, who flanked play-making center Frank Boucher.

These acquisitions weren't enough for Hammond. Smythe's decision not to acquire Babe Dye, when the Toronto St. Pats were trying to trade him, cost Smythe his job, and led Hammond to hire Lester Patrick. But Smythe did not remain out of the NHL for long. Before the end of that 1926-27 season,

Captain Given New Authority

In September 1927, the NHL instituted a new rule that allowed "only the captain of a team to address the referee or judge of play during the progress of a match."

The last great Ottawa Senators team, winners of the Stanley Cup in 1927. Of the twelve skaters who wore the Senators' colors in 1927, eight would eventually be elected to the Hockey Hall of Fame.

bankrolled with money he won betting on an NHL game and on college football, he joined a group that bought the Toronto St. Pats for $160,000. Renamed the Maple Leafs, the team would go on to become one of the most famous in the history of hockey.

The ten-team NHL of 1926-27 was greatly changed, but defensive play still ruled the day, as evidenced by the 84 shutouts that were recorded over the 220-game schedule.

That spring, the Ottawa Senators defeated the Boston Bruins to win Canada's capital its tenth and last Stanley Cup. Four games were played in the finals. Ottawa won games two and four and tied games one and three. Both tie games remained deadlocked despite twenty-minute overtime periods.

Ticket Prices in 1927-28

The most expensive ticket to an NHL game in 1927-28 was to a New York Rangers', New York Americans', or Chicago Black Hawks' contest for $3.50. The least expensive ticket to a game could be secured at Toronto's Mutual Street Arena, where a general admission (standing-room) ticket cost twenty-five cents.

By the autumn of 1927, the NHL, under president Frank Calder, had become firmly established as hockey's major professional league. For 1927-28, the NHL governors lifted team salary caps and raised the transfer price for players who were placed on waivers from $2,500 to $5,000.

The Prince of Wales Trophy would now be awarded to the team finishing first in the American Division; the O'Brien Trophy to the first-place finisher in the Canadian Division.

As the cost of operating an NHL team increased, the Ottawa Senators, who had been one of the mainstays of pro hockey since the late 1800s, appealed to the league for assistance to cover their expenses. To relieve the burden of high salaries and to raise much-needed money, the Senators also began selling off some of the players who had carried the team for so long.

Elsewhere in the league, however, stars who would shine for years were capturing the imagination of the fans. Boston owner Charles Adams had a juggernaut of a team, led by Eddie Shore and Aubrey "Dit" Clapper, the latter of whom played with Ralph "Cooney" Weiland and Norman "Dutch" Gainor. The Canadiens, firmly anchored in goal by George Hainsworth, featured Howie Morenz, "The Stratford Streak," and Aurel Joliat, while the cross-town rival Maroons iced the "S" Line of Albert "Babe" Siebert, Nels Stewart,

At left: Babe Siebert spent fourteen seasons in the NHL, playing for the Maroons, the Rangers, the Bruins, and the Canadiens. Siebert had been hired to coach the Canadiens on his retirement in 1939. However, he drowned during the off-season and never took up the position. The third NHL All-Star Game was held to raise money for his family.

Below: The first NHL marksman to score 300 goals in his career, Nels Stewart was the league's all-time scoring leader until Rocket Richard unseated him on November 8, 1952. A two-time winner of the Hart Trophy, Stewart played his final NHL game on March 24, 1940.

LA PRESSE, MONTREAL, SAMEDI 5 JANVIER 1929

BABE SIEBERT

L'un des piliers de la défense du Montréal, et l'un des plus rapides joueurs de la ligue professionnelle, Siebert est un artiste du hockey. Il est l'un des hommes les plus brillants et les plus effectifs sur le club de M. James Strachan.

Back-up Goaltender Rule Adopted

In November 1928, the NHL's Board of Governors empowered President Calder to loan a team's spare goaltender to another team in the event of injury. The club would be required to compensate the team from which the goaltender was loaned at the rate of $200 per game plus traveling expenses.

and Hooley Smith, backed up by Mervyn "Red" Dutton and, briefly, a young Leighton "Hap" Emms.

The Detroit Cougars, though still struggling, underwent roster upheaval after Jack Adams retired from the Senators and took over Detroit's management and coaching, showing an immediate zest for trading. The powerful Rangers, led by the Cook brothers and the gentlemanly Frank Boucher, remained intact with Taffy Abel and Ching Johnson on defense. New York's other team, the Americans, still had Lionel Conacher, a superb athlete who, much to the displeasure of coach Newsy Lalonde, had developed a liking for New York nightlife.

Pittsburgh, like Ottawa, had trouble drawing crowds, while Chicago continued to employ a largely veteran roster, since many players left over from the Portland team had formed the nucleus of the Black Hawks. Meanwhile in Toronto, Conn Smythe, still smarting from his New York experience and hell-bent on building a winner, added Art Duncan and Tommy Gorman to a defense corps anchored by Hap Day. Late in the season, Joe Primeau, who would prove to be one of the NHL's top forwards in the 1930s, played his first games with the Leafs.

To keep travel and payroll costs down in 1927-28, teams were restricted to twelve-man rosters, which meant that two or three injuries could severely impair a team's effectiveness. Perhaps an even bigger problem was that defensive skills were dominating hockey, and scoring chances had been drastically reduced, resulting in low-scoring games that fans found tedious to watch. Firing the puck to the other end of the rink was still considered an effective means of relieving pressure, and teams stationed checkers in their defensive zone ready to meet puck-carriers as they crossed the blue line. Offensive production was so stifled that, in 1927-28, George Hainsworth of the Montreal Canadiens recorded 13 shutouts in 44 games and a league-leading 1.05 goals-against average. Hainsworth's efforts earned him his second consecutive Vezina Trophy, but Alex Connell of Ottawa and Hal Winkler of Boston topped Hainsworth with 15 shutouts each. Connell established an NHL record of six consecutive shutouts, which still stands.

Although goals-against averages were low, goaltending wasn't getting easier. Though forward passing was not permitted in the offensive zone, there was no offside restriction, so that forwards could set up shop around the crease, making life difficult for a goalie, even before the puck-carrier had come across the blue line. The average number of goals per game was less than four, and, when goalie Lorne Chabot was hurt during the Stanley Cup finals won by the Rangers in 1928, Lester Patrick, the forty-four-year-old coach and manager of the Rangers, was confident enough of his team's ability to keep shots to a minimum that he came off the bench to play goal during a game against the Montreal Maroons. The Rangers became the second U.S.-based club to win the Stanley Cup.

(continued on p. 52)

THE RANGERS' STANLEY CUP WINNERS

by John Halligan

Fans of the New York Rangers, arguably the most loyal and rabid in all of hockey, have suffered through half a century of empty springtimes waiting for a Stanley Cup championship. It wasn't always this way. Their grandparents had it better. Much better.

Yes, Virginia, there were New York Stanley Cups back then. Three of them, in fact, one which came in the second year of the Rangers' existence, 1928! Additional Cups would soon follow in 1933 and 1940 – three Stanley Cups in the team's first fourteen years of play. A remarkable start for a remarkable franchise.

On the ice in those early days, the names were Frank Boucher, Bill and Bunny Cook – hockey's premier forward line – Ching Johnson and Taffy Abel on defense. Lorne Chabot in goal. The "Iron Man," Murray Murdoch, who, true to his nickname, is still alive today. And the boss of the Rangers? One of the most celebrated hockey men of the time, Lester Patrick, the famed Silver Fox.

Off the ice, things were different when the Rangers were founded in 1926, much different. Secretaries made fifteen dollars a week. Sirloin was forty-one cents a pound. Charles Lindbergh, "The Lone Eagle," was in the news. So was Gertrude Ederle, for swimming the English Channel. People were getting their first look at Ernest Hemingway's *The Sun Also Rises* and A. A. Milne's *Winnie the Pooh*.

The movie attraction was *Beau Geste*, with Ronald Colman. And who wasn't fantasizing about Clara Bow, the "It" girl? Broadway had Helen Hayes in *What Every Woman Knows*, and Lynn Fontanne played Eliza in *Pygmalion*.

It was the era of the flapper, and Prohibition was in its seventh year. There were an estimated twenty thousand speakeasies in New York, most of them located between 40th and 60th streets. The Rangers landed smack in the middle, between 49th and 50th streets in a brand new Madison Square Garden, "the world's premier sports arena."

But first, a step back, if only for a calendar year, to 1925.

The Rangers were, in fact, New York's second NHL hockey team, following by one season the appearance of the now-long-defunct New York Americans, who wore star-spangled uniforms and premiered to extremely handsome results at the box office.

Lorne Chabot began his professional career with the new Rangers in 1926-27, and had ten or more shutouts in each of his first three NHL seasons.

Quick to take note of the Amerks success, the Madison Square Garden management team hastily organized a team of its own, and thus was born what is now one of the proudest and most historic of National Hockey League franchises.

Tex Rickard, the Garden's fight-promoter, had become fascinated with hockey, and was convinced the game would continue to flourish at the box office. While it was being assembled, the team was jestingly called "Tex's Rangers," and the latter part of the name stuck.

Toronto hockey man Conn Smythe had been recruited by Rickard to build a team. However, before the team's first season even got started, the two had a falling out, and Lester Patrick was summoned from western Canada to complete the job. And what a job he did.

The two masterminds behind the New York Rangers, Lester Patrick (left) and John Hammond, struck gold early, winning the Stanley Cup in the team's second year.

The Rangers were off and skating to great early success. In their first sixteen seasons, they missed the playoffs only once. They won three regular-season championships, finished second five times, and third on six other occasions. They also won their three Stanley Cups.

This is the story of those magical years, the story of hockey in North America's greatest metropolis.

While Smythe was among the most widely known men of the times in amateur-hockey circles, there was no doubt as to who were the most famous men in professional hockey. They were the Patrick brothers, Lester and Frank, pioneer players, innovators, and builders of the Pacific Coast Hockey Association. So Tex Rickard and Garden president Colonel John Hammond were hardly getting an untested product when they signed Lester to run the Rangers. They were, in fact, getting a forty-two-year-old legend.

Tall, stately, almost magisterial in demeanor, Lester had the appearance of a banker or a lawyer. Well-tailored to a fault, he was a gentleman, a man of presence and dignity.

More important, especially to his Garden bosses, Lester knew hockey and how to sell it in New York. To that end, he courted New York's legendary sportswriters, both individually and collectively, and that got him his nickname, "The Silver Fox." The appellation referred as much to his hockey sagacity, as to the streaks of grey that flecked his thick shock of hair. Ed Daley, then the sports editor of the New York *Herald-Tribune*, coined the monicker after one of Lester's numerous press briefings. "Yesterday," Daley wrote, "I spent a fascinating half hour in the lair of the Silver Fox." It was a name that stayed with Lester throughout his career.

Lester's strategy with the press was a wise one, and one that was dutifully followed by some of his successors at the team's helm, notably Frank Boucher and Emile Francis.

It was the Golden Era of sports in the United States, and New York sportswriters were fascinated with the heroes of the day – Babe Ruth, Jack Dempsey, Bobby Jones, Helen Wills, Bill Tilden, Red Grange, and the king of the jockeys, Earle "A Handy Guy Named" Sande.

Patrick's job was a tough one, battling those headline grabbers, but he tackled it with relish. New York's top sportswriters were hardly enamored of, or even familiar with, the "foreign" game of hockey. Wrote Damon Runyon, perhaps the most famous sportswriter of that era: "Fortunately, hockey is not a game I do not fail to misunderstand."

Eminently familiar with the boxing game, the Garden, hardly surprisingly, assigned two of its boxing press agents to help the Rangers, the first being Johnny Bruno and the second Willis "Jersey" Jones, himself an ex-pug. They were, as Lester was soon to find out, sometimes as much a hindrance as a help. Bruno, for instance, took it upon himself to rename two of the Rangers' players, Oliver Reinikka and goalie Lorne Chabot, in order to appeal to New York's large Italian and Jewish populations. Reinikka, of Finnish descent, became "Ollie Rocco," and Chabot, a French-Canadian, became "Lorne Chabotsky."

Ever the purist, Patrick was said to have choked on his morning coffee when he saw the bogus names in the box score, and that stunt was promptly ended. The next one ended Bruno's tenure as a hockey publicist.

Boxing people were hardly opposed to stretching the truth to gain newspaper space, and Bruno wanted to have the Rangers' captain, Bill Cook, "kidnapped" prior to the first game, which was three days hence. "Of course, we'll have him 'returned' in time for the game," Bruno apparently said. Patrick's reply is not known, but the words "rubbish" and "balderdash" were probably included. Exit Johnny Bruno. Enter Jersey Jones.

Lester Patrick was quick to learn the ways and wiles of big-city life, New York style. But, make no mistake about it, he was hardly a neophyte about the metropolis. In fact, he and brother Frank had been to New York some eighteen years earlier, in the spring of 1908. At that time, Lester, Frank, and a group of Canadian pros, including the famous Fred "Cyclone" Taylor, whom the *New York Times* dubbed "The Ty Cobb of Hockey," came to town for a historic exhibition series against the famous amateur team, the St. Nick's Hockey Club, which played in the seven-thousand-seat St. Nicholas Arena on New York's west side, one of only three artificial ice surfaces in the world in those days.

The occasion was New York City's very first view of professional hockey, and according to Lester Patrick's biographer, Eric Whitehead, it was this pioneering trip that planted in Patrick the notion that hockey could eventually take root in America's largest metropolis.

It was a staunch rival of Lester's – Tommy Gorman, the boss of the New York Americans – who probably best described the relationship between Lester and New York City. "Lester didn't adjust to New York City," Gorman said. "New York adjusted to him."

In a broader sense, Lester's effect on people was succinctly captured by Walter "Babe" Pratt, a lovable and effective defenseman for the champion Rangers of 1939-40. Said Pratt: "You just couldn't be around Lester for long without learning something." New York's sportswriters were finding that out daily.

The late Joe Nichols, one of New York's first hockey writers, who went on to cover the game for almost fifty years for the *New York Times*, said:

Lester Patrick, to the veteran occupants of the press box, was an oracle as well as a leader while he was coaching the Rangers. The young reporter felt every bit the equal of the old-timer in the presence of Lester, when the Silver Fox held one of his "hockey information" panels in the old days, for Lester always had the power of making everybody else feel at ease.

Even Canadian newspapermen, ever more sagacious in the art of hockey than their New York counterparts, were admirers of Lester. Elmer Ferguson, the venerable sportswriter and editor in Montreal, wrote:

Lester's greatest feats were those of a legislative nature, writing into the game the foundation for rules that made hockey a game of breathless, sustained speed and glittering color. He brought to the East a dramatic personality, a vivid imagination and a sincere love for the sport, plus tremendous showmanship.

Born Curtis Lester Patrick, of Scottish-Irish descent, in Drummondville, Quebec, on New Year's Eve of 1883, the Silver Fox grew up in a predominantly French-speaking community and thus was fluently bilingual.

One day a mutual friend teased Frank Patrick about Lester's ease with the French tongue. The friend said, "Your brother speaks better French than you do."

"Yes," replied Frank. "And he speaks better English too."

Bill Chadwick, New York born and bred, who made it into the Hockey Hall of Fame after a stellar officiating career, offers this view of the Silver Fox:

> There were some hangups about Americans in the NHL in those days, but not with Lester. He had a special appreciation for an American in a Canadian game. He got me my first officiating assignment, as a linesman for the New York Americans. Whenever he could, he would watch me and then call me into his office to discuss things I was doing wrong. It was his constructive criticism that got me on my way as an NHL referee.
>
> Lester had an amazing grasp of all the aspects of the game, including my side of it. He was a great advocate of the "slow whistle." He used to say: "Bill, you've got all night to blow that thing, but once you do, you can't call it back. A fast whistle often penalizes the wrong team."

With Lester firmly in charge, the Rangers were ready to take New York in the autumn of 1926. They arrived *en masse* from their training camp at the old Ravina Gardens in Toronto. Most of the players lived in mid-town hotels, a stone's throw from Madison Square Garden.

Recalled Frankie Boucher, the team's nonpareil center and future Hall of Famer:

> We really looked like country bumpkins when we arrived in New York. We all wore caps, but soon changed to hats when we discovered that the only men who wear caps in New York were cab drivers.
>
> People who worked at the Garden used to ask why we weren't wearing snowshoes.

The Rangers were a hit from the very start, both on the ice and at the box office. New Yorkers took an immediate liking to the team. In fact, Ranger games in the 1920s were *the* place to be, and the club attracted a formal "dinner jacket" crowd to the games, which began at 8:45 P.M., coinciding with the curtain time at the nearby Broadway theaters. The fans were often headed by no less a personage than the mayor of New York himself, the Honorable Jimmy Walker, who had been on hand for the Rangers' very first game on November 16, 1926.

On that auspicious night, a crowd of more than thirteen thousand joined the mayor as the Rangers faced off against the Montreal Maroons, the defending Stanley Cup champions. Movie star Lois Moran dropped the ceremonial first puck between Boucher and Maroons star Nels Stewart. Miss Moran was then escorted back to her seat behind the Rangers' bench.

Wrote Ed Sullivan, then a young Broadway reporter for the *Daily News*'s "Talk of the Town" column: "Miss Moran was in the elegant company of Mayor Jimmy Walker and his beauteous companion of the evening, actress Betty Compton." That was the first recorded mention of the romance between the forty-two-year-old playboy mayor and the twenty-two-year-old movie star, who was to become Walker's mistress in the city's most highly publicized love affair.

Despite the formalities and the company of celebrities, the Rangers displayed no opening-night jitters, dispatching the mighty Maroons 1–0 on a goal by Bill Cook, the Rangers' captain, at 10:37 of the second period. The game was described thus in a story by Seabury Lawrence of the *New York Times*:

> In a fast and savagely played hockey game the New York Rangers took up their stand last night and defeated the fast traveling Montreal Maroons by the airtight score of 1–0 on the ice in Madison Square Garden before a big crowd of over 13,000 spectators.
>
> It was the opening game of the season and bristled with fast play and penalties, the latter numbering 18, breaking the American indoor record of 17 hung up last St. Patrick's Day, when the same Maroons and the New York Americans battled it out.
>
> On their first appearance the Rangers made a distinctly favorable impression. Bunny and Bill Cook, playing the wings, and Boucher at center, distinguished themselves by particularly skillful stick work and clever skating. Bunny Cook, a slim, youthful player, displayed some of the most brilliant hockey of the evening and seems to be a player of parts. It fell to Bill, however, to score the only goal of the game, but the pass came from Bunny, which kept it all in the family.

The Rangers went on to have a most successful season, winning the division championship by 11

points over the Boston Bruins. Their overall record was 25–13–6, and only five of the losses came at the Garden. Bill Cook won the Art Ross Trophy with 37 points, 33 of them goals.

In the Stanley Cup playoffs, however, the Rangers were bounced in the opening round by the Bruins, losing a two-game series, 3 goals to 1, total goals being the factor that decided the series that led up to the Stanley Cup final.

All in all, it had been a most enjoyable inaugural season for Patrick's squad. They forged a terrific rivalry with the somewhat-raucous Americans, their co-tenants in the Garden. More importantly, however, they became a hot ticket among celebrities, both sporting stars and entertainers.

Boucher, in his marvelous autobiography *When the Rangers Were Young*, written with Trent Frayne, recalled two fans in particular:

> Many famous New Yorkers followed us: people like Babe Ruth came into the Garden in his flashy beige camel-hair coat and matching cashmere cap; and Lou Gehrig, Babe's running mate on the Yankees, a big, quiet, rusty-haired fellow with a huge cheek dimple and a wide smile. He would often come to the dressing room to visit us.

Over the years, there would be other stars who followed the team's fortunes. Lucille Ball, Desi Arnaz, Humphrey Bogart, George Raft, the Duke and Duchess of Windsor, Edward G. Robinson, Paul Muni, Frederick March, and Cab Calloway were all Rangers fans. For a time, the team was dubbed "The Park Avenue Rangers," because of their high-society following. The Amerks, on the other hand, were "The Bowery Americans."

The Rangers – and their legend – grew quickly, and the team's show-business following, plus their geographic location, soon gave birth to a new nickname: "The Broadway Blueshirts . . . Classiest Team in Hockey." Newspaper advertisements, particularly in Toronto, heralded the arrival of the Rangers in town with just that phrasing.

It was their second season, 1927-28, that became one of the most memorable in Rangers history.

Ivan "Ching' Johnson anchored the Rangers' defense during the franchise's first eleven seasons. For three years, he teamed with Clarence "Taffy" Abel to give the Rangers the league's biggest defense pair.

Coming off their fine initial season, the Rangers stood pat the next year, adding only Alex Gray, a right wing, to the line-up. Patrick's men finished second in the American Division with a record of 19–16–9, which left them four points behind the Bruins. That was good for fifth place in the overall standings, behind the Montreal Canadiens, the Montreal Maroons, the Ottawa Senators, and Boston.

It was in the playoffs that the Rangers caught lightning in a bottle. They dispatched Pittsburgh in two games, six goals to four, in the division quarter-final, and then trimmed Boston in two, five goals to three. That series was billed as a match between hockey's most famous defenseman, Eddie Shore, and Boucher, the game's most gentlemanly player, who had won the Lady Byng Trophy for the first of seven times in eight seasons.

The finals then matched the Rangers with the heavily favored Montreal Maroons. It was a best-of-five series, with all five games being scheduled for the Montreal Forum. Madison Square Garden was unavailable, because of the annual performances there of the Ringling Brothers and Barnum & Bailey Circus, clearly the arena's biggest money-maker at

The 1927-28 New York Rangers, the first New York-based team to win the Stanley Cup. Coach Lester Patrick (center of top row) played an active role in the team's upset victory over the Montreal Maroons.

the time. The Rangers came out flat and lost the opener, 2–0, on April 5. Two days later, the teams met again in a game that will likely live forever in hockey legend. They played through a scoreless first period, but halfway through the second, goalie Lorne Chabot slumped to the ice after being struck above the left eye by a shot from the Maroons' ace, Nels Stewart. Chabot was unable to continue, and Patrick, the team's coach and manager, was desperate for a replacement. Alex Connell, a goaltender for the Ottawa Senators, was in attendance, but the Maroons refused Lester's request to use him as a substitute. The Rangers' net would have to be guarded by a Ranger, it was as simple as that.

Patrick, at forty-four years of age and with a full shock of grey hair, wasted little time in making the decision. He turned from the Rangers' bench and disappeared into the dressing room. He emerged minutes later dressed in Chabot's pads and headed for the Rangers' goal.

As Patrick recounted years later,

Actually we all thought that it was just a mild injury to Chabot's eye and that he would return shortly, but it was worse than we thought and some of the boys said, "Lester, you go in there." But I said no; I didn't want to. However, they persisted, so I donned Chabot's uniform, skates, and what have you, and everything fit perfectly except the skates. I took care of that by putting on an extra pair of socks.

An outstanding defenseman in his time, Lester had even played a little bit of goal, but never regularly. However, Patrick was inspired in his mission. Time and again, he repelled the Maroons, and his teammates were equally inspired with their backchecking. Bill Cook snapped the tie with a third-period tally, and the Maroons finally scored on Patrick, but only after Lester had made two spectacular saves.

Now the game was tied and it was on to sudden-death overtime – the very first overtime game in Rangers' history.

It was a storybook situation indeed, and one that seemed just about impossible from a Rangers standpoint. But just when it appeared that the Maroons would finally prevail, Boucher stole the puck and scored the winning goal.

Only when he saw the jubilation at the other end of the rink did Lester lean back on his net, a tired, middle-aged man who had done the seemingly impossible. Fittingly, his teammates quickly swept him up on their shoulders and skated around the rink.

As startling an achievement as Lester Patrick's was, there are no still photographs of this game. Two posed shots exist, but both were taken after the fact. However, there is a famous poem about the occasion. It was penned by James Burchard, a famous New York hockey writer in the 1940s and 1950s.

Recharged by this dramatic victory, the Rangers went on to win the series, three games to two, and with it their first Stanley Cup. Game three went to the Maroons, 2–0, but the Rangers captured game four, 1–0, and game five, 2–1, on April 14, 1928. A surprisingly large number of New Yorkers had made the journey to Montreal to cheer the Rangers, so the club was hardly without supporters, even in the Montreal Forum.

'Twas in the spring of twenty-eight
A golden Ranger page,
That Lester got a summons
To guard the Blueshirt cage.

Chabot had stopped a fast one,
A bad break for our lads,
The Cup at stake – and no one
To don the Ranger pads.

"We're cooked," lamented Patrick.
"This crisis I had feared."
He leaned upon his newest crutch
And wept inside his beard.

Then suddenly he came to life,
No longer halt or lame.
"Give me the pads," he bellowed.
"I used to play this game."

Then how the Rangers shouted.
How Patrick was acclaimed.
Maroons stood sneering, gloating.
They should have been ashamed.

The final score was two to one.
Old Lester met the test.
The Rangers finally won the Cup,
But Les has since confessed.

"I just spoke up to cheer the
    boys,"
I must have been delirious.
But now in reminiscence,
I'm glad they took me serious.

—*Jim Burchard*

Frank Boucher, on a pass from Ching Johnson, scored the winning goal for the Rangers' first Cup. Recalled Bill Cook many years later: "Had there been a Conn Smythe Trophy (for most valuable player in the playoffs) that year, surely it would have gone to Frank Boucher. He was outstanding throughout the playoffs."

In the custom of the time, hardly any of the Rangers returned to New York to savor their triumph, most of them journeying instead to their year-round homes in Canada. There was one exception, as Eric Whitehead noted in Patrick's biography:

Lester Patrick returned to New York a hero, and nobody embraced him more warmly than did Mayor Jimmy Walker, who loved heroes and their company. Walker was still preening in the afterglow of the colossal tickertape parade he had personally ordered to hail the return of Charles Lindbergh following Lucky Lindy's epic flight to Paris.

Walker, of course, was up front with the new American idol all the way through that incredible parade scene, and he was also up front a few months later with congratulations and a handshake for Babe Ruth, after the Bambino had hit his record 60th homer for the Yankees. And now here he was on the steps of City Hall, beaming and embracing Lester as the crowd cheered and the flashbulbs popped.

Although the Rangers made the playoffs the next four years, five seasons would pass before Stanley Cup number two was secured in 1932-33. Basically, the team was the same team that won in 1928. Only Taffy Abel and Lorne Chabot had been dispatched elsewhere.

President Frank Calder presents the Rangers with their second Stanley Cup after they defeated the Leafs in the 1933 finals. In the Cup-clinching game that year, Bill Cook's overtime winning goal was scored as two Toronto players sat in the penalty box.

The trading of Abel was unpopular with the fans, one of whom, the actor George Raft, indignantly complained that he had wagered and won somewhat handsomely with Abel in the line-up, but without Taffy, he would not be as successful.

The 1932-33 final standings left the Rangers third in the American Division and fourth overall behind Boston, Detroit, Toronto. They drew the Montreal Canadiens in the opening round of the playoffs and ousted the Canadiens in two games, eight goals to five, the first game drawing a record crowd of over eighteen thousand fans to the Garden. The Rangers then made equally short shrift of Detroit, beating the Red Wings in two games, six goals to three. From there it was on to the Stanley Cup finals – the "Classiest Team in Hockey," the Rangers versus the Toronto Maple Leafs. The Cooks and Boucher versus Toronto's famous "Kid Line" – Joe Primeau, Busher Jackson, and Charlie Conacher.

Game one was a rout, 5–1 for the Rangers, but it was to be the team's last home game at the Garden. Hockey was still in competition with the circus for possession of the arena, and the crowd booed lustily when the announcement was made that the rest of the series was to be contested at Maple Leaf Gardens.

Game two went to the Rangers as well, by a score of 3–1, but the Leafs came back to capture game three, 3–2. Game four, played on April 13, was a classic – a scoreless tie through three periods, with Rangers goalie Andy Aitkenhead playing spectacularly in shutting down the Kid Line.

The overtime was a brief one. The Leafs, incredibly enough, let penalties do them in, falling two men short, and Bill Cook scored the game-winner at 7:33 of the extra period.

This time, there was plenty of celebrating. The Rangers were fêted at a sumptuous party at New York's Times Square landmark, the Astor Hotel. The party was thrown by Madison Square Garden president Bill Carey, who had taken the position over that very season from John Hammond.

One very noticeable absentee at the Astor bash was Jimmy Walker, who was no longer mayor by then, having been caught in a graft scandal that turned up secret bank accounts and led to fifteen

Bill Cook, captain of the Broadway Blues from 1926 to 1937, was the first Ranger to lead the NHL in scoring, compiling 37 points in 1926-27.

criminal charges. Walker had resigned and fled to self-exile in England.

The party served not only as a salute to the champion Rangers, but Carey also used it to introduce the Rangers to their new president, General John Reed Kilpatrick, a distinguished military hero and All-America football star at Yale. It was Kilpatrick, a large, genial man who loved to socialize, who would run the Rangers for the next quarter of a century.

Sage businessman that he was, "The General," as he was widely known, quickly made the acquaintance of Lester Patrick. Being of similar natures, the General and Lester hit it off famously, and that meant that the Rangers were in solid, knowledgeable hands for the foreseeable future.

It had been seven years since the birth of the Rangers, and the team had been a relatively mature one when it started, so Lester certainly felt the need to retool if the Rangers were to maintain their excellent caliber of play. What Lester didn't know was that he would find two components of this rebuilding right in his own household, in the persons of his sons Lynn, who would become an All-Star left wing, and Murray, or "Muzz," who would become a popular, bruising defenseman.

Some of the "originals," notably Boucher and Bill Cook, were still hanging on, but others (Murdoch, Johnson, and Bun Cook) retired from active play as the Rangers slipped into mediocrity during the mid-1930s.

Patrick's youth movement was in full swing by 1936-37. A pair of stellar brothers – Neil Colville, a center, and Mac Colville, a right wing – more or less replaced the aging Cooks. Their left wing was Alex Shibicky, and the trio was known as "The Bread Line" during the height of the American Depression. Fiery Phil Watson, a character to the present day, centered the second line, with Lynn Patrick on the left and Bryan Hextall, Sr., a superstar-to-be, on the right.

After having several goaltenders in their formative years, the Rangers finally had a permanent netminder. His name was Davey Kerr, and he would go on to record forty shutouts in seven seasons and win the Vezina Trophy as the NHL's top goalie in the Cup-winning campaign of 1939-40. He also made the cover of *Time* magazine on March 14, 1938, something no other hockey player would manage until Maurice "The Rocket" Richard did it some twenty years later.

The defensemen were new as well. Bruising Art Coulter was the team's new captain, joined by Muzz Patrick, Ott Heller, and the fun-loving Babe Pratt. It was Pratt who once described Lester Patrick as "not exactly cheap, but certainly adjacent to cheap," alluding to Lester's sharp eye with regard to matters financial.

To be sure, this was a fun-loving bunch. But it was Pratt, if only a touch more than the others, who positively loved what he saw in New York. Years later, he recalled his arrival in the city. "I knew I had come a long way from Manitoba when we pulled into Penn Station and hopped a bus to the Garden. I looked out at all those beautiful bright lights of Broadway, and said to myself, 'Babe, you are going to personally look behind every single one.'" No doubt he did – and with lots of company.

Like their counterparts of a decade earlier, the new Rangers were making – and leaving – their own mark on Broadway. For the most part, Lester let them be, but on occasion he had to put his foot down. For instance, when his son Muzz's name made Walter Winchell's column as part of an item regarding a late-night party in a popular nightclub.

Lester was understandably livid, and hailed Muzz into his office the next morning. As Eric Whitehead related in *The Patricks*, the conversation went like this:

"Muzz, have you seen this in Winchell's column?"

"Yes. It's well written, isn't it?"

Just as Lester was about to blow his stack, Muzz grinned and added: "Come on, Lester. Look at it this way. How many Rangers have ever made Winchell's column? Not even Pratt, and you've got to admit that's something." Ever conscious of the value of the press, Lester had to laugh at that one.

Quite unlike their counterparts around the NHL, the Rangers were in a unique situation. The players lived – and worked – in the heart of North America's biggest metropolis. Their practice rink was an undersized figure-skating rink on the fifth floor of the Garden, and one end was only half as wide as the other, because of the installation of an elevator.

Most of the Rangers, whether married or single, lived in mid-town hotels. Despite the elements – and the temptations – of big-city life, the management was not about to change anything. After all, the club was advancing solidly towards a third Stanley Cup championship.

As their predecessors had, the new breed of Rangers continued to attract a show-business crowd, personally and professionally. Metro-Goldwyn-Mayer even planned a hockey movie called *The Great Canadian*, starring Clark Gable as the slick-skating hero, with Myrna Loy the female lead.

Location shots were being filmed at the Garden, and MGM had arranged for Watson to double for Gable and for Pratt to double for the film's villain. Watson even grew a pencil-thin moustache for the shoot. Although the movie was eventually canceled, and Watson was cheated of his movie debut, he did recover. Gable also survived, turning up soon there-

after in a film called *Gone with the Wind*.

The fall of 1939 brought uncertainty, when England declared war on Germany just before the start of the hockey season. The world would be at war for six years, and eventually the war would deeply affect the Rangers – and all of professional hockey – but not right away.

Making his youth movement complete, Lester Patrick himself stepped aside as the only coach the Rangers had known. Not at all surprisingly, he handed the reins to Frank Boucher, whose marvelous playing career had ended a year earlier and who had spent the past season coaching the Eastern League's New York Rovers. The Rovers were the second rung in Lester's unique "Three R" system, which included the Philadelphia Ramblers at the bottom and the Rangers at the top. It was directly through that "feeder" system that the Rangers had developed virtually all the talent that stocked its 1939-40 squad.

The Rangers finished the 1939-40 season with their most wins ever to that date, twenty-seven, good for second place in the seven-team league, just three points behind the Boston Bruins.

The highlight of the regular season, however, was a remarkable nineteen-game unbeaten streak that ran from November 23, 1939, to January 14, 1940 (fourteen wins and five ties), and that still stands as a team record.

That winning streak proved what a remarkably well-balanced club the Blueshirts had assembled. In addition to the Colvilles, the Patricks, Kerr, Hextall, Shibicky, Watson, Coulter, and Heller, there were other key players. Little Clint "Snuffy" Smith, the smallest of the bunch at five feet seven inches, had run off a remarkable string of eighty-five consecutive games without incurring a penalty, and Alfie Pike, a strong, silent centerman, who was then only a rookie, would go on to a stellar career for the Rangers. Add left wingers Wilfred "Dutch" Hiller, the team's fastest skater, and Kilby Macdonald, who had won the Calder Trophy as the NHL rookie of the year, and you had a formidable cast indeed.

Surviving members of the team recall an extremely close bond, a classic sense of camaraderie that held them together. "We had a lot of harmony on that particular team," recalls Shibicky, who played every game that season, including six in the finals, with a broken bone in his ankle. "Everybody dug in for each other."

Adds Pike, "You travel by train, twenty hours at a clip, and you have to get along. We used to have a saying: 'Once a Ranger, Always a Ranger.'"

As much as anyone, it was coach Boucher, sometimes to a fault, who instilled the special sense of closeness in the club. Frank could still be "one of the boys." Says Mac Colville: "Frank was a good egg to have around. He got the guys feeling good."

And, there was Coulter, the captain, who knew a bit about team psychology himself. "Sometimes, I would create situations just to get a rise out of the guys," he recalls. "It would work, too. They would start buzzing like bees, and when we got buzzing, we could beat anybody."

Fittingly enough, the Rangers and the Bruins, just a train ride apart, drew each other in the first round of the 1939-40 playoffs. Total-goals series having been abandoned, this series was now best four-of-seven. It was too early for the circus to move into the Garden, so the Rangers got their fair share of home games, winning the opener 4–0, but dropping the next two in Boston, 4–2 and 4–3.

Goaltender Davey Kerr and defenseman Babe Pratt combine to thwart Eddie Wiseman of the Bruins during the 1940 semi-finals.

Goalie Kerr, winner of the Vezina Trophy, then posted back-to-back 1–0 shutouts for the New Yorkers (the first in New York, the second in Beantown), marking the only time in Rangers' history that a goalie turned successive shutouts in the playoffs. Buoyed by Kerr's heroics, the Rangers won the series, four games to two, with a convincing 4–1 victory at the Garden on March 30.

So it was on to the finals, the Rangers versus the Toronto Maple Leafs, with the Rangers as the favorites, having outdistanced the Leafs by eleven points during the regular season.

The first two games were set for Madison Square Garden, back to back on April 2 and 3, 1940. With Kerr still working his magic, the Rangers won them both, the first 2–1, on Alf Pike's overtime goal, and the second 6–2. As the teams dressed after game

Left to right: Bryan Hextall, Phil Watson, and Lynn Patrick made important contributions to the Rangers' 1940 Stanley Cup victory.

two was over, workmen were already dismantling the boards and melting the ice. The circus was coming to town. The rest of the series would be played at Maple Leaf Gardens in Toronto.

The Leafs quickly rebounded, winning 2–1 in game three, and 3–0 behind goalie Turk Broda in game four. The turning point came in game five, a tight-checking contest that went into overtime. The unlikely hero was defenseman Muzz Patrick, whose goal at 11:43 of the extra session gave the Rangers a 2–1 victory on April 11.

That set the stage for game six, two nights later, Saturday, April 13. Fans from New York, as they had years earlier, journeyed to Toronto by train. The New York Central Railroad made a promotion of the trip, calling it the "Hockey Week-end Excursion": Grand Central Station in New York to Union Station, Toronto. Round-trip fare: $31.15.

The Rangers fell behind 2–0 after two periods of game six, but battled back to tie on third-period goals by Neil Colville and Alf Pike. Then it was on to overtime, and although it is now more than half a century ago, Dutch Hiller says: "I can remember it as though it was yesterday."

What Hiller remembers, barely two minutes into overtime, is muscling a Leaf off the puck behind the Toronto net and zipping a pass to Watson near the Toronto blue line. "It was kind of a fast play, bang-bang, just like that," recalls Watson, who slipped the puck to Hextall, the ever-dangerous, left-handed-shooting right wing. "Bryan came burning in like an elephant," Watson remembers. The Rangers were to be champions again; Hextall's winning shot was a hard backhander, high to the right on Turk Broda, who moved to stop the puck, but missed.

Suddenly the Rangers were hollering and hugging. The Cup was theirs – and so are the memories, half a century later.

Toronto's coach in 1940 was the legendary Hall-of-Famer Dick Irvin, Sr., whose son, Dick, Jr., was a

Hextall, who scored the Cup-winning goal at 2:07 of overtime in game six of the 1940 finals, receives congratulations from coach Frank Boucher.

wide-eyed eight-year-old in the stands that night at Maple Leaf Gardens. Dick, Jr., who would go on to forge a Hall of Fame career himself as a broadcaster, recalls the moment vividly. "I cried," he says. "I was crushed. When it was over, I remember the players didn't line up to shake hands the way they do today. They gathered in a little circle, like it was a cocktail party."

Fittingly enough, a real party did follow, in the Tudor Room of the Royal York Hotel. General Kilpatrick, in an exuberant mood to be sure, made a rare dressing-room appearance and invited the entire team – and their friends – to the party. And what a party it was. Waiters in tuxedos. Players in suits and ties. Champagne replacing the usual beverage of choice, which was beer.

Muzz Patrick still remembers the Stanley Cup perched on a table in the Royal York, and how the players passed it around, held it for a moment, and drank champagne from it.

Those were the days.

Art Ross (center) defines a few defensive techniques, with four of his valued rearguards looking on. Eddie Shore, the finest defenseman of his era, stands to Ross's right.

Goals were even scarcer in 1928-29, dropping to 2.80 per game for both teams. Only two players – Ace Bailey of the Leafs and Nels Stewart of the Maroons – scored more than 20 goals over the 44-game regular season. All but two first-string goaltenders recorded at least 10 shutouts, George Hainsworth leading the league with 22. Hainsworth also posted a goals-against average of 0.92, which earned him his third Vezina Trophy.

The playoff format was further refined. First-, second-, and third-place clubs played their counterparts in the other division. The first-place clubs played a best-of-five series, the winner of which advanced to the finals. The second- and third-place clubs played two-game, total-goals series, with the winners meeting in a best-of-three semi-final round. (This semi-final would be changed to a two-game, total-goals series in 1931-32.) The winner of the semi-final would face the victorious first-place club in a best-of-three Cup final. This unusual format guaranteed that the first-place finishers in each division would not meet in the Stanley Cup finals.

The Canadiens and Boston were the top teams in their respective divisions over the regular season, and the two met in the revamped best-of-five semi-final, which was won by the Bruins. Boston eventually faced the Rangers in the first Stanley Cup final between two U.S.-based teams, which saw the Bruins win their first Stanley Cup. Boston got goals from Dit Clapper, Dutch Gainor, Harry Oliver, and Bill Carson to defeat New York by scores of 2–0 and 2–1 in the best-of-three final.

Before the start of the 1929-30 season, significant rule changes were made to counter the emphatic defensive trend and to soup up offensive play.

The 1929 Pittsburgh Pirates. Formed from a nucleus of players that were part of a club that won the U.S. national amateur championship, the Pirates finished in third place with an 19–16–1 record in 1925-26, their first NHL season. By 1929, however, the club resided in the NHL's basement, and after a 5–36–3 mark in 1929-30, was shifted to Philadelphia.

Forward passing was now permitted in the offensive zone in addition to the defensive and neutral zones, but the puck had to be carried over both blue lines. The new rules also stipulated that no more than three defenders, including the goalie, were allowed behind the blue line until after the attacking team moved the puck into the defenders' zone.

Although the changes were designed to please fans, initial reviews were mixed. Many felt the faster play was reminiscent of old-fashioned river hockey and discouraged the sometimes riotous bashing that had been so much a part of defensive NHL hockey in the 1920s.

It was never questioned that the changes created offense. Indeed, league governors were concerned that the pendulum had swung too far. After 66 of the season's 220 games had been played, the average number of goals scored per game had jumped to 6.91 from the previous season's average of less than three. This increase was so drastic that, beginning with games played on December 21, 1929, the NHL introduced an offside rule that obliged forwards to wait until the puck crossed their opponents' blue line before they could follow it in to carry on an attack. This proved to be a key step in the development of the modern game.

Goaltenders, of course, bore the brunt of these experiments with new rules. Shots on goal and good scoring chances increased, making the goaltender's job more hazardous. To protect a broken nose, Clint Benedict of the Maroons tried out a leather facemask. The mask didn't work; Benedict was re-injured while wearing it and retired from the game.

Netminders' statistics also took a battering. The number of shutouts had dropped from 120 to 26 – almost the number that Hainsworth alone had recorded the previous season. Cooney Weiland and Dit Clapper of the Bruins and Howie Morenz of the Canadiens reached the 40-goal plateau, the first players to do so since Joe Malone scored 44 in the league's first season.

In the playoffs, Boston advanced to the Cup finals by defeating the Maroons three games to one in a series between the first-place finishers in each division. The Canadiens and Rangers were victorious in two-game, total-goal series with the Black Hawks and Senators, with the Canadiens

Action from 1929-30 between the Boston Bruins and the New York Rangers. The Bruins recorded the highest winning percentage (.875 based on 38W–5L–1T) in NHL history that season.

Press Box

The press box had its formal beginnings in the NHL during the 1928-29 season when the league made it mandatory for all teams to have facilities at its rink for visiting media. Teams were directed by President Calder to have "at least ten centrally located seats from which all parts of the rink are plainly visible, adjacent to telegraph wires and telephone communication with minor officials."

then sweeping the Rangers in two straight games to earn a berth in the finals. The Bruins were heavily favored in the best-of-three final series, but the Canadiens, led by Morenz and Alfred "Pit" Lepine, defeated Boston in two straight games to win the Stanley Cup.

The new emphasis on offense placed a premium on cohesive team play. Forward lines came to play together for entire seasons, capturing fan imagination and laying the groundwork for the team approach that would characterize the future of the game. Boston's Weiland, Clapper, and Gainor became known as the Dynamite Line, while in New York, the line of Frank Boucher and the Cook brothers became a mainstay of the league. The Maroons employed the "S" Line (Siebert, Stewart, and Smith), and Morenz and Joliat of the Canadiens played with Johnny "Black Cat" Gagnon. In Toronto, the Maple Leafs' roster included a number of players from the Ravinas, a local amateur team put together by another Toronto hockey fanatic, Frank Selke. To get access to the Ravinas, Conn Smythe hired Selke as a scout and promotions manager. The amateur club provided the new team with players such as Reginald "Red" Horner and two rookies, Charlie Conacher and Harvey "Busher" Jackson, who would flank center Joe Primeau on the renowned Kid Line.

Shown here in an illustration from the Montreal newspaper La Presse, *diminutive right winger Johnny Gagnon was the Canadiens' leading playoff scorer as a rookie during the Habs' Cup-winning 1930-31 season.*

Top forward combinations on other clubs included Ottawa's Hec Kilrea, Joe Lamb, and Frank Finnigan; Chicago's Johnny Gottselig, Tom Cook, and Rosie "Lolo" Couture; and Detroit's Herbie Lewis, Ebbie Goodfellow, and Carson Cooper.

Despite the onslaught of the greatest economic depression the world had ever known, the price of hockey stars was rising. In 1930, using gambling winnings from a horse race, Conn Smythe of the Maple Leafs bought King Clancy from the financially strapped Ottawa Senators for the then-outrageous price of $35,000 plus two players. A year later, the Montreal Maroons would offer $40,000 for the Bruins' Eddie Shore, but Boston manager Art Ross would reject the offer.

Prior to the 1930-31 season, the Maroons traded Red Dutton to the Americans for Lionel Conacher. Conacher, notwithstanding his reputation for enjoying the good life, was still a sound hockey player, and the Maroons' management hoped that he would facilitate their young players' transition to the professional game.

Despite the sale of Clancy, financial woes continued to hobble the Ottawa Senators. Pittsburgh, also facing financial problems, moved to Philadelphia, where the team's name was changed to the Quakers; but the move failed to save the franchise. Both the Quakers and the Senators suspended operations in the spring of 1931. Ottawa and Philadelphia leased their rosters to the league for $25,000 and $20,000 respectively, and the league divided them up among its member clubs.

Charlie Conacher of the Maple Leafs was the NHL's top goal-scorer with 31,

LA PRESSE, MONTREAL, SAMEDI 20 DECEMBRE 1930

JOHNNY GAGNON

followed by Bill Cook of the Rangers with 30. Despite missing five games due to injury, the Canadiens' Howie Morenz was the league's point-scoring champion with 28 goals and 23 assists for 51 points, followed by Ebbie Goodfellow of Detroit, who scored 25 goals and finished with 48. At the urging of local reporters, who felt that a name change would bring the club better luck, the Detroit franchise changed its name from Cougars to Falcons.

The Chicago Black Hawks reached the Stanley Cup finals for the first time in franchise history in 1930-31, but lost to the Canadiens in a tight five-game final. Despite this success, the Hawks fired coach Dick Irvin before the start of the 1931-32 campaign. Irvin was soon hired as a replacement for coach Art Duncan in Toronto.

(continued on p. 63)

The Toronto Maple Leafs' Kid Line of (left to right) Charlie Conacher, Joe Primeau, and Busher Jackson. Formed during the 1929-30 season, the "Kids" had their finest season in 1931-32, when they finished 1–2–4 in league scoring.

SHORE, MORENZ, AND CLANCY

by Percival Leary
South Grouse Nursing Home,
South Grouse, Ontario
as told to Paul Quarrington

I imagine that elsewhere in this book is a chapter, more likely an entire section, devoted to myself, Percival Leary, "King of the Ice." But before you go thumbing around trying to locate it (look up the 1919 Stanley Cup Championship) you should take a while to hear what I'm going to tell you about three mooks I played the game with. You see, the people who made this book got on the blower a short while back, asked if I wouldn't mind being interviewed, and I said I wouldn't, the social calendar here at the South Grouse not being what you'd call chock-a-block. So there is currently a young man pointing a tape recorder at my wrinkled puss. At least, he maintains it's a tape recorder, and I'm obliged to take him on faith.

The three gooms in question are Shore, Morenz, and Clancy. Eddie, Howie, Francis. Boston, Montreal, Toronto. I knew them all. In fact, I would have been nowhere near as unsightly a man as I am now had it not been for Eddie Shore. You maybe notice that my left ear looks like someone tried to fold it up and mail it to his great-aunt. That someone was named Shore.

Mind you, I shouldn't complain. You ought to have seen Eddie.

The ancients here at the South Grouse Nursing Home are very fond of horror motion pictures, trying to gird their loins for the Hereafter, I suppose, but even those movie ghoulies look presentable compared to Shore. It wasn't nature that had rendered him untoothsome, it was battle. The stitches in his face alone numbered 947. His nose had been broken fourteen times, his jaw cracked twice. We were all tough enough back then, I suppose, but Eddie pushed things in that regard.

He was born in a place called Fort Qu'Appelle, Saskatchewan. He knew about cattle and wild horses from there. In fact, I'm not convinced there was anything *but* cattle and wild horses out there, 'cause when Eddie finally blew into Boston in 1926 (they'd plucked him from the old Western Hockey League when it bellied-up), he seemed singularly unlearned in the ways of human beings. I don't mean he was stupid, which he wasn't, but he was, let's say, *otherwise*. Different, if you see what I mean. The first thing he does in training camp is take a series of runs at Billy Couture, a grisly side of beef himself. When they come to blows, Shore ends up with his ear

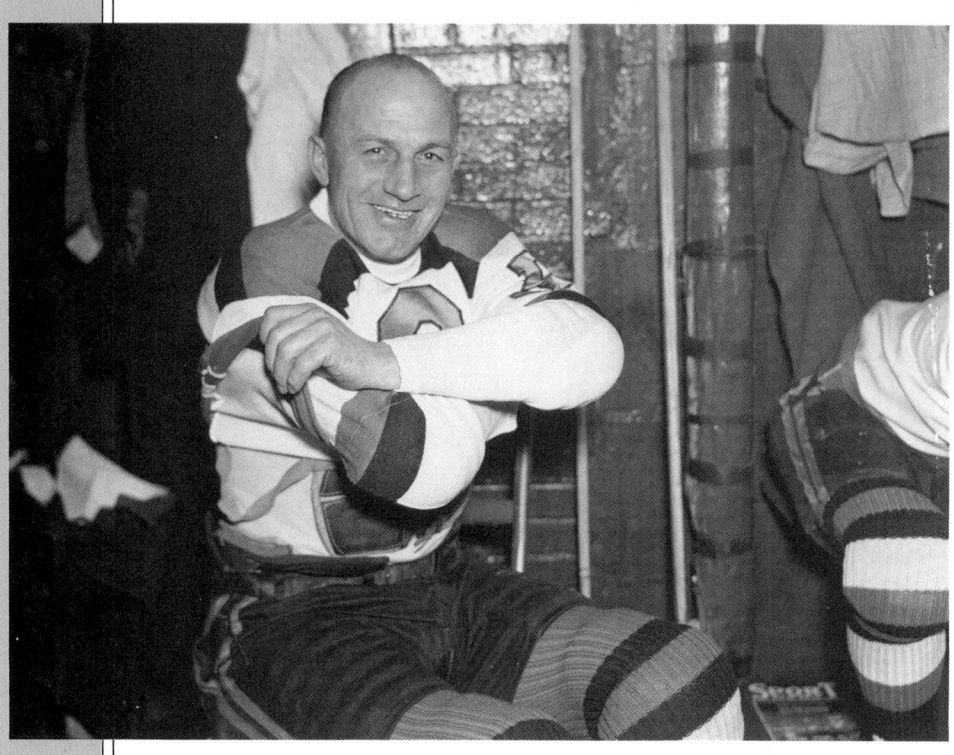

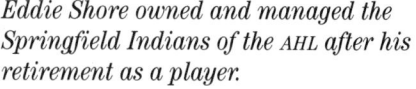
Eddie Shore owned and managed the Springfield Indians of the AHL after his retirement as a player.

sliced and dangling from the side of his head. The Bruins' team doctor says it will have to come off, but Shore states he wants another opinion, like the complaint at hand is dyspepsia instead of a dangling earflap. Eddie finally finds a doctor willing to try his hand at stitching it, so Shore sits down on a little stool and calmly removes a pocket mirror, angling it so he can watch the procedure.

The Bruins knew they'd got themselves something special.

Mind you, there were already stories circulating to the effect that Eddie was, as the old mother would have it, a wee bit addled. Like the time someone caught him on the leg with a skate, carved him up for fourteen stitches. Doctor told him to stay off the leg. Edward had scant respect for doctors. The next game Shore played full-out, popping all the stitches. He ended up with his hockey pants soaked in blood. Another time, his team, the Melville Millionaires, was embroiled in a championship match with Winnipeg. The coach told Eddie not to take a penalty, no matter what happened. Eddie complied and abandoned the more reciprocal aspects of his game. The Winnipegonians figured out what was going on and came at Shore hard and bullish. Eddie played a full fifty minutes, that is, until he was rendered insensate for the third time, at which point they hauled him unconscious into the dressing room. He'd broken his jaw, his nose, and lost six teeth. Of course, he never did draw a penalty.

Mind you, in his second season with the Bruins he got I think it was 166 minutes in penalties, and although I realize that some overly exuberant boys have broken this record recently, it stood for years.

Some of the most famous tales about Eddie concern his bullheaded determination to get to games. He was once in Boston when the rest of the team was in Montreal. He hired a chauffeur-driven car, chauffeur-driven until the chauffeur decided he didn't much care for the blizzard that was raging, at which point Eddie installed the driver in the back seat and got behind the wheel himself. The windshield got blown out, but Shore just squinted and kept on going. The car went into a ditch, but Shore just found some horses and hauled it out. Eddie made it to Montreal in time to pot the winner. Another time,

in New York City, Eddie broke three ribs and contracted a fever so high they thought it was prudent to hospitalize him. The doctor left Eddie alone in a hotel while he went to register him but, when the doc got back, Eddie had boarded a train for Montreal, where the Bruins had their next game.

I don't think it's mere coincidence that Montreal was the destination in both those stories. You see, Shore played defense, which is to say, if you had the puck and he was the only thing standing 'twixt you and the goal, little thoughts would run through your mind. You'd consider career changes, is what I'm saying, and if you did manage to get by him, you'd only make him mad. But there was one player who used to get by him, in fact Eddie would be the first to tell you that this man was the hardest in the whole league to stop, and that man would be the Montreal Canadiens' Howie Morenz.

It was Howie Morenz who did the following to Eddie: Howie was coming down the ice, which he did at a clip you had to see to believe. We called Howie Morenz the Stratford Streak, the Mitchell Meteor, the Canadien Comet. The French called him *l'homme éclair*, which I assume runs along the same track, although it does beg the question, what the jesus are those chocolate things we been eating? The point is, Howie was fast, and if you don't believe it, listen up. First thing, Shore and his defensemate decide to sandwich Morenz, except he darts through and they collide like mountains. Then Howie fires at the net, misses by a hair, and while Morenz blows around back of the net, the puck pops out and lands right on Eddie's blade. Well, you didn't have to send Shore a written invite, that man was gone, and he was a hell of a skater himself. He charges toward the Montreal net on a clear-cut breakaway, and while he's deciding on a suitable course of goaler befuddlement, Howie Morenz appears out of nowhere – *in front of him* – and relieves Shore of the rubber.

Mitchell, Ontario, is where Morenz was born (he moved to Stratford, thirteen miles away, when he was a sprout of nine), and he came to the attention of the Canadiens' high muck-a-muck, Léo Dandurand, when he scored nine goals as an amateur in a single game. Looking into the matter, Léo discovered this lad was quite the star in his hometown. Such was

Howie Morenz, who scored the second goal for the All-Stars during the Ace Bailey Benefit Game in 1934, was known for his finesse and elegance as a player.

Howie's shinny-playing prowess that there was an actual instance of the other team *trying to get him arrested*. It seems a member of the local constabulary (the Stratford lads were playing away, in Preston) showed up one time between periods, wanting to haul Howie to the hoosegow on the charge of malicious damage to property. Turns out that whilst rounding the net at his usual clip, Morenz sliced the toes of the goal-judge's galoshes.

The thing I remember best about Howie, aside from his shinny-playing brilliance, was this: if you gave the man half an hour with nothing better to do, he'd grow a beard. Morenz would shave a couple of times a day, and he'd also change his clothes a couple times a day, sometimes thrice, exchanging one set of fancy duds for another, Morenz being something of a fashion horse. Howie Morenz was a happy-go-lucky sort, which doesn't get played up much these days, largely owing to the conjecture surrounding his final days. But I'm here to tell you that Morenz enjoyed life. He used to play the uke, he liked to sing, and he carried on what the newspapermen used to call an intense love affair with Montreal, which meant, don't bother waiting up. Not that

he was a great misbehaver or anything, he just didn't seem to care much for sleep. If his team should lose, Howie would be up all night, walking the streets morosely and dwelling on it. If his team should win, a far likelier outcome, then Howie would be up all night being, well, happy-go-lucky.

Mind you, you want to talk happy-go-lucky, I should get around to the last of the three, Clancy. Francis, Frank, whatever. They called him "King," just as they called me King, although in Clancy's case it was kind of an inherited thing. His father, Thomas, was a well-known footballer around Ottawa, also called King, and I understand the elder Clancy had the stature to pull it off. Somehow the handle got passed on to his son, even though Francis Clancy only weighed 135 pounds. But I remember what Conn Smythe said about him, he said, "Clancy may only weigh one-thirty-five, but 125 of it is heart." And he was one happy-go-lucky son-of-a-gun. I imagine that if you look up *happy-go-lucky* in a dictionary they got a picture of Frank "King" Clancy. When he first signed on with the Maple Leafs, Smythe asked him what he wanted to be paid. "Anything you say," replied Clancy.

That would have been 1930. Clancy was already a star, up in Ottawa with the Senators. Conn Smythe wanted Clancy, but couldn't afford to deal for him. What altered the course of hockey history is that Smythe owned this racehorse named Rare Jewel, and the beast was indeed rare, in that you don't see many such sway-backed nags. So Conn put down some money on the creature to win such-and-such a race, and probably no one was more surprised than Smythe when that horse did just that, paying off at a hundred to one. So then Smythe dealt for King Clancy, $35,000 it cost him, which I suppose these days you might spend taking a prospect to dinner, but at the time it was much ballyhooed. That was the most money had ever exchanged hands in connection with a hockey player. The next year, you know, Conn Smythe offered more than *twice* that, 75,000 clams, to Montreal, but the Canadiens weren't about to part with the Mitchell Meteor. Howie Morenz was at the top of his game, he'd potted 40 goals in just 44 games, and I don't care how you peel that particular potato, that's astounding. But I remember something

somebody said about Morenz back then. "The kid's *too* fast," is what they said. "He'll burn himself out."

Morenz's first game with Montreal was against the Ottawa Senators, whilst Clancy was still anchoring their back end. The King had heard a lot about this kid from Stratford, but tended to dismiss it mostly as hyperbole. So Morenz got the puck and lit out for enemy territories. Clancy readied himself, got set nicely, and waited for Howie to make one of his highly touted little dekes.

Morenz went right over him, knocked King on his doormat.

King's defense partner with the Senators was Frank Boucher. One night, that pair found themselves protecting the back-end whilst the Mitchell Meteor was making one of his rushes. Well, Morenz blows by, pots a goal, and Boucher and Clancy look at each other for a moment, and then Boucher wonders aloud, "What did he do, go around you?"

"I don't think so," opines King. "Seems to me he came right up between us." They bandied the point about for a while, neither one coming any closer to knowing what in the world had transpired.

Your Clancy wasn't that much of a puck-potter. I'll tell you how bad he was: his first NHL goal didn't even go in the net, at least not in any acceptable manner. King took a wild shot that the goal-judge counted as a tally, waving the handkerchief over his head, although it was clear to everyone else in the building that the rubber had popped through the mesh on the side.

Some of the best stories have to do with King Clancy and Eddie Shore. Those two, they couldn't have been more different, despite them both being defensemen. Shore would flatten you, Clancy would bother and bedevil you. The end result was the same: if you did manage to get anywhere near the goal, you did so without the company of the puck. Sometimes it seemed like Clancy's real mission in life was to vex Shore. I remember once, Clancy pushed Eddie into the boards. Shore bounced off and dropped his gloves, but before he knew it King Clancy had grabbed his hand and was pumping it up and down. "Why hello, Eddie," he says. "How are you tonight?"

Another time, those two collided near center-ice. They'd both built up a pretty healthy head of steam,

so when they hit they tumbled to the ice. Clancy gets up first – he was nothing if not resilient – and he spies Shore on hands and knees. Well, King's enthusiasm gets the better of him; he hauls off and whacks Eddie across the wattles. Shore just continues getting up, staring grimly at the King, and when he has reached his full height he says, "All right, Clancy. Let's see you try that again."

"Okay, Eddie," says King. "Get back down on your hands and knees."

Of course, there is one story concerning those two that's not very good, but I imagine you want me to tell it. As it happens, I was there, because this was in 1934, after I'd broken my leg, so I was spending a lot of time just watching hockey games. The Bruins were playing the Leafs, and the Toronto franchise ended up two men down, thanks to injudicious conduct. So the Maple Leafs were playing with Clancy and Red Horner on the back end, Ace Bailey the lone forward. Now what happened next is a matter of some question, but I'll tell you what I seen and think. Eddie Shore was on the ice defending for the Boys from Beantown, and all of a sudden he was pushed into the boards by you-know-who, the player somebody called 135 pounds of muscle and conversation. So Clancy pushes Shore into the boards,

After the Ace Bailey "incident" in 1933, the entire Boston team followed Eddie Shore's cue and wore helmets for the remainder of the season.

relieves him of the puck, and then rushes up-ice for a shot at the Boston net. Ace Bailey fell into position beside the other defenseman, Clancy's attack comes to naught, the whistle is blown, and by this time Shore has just finished extricating himself from the boards. Bailey is doubled over, trying to catch his breath, and when Shore saw him his eyes turned black. Now, you can't tell me that Eddie didn't think he was looking at Clancy, and while that doesn't excuse what he did next, it makes it a bit more understandable. Shore charged him from behind, caught Bailey with his shoulder, sent him flying into the air. Ace dropped and then ceased to move. So Horner comes over and says, "Why the hell did you do that, Eddie?" Apparently Eddie just smiled, adding fuel to the theory that Shore figured he'd just dropped King Clancy, and Red lofts his stick and connects off Eddie's head. Shore dropped, blood started pouring out on to the ice. Shore's looked like the more serious injury – I mean, blood covered the ice for about three feet in all directions, but after the game we all learnt that Ace Bailey was knocking on the Big Door. Now, he didn't die, thank the Good Lad upstairs, but his hockey career was over.

They had a special ceremony for Ace during the all-star benefit game we held for him. Bailey came out on the ice, wearing dark glasses, walking very gingerly. He seemed to have aged tremendously during the few months he'd been out of the game. He moved along the line of players, shaking hands, and the audience all fell silent as he arrived at Shore. Well, those men embraced, and all the shinnyboys began to bang their sticks on the ice. Just thinking about it brings a lump to my throat, and I am the least sentimental of men.

I might as well get the bad stories over with all at once.

It seemed like that fellow might have been right, who said that Howie Morenz might burn himself out, just like the meteor he was named for. He'd dropped way down in the scoring, forty-eighth in the league or something, and he was dealt to Chicago. But that just didn't seem right, and in 1936 he came back to wear the Canadien red, white, and blue. He was

Howie Morenz in a hospital bed after suffering his career-ending injury.

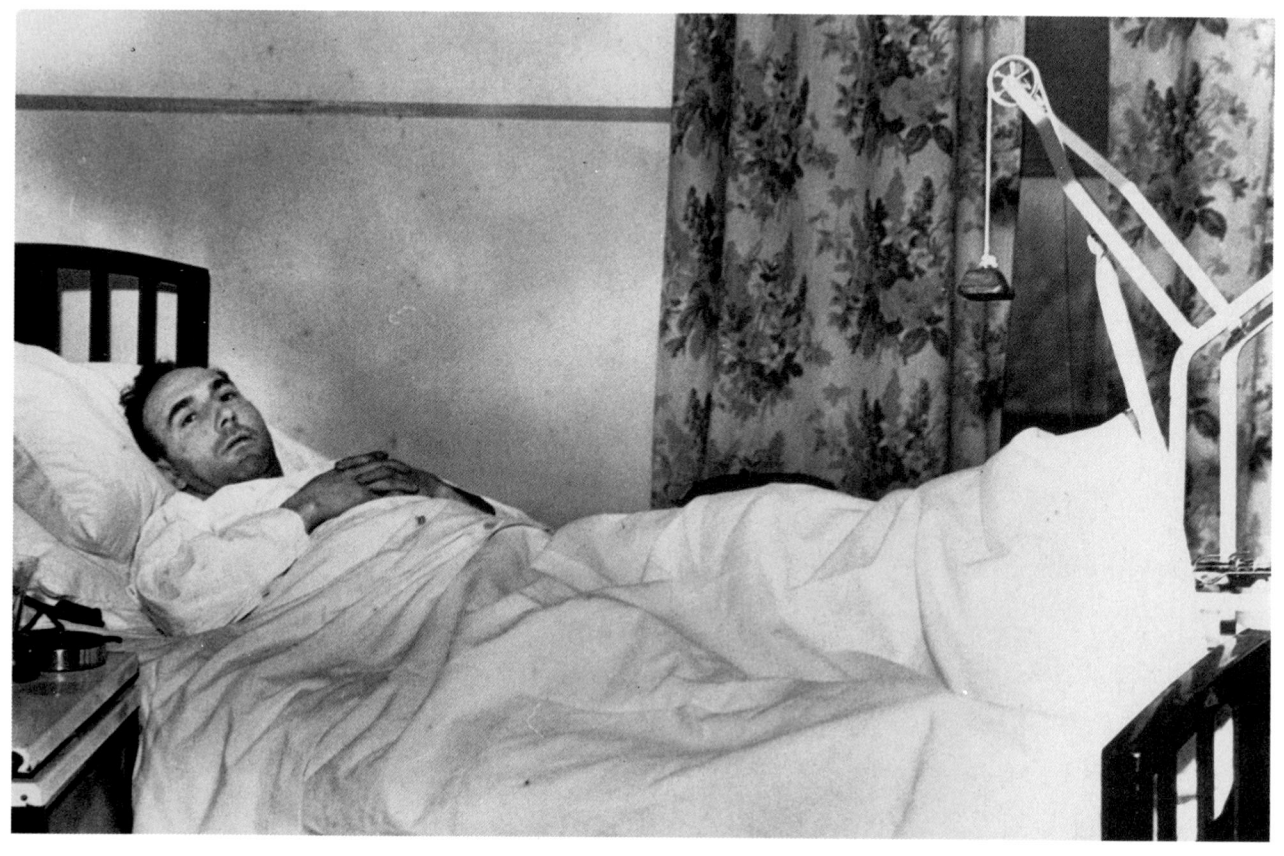

nowhere near the player he'd been, but every so often Howie would light out at a hell of a clip, and on January 28, 1937, he was doing just that when he caught the blade of his skate along the boards. To say he broke his leg would be something of an understatement. I believe he snapped it in four different places. He was laid up in hospital for about six weeks, and then Howie Morenz died.

Twenty-five thousand people filed by his casket lying in state in the Montreal Forum.

Now, many people ask me, they say, Leary, what the jesus happened? Well, the official reports cited something called a coronary embolism. His heart exploded. Other people think that his heart didn't explode, they think it just plain broke, because his career was just about over anyway, and his broken left leg certainly made sure of that, and a lot of people think that the Stratford Streak just couldn't conceive of a life without the game of hockey. This is why there's a widespread impression that Morenz was a moody, morose sort, because anyone who is popularly believed to have willed himself to death ain't likely to be Mr. Sunshine.

But there's those among us who gave at least a little consideration to the notion that what did Howie in was Life – in even larger dollops than he was used to. As somebody put it, that hospital resembled nothing more than Times Square on a Saturday night. There were people through there every minute, huge clutches paying no mind to the posted visiting hours. The nurses and doctors were frantic trying to get Morenz some peace and quiet, frantic and very unsuccessful. I myself get one visitor per week in this place, my son the gormless Clifford, and even that solitary half-hour leaves me exhausted and spirit-sapped, so I can't begin to fathom what Howie Morenz went through. Anyway, it solved his problem of living a life after hockey, a problem every man-jack of us has.

Clancy, now he came back as a coach and a referee. He officiated for eleven years and only handed out a total of five misconducts. He coached for the Maple Leafs, and then he became an assistant to the general manager, and then the vice-

King Clancy during his three-year stint as Toronto head coach during the 1950s.

president, and he was with the Maple Leafs right up until his death in 1986. Clancy was a Toronto boy, through and through, and it didn't matter if he was born in Bytown, just as Shore was a Beantowner and Morenz the King of Mont Royal. And I want to make this point, those three teams were among the best that ever were.

Let's take Clancy's Toronto Maple Leafs for first. This was the team had the famous Kid Line: Busher Jackson, Gentleman Joe Primeau, and Charlie Conacher. They had fellows like Ace Bailey, Baldy Cotton, Hap Day, and Red Horner. They were imbued by the spirit of Clancy, which means they didn't take life all that serious, which got them nicknamed the Gashouse Gang on Ice, after baseball's prankish St. Louis Cardinals.

By the Courtesy of Eno's "Fruit Salt"

Now Morenz's Canadiens, they were the ones who first got called the Flying Frenchmen. They were all speedy, Pit Lepine, Wildor Larochelle, Black Cat Gagnon, and of course, you can't discuss Morenz for long without mentioning the little pipsqueak alongside, Aurel Joliat, who could match Howie step for step, and some fellows would argue ofttimes got the better of him.

The Boston Bruins, as you know, still have a reputation for being tough mean sons-of-bees, and they first earned that back in the days of Eddie Shore. They had some fair talent up front, Cooney Weiland, Perk Galbraith, but mostly the Bruins were stingy about giving up points, which had to do with Shore, Lionel Hitchman, and a pint-sized goalie name of Tiny Thompson.

When Eddie hung up the blades he'd amassed a mind-boggling assemblage of honors: four Hart trophies, four times a first-string All-Star, all manner of things. Just before he left his playing days behind, Eddie got crafty and purchased the Springfield Indians of the American League. He ran things in Springfield with a typically iron Shore glove. One example springs to mind: Eddie had himself a goalie who liked to go down too much. Eddie's solution was to loop a noose around the fellow's neck, tie the other end to the crossbar, so that any flopping would be the lad's last. Eventually this sort of conduct caused the rebellious Indians to secure the services of a young lawyer, a fellow named Eagleson, and . . .

I guess you can read all about it in the pages to come. I ain't up to thinking about it. I like recalling the olden days of sports, golden days they were. Just think about it. Baseball had Babe Ruth. Football had Red Grange. And hockey, we were lucky, we had three of them: Shore, Morenz, and Clancy.

Time for my nap.

Clancy played a major role in the Leafs' return to the Cup finals in 1936 by using one of his greatest assets – the gift of gab. In the first round against Boston, Clancy persuaded Eddie Shore that the Bruins were victims of a bad call by referee Odie Cleghorn. Shore agreed and berated the ref, earning a prolonged stay in the penalty box. With the Bruins' best defender off the ice, the Leafs scored three power-play goals to win the game and the series.

The Boston Bruins' NHL governor, Charles Adams, disliked the fact that defending teams often "iced" the puck, shooting it the length of the rink when they were under pressure. He had long advocated a rule calling for a face-off in the defending team's zone when icing occurred, reasoning that it would cut down on the practice and improve the pace of the game. His idea did not appeal to those of the league's governors who represented weaker teams and saw icing as a useful defense against powerful clubs like the Bruins. Adams's annoyance reached its zenith following a game in Boston in which the visiting Americans had iced the puck sixty-one times en route to a 3–2 win. When the league shrugged off his complaints, he promised that the next time the Bruins played the Americans in New York, he would see to it that his team put on a similar snoozer for the New York fans. He lived up to his word, too. The Bruins iced the puck eighty-seven times in a scoreless game.

Adams's tactic had a predictable result. Already jealous of the Bruins' success, other teams began clamoring that Adams be fined anywhere from $1,000 to $10,000 for his actions. President Calder, who had attended the game in question, turned down the plaintiffs' demands, pointing out that Adams had broken no rules. Perhaps to reinforce his decision, Calder observed that the game hadn't been the worst he had ever seen (it's hard to imagine what could be worse than a game in which the icings perpetrated by one team occurred every forty seconds or so). In any event, the Adams-backed icing rule would be added to the NHL rule book for the 1937-38 season.

One change that didn't stick was an attempt to change the shape of the puck. Art Ross, following his success in designing a goal net and frame that had become the league standard, came up with a puck that had rounded edges. When the new model was tried in games, however, goaltenders complained that it took some strange dips and curves. It was abandoned in favor of the traditional model. The rejection didn't discourage Ross from seeking ways to improve equipment, however. Before World War II, he came up with a hockey stick that had a metal handle and replaceable wooden blades. Although it did not catch on at the time, it was a forerunner of the model used by many of today's NHL players.

With the increasing number of teams and games, on-ice officiating became a full-time career. Many of the applicants for officiating jobs were retired players who felt that they knew the game as well as anyone. Even goalie Clint Benedict had a one-game stint as a referee before retiring. But perhaps the most interesting appointment to the job was Odie Cleghorn, half of the brother team that had once been castigated as the rowdiest in the game.

While Ottawa and Pittsburgh proved victims of tough economic times, Conn Smythe in Toronto was proving that economic miracles could happen. In 1931, he opened his new Maple Leaf Gardens, a few blocks up Church

Roy "Shrimp" Worters, the diminutive goaltender for the New York Americans, came up big in the nets in 1929, winning the Hart Trophy with a miniscule goals-against average of 1.21. Worters added the Vezina Trophy to his mantelpiece in 1931, leading the NHL with a GAA of 1.68.

Players Identified by Numbers on Sweaters

Beginning in 1930 it became mandatory for each player to wear a number, measuring at least ten inches in height, on the back of his sweater.

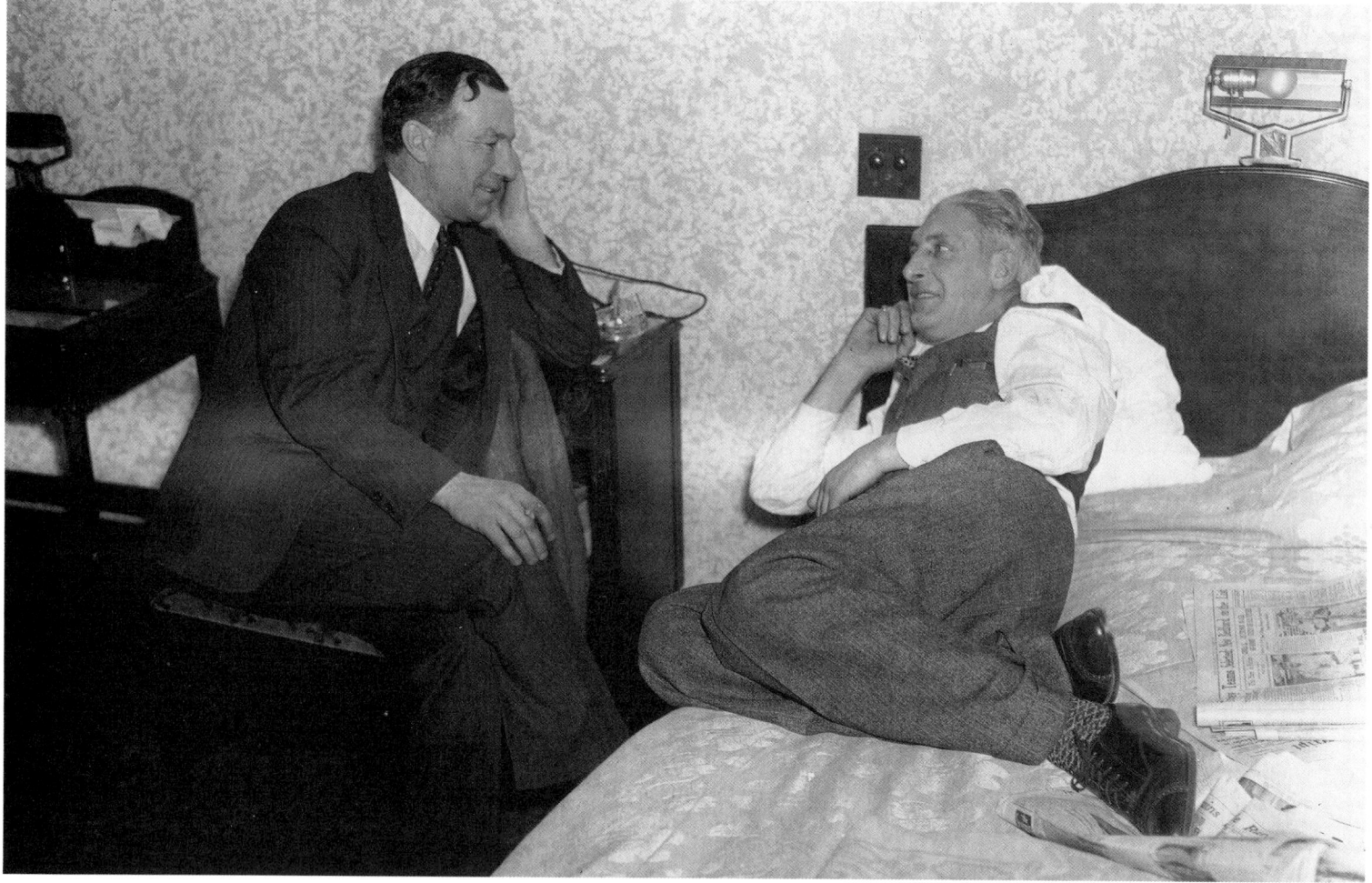

Art Ross and Lester Patrick, perhaps the NHL's most influential architects in the game's growing years, both devoted more than half a century to the game as players, coaches, and managers. Ross built the Boston Bruins into Stanley Cup champions, while Patrick's New York Rangers won the Stanley Cup in their second year in the NHL.

New Clock Introduced

At the March 1931 NHL Board of Governors meeting in New York, a demonstration of a four-faced electric clock was given by A. B. Conmee of the Port Arthur Shipbuilding Company.

Street (and considerably upscale) from the old Mutual Street Arena. Over the years, the new structure would become the most famous hockey building in the world. In 1931, it was state of the art, and was a money-maker almost from the start, contributing handsomely to the financing of Smythe's tactic of buying the players he needed to build the Leafs.

Perhaps inspired by their new surroundings, the Leafs won the Stanley Cup in three straight games against the Rangers in the spring of 1932. They accomplished the feat by winning in three different arenas. Game one was played in New York, but because Madison Square Garden was subsequently occupied by the circus, the Rangers were forced to play game two in the Boston Garden. The Leafs' third win came in Maple Leaf Gardens. The big-top's disruption of the Rangers' spring activities would become a yearly frustration for decades to come.

As the Depression wore on, it began taking its toll on the weaker franchises. Pittsburgh/Philadelphia finally dropped out for good. (Ottawa would return to action after a year of inactivity, forcing the return of all players the Senators had leased around the league – apart from those the team sold outright to raise cash.) As the season progressed, the New York Americans, playing in Madison Square Garden (owned by the Rangers), complained that their contract with the Garden made it difficult for them to make money. The league administration began to negotiate volume discounts with railways and hotels to help defray traveling costs.

As teams tried to stay on budget, some of their stars weren't being paid what they thought they were worth. The Rangers' Frank Boucher, a multiple-winner of the Lady Byng Trophy, wasn't above walking out on the team as a means of forcing management to improve his contract. The Maroons' Hooley Smith and Babe Siebert of the Rangers held out as well. Concerned that others would emulate these stars, leading to a run on the owners' vaults, Calder announced that he would suspend players who refused to sign a fair contract.

The league governors, who were either team owners or their proxies, were unanimous in their opposition to wholesale increases in player salaries heading into the 1931-32 season, but deeply divided on other issues. Toronto's Conn Smythe and Boston's Art Ross feuded frequently, as did Bruins' owner Charles Adams and Canadiens' co-owner and manager Léo Dandurand. Adams, it seemed, was born to spat. When president Calder fined him $1,000 to try to put an end to his constant baiting of referees and other league officials, Adams resigned as a governor so that he could continue his criticism.

Chicago's owner, Manor House Coffee heir Fred McLaughlin, decided that Calder was taking too many liberties and started a petition among owners to rein him in. McLaughlin's position was that, as league president, Calder was an employee of the owners and therefore shouldn't be levying fines against them. In the end, the petition came to nothing. McLaughlin, who also acted as the Black Hawks' general manager, had a propensity for changing coaches. Fourteen men, several of whom had little, if any, previous coaching experience, would pace behind the Hawks' bench in the franchise's first thirteen seasons.

A less significant problem arose over Detroit's new uniforms. The club had changed its name from the Falcons to the Red Wings and had acquired new red jerseys, which turned out to be very close in color to the red of the Canadiens'. The confusion this created was alleviated by Detroit wearing white pullovers over their game sweaters when they visited Montreal. To prevent similar problems in the future, the league ruled that a visiting team had to wear white pullovers if its uniforms were the same color as those of its opponent.

Beginning on January 1, 1933, radio broadcasts of games from Toronto's Maple Leaf Gardens could be heard across Canada on twenty stations. With play-by-play by Foster Hewitt, these games would soon attract listening audiences of more than one million people. Hewitt, who had pioneered hockey on radio in 1923, called the play from "the gondola," a custom-built broadcast booth located fifty-six feet above the ice at the Gardens. Hewitt's

Playoff Per Diem

The league adopted a uniform per diem of $5.00 per man for meals and $2.50 per man for lodgings for the 1931 Stanley Cup playoffs.

Formal Definition of Assist Adopted

Before the beginning of the 1931-32 season a formal definition of an assist was adopted for the first time by the NHL's Board of Governors. It read as follows: "A goal shall be credited in the scoring records of a player who shall have propelled the puck into the opponent's goal. When such goal shall have been scored as a result of an act of a player of the same side, such player shall be credited in the scoring records with an 'assist.' An assist may not be credited, however, to a player unless the act of 'assistance' took place within the defending zone of the opposing team. If a goal was scored from a rebound from a goal-keeper or from any part of the goal, credit for an 'assist' shall be given to the player whose shot caused such rebound."

Foster Hewitt in his broad-caster's perch high above the ice of Maple Leaf Gardens. Although he never played pro-fessional hockey, Hewitt proved to be the game's greatest ambassador, bring-ing the action into living rooms across Canada – and throughout what was then the separate British colony of Newfoundland – every Satur-day night.

"He shoots . . . he scores!" would soon become the most widely recognized phrase in Canada.

The Canadian Press wire service initiated a rookie-of-the-year award for 1932-33. This award, which was won by Carl Voss of the Red Wings, was the predecessor of the Calder Trophy, first awarded in 1936-37.

In the first round of the playoffs, overtime was required in four of the five games needed to determine a winner in the first-place finishers' series between the Bruins and Maple Leafs. The Leafs advanced to the finals on Ken Doraty's goal after 104 minutes and 46 seconds of extra time. This eclipsed by 36 minutes the league mark for longest overtime game. The Red Wings and the Rangers won two-game, total-goals series to qualify for the semi-finals, won by the Rangers six goals to three. In the finals, the Rangers defeated the Leafs three games to one to win their second Stanley Cup and become the first third-place team to win in the playoffs.

Shortly after the end of the post-season, president Calder appointed Lester Patrick, Eddie Gerard, Jack Adams, and Newsy Lalonde to a commit-tee to review the rules and operating procedures of the NHL. Frank Patrick was appointed to the new position of NHL managing director, whose responsibilities included the maintenance and supervision of the league's officiating staff. At the same time, a salary cap of $65,000 per team was imposed, to help owners control their payrolls.

By the start of the 1933-34 season, the NHL was beginning to take on a different look, partly as a result of the economics of the time. The Detroit franchise, which had gone into receivership in 1932, had been bought by Olympia Incorporated, a company controlled by James Norris, Sr., and his son, James D. Norris. The Ottawa Senators, though vowing to start the season, were on shaky financial footing. So were the New York Americans, but the rumor that the Americans and Senators might amalgamate was quickly extinguished by Calder. In Montreal, there was concern about the Maroons' poor crowds at the Forum, which they shared with the Canadiens.

The Bruins' superb rushing defenseman Eddie Shore, coming off a season for which he was awarded the Hart Trophy as the league's most valuable player, was unwilling to accept a reduced salary offered by Art Ross and held out for the first three games of the season. Shore finally met with NHL president Calder and signed a $7,500 contract in the Bonaventure train station in Montreal.

Maximum Player Salary Adopted during Depression

In 1932, the NHL's Board of Governors directed that no team should have a total payroll for players in excess of $70,000, while no individual player should be paid more than $7,500.

Two years later the maximum team salary was set at $62,500, with the maximum individual salary rolled back to $7,000.

The Montreal Canadiens of 1933-34 with their two most famous sons, Aurel Joliat and Howie Morenz, flanking goaltender Lorne Chabot. When Morenz was traded to Chicago the next season, it marked the end of an era for "the Flying Frenchmen."

By 1933-34, Shore's reputation as one of the NHL's toughest and most skilled players was well established. It seemed he was at the center of every *contretemps* that took place on the ice. The most infamous of these, one of the darkest in hockey, took place in Boston on December 12, 1933. Shore, having attempted one of his hallmark rink-long rushes, was tripped by King Clancy before he could shoot. Mistaking Toronto's Ace Bailey for Clancy, Shore retaliated by checking Bailey from behind as he came out of the Toronto end. Unfortunately, Bailey fell and hit his head on the ice and fractured his skull. It was ten days before doctors were sure Bailey would live, and though he recovered, his hockey career was finished. Ironically, former tough guy Odie Cleghorn was the referee on the night of the incident in Boston.

The aftermath of the battle saw Shore suspended for sixteen games. Conn Smythe thought Shore got off lightly, and later insisted that Boston indemnify the Leafs for the loss of their star player. For good measure, Smythe also wanted the Bruins to cover the the costs the Leafs incurred while Bailey recuperated. Boston's Art Ross, at least Smythe's equal in playing to the press, countered by noting how repentant Shore was and claimed that his feelings of guilt were punishment enough. (Shore, meanwhile, was vacationing in Bermuda during his suspension.)

In the end, the Bailey–Shore incident was the impetus for the NHL's first All-Star Game. This game, which Bailey attended, saw the Maple Leafs defeat an NHL all-star team 7–3 on February 14, 1934. The affair raised more than $20,000 for a trust fund in Bailey's name. A benefit game in Boston added another $6,764 to the fund. In March, Bailey was well enough to drop the puck for a ceremonial face-off in a game between Toronto and Boston. But the game itself was almost overshadowed by the touching moment

The first NHL All-Star Team that played the Toronto Maple Leafs in a benefit game for the injured Ace Bailey. Top row, left to right: Charlie Gardiner, Red Dutton, Eddie Shore, Allan Shields, (referee), Frank Finnigan, Lionel Conacher, Ching Johnson, Nels Stewart. Front row, left to right: Normie Himes, Larry Aurie, Hooley Smith, Jimmy Ward, Lester Patrick, unidentified, Bill Cook, Howie Morenz, Aurel Joliat, Herbie Lewis. The mascot is Howie Morenz, Jr.

when Eddie Shore slowly skated up and shook Bailey's hand.

In the spring of that year, Chicago, led by Vezina Trophy-winning goaltender Charlie Gardiner, defeated Detroit to win its first Stanley Cup. The series featured the match-up of two top lines: the Black Hawks' Harold "Mush" March, Elwyn "Doc" Romnes, and Paul Thompson, and the Red Wings' Larry Aurie, Cooney Weiland, and Herbie Lewis. March had two overtime goals in the playoffs, including the only goal in the Cup-clinching game. Despite winning the Cup, the Black Hawks' performance wasn't good enough for their owner McLaughlin. Shortly afterwards, he fired coach Tommy Gorman, who immediately got a job with the Maroons.

In the off-season, Charlie Gardiner died of a brain tumor. He was thirty years old.

In the fall of 1934, financial woes forced the Ottawa Senators to move to St. Louis, where the team was renamed the Eagles. Despite the new location, business remained bad, and the Eagles were forced to sell off their better players to raise money. This resulted in a last-place finish and a farewell to the league at the end of the 1934-35 season. Meanwhile, the New York Americans' players were complaining that they weren't getting paid. The state of the economy was reflected in the NHL's decision to lower the salary cap to $62,500 per team and $7,000 per player. In an effort to stay within that limit, several high-salaried stars were traded, including Howie Morenz, the Canadiens' perennial scoring leader, who ended up in Chicago. Lionel Conacher followed coach Tommy Gorman from the Black Hawks to the Maroons.

On the last night of the season, Toronto's Charlie Conacher won his fourth goal-scoring title in a game refereed by Babe Dye, who, before becoming an

Charlie Gardiner, considered by many to be the finest goaltender of his generation, spent seven outstanding seasons in the NHL, winning the Vezina Trophy in 1932 and 1934 and leading the Chicago Black Hawks to their first Stanley Cup title in 1934.

This fedora-flourishing flock of fellows is the Toronto Maple Leafs of 1934, posing elegantly in front of their state-of-the-art ice palace, Maple Leaf Gardens.

official, had himself won the title on three occasions. It is noteworthy that Frank Boucher won his seventh Lady Byng Trophy in the past eight seasons.

In the playoffs, Toronto needed four games to eliminate Boston and qualify for the finals. The Montreal Maroons defeated Chicago and the Rangers to earn a date with the Maple Leafs. In the Maroons' first two-game, total-goals series, both contests with the Black Hawks were scoreless after regulation time. In overtime in game two, a major penalty called against Chicago's Lolo Couture gave the Maroons a power-play that was converted by Lawrence "Baldy" Northcott into the only goal of the series. In the finals, the Maroons defeated Toronto in three straight games to win their second Stanley Cup. Tommy Gorman became the only coach to win the Cup in successive years with different teams.

Unsettled conditions prevailed into the 1935-36 season, when Dandurand and Joseph Cattarinich sold the Canadiens to a group led by Ernest Savard. It is possible that Dandurand and Cattarinich thought they were dealing away an aging and unproductive line-up, but, while Savard couldn't have known it at the time, one of the hidden treasures on the Canadiens' roster was rookie Hector "Toe" Blake, who had originally signed with the Maroons but had been traded to the Habs for goaltender Lorne Chabot.

Elsewhere around the league, the Americans were still in financial difficulty and had to be bailed out by the NHL, which took over operation of the team. Even the Maroons, the previous year's Stanley Cup winners, were struggling to draw fans to the Forum, and the Canadiens weren't drawing well either. Many of the league's owners and managers believed that Montreal could no longer support two NHL teams.

The Cook Brothers (Bun and Bill) joined crafty centerman Frank Boucher to form a productive forward line that played together for ten seasons.

The Forum in Montreal was the site of a unique late-season skirmish involving two league governors and NHL president Calder. Toronto's Conn Smythe became involved in a shouting match with Canadiens' playing-coach Sylvio Mantha and followed him into the penalty box to continue his protests. With the arrival of referee Mike Rodden, Canadiens' owner Ernest Savard, and president Calder, fans were treated to the unusual spectacle of two of the league's governors and its president in the penalty box during a game.

In New York, Lester Patrick broke up the Rangers' forward line of the Cook brothers and Frank Boucher that had been together for ten years and had amassed more than 1,100 points. The Bruins traded Marty Barry to Detroit to reacquire Cooney Weiland and reunited him with Dit Clapper to re-form two-thirds of the old Dynamite Line. The Detroit Red Wings had rebounded from a last-place finish in 1934-35 to finish first in the American Division. The acquisition of Marty Barry enabled Jack Adams to create one of the league's top forward lines, as Barry centered Larry Aurie and Herbie Lewis.

In the playoffs, the Red Wings swept the Maroons to win the best-of-five series between the first-place clubs in each division. The first game of this

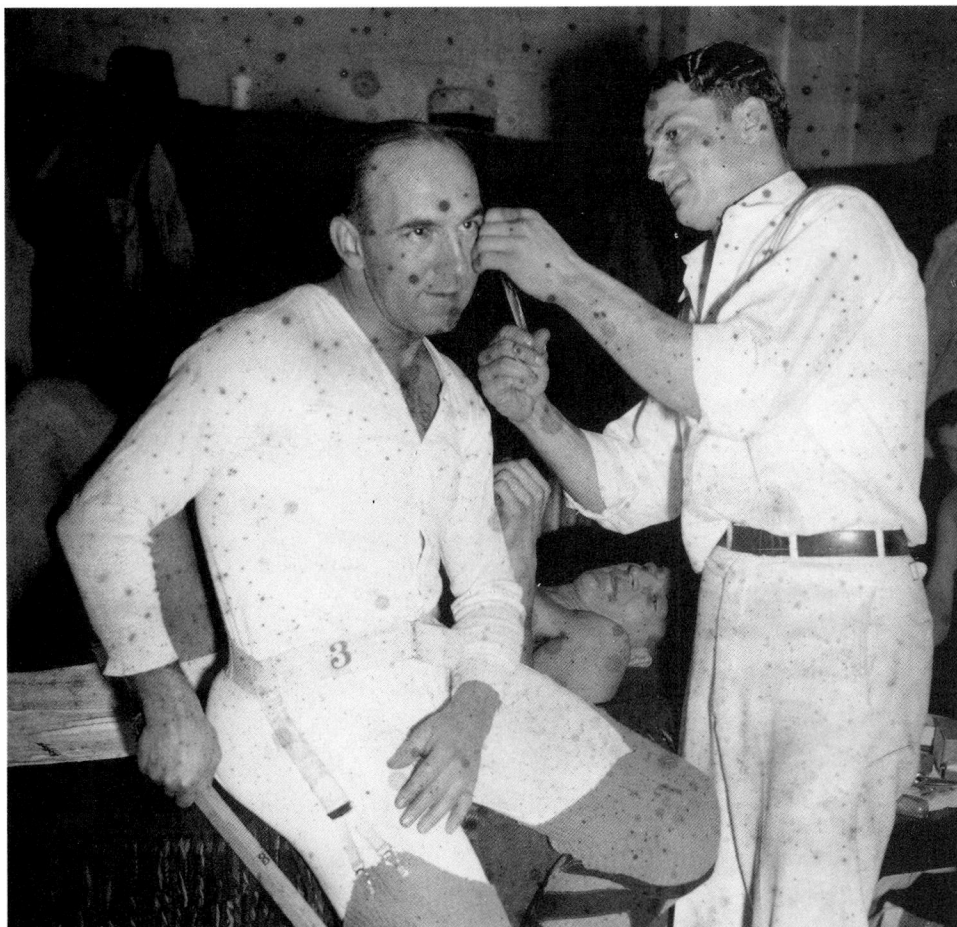

Howie Morenz receives a cosmetic touch-up from a Chicago Black Hawks' trainer shortly after arriving in the Windy City in 1934. Morenz, who was traded to the New York Rangers midway through the 1935-36 season, returned to the Montreal Canadiens for 1936-37.

series was a marathon overtime encounter that finally ended after 116 minutes and 30 seconds of extra time when Detroit rookie Mud Bruneteau scored the only goal of the contest. In other first-round series, Toronto eliminated Boston and the New York Americans upset heavily favored Chicago seven goals to five. Roy Worters was a standout in goal for the Americans, but the dark-horse team of 1936 was eliminated in three games by the Maple Leafs. In the Stanley Cup finals, the Red Wings won games one and two and appeared to be in position to sweep the series when, in game three, trailing 3–0 after two periods, the Leafs scored three goals to force overtime. Frank "Buzz" Boll got the winner for the Leafs after just thirty-one seconds of overtime. This established a new record as the shortest overtime game in Stanley Cup play. The Wings bounced back to win game four 3–2, clinching their first Stanley Cup.

The final Cup game of 1936 was the last for Toronto's Joe Primeau, who retired after the series. Primeau, who had seven points in the 1936 playoffs, was the first of Toronto's Kid Line of Primeau, Charlie Conacher, and Busher Jackson to retire.

At the spring meetings of that year, the NHL moved to boost the fortunes of the struggling Canadiens franchise by ruling that the Habs would have first

Medals Given to Stanley Cup Champions in Early Years

Starting with the 1936 playoffs, each member of the Stanley Cup-winning team received a medal from the league. This tradition was later replaced with the presentation of a miniature of the Stanley Cup to each member of the championship team.

Blinco First NHLer to Wear Glasses while Playing

Montreal Maroons' center Russ Blinco made hockey history during the 1936-37 season when he became the first NHL player to wear glasses in a game.

Olympic Apps

Syl Apps, who signed with the Toronto Maple Leafs prior to the Leafs' Western Canada exhibition tour in April 1936, competed for Canada in the 1936 Olympics, finishing sixth in the pole-vault event.

claim on all unsigned French-Canadian players for the next three years. Any other team wishing to employ a player of French-Canadian descent would have to notify the Canadiens, who would then have two weeks to decide if they wanted the player.

A modification to the playoff format replaced the two-game, total-goals format with best-of-three series. The Stanley Cup finals were changed from best-of-three to best-of-five.

During the 1936-37 season, Howie Morenz, after stops in Chicago and New York, returned to the Canadiens to play again with the seemingly ageless Aurel Joliat and Johnny Gagnon. Although fans were pleased to see the veterans together again, there was no question that all three were in the last stages of their glorious careers. Increasingly, the Canadiens' future was in the hands of young stars such as Toe Blake.

In Toronto, former all-star and shutout king George Hainsworth was replaced in the nets by Walter "Turk" Broda. Rookie center Sylvanus Apps was showing promise working with another first-year player, left wing Gordie Drillon, whose natural scoring touch was a perfect complement to Apps's playmaking skills. Apps would go on to finish second in scoring and win the new Calder Trophy, awarded to the league's top rookie. In the last game of the regular season in Boston, linemates Milt Schmidt and Woodrow "Woody" Dumart were joined by Bob Bauer to form the famed Kraut Line.

Two of the league's top players suffered dramatic injuries, both on the same night. On January 28, 1937, Eddie Shore suffered a cracked vertebra in a collision with the boards in Madison Square Garden and was out for the season after playing just 20 games. That same night, Howie Morenz, while

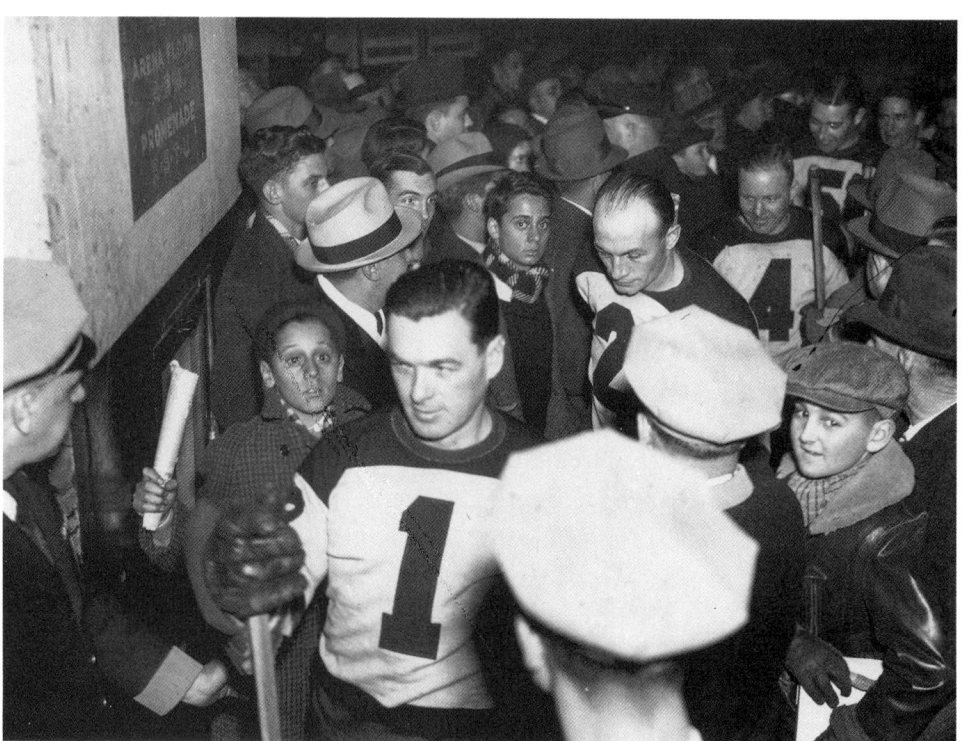

The Boston Bruins, led by Tiny Thompson (1) and Eddie Shore (2), prepare to leave the ice. The Bruins won their second Stanley Cup in 1939, which was Shore's last full season with the team.

being checked by Earl Seibert, caught the tip of his skate in the boards of the Montreal Forum, badly breaking his leg above the ankle. After five weeks in hospital, he died unexpectedly of a heart attack on March 8.

The sudden loss of Morenz, who was the NHL's glittering superstar of the late 1920s and early 1930s and the first three-time winner of the Hart Trophy, was deeply felt by hockey fans in Montreal. Thousands filed by his casket as Morenz's body lay in state in the Forum, and many more – some estimate as many as 100,000 people – lined the route of the funeral procession that took his body from the Forum to the cemetery.

Art Ross made headlines when, accused of having his Bruins play so defensively that they bored fans, he offered $1,000 to anyone who could prove the accusation, though he shrewdly didn't define what would constitute such "proof" and was never taken up on his offer. That same season, Chicago owner Fred McLaughlin demonstrated that firing winning coaches was not his only idiosyncrasy when, with five games left in the regular season, he announced that he would convert his team to one made up entirely of American-born players. Despite the protests of Detroit's Jack Adams, Boston's Art Ross, and the Rangers' Lester Patrick, in the end, McLaughlin iced a team on which only half the players were American. But the team did not do well, winning just one game (against the Rangers), in which no American player scored.

Left winger Dave "Sweeney" Schriner of the New York Americans won his second point-scoring championship, finishing with 21 goals and 25 assists for 46 points. The Red Wings were the NHL's top club, finishing with 59 points, six better than second-place Boston in the American Division. The Canadiens were first in the Canadian Division, one point ahead of the Maroons. The Rangers and Maple Leafs qualified for the playoffs, finishing in third place in their respective divisions.

Thousands gathered in the Montreal Forum to pay their respects to Howie Morenz, who died on March 8, 1937. At the peak of his powers in the late 1920s, Morenz was known as "the Babe Ruth of Hockey." The NHL's second All-Star Game was played on November 2, 1937, to raise money for Morenz's family.

Red Wings, Canadiens Meet in Europe

During the mid-1930s, the Detroit Red Wings and Montreal Canadiens traveled to Britain aboard the sailing vessel *Ausonia* for a series of exhibition games.

Calder Trophy Originally Awarded for Golfing Prowess

The Calder Memorial Trophy, presented annually to the NHL's outstanding first-year player since 1936-37, had its origins in the late 1920s, when it was presented for the best net score during the league's annual golf tournament. Some of the early winners included Sprague Cleghorn (1928), Conn Smythe (1929), and Lionel Hitchman (1930).

The best-of-five series between first-place finishers went the limit, with the Red Wings needing a goal in the third overtime period from Hec Kilrea to eliminate the Canadiens. Detroit goaltender Normie Smith was injured in game three, necessitating the call-up of minor-leaguer Earl Robertson, who played in the Red Wings' 3–1 loss to the Habs in game four.

Detroit's final-series opponent would prove to be the Rangers. Goaltender Davey Kerr allowed just one goal in the four games required to eliminate the Maple Leafs and Maroons in two-game series sweeps.

In the finals, the Red Wings captured their second consecutive Stanley Cup in a five-game final series that featured two shutouts by Robertson and one by Kerr. In the final game of the series, the Red Wings broke through. Marty Barry had two goals and John Sorrell one as the Rangers were eliminated by a 3–0 score.

To raise money for Howie Morenz's family, a memorial game was held in November of 1937. A combined squad made up of members of the Canadiens and Maroons played an all-star team made up of players from the NHL's six other clubs. Cecil Hart of the Canadiens coached the combined Canadiens–Maroons team. King Clancy, who took over as coach of the Maroons, played for the Montreal squad in what was his last appearance as a player in an NHL game. The NHL All-Stars won 6–5 as twenty thousand dollars were raised for the Morenzes.

By 1938, many of the NHL's early stars were turning to coaching, but a few persisted as players. Aurel Joliat, then in his sixteenth season, seemed

The 1937-38 Chicago Black Hawks were longshot Stanley Cup winners after finishing the regular season in fourth place with a 14–25–9 record. They are the NHL's only Stanley Cup-winning team to finish the regular season below the .500 mark.

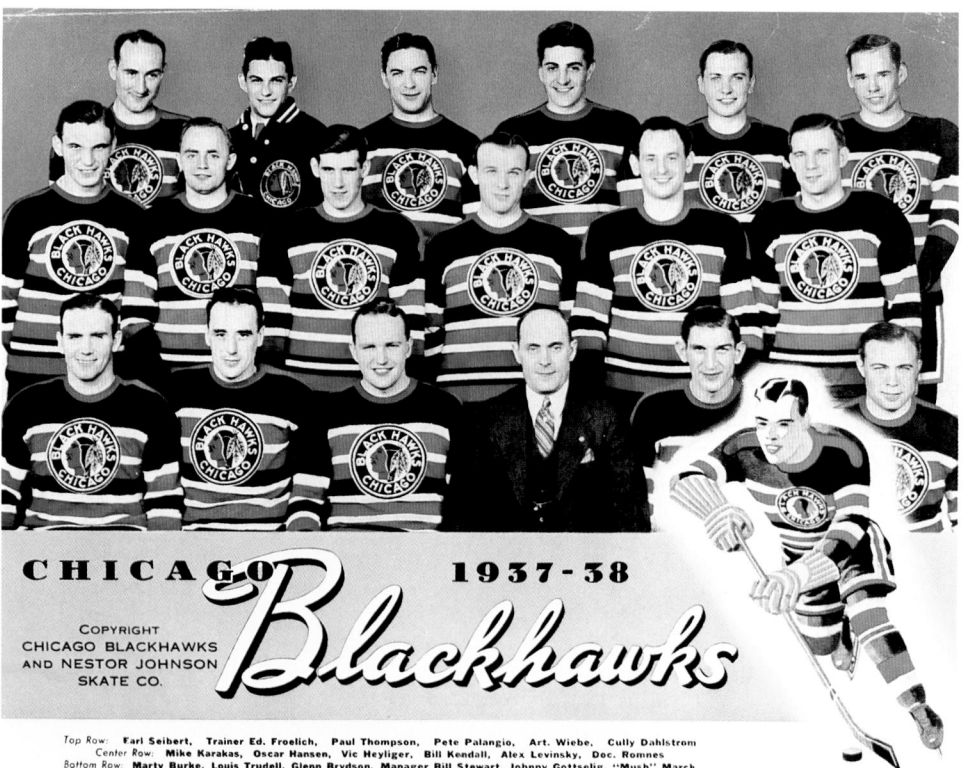

CHICAGO   1937-38
COPYRIGHT
CHICAGO BLACKHAWKS
AND NESTOR JOHNSON
SKATE CO.
Blackhawks

Top Row: **Earl Seibert, Trainer Ed. Froelich, Paul Thompson, Pete Palangio, Art Wiebe, Cully Dahlstrom**
Center Row: **Mike Karakas, Oscar Hansen, Vic Heyliger, Bill Kendall, Alex Levinsky, Doc. Romnes**
Bottom Row: **Marty Burke, Louis Trudell, Glenn Brydson, Manager Bill Stewart, Johnny Gottselig, ''Mush'' March**

ageless. Career goal-scoring leader Nels Stewart of the New York Americans got his 300th, and Eddie Shore, his back finally healed, won his fourth Hart Trophy.

Tommy Gorman had moved up to the general manager's job with the Maroons, having hired King Clancy as coach. Clancy's tenure with the Maroons was brief, as he proved more interested in hanging out and enjoying himself with his players than disciplining them. (Ironically, after leaving the Maroons, he turned to refereeing.) The Maroons' players, though, were not happy to see Gorman take over again as coach, as his hard-headed disciplinary attitude and his insistence on early-morning practices were predictably unpopular.

The Bruins and Rangers were the NHL's top two clubs in the regular season and finished in first and second place in the American Division. Chicago finished third with just 37 points. The Maple Leafs topped the Canadian Division, eight points up on the Americans and Canadiens. The Leafs had the league's two top scorers, as Gordie Drillon finished with 52 points and Syl Apps, 50. Boston's Cecil "Tiny" Thompson won his second Vezina Trophy, allowing just 89 goals-against in 48 games.

The Bruins were upset in the first round of the playoffs as the Leafs swept Boston in three straight games. Toronto goaltender Walter "Turk" Broda allowed just three goals-against in the series. Drillon got the overtime winner in game three. The Black Hawks reached the finals by defeating the Canadiens and Americans, but lost goaltender Mike Karakas, who broke his

Sponsorship of Amateur Teams Adopted

In June 1938 the league gave its approval for member clubs to "designate, assist and finance" one amateur, junior, or senior club in the United States or Canada. A year later, the rule was amended to allow for sponsorship of two amateur clubs.

Sponsorship of junior teams was discontinued in 1966.

big toe in the last game of the semi-finals. Forced to use back-up goaltenders in games one and two, the Black Hawks gained a split before Karakas returned wearing a steel-toed skate. Karakas held the Leafs to just one goal in each of the next two games, as the Black Hawks' much-improved half-American roster captured the 1938 Stanley Cup.

Last-place finishers in 1937-38, the Montreal Maroons were drawing poorly and were suffering grave financial problems. The league allowed the Maroons to suspend operations for a season, provided they disposed of all their player contracts or signing rights by December 1, 1938.

The loss of the Maroons, coupled with the precarious financial health of the New York Americans, forced the NHL to amalgamate its teams into a single seven-team group. To absorb the players from the defunct teams, the league increased the roster size from fourteen to fifteen, plus a goalie. Always the innovator, Lester Patrick of the Rangers used the larger roster to experiment with five-man units and fancy passing patterns. Chicago's Fred McLaughlin continued to change coaches, firing Bill Stewart, the ex-referee and major-league baseball umpire who had led the Hawks to the Stanley Cup the previous spring.

Reduced to one division, the NHL restructured its playoff format. Six of the league's seven clubs would qualify for post-season play. The first and second-place clubs would play a seven-game semi-final. The third- and fourth-place finishers would play a best-of-three quarter-final, as would the fifth- and sixth-place clubs. The quarter-final winners would then meet in a

The New York Americans and the Boston Bruins scramble for possession of a loose puck during action in the 1939-40 season. The Bruins, with Frank Brimsek in nets, returned to the Stanley Cup winners' circle in 1941.

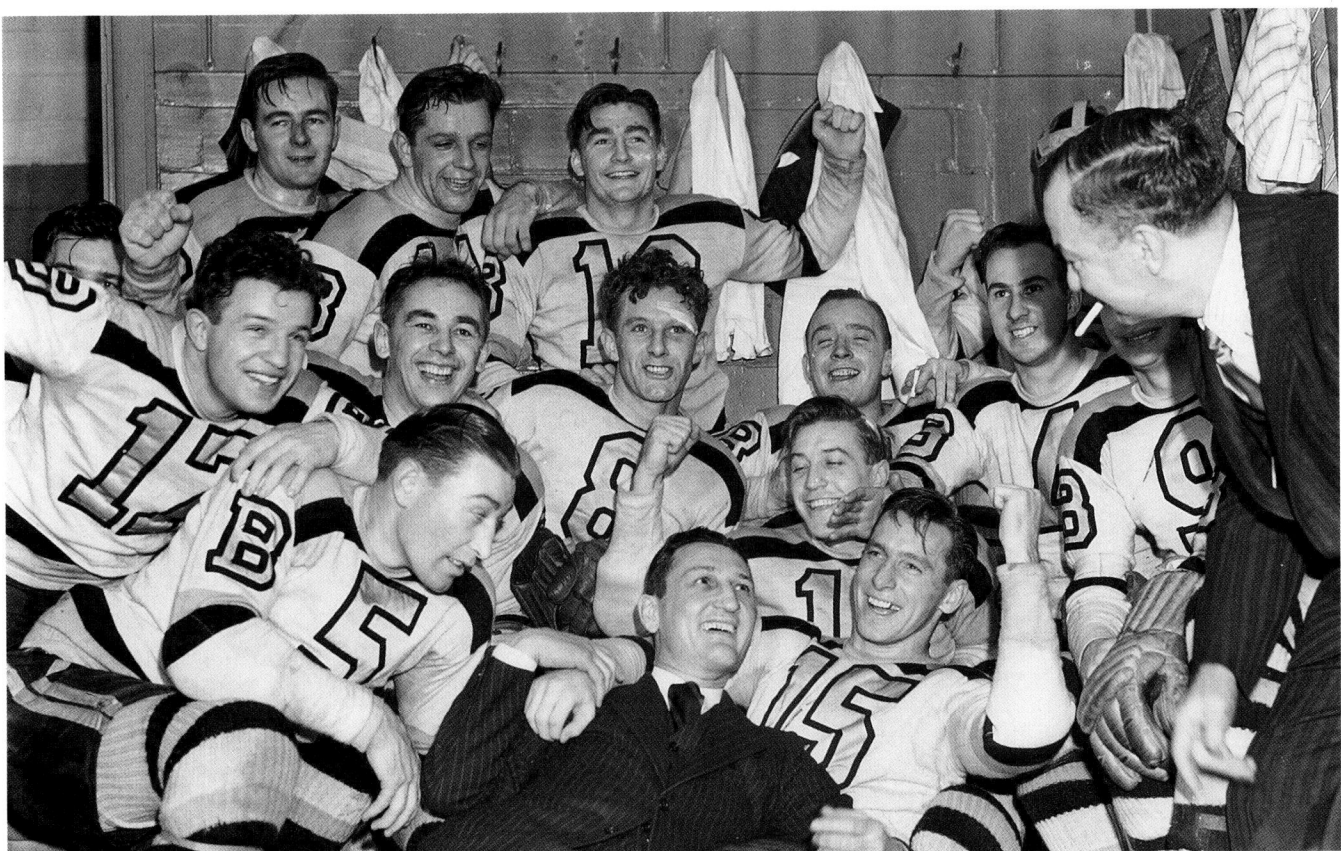

three-game semi-final series. The Stanley Cup finals would be a best-of-seven series.

The biggest impact on the league was made by a newcomer, goaltender Frank Brimsek, who had been signed for Boston by Art Ross. The Bruins placed Cooney Weiland and Dit Clapper on a line with Roy Conacher and still had the redoubtable Eddie Shore on defense. But it was Brimsek's goalkeeping that made the difference; Boston won twelve of their first fifteen games, six of them by shutouts, and went on to win the Prince of Wales Trophy as the league's regular-season champion. The Bruins finished sixteen points ahead of the second-place New York Rangers.

The Rangers proved to be much better competition for the Bruins than the regular-season margin between the two clubs indicated. The NHL's first best-of-seven series went the limit, with Boston's Mel Hill scoring three overtime game winners. Hill's exploits earned him the nickname "Sudden Death." The third-place Leafs earned the other spot in the finals, eliminating the Americans and Red Wings. In the final series, Frank Brimsek and the Bruins held the Leafs to just six goals in five games as the Bruins won their first Stanley Cup in ten seasons.

Despite its economic hardships (which were gradually resolving themselves), the NHL had come a long way in the twenty-two years since its founding. The game had moved from small wooden arenas with rutted natural ice to mammoth new buildings capable of holding crowds of up to

The Boston Bruins raise a victory cheer in the dressing room following their four-game sweep of Detroit in the Stanley Cup finals of 1941. It was a taste of prosperity the Bruins would have to savor for twenty-nine years.

Green Light Introduced in 1938

In November 1938 the League passed a resolution requiring that all rinks be equipped with a "timing-lighting device" behind the goal, showing a green light at the expiry of each period. The new equipment made it impossible for the red goal light to be illuminated once the green light was on.

Toronto was the first NHL club to have such a light installed in its rink — in March 1936.

fifteen thousand. Rule changes had steadily speeded up play; improved equipment accentuated the skills of the athletes; and the growth of radio and newspaper coverage transformed hockey players, some of them from the smallest hamlets in Canada, into celebrities.

Although war had broken out in Europe, the NHL decided in the fall of 1939 to continue operations with as little disruption as possible. In late October, the league played its third all-star benefit game to raise money for the family of Albert "Babe" Siebert, who had drowned the previous August. Siebert had been part of the "S" Line with the Maroons in the early 1930s before switching to defense, where he earned three consecutive First All-Star Team berths beginning in 1936.

In New York, the Americans tried to solve a cash shortage by peddling off their best player, Sweeney Schriner, to Toronto. In return, the Americans received cash and four Toronto players, including Busher Jackson.

Over the years, the New York Americans had become something of a haven for fading stars. In 1939, they picked up Charlie Conacher from Detroit, and Eddie Shore in a mid-season trade with Boston. Nels Stewart, too, was entering his fifth season with the Amerks.

Across the hallway at Madison Square Garden, Lester Patrick stepped down as coach of the Rangers in favor of Frank Boucher, for whom Patrick's sons, Lynn and Murray, would play effectively all season. In Boston, Art Ross gave up the Bruins' coaching job to Cooney Weiland. Relinquishing his coaching duties didn't diminish Ross's feud with Conn Smythe. Prior to a game in Boston, Smythe decided to enliven events by running a newspaper ad, suggesting that Boston's defensive style was an insult to fans. Those who wished to see the game played properly, Smythe promised, could come out to see the way the Leafs played against Boston. Ross, however, had the last laugh – the Bruins won the game.

An era came to an end in the first round of the 1940 Stanley Cup playoffs when Eddie Shore played his last NHL game. Before the season began, Shore had announced that he had purchased the Springfield (Massachusetts) Indians of the American Hockey League and that he planned to play home games for both the Indians and the Boston Bruins. This unusual arrangement did not work, giving rise to Shore's trade to the Americans, where he finished his NHL career in the post-season. Shore's old Toronto adversary, Red Horner, also "hung 'em up" after the 1939-40 season.

The Bruins' loss of Eddie Shore did not hinder them in 1939-40. Led by the Kraut Line of Dumart, Schmidt, and Bauer, along with Bill Cowley and goaltender Frank Brimsek, the team finished in first place for the third consecutive season. The three members of the Kraut Line topped the scoring list.

In the playoffs, the second-place Rangers eliminated the Bruins in six games as Davey Kerr registered three shutouts. In the quarter-final series

Babe Pratt (left) and Muzz Patrick display their defensive form during the Rangers' Cup-winning season of 1940. Pratt, one of the game's premier rushing defensemen, was eventually traded to Toronto, where he captured the Hart Trophy in 1944.

between Chicago and Toronto, the Black Hawks were eliminated in two straight games. For game one of the series, the Hawks traveled to Toronto by airplane instead of by overnight Pullman car. Detroit eliminated the Americans in the other quarter-final, before bowing to the Leafs in two straight games. In the finals, the Rangers needed six games – including three wins in overtime – to win the Stanley Cup. Bryan Hextall scored the Cup-winning goal after two minutes of overtime in game six.

While crowds continued to turn out for games, there was speculation in 1940 that the New York Americans, then under the stewardship of the league, might not operate the following year. At the conclusion of the season, full responsibility for the Americans was turned over to their manager Red Dutton, who was charged with improving the club's financial situation and its on-ice performance. During the 1940-41 season, Dutton showed that he was, in fact, in charge of the club when he suspended Hooley Smith for questioning his coaching.

North of the border, coach Dick Irvin of the Leafs moved to the Canadiens, and was replaced in Toronto by Hap Day, who had been dragooned from the officiating corps. There were signs of Dick Irvin's frustration during his first season with the flagging Canadiens. At one point, he complained that the Leafs were playing a "clutch-and-grab" game, apparently forgetting that the Toronto team was still playing the style of hockey he had taught in his years in Toronto. He also attempted to keep the Canadiens' goals-against down by platooning goaltenders at seven-minute intervals. But his efforts were to no avail: the Canadiens finished second-last in the standings and then lost to Chicago in the first round of the 1940-41 playoffs.

Irvin wasn't the only innovator among coaches. On March 16, 1941, late in a game against Toronto and down by one goal, Chicago coach Paul Thompson used the opportunity of a Toronto penalty to replace his goaltender with a forward to give the Black Hawks a two-man advantage while leaving the net undefended. Although the tactic didn't work in its inaugural application, the Leafs would also use it during the playoffs, and before long, it would become a standard practice in the NHL. Earlier in March, Chicago goaltender Sam Lopresti faced a single-game record 83 shots in a game against the Bruins. Lopresti played well, but the Black Hawks lost 3–2.

The Bruins again finished in first place, five points ahead of the Leafs, and set a league record by going twenty-three games without a defeat. Bill Cowley was the league's top scorer, finishing with 62 points. Five players – Hextall, Drillon, Apps, Lynn Patrick, and Syd Howe – were tied for second with 44 points.

The Bruins eliminated the Maple Leafs in a thrilling seven-game series between first-place finishers. Three of Boston's wins were by 2–1 scores. Detroit eliminated the Rangers and Black Hawks to qualify for the finals, but the Bruins, led by three goals from Milt Schmidt and right winger Eddie

Experiment with New Faceoff Technique

In January 1941 teams experimented with a new faceoff technique during practices for a period of one month. Instead of the traditional dropping of the puck by the official, the puck would be placed on the ice and the opposing centers would place their sticks on the ice twelve inches away from the puck. The experiment was advanced in the belief that the linesman would be in a much better position to call the play as the puck came out of the defensive zone. When the two-linesman system was adopted for the 1941-42 season, a new faceoff procedure proved unnecessary.

Above: A brief history of the Boston Garden, from broadcaster Ryan to organist Kiley, presented through the cartoonist's pen. Below: Mervyn "Red" Dutton poses with members of the Brooklyn Americans during the franchise's final campaign.

Wiseman, swept the Red Wings in four straight games. This was the first playoff series in the seven-game format to end in a sweep.

During the 1941-42 season, the NHL was still burdened with a weak Americans' franchise. Red Dutton's efforts to spark local interest in the team included changing its name from the New York Americans to the Brooklyn Americans. While home games would continue to be played in Madison Square Garden, the team practiced in Brooklyn. Dutton moved to Brooklyn himself, and urged his players to do the same, but these efforts went unrewarded and the cash-strapped franchise began dealing away stars whose salaries it couldn't afford, swapping them for cash and younger players. Two of the newcomers, Ken Mosdell and former Olympic-team player Harry Watson, would become names to be reckoned with in the NHL, but their success would be achieved later in their careers with other clubs. The strain of failure told on Dutton over the course of the season: he was fined three times for outbursts of temper, and eventually gave up coaching, no doubt to preserve his sanity.

By early 1942, the war in Europe began to affect the NHL. Boston especially was devastated when the entire Kraut Line was called up for military service in February. In Toronto, Conn Smythe was preparing to turn over the reins of the Leafs to his colleague Frank Selke while he went to war as leader of a battalion.

As more and more players joined up and headed to Europe, newcomers got their first taste of NHL action. Among the most impressive were Emile "Butch" Bouchard, a burly defenseman who joined the Canadiens, and Chicago's Bill Mosienko, who scored two goals in twenty-one seconds in his first game for the Black Hawks.

Although the Rangers were regular-season champions, the best hockey of 1941-42 was played between Detroit and Toronto in the Stanley Cup finals. Having eliminated the talented Rangers in the first round of the playoffs, the Leafs were expected to defeat the Red Wings easily. But that wasn't the way things went. Unable to score more than two goals in any of the first three games, Toronto lost all three and appeared to be finished.

For game four in Detroit, coach Hap Day benched Gordie Drillon, one of the team's top scorers, and Bucko McDonald, a thumping defenseman. In their places, Day dressed Don Metz and Hank Goldup. Although the additions didn't dominate play, the Leafs earned a reprieve, winning 4–3 and holding the Detroit line of Eddie Wares, Sid Abel, and Don Grosso to a single goal. Frustrated at losing what he had expected to be the Cup-winning game at home, Jack Adams ran onto the ice to protest penalties to Grosso and Wares towards the end of the game and was suspended indefinitely.

It remained to be seen, however, whether Toronto could continue its strong play. Having won without Drillon and McDonald, Day wasn't about to

Boston Game Delayed for Roosevelt Address

Throughout its seventy-five-year history, the NHL has had games delayed for numerous reasons — from the weather to player injuries. On December 9, 1941, at Boston Garden, the contest between the Bruins and the Chicago Black Hawks was delayed as President Roosevelt announced to the nation that war had been declared.

More than ten thousand fans listened in silence to the twenty-eight-minute radio broadcast. Players from both clubs sat on their respective benches wrapped in blankets while play was held up.

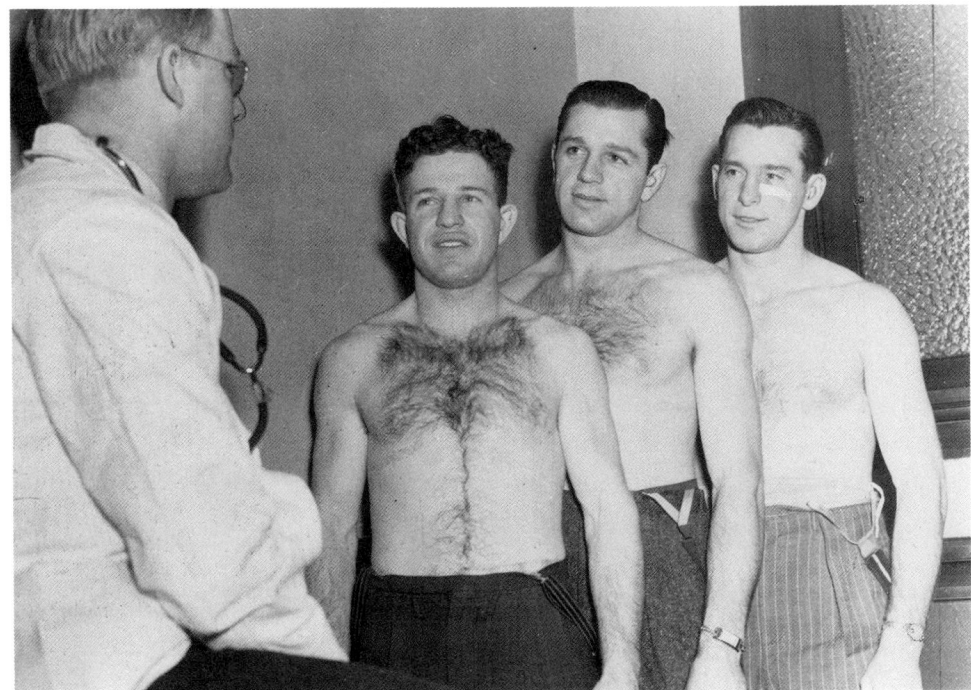

The Boston Bruins' famous trio of (left to right) Bobby Bauer, Woody Dumart, and Milt Schmidt, known collectively as the Kraut Line, prepare to take their medical checkups after joining the Canadian Armed Forces in World War II. More than eighty NHL players joined up to fight overseas.

Consolidation to Canada Rumored in '42

Newspapers in Montreal, Quebec, Toronto, and New York all carried reports, in March 1942, that the NHL was going to consolidate its franchises to Canada for the 1942-43 season. According to the reports, Chicago was destined to become the second franchise in Montreal; the New York Rangers would relocate to Toronto; Detroit would move across the river to Windsor, Ontario; Boston would operate out of Hamilton; and the Brooklyn Americans would play in Ottawa.

The reported reason for such action was that no more passports would be issued to professional athletes by the Canadian government.

put them back into the line-up. His resistance to doing so was rewarded in game five as substitute Metz scored three goals, and the Leafs galloped off with a 9–3 win over the Adams-less Wings. Game six turned out to be more of the same, as the Leafs won 3–0 in front of a flawless Turk Broda in goal, setting up, potentially, one of the most startling turnarounds in the history of hockey.

Toronto fans gave game seven of the 1942 finals the attention it deserved: a record 16,218 showed up at Maple Leaf Gardens. For two periods it looked as if the Leafs' miracles could be over as the Wings led by a goal and were playing strongly. Before the final period, however, Conn Smythe paid a visit to the Toronto dressing room to exhort his troops for the last time before he headed overseas. This apparently inspired them, and the Leafs came out flying, scoring three goals to complete their spectacular comeback and win the Stanley Cup. The Leafs' win marked the only time in big-league sports history that a team came back from a three-games-to-none deficit in a championship final.

At the spring meetings of 1942, the league subsidized the Brooklyn Americans' continuing losses and attempted to arrange a new contract with Madison Square Garden for the following season. But no deal could be

King Clancy, who spent twenty years in the NHL as a player and a coach, also served as a referee during the 1940s. Here he gives a hand to injured Red Wings' defenseman Jimmy Orlando. Of special note is the "V for Victory" symbol on Orlando's jersey.

struck, forcing the Americans to suspend operations; the league covered their losses.

Reduced to six franchises for 1942-43, the NHL continued operations with the blessing of the Canadian government, which saw hockey as a distraction from the pressures of the war abroad. Because military service had reduced the number of NHL-quality players available, the league elected to reduce playing rosters by one, to fourteen per team. Acknowledging wartime travel restrictions, overtime was eliminated in regular-season play so that overnight trains would not have to wait for teams to finish games that went into overtime.

By 1942-43, enlistments and military call-ups put some eighty NHL players in the armed services, leaving gaping holes in line-ups throughout the league. Toronto lost Syl Apps, the Canadiens lost both Terry and Kenny Reardon. And while the arrival of newcomer Maurice "The Rocket" Richard seemed to help – no less a figure than Newsy Lalonde pronounced him a future star – Richard was out of action with a broken leg by mid-season.

Perhaps the biggest loss to the league was that of Frank Calder, who died in February at sixty-six, following a heart attack. Calder's contribution to the NHL had been enormous. He had served as league president from the NHL's

Dick Irvin (right) coached the Toronto Maple Leafs into the Stanley Cup finals on seven occasions, but captured the championship only once. In 1940, he was named the coach of the Montreal Canadiens and, with superstar Maurice Richard (left) performing his playoff magic, the Habs would win three Cups during Irvin's reign.

Youngest NHLer

Armand "Bep" Guidolin was the youngest player ever to play in the NHL. Guidolin was only sixteen years old when he made his NHL debut for Boston in November, 1942. Guidolin went on to play nine years for Boston, Detroit, and Chicago.

League president Frank Calder poses with referee Mel Harwood, (left) and linesmen Don McFadyen and Doug Young prior to a semi-final game between the Leafs and the Rangers on March 28, 1942. Harwood would later be involved in an on-ice confrontation with Detroit coach and general manager Jack Adams following game four of the Stanley Cup finals.

beginning in 1917, and was held in such respect that his re-election each year was never questioned.

The NHL appointed Red Dutton, former manager and coach of the defunct Americans, as interim president, to be assisted by Toronto governor J. P. Bickell and by Lester Patrick.

Almost as quickly as it lost players, the league was also losing on-ice officials to the armed forces. Veteran referee Mickey Ion was appointed to scout out new prospects. Ion's solution was to appeal to retired players. One of those he enticed was Red Horner, the former Leaf captain and one of the most penalized players of his era. Others included King Clancy, Bill Chadwick, Charlie McVeigh, and Aurel Joliat, the diminutive veteran of the Canadiens, who had officiated in the comeback Stanley Cup final between Toronto and Detroit the previous spring.

Clancy and Joliat both played sixteen years in the league, but, in 1942-43, Dit Clapper became the NHL player with the most years of service, playing in his seventeenth campaign with the Bruins.

In addition to all the other changes that were occurring in the game, there was a clear trend emerging toward more offense. By the season's end, Toronto's 198 goals eclipsed the previous record of 179 set by Boston in 1930-31; in fact, four of the NHL's six teams equaled or bettered the old mark.

The six-team league's new playoff structure called for semi-finals in which the first-place finisher would play the team that finished third, and second-place would play fourth. The winners of these two series would meet in the Stanley Cup finals. All series were best-of-seven. In the 1943 semi-finals, third-place Detroit rebounded from its shocking loss to the Leafs the previous season, defeating Toronto in six games. In the other semi-final series, the Bruins eliminated the Canadiens in five games before being swept in four straight games by the Red Wings. Detroit's Johnny Mowers led all playoff goaltenders, with an average of 1.94 goals-against.

At the beginning of the 1943-44 season, the center-ice red line was introduced in an attempt to speed up play and reduce offsides. Before the red-line rule, a team coming out of its defensive zone could not pass the puck forward across its own blue line; the puck could be passed up to the line, but had to be carried into the neutral zone before another pass could be made. The new rule allowed a team coming out of its own end to pass the puck right up to center-ice, greatly enhancing its ability to clear its own zone and launch an attack. The puck could not be passed across the red line, however, unless the player originating the pass had already crossed his own blue line.

Allowing forward passes over a team's own blue line would soon reward those clubs most adept at rapid transition from defense to offense and would accelerate the evolution of NHL hockey from a stickhandling to a passing game. Combined with the offside rule of 1929-30, liberalized forward-passing rules mark the beginning of modern hockey.

Red Garrett Award

Dudley "Red" Garrett, who played with the New York Rangers in 1943, was the first NHL player to die in action during World War II. The American Hockey League's rookie-of-the-year award is named in Garrett's honor.

Frank "King" Clancy was actively involved in the game of hockey as a player, coach, referee, and executive for over seventy years. The goodwill ambassador of Maple Leaf Gardens from 1956 to 1986, Clancy was once asked by Conn Smythe what he did all day. Clancy pondered the query and replied honestly: "Nothing." Smythe, without missing a beat, answered, "Well keep it up. You're doing a great job."

Six-Team Stars

THE ADDITION OF THE CENTER-ICE RED LINE IN 1943 WAS TAILOR-MADE for the fast-skating team that Dick Irvin had been building in Montreal. The Habs' free-wheeling Punch Line – Maurice Richard, Toe Blake, and Elmer Lach – would take advantage of the innovation and remain one of the NHL's top forward units for the next five seasons. The 1943-44 season also marked the NHL debut of Bill Durnan, the ambidextrous netminder who would backstop the Canadiens to four consecutive first-place finishes.

To cope with the wartime player shortage, the league cut rosters to thirteen skaters plus a goalie, but all of the NHL's clubs were forced to make do with veterans and with youngsters who hadn't gained the usual minor-league seasoning. There were, of course, bright spots among the replacements. Desperate for goaltending, Detroit briefly employed seventeen-year-old Harry Lumley in 1943. While the young goalie didn't stay with the Red Wings that season, he demonstrated that he had the skills to play in the NHL. Detroit finished second to Montreal and benefited from career goal-scoring highs by two veterans: Carl Liscombe with 36 goals and Syd Howe with 32.

In Boston, thirty-seven-year-old Dit Clapper continued to anchor the Bruins' defense in his eighteenth NHL season, while Toronto's Ted "Teeder" Kennedy was beginning what would become a fourteen-year career with the Leafs. The Black Hawks finished in fourth place with 49 points and placed three scorers in the league's top ten. Linemates Doug Bentley, Clint Smith, and Bill Mosienko each had seventy points or more. Bentley led the league with 38 goals; Smith was the top assist-getter with 49.

The once-powerful Rangers had fallen on hard times, weakened by the loss of six first-string players to the armed forces. Lester Patrick had to be talked out of suspending the franchise until the war ended. His decision to convert his coach Frank Boucher into a playing coach after Boucher had been off skates for five seasons didn't help much either.

Opposite: Frank Mahovlich, known as the "Big M" because of his loping stride and long reach, attempts to slow down Gordie Howe, whose smooth skating style disguised his speed and strength.

Below: The dominant goaltenders of their era, Bill Durnan (left) and Turk Broda. Durnan won six Vezina trophies in seven years, while Broda won the award in 1948, the only year Durnan didn't.

Play had definitely deteriorated, but the fans didn't seem to mind. The league's arenas were filled to capacity most nights, especially when the Canadiens were in town. So proficient were the Habs that they finished the season 25 points ahead of the second-place Red Wings, scoring a record 234 goals on the way. Bill Durnan won the first of what would prove to be four consecutive Vezina trophies. Three players – Boston's Herb Cain, Chicago's Doug Bentley, and Toronto's Lorne Carr – eclipsed the league's single-season scoring record of 73 points.

The Canadien's regular-season dominance continued in the Stanley Cup playoffs, as they lost only their first game to Toronto before winning the next four from the Leafs and sweeping the Black Hawks to win the Stanley Cup.

The Canadiens' young star, Rocket Richard, showed the first true signs of his prodigious abilities in the 1944 playoffs, scoring twelve goals in nine games. Five of these goals were scored in a record-setting performance against the Leafs in game two of the semi-finals.

Though critics of the center-ice red line claimed it resulted in too much scoring, there was no denying it was good box office, and no move was made to change it.

Before the start of the 1944-45 season, concern was raised that assists were being given out indiscriminately by official scorers at NHL games. League president Red Dutton wrote to each club, urging that scorers be somewhat less liberal in the awarding of assists.

In what turned out to be the last wartime NHL season, rookies continued to excel. Detroit made Harry Lumley its first-string goaltender and had combative little Ted Lindsay playing forward. Jack Adams further strengthened his team by trading with Chicago for ten-time all-star defenseman Earl Seibert (not to be confused with Albert "Babe" Siebert).

Certainly the Red Wings were stronger, and at the halfway point, they were tied with the Canadiens for the league lead. In Toronto, the Leafs had replaced Turk Broda with Frank McCool, and had welcomed back stars Wally Stanowski and Sweeney Schriner from overseas to fill out a roster that featured youngsters like Kennedy and Bill Ezinicki. The Leafs were improved, but their third-place finish left them well back of the powerful Red Wings and Canadiens.

Among the returning servicemen, one of the most significant was Conn Smythe. He played an important role in persuading Red Dutton to stay on as president of the NHL and also showed that the war hadn't diminished his ability to make headlines. On seeing Maurice Richard play, he announced that he would pay $25,000 to acquire him for the Leafs – and $1,000 to anyone who could negotiate the sale. And though there was little possibility of a deal, he also offered $30,000 each for Milt Schmidt and Neil Colville, who were both still in the army.

The major on-ice event of the 1944-45 season was the performance of

Rocket Richard, whose goal-scoring pace led many to compare him to the late Howie Morenz. Richard played the year at a goal-a-game clip, eventually winding up with a single-season record 50 goals in 50 games. Until that season, no player had reached even the 40-goal plateau since Cooney Weiland of the Bruins scored 43 in 1929-30. The Rocket, already earning his reputation as a player who scored big goals in crucial games, didn't fatten his totals on weak teams; he scored more against second- and third-place Toronto and Detroit than any other clubs. Despite Richard's emergence, Montreal did not repeat as Stanley Cup champions. The Canadiens were beaten in the semi-finals by Toronto, who went on to beat the Red Wings for the Stanley Cup.

The Bentley brothers, Doug (left) and Max, were team-mates in Chicago from 1940-41 until Max's much-discussed trade to the Leafs in 1947-48. Doug was the NHL's top goal-scorer in 1942-43 and 1943-44; Max was the league's leading point-getter in 1945-46 and 1946-47, and also won the Hart Trophy in 1946.

With the war's end, hockey fans looked forward to the return of many players from service overseas, and the NHL's governors decided to retain many of the rule and format changes that had been enacted during the war. Regular-season overtime, which had been eliminated due to restricted train

Last Minute of Play

The "last minute of play" announcement for each period began in the 1945-46 season.

schedules during the war years, was not reinstituted for 1945-46. And the center-ice red line, which had proven to be a popular addition, would be retained. Following its introduction in 1943, the number of goals scored rose to 1,225 from the previous year's 1,083, and the number of assists awarded increased to 1,748 from 1,647.

Despite initial optimism when the 1945-46 season opened in October – the earliest start ever – it was soon evident that those who had left the game to serve overseas would need time to regain their form. But as the season progressed, top forward lines began to re-emerge. Montreal's Punch Line, which had been together since 1943-44, remained potent and, toward the end of the season, the Kraut Line was reunited in Boston. Chicago had discovered a new combination in the Pony Line, made up of the Bentley brothers, Max and Doug, and Bill Mosienko. While crowds during the war had been surprisingly good, they only grew stronger in the booming postwar economy.

If there was a blot on the season, it was the revelation that Toronto defenseman Walter "Babe" Pratt – winner of the Hart Trophy in 1944 – had bet on hockey games. Wagering had been a part of the game for as long as anyone could remember. Indeed, Conn Smythe founded the Leafs with money gained largely at the race-track, and Lionel Conacher, who would later become a member of Parliament, opined that, had there been restrictions on betting during his days with the Montreal Maroons, the entire team would have been called up on the carpet. Nonetheless, president Red Dutton was determined to stamp out the practice and expelled Pratt from the NHL. In his hearing before the league, a chagrined Pratt acknowledged that he had been warned by team officials, and in his own defense, denied betting against his own team. Ultimately, Dutton and the governors figured they had made their point and reinstated Pratt after he had missed nine games.

The Canadiens were the NHL's top team in 1945-46. Of all the league's clubs, the Habs had lost the fewest players to military service, so their postwar reconstruction job was relatively easy. The Leafs, winners of the Stanley Cup during the last year of the war, tumbled out of the playoffs, clearing the way for the Canadiens to win both the Prince of Wales Trophy and the Stanley Cup. During the playoffs, the Habs lost only once, as their powerful Punch Line scored nineteen goals in nine games.

Beyond shifts in the league standings and playoff picture, the 1945-46 season revealed signs of immutable change in the NHL. Many of the older players, whose careers had been prolonged by the war, found it difficult to earn regular playing time. The durable Dit Clapper was hanging on as playing coach of the Bruins, but was obviously facing the end of his outstanding career.

Changes in playing rosters were matched by changes in coaching and management. Sixty-year-old Art Ross retired from coaching, and league managing director Frank Patrick, also now sixty, suffered a heart attack. His

Red Dutton became the NHL's second president, serving a three-year term from 1943 to 1946.

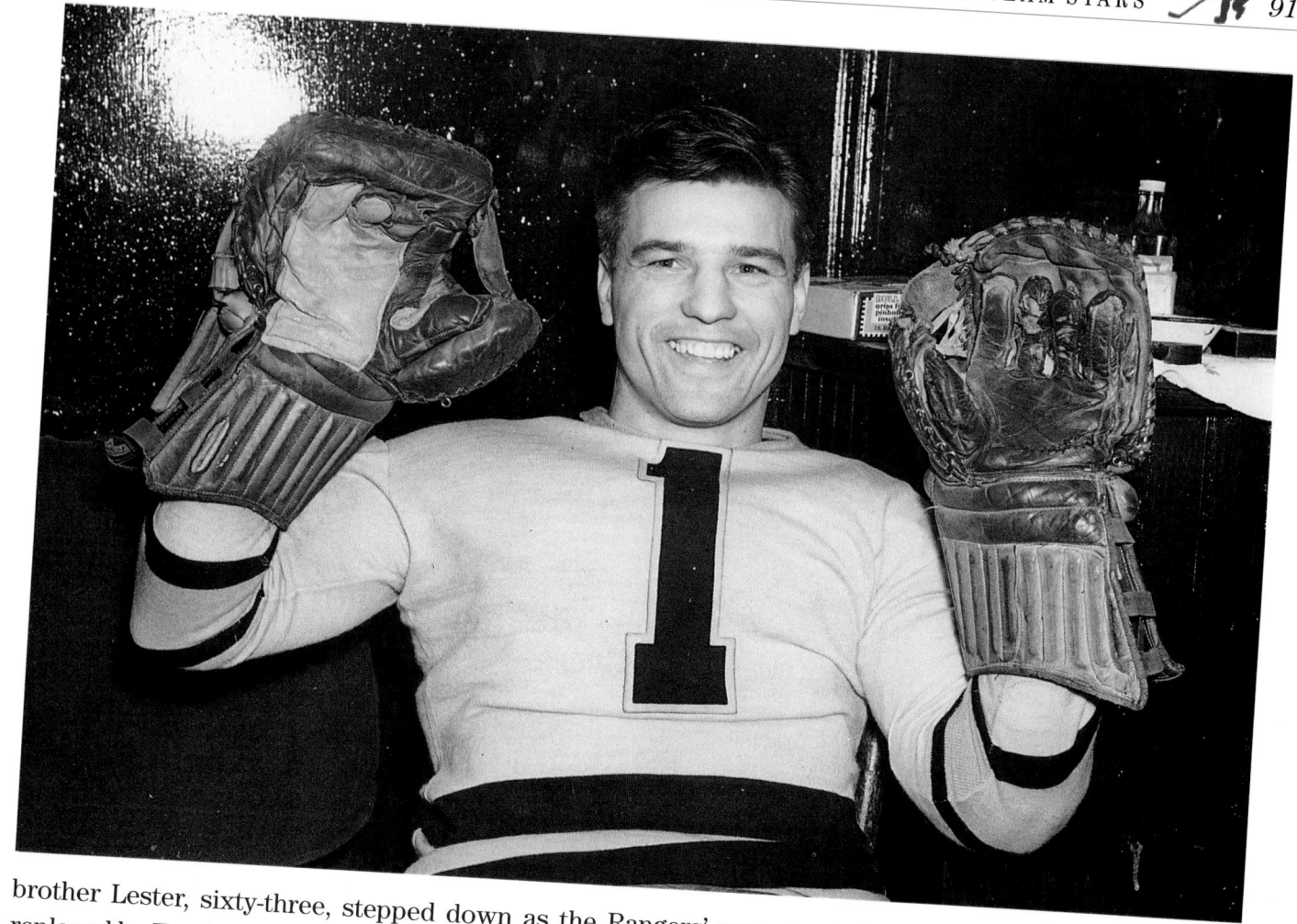

Frank Brimsek, who recorded 40 shutouts in ten seasons to earn his well-deserved moniker "Mr. Zero," exhibits the tools of his trade: primitive prototypes of the blocker and trapper that would become standard pieces of a goaltender's arsenal.

brother Lester, sixty-three, stepped down as the Rangers' manager to be replaced by Frank Boucher. Conn Smythe's war injuries forced him to spend much of the season away from his beloved team.

It was apparent that the NHL's pioneering builders were giving way to a new generation. Like the rest of society, the NHL was on the verge of a period of prosperity and accelerated change.

In the opinion of Red Dutton, who had attempted to save the New York/Brooklyn Americans and then had reluctantly operated as league president during the war, the new era called for a change at the top. As his successor, he recommended Clarence Campbell.

It would have been difficult for the six league governors to turn down a man of Campbell's credentials. He was a talented amateur player and had done a stint as a referee in the NHL. His academic credentials were impeccable as well. After graduating from the University of Alberta, he had attended Oxford University as a Rhodes Scholar. He served in the armed forces during the war, and then returned to practice law in Montreal. His election gave the NHL its third president.

It was not long before Campbell was overseeing further changes. John Carmichael of the *Chicago Daily News*, with support from Chicago manager

National Anthem

Although several teams had played their country's national anthem prior to games several years earlier, the NHL did not institute a rule requiring the home team's national anthem to be played until 1946.

Bill Tobin, suggested that a game between the league all-stars and the previous year's champions be played each fall as a kick-off to the season. The idea was that 25 per cent of the proceeds of the game would be given to the Players' Emergency Fund, forerunner to the NHL pension plan, and the rest to local charities. Campbell readily agreed to the idea, and the NHL's All-Star Game was born.

By the fall of 1946, the quality of play in the NHL was bolstered not only by the return from military service of players who had earlier shown no more than hints of their future stardom, but also by the emergence of talent from thriving junior and minor leagues. And owners and managers continued to juggle their roster with an eye to improvement.

The NHL's regular-season schedule was expanded from fifty to sixty games. Each of the league's six clubs would play its five rivals twelve times each, six games at home and six games on the road.

Toronto's Conn Smythe, who had seen the Leafs finish out of the playoffs the previous season and had been embarrassed by the gambling charges brought against Babe Pratt, shipped the fading star to Boston. Art Ross eventually sent Pratt to the minors, ending his big-league career. Frank

Frank Selke, the designer of hockey dynasties in Montreal and Toronto, shares a few hockey secrets with Leafs captain Syl Apps. Apps was an unselfish player who had only one individual objective: to score 200 goals. On the last day of the 1948 season, he scored a hat-trick to give him 201 career goals, and he immediately retired.

Selke, Smythe's long-time cohort in Toronto, left to manage the Canadiens, who looked as strong as the previous season's Cup winner.

Chicago still had its Pony Line (the Bentley brothers and Mosienko), and coach Johnny Gottselig had discovered a winner in rookie defenseman Bill Gadsby. Emile "The Cat" Francis also joined the Black Hawks in goal. In Detroit, Jack Adams was set with Ted Lindsay and Sid Abel up front, Harry Lumley in goal, and Bill Quackenbush on defense. But the best news in Motor City was the play of a big kid from Saskatchewan, Gordie Howe, who scored in his first game of the season.

New York, without Muzz and Lynn Patrick, who had retired, was short of players and would have trouble filling its roster. A bright spot was goaltender Chuck Rayner, one of the first at his position to wander about the ice to field pucks and make plays. In one game against Toronto, Rayner actually went to the Toronto blue line to get involved in the play. On another night, after an opponent had pulled its goalie, he nearly became the first netminder to score, when he fielded a puck in his own end and shot it down the ice, narrowly missing the opposing team's goal.

Although the Maple Leafs had lost Sweeney Schriner, Lorne Carr, and Bob Davidson, the core of the team was built around veterans Syl Apps, Don and Nick Metz, and Ted Kennedy. Leaf youngsters included a hard-rock defenseman named Bill Barilko, tough Bill Ezinicki, and war veteran Howie Meeker, who would have a five-goal game against Chicago on January 8, 1947. Despite their performance a year earlier, the Leafs looked like the team to beat, and over the course of the season, proved it.

Babe Pratt's gambling suspension had launched Smythe on a clean-up campaign to stop the taking of bets by bookies who congregated in a section of Maple Leaf Gardens' concourse known as the "Bull Ring." Although Smythe successfully cleared the gamblers out of the building, they didn't go far. During the season, police raids of five establishments around town led to charges against five gaming-house operators and forty-six of their customers. The police seized $17,000 in wagers, a considerable sum at the time.

The rivalry between Toronto and Montreal heated up with the departure of Frank Selke for the Canadiens. Conn Smythe tried to put pressure on the Canadiens by declaring them the team to beat. For his part, Frank Selke became so exasperated at the Leafs' "clutch-and-grab" tactics that he promised to add a wrestler to the Canadiens' line-up when playing Toronto. Smythe impishly said he would counter that with his own ringer in the person of "Whipper" Billy Watson, then regarded as the best wrestler in the country. Neither went through with his threat.

As the list of retired or departed NHL stars grew, the Hockey Hall of Fame, started in Kingston, Ontario, began honoring the game's greats. Eligibility rules for the Hall of Fame were bent to allow the admission of twenty-year veteran Dit Clapper. Clapper, who played in six games while coaching the Bruins in 1946-47, was technically still active as a player when he was

Origins of Trophy for NHL Leading Scorer

A trophy for the NHL's leading regular-season scorer was first contemplated almost ten years before Boston Bruins' former manager and coach Arthur Howie Ross donated the Art Ross Trophy to the League in 1947. Charlie Conacher, who was sidelined with a hand injury for most of the 1936-37 season, first made the suggestion while writing a guest column for a Toronto newspaper in February, 1937.

The 1948 First All-Star Team, November 3, 1948. Left to right: coach Tommy Ivan, "Black" Jack Stewart, Elmer Lach, Bill Quacken-bush, president Clarence Campbell, Maurice Richard, and Ted Lindsay.

Rayner's Rushes

In a game against the Montreal Canadiens on February 1, 1947, goalie Chuck Rayner made three "mad dashes" into the Habs' zone, attempting to score the tying goal in a 2-1 Rangers' loss. Rayner is credited with scoring several goals, none of which occurred during NHL action.

inducted into the Hall of Fame in the autumn of 1947.

Although Smythe's claim that the Canadiens were the class of the league seemed to be borne out when they won the Prince of Wales Trophy, the Leafs prevailed to win the Stanley Cup. Toronto had thus completed a remarkable three-year cycle, winning the Cup in 1945, finishing out of the playoffs in 1946, and winning it again in 1947.

Quality rookies continued to flood into the NHL in 1947-48. Doug Harvey and Floyd Curry played their first games for the Canadiens and, in Detroit, Tommy Ivan, who had replaced Jack Adams as coach, installed a young Leonard "Red" Kelly on defense.

In Chicago, it had been some time since the Black Hawks had performed well, and it was dawning on Hawks' president Bill Tobin that coach Johnny Gottselig, a former star left winger, was the problem. His solution was to move Gottselig up to manager and bring in Charlie Conacher as coach. Tobin also saw a chance to fill out his roster by giving up quality for quantity. Conn Smythe, who had long coveted Max Bentley, packaged Gus Bodnar, Bud Poile, Gaye Stewart, Bob Goldham, and Ernie Dickens and shipped the five to Chicago for Bentley and Cy Thomas.

The trade was a blockbuster that rivaled Smythe's purchase of King

Clancy from Ottawa in 1930. Aficionados argued over who got the best of the deal, and for some time it looked as if the Black Hawks had trumped the Leafs. Stewart and Poile were both good scorers, and Bodnar and Goldham were promising youngsters. However, the key to the trade was Bentley. Though not as robust as his brother Doug, he was the smooth playmaker that the Leafs needed to reach the top of the standings.

With the regular-season schedule up to sixty games, continuing injuries began to worry some of the league's managers. At one point, Frank Boucher recommended that goaltenders wear facemasks, and as postwar plastics began to find consumer applications, even Rocket Richard and Elmer Lach tried crude plastic helmets.

In March 1948, Clarence Campbell announced that Billy Taylor, recently traded to the Rangers by the Bruins, had been expelled from the league for gambling. Campbell also suspended Taylor's one-time Bruin teammate, Don Gallinger, for the same offense. Coming on the heels of the Babe Pratt affair and the gambling-house raids in Toronto, the Taylor and Gallinger announcements marked some of the darkest days for the NHL.

On the ice, Elmer Lach of the Canadiens became the first winner of the Art Ross Trophy. Boston's long-time manager, who had been a star player himself forty years before, presented the trophy to the league to be awarded annually to the NHL's top scorer in regular-season play. Lach won the award with 30 goals and 31 assists for 61 points, finishing one point ahead of Buddy O'Connor of the Rangers.

The Leafs won the Prince of Wales Trophy and then swept to their second successive Stanley Cup in front of Turk Broda, who had interrupted Bill Durnan's string of four consecutive Vezina Trophy wins. The Leafs' attack was led by Ted Kennedy, Max Bentley, and Syl Apps, none of whom took a penalty during the entire Stanley Cup playoffs.

In the meantime, persistent entrepreneurs in Philadelphia were attempting to resurrect the Montreal Maroons franchise and move it to the "City of Brotherly Love." The governors rejected this proposal, and also turned down a submission from Los Angeles on the grounds that the applicants didn't own an arena. Neither did it escape notice that traveling to California by train would have made a difficult schedule for existing teams – and a nearly impossible one for the Los Angeles entry. When the Los Angeles group made a second bid during the fall of 1948, president Campbell set the condition that a new team would have to have a fifteen-thousand-seat arena.

The opening games of the 1948-49 season were played in scorching heat that revealed faults in the ice-making plants in the NHL's existing facilities. During a breakdown of ice-making equipment at a game in Toronto, concrete began showing through the ice. To equalize the impact of the problem for each team, the referee had the teams switch ends halfway through the final period. On another night in Boston, unseasonably warm weather made the

Goaltending Innovation

Two Hall-of-Fame members are credited with introducing important pieces of equipment for goaltenders. Frank Brimsek was the first goalie to modify his stick-hand glove so that he could block shots with the back of his hand. Emile "The Cat" Francis is credited with introducing the "trapper-style" glove to the goaltender's arsenal. In a game against Detroit during the 1948 season, Francis appeared in nets using a baseball-style first-baseman's mit. Despite protests from Jack Adams, referee King Clancy allowed Francis to use the equipment, and the NHL endorsed it later that year.

Elmer Lach played fourteen seasons with the Canadiens, winning the Art Ross Trophy twice (1945 and 1948) and the Hart Trophy once (1945).

ice surface so foggy that the officials decided to postpone the game until the following night.

As the season progressed, tempers frequently became heated as well. In a game between arch-rivals Toronto and Montreal, referee King Clancy handed out a record ten major penalties.

By the mid-point of the 1948-49 season, only eleven points separated the first-place team from the last. And while Chicago remained in the league cellar, the players that coach Charlie Conacher had received from Toronto in the Max Bentley deal showed signs of finally fitting together. Toronto, winner of the Stanley Cup the previous year, was mired in fifth place, prompting coach Hap Day and manager Conn Smythe to make a pitch to the Canadiens for Maurice Richard; the two were turned down by Frank Selke. In Boston, Dit Clapper's successor behind the bench, George Boucher, was replaced by Lynn Patrick, who, at thirty-six, was the youngest head coach in the league.

Detroit, led by Sid Abel, Ted Lindsay, and Gordie Howe – a forward unit known as the Production Line – finished in first place with 75 points, nine better than second-place Boston. The Bruins' top scorer was Grant "Knobby" Warwick, a former Calder Trophy-winner who, after the end of his NHL career, would lead the Penticton (British Columbia) Vs to the International Ice Hockey Federation World Amateur Championships in 1955. The third-place Canadiens were the league's best defensive club. Bill Durnan recorded four straight shutouts on his way to a ten-shutout season, earning his fifth Vezina Trophy and fifth all-star selection in six years. His job was made easier by a strong defense, led by Doug Harvey, Butch Bouchard, and Kenny Reardon.

The league's top two scorers both played for the fifth-place Black Hawks. Roy Conacher – a younger brother of Charlie and Lionel – won the Art Ross Trophy with 68 points. Runner-up Doug Bentley had 66.

In the semi-finals series between the Red Wings and Canadiens, Max McNab got the winning goal for Detroit in triple overtime in game one. The Wings would go on to win this series in seven games, earning a berth in the finals against the fourth-place Maple Leafs, who had eliminated Boston in five games. In the finals, the Leafs held the Red Wings to just five goals in engineering a four-game sweep to become the first fourth-place club to win the Cup and the first NHL club to win the trophy in three consecutive seasons.

Despite the Leafs' success, the Red Wings' first-place finish and final series appearance served notice that a new era of power had arrived in the NHL. It would be 1955-56 before a team other than Detroit would finish atop the NHL standings.

At the end of the 1948-49 season, the NHL increased its regular-season schedule from sixty to seventy games, so that each of the league's six clubs

would play its five opponents fourteen times – seven games at home and seven on the road. To help teams weather the increased workload, rosters were expanded to seventeen skaters plus a goaltender.

King Clancy was hired as the NHL's head referee after the 1949 playoffs, but he resigned to take a front-office job with the Maple Leafs in 1950. In his stead, the NHL appointed Carl Voss as its first referee-in-chief. Voss was an experienced referee who had played for eight NHL teams in eight seasons. He also had the distinction of being the first Toronto Maple Leaf: he had signed the club's baptismal contract after Conn Smythe purchased the team and changed its name.

The 1949-50 season would belong to the Red Wings, though manager Jack Adams couldn't resist tinkering with his line-up, trading all-star rearguard Bill Quackenbush to Boston. One of the NHL's most effective rushing defensemen, Quackenbush had distinguished himself as one of the league's least-penalized players, winning the Lady Byng Trophy in 1949 with a penalty-free season. It's possible that Adams, who also had the mild-mannered Red Kelly playing defense, wanted a little more aggressiveness at the position – though it's hard to imagine that any team employing Ted Lindsay needed to be any tougher.

The Canadiens, led by the mercurial Richard and his 43 goals, finished second to Detroit. Early in the season, three Montreal players had faced assault charges after fighting with heckling fans in rinkside seats in the Chicago Stadium. One fan had reached over to grab Montreal's Ken Reardon by the sweater, igniting the fracas. Chicago club president Bill Tobin eventually posted $200 bail, and the charges were thrown out of court when a judge ruled that the fans had overstepped their prerogative to jeer the opposition.

Relations between the press and the coaches and players were usually cordial, as newspapermen often traveled on overnight trains with the teams they covered. On occasion, though, there were blow-ups. Chicago coach Charlie Conacher, showing some of the stress of handling a perennially weak team, went so far as to belt reporter Lew Walter to express his objection to something the newspaperman had said.

The press also became embroiled in league affairs when Ken Reardon of the Canadiens vowed to a magazine writer that he would seek revenge against Toronto's Cal Gardner for a cross-check that had cut him. This quickly attracted the attention of NHL president Clarence Campbell, who summarily demanded that Reardon (who had been one of the combatants charged in Chicago) post a $1,000 peace-keeping bond. One can only imagine how tempting it must have been for Gardner to taunt the Montreal rearguard in subsequent games between the two teams.

Conn Smythe, who never hesitated to join coach Day behind the Leaf bench when he felt his presence was needed, grew increasingly distressed at the poor performance of his club. He decided that the Leafs suffered from poor physical conditioning. The first to feel his wrath was goaltender Turk

Hockey Doubleheaders

During the 1949-50 season, the NHL experimented for the first time with so-called "doubleheaders," as teams played games on consecutive nights in one city. The primary reason for the change in scheduling was to help teams reduce their travel costs.

Before 1949, however, there was at least one occasion when teams played two games on the same day. The New York Americans and New York Rangers played pre-season games at 2:00 PM and 9:00 PM on October 30, 1937, at Saskatoon. The back-to-back contests were scheduled to accommodate overflow crowds.

Broda, who was ordered off the team until he cut his grocery intake enough to lose some weight. In his place, Smythe brought up minor-leaguer Gil Mayer and bought Al Rollins from the AHL's Cleveland Barons. He also ordered Sid Smith, Vic Lynn, and Harry Watson to shed some pounds.

The press of the day had a splendid time following the story: news photos showed Broda sitting down to a tiny portion while his family tucked into normal-sized meals. It wasn't lost on the press either that the Leafs now had the "long" (Rollins at six feet, two inches), the "short" (Mayer at five feet, six inches), and the "fat" (Broda). Rollins even came up with a shutout in his short stay with the Leafs. But Smythe wasn't so eager for publicity that he was prepared to tempt fate. Broda, ten pounds lighter, was soon restored to his position, and gained a shutout in his first game back. All the Leafs seemed to have extra energy after Smythe's weight-loss campaign and, more importantly, the players' public dieting bumped football from the sports pages, which many argued was Smythe's true objective.

The real story of the season, however, was in Detroit. Led by the Production Line, by defensemen Red Kelly and Leo Reise, and by goaltender Harry Lumley, the Red Wings were on the verge of realizing their considerable potential. Their depth was impressive. When Lumley was briefly injured, a youngster named Terry Sawchuk was called up from Detroit's Indianapolis farm team and promptly recorded a shutout in the NHL.

At the end of the season, the Red Wings captured the Prince of Wales Trophy by eleven points, and Lindsay, Abel, and Howe were one-two-three in scoring. Goaltender Charlie Rayner of the New York Rangers won the Hart Trophy, joining Roy Worters of the 1928-29 New York Americans to become only the second goaltender to be named most valuable player.

In the playoffs, the Red Wings defeated the Maple Leafs in the semi-finals, despite losing Gordie Howe who, during the first game, suffered a near-tragic collision with Toronto's Ted Kennedy. Howe was hospitalized with a broken nose and cheekbone and a severe concussion. Although Kennedy was one of the league's cleanest players (no penalty was called on the play), Detroit chose to transform the incident into a vendetta, resulting in a penalty-riddled series, in which goaltenders Turk Broda of the Leafs and Harry Lumley of the Red Wings took turns shutting out their rivals. In seven games, Broda recorded three shutouts and Lumley two.

The Rangers, meanwhile, beat Montreal in the other semi-final series, earning the right to meet the Red Wings in the Cup finals. Because the circus was once again in Madison Square Garden, the Rangers elected to play games two and three in Toronto. Three of the games went to overtime, with the Rangers winning games four and five on goals by Don "Bones" Raleigh. The Red Wings won game seven and the Stanley Cup on Pete Babando's goal midway through the second overtime period. This was the first Stanley Cup final that was decided in overtime in the seventh game.

(continued on p.106)

Goaltender Chuck Rayner, the "Bonnie Prince Charlie" of the New York Rangers, won the Hart Trophy as league MVP in 1950, the year he led the Rangers into the Stanley Cup finals.

POWER AND PRODUCTION: JACK ADAMS'S RED WINGS

by Trent Frayne

Four names, maybe five, leap immediately to the minds of long-time hockey fans in any contemplation of the 1950s Detroit Red Wings. This is the team, remember, that topped the standings for seven straight seasons, a mark that still adorns the record book. This is the team that reached the finals five times in those seven years and lost only once. Talk about dynasties.

Off the top, Gordie Howe. Was there ever another like him? Almost from the moment he joined the Red Wings at age eighteen, it was apparent that he could do every-thing—skate, shoot, check, stick-handle, kill penalties, and, most important of all, put the puck in the net. He could do this shooting right-handed, his natural side, and left-handed, too, for he was ambidex-trous.

The revered Montreal goaltender Bill Durnan was also ambidex-trous. One night on a breakaway, Howe banged a shot off the goalpost and then, passing the net, reached out left-handed and skidded the rebound past Durnan into the cage.

"Geez," muttered the puddin'-faced Detroit coach Jack Adams after the fact, "whoever saw one ambidextrous guy beat another ambidextrous guy before?"

Next, Ted Lindsay. Terrible Ted, they called him, because he rushed in where angels feared to tread. Ted was a skilled, sinewy fellow, only five foot eight and 165 pounds, but he wouldn't back away from a cheetah (or even an honest man). In seventeen NHL seasons he scored 379 goals, earning eight First All-Star Team selections at left wing.

He and Bill Ezinicki, a fire hydrant who roamed right wing for the Maple Leafs and later the Bruins, often went toe-to-toe. One night they exchanged a few rudimentary taps by way of saying hello, and then somehow the dams burst. Then they threw down their sticks and gloves and hammered away. They did this non-stop for three riotous minutes.

Ezinicki needed eleven stitches to close a cut from eyebrow to hairline. He needed four more on the side of his head, and four more on the inside of his mouth. Also, he had one tooth broken off. Lindsay, remarkably, required only one stitch but, significantly, needed extensive treatment for a scarred and bruised right hand, which he couldn't close for ten days.

Sid Abel. Mostly people remember Bootnose Abel

Gordie Howe tips his hat to commemorate one of his nineteen three-goal games.

Ted Lindsay escapes the grasp of this Leaf defender as he motors his way toward the Toronto zone. Lindsay won the Art Ross Trophy in 1950.

his face only inches above the ice. In this fashion he peered through goalmouth traffic and derailed incoming point blasts. His 103 shutouts top the goaltenders on the all-time list.

Sawchuk was a man tortured by insecurity and shocking injury. He played twenty-one seasons at Detroit, Boston, Detroit again, Toronto, Los Angeles, Detroit once more, and New York, and it seemed he faced a crisis at every stop. He was admittedly overweight – his weight once soared to 229 – but a few years later I watched him step on the scales after a tough playoff game in Toronto, his body a mass of blue and yellow and purple welts and bruises, and the needle stopped at 157, a spread of 72 pounds on a big-boned five-foot-eleven frame.

Terry had some four hundred stitches in his face and head, including three in his right eyeball, before he adopted a mask in 1962. He broke bones, had concussions, arthritis, charley horses, mononucleosis. Surgery was necessary one time for a collapsed lung pierced in a car accident. He developed a spinal condition called lordosis that was so painful he could sleep only in two-hour stretches. In 1966, when his left side went numb, he thought he'd had a stroke. It turned out to be two herniated discs in his back. An operation could have ended his career, but he had it done anyway, and it didn't. He was believed to be on the brink of a nervous breakdown in 1957; he took the last part of the season off and was back the next – a morose, nervous, short-tempered man, who died at forty in May of 1970 after emergency surgery in New York to remove a collection of blood from his liver.

This, then, is the automatic quartet that springs to the minds of fans of the 1950s Red Wings: the Production Line of Abel, Lindsay, and Howe, and the peerless goaltender Sawchuk.

And then there's the remarkable Red Kelly, a big-boned, rock-hard defenseman, who, paradoxically, is remembered as a frequent winner of the Lady Byng Trophy, a bauble of peace. He was the original winner of the Norris Trophy in 1954 as the league's top defenseman and played on the four Red Wing Stanley Cup-winning teams in their 1950s run.

The hand that held the baton orchestrating the seven-year sweep during the 1950s belonged to this

as the center for Howe and Lindsay. It was an era when forward lines stayed together as units, and some of them had special names – the Punch Line, the Kraut Line, the Kid Line. This line, being from Detroit, was dubbed the Production Line.

But Abel was more than just a center for two superstars. In his own right he had won the Hart Trophy as the league's most valuable player in 1949, and way back in 1942, as the left winger on a line with Count Grosso and Eddie Wares, he had made the league's Second All-Star Team.

The fourth guy is Terry Sawchuk. What a star-struck victim he was, quite possibly the best goaltender of all time, a maskless star with big hands, fast reflexes, and an unorthodox, gorilla-like crouch, in which his legs were stiff from hips to ankles, same combustible operator, Jack Adams – fat, red-faced, bombastic, impulsive. In that swashbuckling period the Red Wings were dominating, pugnacious, and arrogant, every bit as intimidating in their own rink, the Olympia, as the Philadelphia Broad Street Bullies became a couple of decades later. They carried their sticks like lances and plastered visiting players against the boards as though they were advertisements.

Adams wasn't much for Lady Byng winners. He tolerated Kelly because there were heavy-handed hewers of wood backing Red up, tough nuts such as Benny Woit, Tony Leswick, Marty Pavelich, Vic Stasiuk, Leo Reise, and Marcel Pronovost.

I remember games in the Olympia, when the Maple Leafs and the Red Wings tangled, that had me wincing, and I was many pews removed, in the safety of the pressbox up under the roof. The picture I retain is of players cruising with sticks aloft – "a tiny, moving forest," I remember calling it (it wasn't much of a phrase, but it was how I saw those endlessly raised sticks).

I got to know Adams quite well, because Ralph Allen, the editor of *Maclean's* magazine at the time, sent me to Detroit to do a two-part article under Adams's name, an abbreviated autobiography. Adams was a man with a frequent, humorless laugh, a sort of reflex at the end of sentences. He'd introduce me to people at luncheons or golf clubs or the ball park, wherever he happened to take us, by saying, "He's writing my life story," and then giving that nervous little chuckle. In his time, Adams had been a fiery player for the old Toronto Arenas, who preceded the St. Pats, who preceded the Maple Leafs. He recalled that the team trainer kept a pail of cold water and a sponge at the bench, and when a player was cut, he skated to the boards, where the trainer sloshed off the blood, put some sticking plaster over the cut, patted the guy on the shoulder, and sent him out for more lumps.

After one game Adams was so cut up that his own sister, a nurse at the Montreal General, didn't recognize him until she'd cleaned up his bloodied kisser. Of that game the Toronto *Mail* reported:

The Arenas refused to quit and that tells the whole story. For the entire first period the Canadiens hammered and battered these game youngsters. They put Ken Randall out of the game for keeps, cut Jack Adams's head to ribbons, battered Rusty Crawford from head to foot, sent Harry Mummery hobbling off halfway through the period with one leg limp from a sweeping slash, broke the teeth of goalkeeper Harry Holmes, knocked out Harry Meeking and Alf Skinner, and bumped every other opposing player on the ice – but the Arenas didn't quit. It was the most punishing game ever played in an NHL final, and Canadiens made punishing play the main issue. An unforgettable picture was of chunky Jack Adams dashing up and down the boards with blood streaming from cuts over his eyes and ears.

In retrospect, the notion grows that Jack Adams was the foremost trader of hockey players in the game's history. He did nothing so spectacular as the

Red Kelly, first winner of the Norris Trophy, awarded to the NHL's top defenseman, captured the award in 1954 and was runner-up to Doug Harvey the following season.

move by which Edmonton's Peter Pocklington sent Canada's national treasure, Wayne Gretzky, out of the country, or Léo Dandurand's decision to ship the deified Howie Morenz from the Montreal Forum to Chicago late in the immortal one's career, or even the modest swap by Conn Smythe of five Maple Leaf players to the Black Hawks for the mighty mite Max Bentley. But in quantity and a certain amount of quality, Adams was hard to beat during Detroit's seven-year reign in the 1950s. In the spring of 1949, Detroit's Bill Quackenbush, a calm, blond-haired pillar on the Detroit blue line, became the first defenseman to win the Lady Byng Trophy, so decidedly the best that he polled 52 points of a possible 54. Of greater impact, he also won the Hart Trophy that spring. But now, beginning a new decade, Adams sent this paragon of defensemen to Boston, along with forward Pete Horeck, for four players: Pete Babando, Jimmy Peters, Clare Martin, and Lloyd Durham. The Wings had been on top in the standings the previous spring, but had been laced in straight games in the Stanley Cup finals by Toronto. Thus, explaining the swap, Adams said, "We want that Cup. We have defensemen, but we don't have forwards. You can be sure I hate to lose Quackenbush."

All season long, and in the spring as well, the move paid dividends. The Red Wings finished in first place for the second successive year. In the spring, in the Cup finals, heavily favored Detroit had all it could handle against the surprising New York Rangers. In the seventh game and in the second overtime period, who should score the Cup-winning goal but one of the players that Adams had traded for, Pete Babando.

The spring of 1950 was memorable for another incident in the Detroit saga – the near-death of Gordie Howe. There have been several versions of what happened that night in the Olympia when the Red Wings were engaged with the Maple Leafs in the semi-finals. Back then, the team's star center was Ted "Teeder" Kennedy. As it happened, I shared a breakfast table with Kennedy and King Clancy thirty-four years after the incident.

Talking hockey, Clancy recalled Howe's near-fatal injury. In trying to check Kennedy along the boards,

Howe had missed his man, King said, had crashed against the boards, and was carried, bleeding, from the ice on a stretcher. He had a deep cut near his right eye, a fractured nose, a possible fractured cheekbone, a possible fractured skull, and even possible brain damage. After a team of doctors performed a ninety-minute operation to save Howe's life, his condition was called serious but stable.

King went back to his pancakes and syrup, and Kennedy took up the tale. "In Detroit they blamed me for butt-ending Gordie, though in truth I didn't lay a glove on him," Teeder said. "The furor upset several of our players, and probably turned the series around against us. We had won three Stanley Cups in a row, but we lost this series in seven games, the last one 1–0 in overtime. Then we won the Cup again in 1951 so, really, except for the Howe incident, we'd likely have become the first team to win the Stanley Cup five straight years."

Big Gordie, of course, recovered. Indeed, he recovered rapidly. The night Pete Babando scored the Cup-winner, Howe was there, seated near the Detroit bench, and the roaring Olympia crowd demanded that he rise and make his way to the ice.

The following summer, in July of 1950, undeterred by his Stanley Cup triumph, Trader Jack was back at it. Remarkably, in a nine-player deal with Chicago, he sent away five members of that championship line-up, including the playoff hero, Babando. Also, with a kid named Sawchuk on the rise at the Indianapolis farm, Adams felt no compunction in shipping away the tubby, apple-cheeked Cup goaltender, Harry Lumley. And with a similar lack of compassion, away went "Black Jack" Stewart, the veteran, king-sized defensive star, and two lesser lights, Al Dewsbury and Don Morrison. In return, Adams didn't appear to get all that much: the forwards Gaye Stewart and Metro Prystai, the great puck-stopping defenseman Bob Goldham, and the Hawks' farm-club goaltender at Kansas City, "Sugar Jim" Henry, who was immediately dispatched to the Indianapolis farm to replace young Sawchuk.

The departed defenseman, Jack Stewart – handsome, black-haired, and an elegant dresser – could hit with terrific force, a rib-rattler of grim applica-

Sid Abel (right) celebrates his 100th career goal with "Black Jack" Stewart. Abel later coached in Chicago, Detroit, Kansas City, and St. Louis.

tion. His best playing weight was 185 pounds, but he was regarded by Adams as one of the strongest players he'd ever seen. Though an off-ice fashion-plate, Black Jack was as marked as an old fighter, scarred over both eyes, with a large semicircular scar under his right eye and another big one down his right cheek. He carried 201 stitches that over the seasons had closed forty-eight wounds in his physiognomy.

But Adams knew what he was doing, apparently. The Red Wings finished on top again, and the youngster Sawchuk played the full schedule of 70 games, recorded 11 shutouts, and put up a glittering goals-against average of 1.98.

The Wings were kayoed early in the playoffs, however. That was the spring when Rocket Richard made another of his indelible impressions on the history books, the spring when he scored two goals in marathon overtime when the Canadiens opened

the semi-final by winning twice on Detroit ice. He slammed the first one past Sawchuk after sixty-one minutes of overtime, and two nights later he repeated the process after forty-two minutes of extra time.

His team sidelined, Trader Jack fidgeted until July before brightening up his summer with another pair of headline swaps. First he sent Gaye Stewart to the Rangers for the little pest Tony Leswick, then he peddled the goaltender Jim Henry to Boston. These deals merely whetted Jack's appetite for a new departure: he negotiated the largest cash deal for players in NHL history, collecting $75,000, an enormous sum, from the Black Hawks for six players: Jim McFadden, Clare Raglan, Max McNab, George Gee, Jimmy Peters, and Clare Martin.

Terry Sawchuk is annointed with some ceremonial bubbly from the bowl of Lord Stanley's mug in 1954.

Still, not all of Adams's swaps were made in heaven. Unloading Sugar Jim Henry cost him heavily in the playoffs of 1953 when the Wings met the Bruins. They lathered them by 7–0 in the first game but, backstopped brilliantly by Henry, the Bruins prevailed in six games. Henry was bombarded by 228 shots to a mere 140 aimed at Terry Sawchuk.

Though the Red Wings achieved their sixth and seventh straight first-place finishes, and two more Stanley Cup championships in 1954 and 1955, Trader Jack was insatiable. In May of 1955 he dispatched Tony Leswick, Glen Skov, Johnny Wilson, and Benny Woit to Chicago in an eight-player swap that netted him Jerry Toppazzini, Johnny McCormack, Dave Creighton, and Bucky Hollingworth. Then, less than a month later, he engineered a nine-player transaction with Boston. From the Bruins

he brought in the team's captain, Ed Sandford, along with Réal Chevrefils, Norm Corcoran, Warren Godfrey, and Gilles Boisvert. The players Jack dealt away to corral this gang were Vic Stasiuk, Lorne Davis, Marcel Bonin, and, incredibly, the sensational Sawchuk.

Terry, sensitive and insecure, was shocked. The trade eroded his confidence. At the time, by coincidence, I was at his home in Union Lake, a Detroit suburb, to do an article about him, and his agitation was clearly apparent. He had been pads deep in praise following his third Vezina Trophy in his first four years in the NHL and had backstopped two successive Stanley Cup wins, yet he was sent packing.

Near the home where Terry lived with his wife,

Pat, and their children, there was a municipal golf course operated by his father-in-law, Ed Morey. Terry and Pat played nearly every day, sometimes as many as twenty-seven holes. One steamy night at the club, the frogs croaking and insects buzzing beyond us, Terry and I sat in a wide screened-in porch drinking beer and talking. He was pained that Adams had picked the Indianapolis farmhand, Glenn Hall, to play goal for the Wings over him. Why had he been traded, he wondered, and not the untried Hall?

"Does it mean I'm washed up?" he asked three or four times. I assured him he wasn't, but what did I know?

Anyway, he went to Boston, stayed two seasons, and was then suddenly brought back to Detroit when the mercurial Adams grew disenchanted with Glenn Hall and banished him to the Black Hawks. After that, of course, Terry went on and on. In action he was the most acrobatic goaltender of his time. He didn't move so much as he exploded into a desperate release of energy – down the glove, up the arm, over the stick, up the leg pad; he sometimes seemed a human pinwheel. He played the whole game in pent-up tension, shouting at his teammates, crouching, straightening, diving, scrambling, his pale face drawn and tense before he covered it with a mask.

Things were never easy for him, even as a child. His dad, Louis, was a tinsmith in Winnipeg. His brother Mike played goal at school so, as Terry said that night on the screened-in clubhouse porch, "the pads were always around the house and I fell into them." He was ten when Mike died of a heart ailment at seventeen. Another brother, Roger, died of pneumonia. By fourteen Terry had worked in a foundry and for a sheet-metal company installing canopies over giant ovens in bakeries. Is it any wonder he grew to be an agitated, apprehensive, even haunted, adult?

That massive turnover of players in the summer of 1955, in which seventeen of them swapped sweaters, turned out to be Trader Jack's swan song. He was to make a terrible mistake in 1959 when he traded Red Kelly to Toronto for journeyman defenseman Marc Réaume. (The trade was done because Red had revealed to a magazine writer that during the previous season Adams had asked him to play on a cracked ankle, and Red had done so.)

But that summer of 1955 was really Trader Jack's last hurrah. The Red Wings, once so dominating, fell to a distant second place the following spring, and they haven't won the Stanley Cup since.

The 1955 Detroit Red Wings, the last Motor City squad to win the Stanley Cup.

Heading into the 1950-51 season, it looked as if Jack Adams had built a near-invincible juggernaut in Detroit. At the other end of the standings, the lowly Chicago Black Hawks so frustrated Charlie Conacher that he quit as coach and was replaced by Ebbie Goodfellow. The Bruins, too, were in poor shape. Even the Canadiens, depleted by a host of departures, were forced to rebuild. Goaltender Gerry McNeil would be counted on to replace all-star Bill Durnan, who had retired a six-time Vezina Trophy-winner after seven seasons with the Habs.

In Toronto, where Joe Primeau replaced Hap Day as coach, the Leafs decided to split goaltending responsibilities between Turk Broda and Al Rollins. This platooning system worked well and foreshadowed the two-goaltender systems widely used in the NHL by the mid-1960s. Rollins went on to win the Vezina Trophy, playing in forty games.

In New York, the Rangers never regained the previous season's winning form, as crowds in Madison Square Garden dwindled to a ten-year low of 6,800 for a game against the Bruins. Neil Colville, who had succeeded Lynn Patrick as coach, was so desperate that he even experimented with hypnotism to get some of his players back on track.

In the blockbuster trade of the off-season, Detroit had sent Harry Lumley, "Black Jack" Stewart, Al Dewsbury, Don Morrison and Pete Babando to Chicago in exchange for goalie "Sugar Jim" Henry, Bob Goldham, Gaye Stewart, and Metro Prystai. (Babando, an American-born player, became the first NHLer drafted to fight in the Korean War.) The key to the trade, from Detroit's point of view, had been the strong play of young Terry Sawchuk the previous season, which had made Lumley expendable. The Red Wings had also promoted Marcel Pronovost and Glen Skov from the minors. The club was strong enough to defeat the NHL's best by a lopsided 7–1 score in the annual pre-season All-Star Game.

As the season progressed, the Canadiens gave brief trials to two junior stars, Jean Béliveau and Bernie "Boom-Boom" Geoffrion, both of whom shone in their debuts. Prying Béliveau away from the junior Quebec Citadels for whom he played, however, proved impossible. The Canadiens' offer of two players was scoffed at by the owner of the Quebec team, where Béliveau was not only the star attraction, but was rumored to be earning the equivalent of an NHL salary.

By the halfway point in the season, Toronto and Detroit had opened a huge lead on the rest of the league. The remaining four teams were virtually tied, making competition for the remaining two playoff positions intense.

Although Rocket Richard continued to excel for the Canadiens, surpassing Howie Morenz and Aurel Joliat to become the Canadiens' all-time leading goal-scorer, he was never far from difficulties with the league. In the lobby of New York's Picadilly Hotel, for instance, he accosted a referee who had given him a game misconduct the previous night. President Campbell fined him $500.

First Hockey Telecast

The first NHL game televised by the Canadian Broadcasting Corporation featured the Montreal Canadiens and the Toronto Maple Leafs on March 21, 1951. The telecast from Maple Leaf Gardens was viewed by only six people, however, as the CBC had their cameras transmitting pictures to a television in the radio control room of the Gardens. Foster Hewitt gave a play-by-play description of the first period of the game before resuming his radio broadcast. The experiment was deemed an overwhelming success.

The Red Wings ended the season atop the standings. Sawchuk won the Calder Trophy as the league's top rookie with a glittering 1.99 goals-against average and 11 shutouts. Rookie awards were nothing new for Sawchuk, who had rocketed through the minors, winning freshman accolades in the AHL and USHL. There were many who felt that in playing every game of the schedule, Sawchuk should also have won the Vezina Trophy, which went to Toronto's Al Rollins, whose goals-against average was better than Sawchuk's, although he appeared in just forty games. Detroit owner James Norris felt that Sawchuk deserved the Vezina; he gave his goalie a $1,000 bonus to match the monetary award that accompanied the trophy. Gordie Howe (the only NHL player to wear a helmet, following his near-disastrous accident the previous season) had 43 goals and 43 assists for 86 points to win the first of four consecutive Art Ross trophies. Howe's point total established a single-season point-scoring record, surpassing Herbie Cain's 1943-44 mark of 82 points. Red Kelly received the Lady Byng Trophy for gentlemanly conduct.

Milt Schmidt of the fourth-place Boston Bruins won the Hart Trophy as league MVP. Schmidt played on a line with Woody Dumart and Bill Ezinicki, who along with Vic Lynn, came over from the Leafs in exchange for Leo Boivin, Fern Flaman, Phil Maloney, and Ken Smith.

The final scoring list told the tale of the season. Except for Richard and Schmidt, all the others in the top ten were either Leafs or Red Wings. Detroit, which became the first NHL team to finish with more than 100 points in a season, finished six points ahead of second-place Toronto and 36 points ahead of the third-place Canadiens.

For all their success in league play, though, the Wings were a flop in the playoffs. They dropped the semi-final round to Montreal in six games, despite deploying their checking winger Marty Pavelich to shadow Maurice Richard. Toronto, after quickly dispatching Boston, faced Montreal in the finals. Although the Leafs won the Stanley Cup in five games, the series was a close one – in fact, it was the only series in NHL history in which all games went into overtime. Leaf defenseman Bill Barilko, who would die in an airplane crash that summer, scored the Cup-winning goal. Toronto coach Joe Primeau continued his string of successes behind the bench, adding a Stanley Cup to his junior Memorial Cup and senior Allan Cup championships.

The 1950-51 season saw the first experimental television broadcast of an NHL game in Canada – on March 21, 1951, when the Leafs and Canadiens played in Maple Leaf Gardens. With regular television coverage slated to begin in 1952, NHL clubs agreed that, beginning with the 1951-52 season, opposing teams would wear contrasting uniforms, either white or colored, to help viewers of black-and-white television follow the game. The Canadiens and Rangers adopted colored uniforms for use at home; the other four clubs chose to wear white in their home rinks. Three seasons later, the

Milt Schmidt, who spent thirty-seven years with Boston as a player and coach, captured the Hart Trophy in 1951 when he compiled 61 points for the Bruins, the second-highest total of his career.

league would further amend these uniform requirements, stipulating that, as of January 1, 1956, all clubs would wear colored uniforms when playing at home.

At the same time, the league made minor rule changes. Icing calls were nullified if a goaltender touched the puck after it crossed the goal-line, and the goal crease was expanded a foot in each direction, making it four feet by eight feet. Face-off circles were increased from a ten-foot to a fifteen-foot radius. Although Detroit sportswriters advocated discounting from goaltenders' averages any goals scored into an open net, the rule was not officially adopted.

A few hockey men still wanted to rid the game of the center-ice red line, which had been introduced as a stop-gap measure during the player shortages of the war years. Despite arguments that the red line de-emphasized stickhandling by permitting longer passes as a team emerged from its defensive zone, the NHL's icing rules fit with the red line's existence and worked very well – so the center line stayed.

Following the 1950-51 season, it was apparent that a chasm had grown between the NHL's top three teams – Detroit, Montreal, and Toronto – and the rest of the league. Things did not change much in 1951-52. The Red Wings, who twice in the previous three seasons had won the Prince of Wales Trophy as league champions, only to lose in the playoffs, finally emerged as true champions. Jack Adams had an eye for talent; it seemed everyone he brought up from the minors turned into a star. And those the Red Wings' farm system didn't develop were acquired through trades. The Wings'

Ted Kennedy, captain of the Toronto Maple Leafs, greets Princess Elizabeth and the Duke of Edinburgh.

Pony Line right winger Bill Mosienko scored a record three goals in twenty-one seconds in a 7–6 win over the New York Rangers on the final day of the 1951-52 season. Mosienko, who was set up by Gus Bodnar on all three markers, narrowly missed adding a fourth goal when he rang a shot off the post seconds later. The victim of Mosienko's barrage, Rangers' netminder Lorne Anderson, never played another NHL game.

explosive Production Line was backed up by forwards such as Glen Skov, Tony Leswick, Johnny Wilson, Metro Prystai, and a smooth young newcomer, Alex Delvecchio. On defense, Red Kelly and Marcel Pronovost prevailed.

Montreal, led by the stormy genius of Rocket Richard, had added scoring-punch with Dickie Moore and eventual Calder Trophy-winner Bernie Geoffrion. Richard and Moore were centered by playmaker Elmer Lach. However, a groin injury that sidelined Richard for six weeks late in the season hindered the Canadiens' chances. Toronto added a young George Armstrong to its line-up, but could no longer keep pace with Detroit and Montreal.

Chicago and Boston continued to fade on the ice and at the gate. In Boston, Weston Adams, who had taken over from his father, Charles, resigned when the Boston Garden bought 60 per cent of the team, but new ownership didn't change the club's fortunes. The night of Woody Dumart's 100th goal in a Bruin uniform, there were fewer than five thousand fans in the seats.

In Chicago, where Charlie Conacher's son Pete briefly joined his uncles Roy and Jim on the roster, the team continued to draw poorly. The highlight of the season occurred in the Hawks' final game, when Bill Mosienko scored three goals in twenty-one seconds, a record that still stands in the NHL's

Chicago Experiments with Afternoon Games

Citing attendance figures that had averaged only eight thousand per game, the Chicago Black Hawks began experimenting with afternoon contests during the 1951-52 season. Black Hawks' general manager Bill Tobin believed that weekend prime-time television was proving to be more attractive to Chicagoans than a trip to the Stadium. The first two matinee games proved Tobin's point, as crowds of 13,600 and 13,900 watched the Black Hawks.

Detroit marksmen Tony Leswick (left) and Ted Lindsay surround goaltender Terry Sawchuk after the Wings defeated the Canadiens 3–1 in the opening game of the 1952 Stanley Cup finals. Although Lindsay and Leswick both scored key goals for the Wings, Sawchuk was the hero of this series, allowing only two goals in four games as Detroit swept the Habs in four straight.

Red Wings, Black Hawks Meet in Indianapolis

On December 6, 1952, the Chicago Black Hawks hosted the Detroit Red Wings for a regular-season game in Indianapolis. The game had been rescheduled from November 4 after Chicago management requested a postponement because of the U.S. election. The Stadium could not be secured for the rescheduled game because of previous bookings.

seventy-fifth anniversary season. He victimized Rangers' goaltender Lorne Anderson, who never played another game in the NHL. In New York, a coaching change that brought in former star Bill Cook failed to have much impact on the team's performance.

The Red Wings swept to their fourth consecutive league championship and second 100-point season, finishing 22 points ahead of the second-place Canadiens. In the playoffs, the Red Wings swept the Leafs and the Canadiens eliminated the Bruins in seven games. Maurice Richard scored what many consider to be the most electrifying playoff goal of his career in the final game of the Habs' series with the Bruins, going end-to-end to beat Boston netminder Sugar Jim Henry. Richard had been knocked unconscious in the first period and remained on the Canadiens' bench until late in the game with the score tied 1–1.

In the finals, the Red Wings were too strong for the Canadiens, and again swept the series to become the first club to win the Stanley Cup in the minimum eight games. Terry Sawchuk was marvelous in goal for Detroit, holding the Leafs and the Canadiens to a total of five goals in the post-season. His 0.62 goals-against average in the playoffs stands as an NHL record.

Detroit, with four consecutive first-place finishes, was again the team to beat in 1952-53. The arrival of Alex Delvecchio allowed the Red Wings to sell Sid Abel to the Black Hawks, where he served as playing coach. If Howe missed his old linemate, it didn't show; he poured in 49 goals, barely missing the single-season record of 50 held by Rocket Richard. Owner James Norris,

Sr., who had been responsible for much of the franchise's success, died in December of 1952. He was replaced as president of the club by his daughter, Marguerite, who became the NHL's first female executive.

Montreal received first-rate goaltending from Gerry McNeil, who, along with Toronto's Harry Lumley, posted ten shutouts in 1952-53. Despite McNeil's success, playing goal for the Canadiens wasn't always a simple assignment. Despite all-stars Doug Harvey and Butch Bouchard on defense, the Canadiens' firewagon style emphasized offense, which left the team vulnerable to counter-attacks. As well, the fiery performance of the likes of Richard and Geoffrion frequently left the Habs short-handed. A newcomer named Jacques Plante, who turned out to be, of all things, an offensive-minded goaltender, was added to spell off McNeil, and proved to be the perfect complement to the Canadiens' style.

The Canadiens had not given up on their efforts to add Quebec junior and senior hockey sensation Jean Béliveau to their roster. He joined the Canadiens for another mid-season tryout, scored five goals in three games, and returned to Quebec City.

In addition to Jacques Plante, two more future Hall of Fame goaltenders made their NHL debuts in 1952-53. Glenn Hall, who backed up Sawchuk, appeared in six games for Detroit, while Lorne "Gump" Worsley, who played in 50 games, became the Rangers' first-string goalie. New York substantially rejuvenated its roster, adding Harry Howell on defense, and Andy Bathgate, Dean Prentice, and Ron Murphy up front.

In Toronto, the Leafs filled openings with Leo Boivin, Tim Horton, Eric Nesterenko, and Ron Stewart. During the season, the Leafs' magnificent center Max Bentley left the team, suffering from depression, but was able to return in March. The Leafs also decided to bolster their goaltending by trading Al Rollins to Chicago for Harry Lumley. Boston's Fleming Mackell scored 27 goals and was named to the First All-Star Team at center. Bill Quackenbush earned his fifth all-star selection on defense. He was joined on the Second All-Star Team's defense by Chicago's Bill Gadsby. The Black Hawks' line-up also boasted two of the NHL's ten 20-goal scorers in Jim McFadden and Jimmy Peters.

The regular season ended with Detroit in first place, 15 points ahead of the Canadiens. The Wings topped the NHL in goals scored with 222 (Chicago was second with 169), and in goals-against with 133 (Montreal was second with 148). This statistical superiority didn't help the Red Wings in the semi-finals, however, as Boston upset the league champions in six games. The Bruins advanced to meet the Canadiens in the Stanley Cup finals, losing in five games. The series' final match went into overtime and was decided when the Canadiens' Elmer Lach scored to give the Habs a 1–0 win and their first Cup since 1946.

Native Black Hawk

The first full-blooded Native Canadian to play in the NHL was Fred Saskamoose, who made his NHL debut with Chicago in 1954. The first black to play in the NHL was Willie O'Ree, who made his first appearance with the Boston Bruins on January 18, 1958, in a game against the Montreal Canadiens.

Bill Quackenbush won the Lady Byng Trophy in 1949, playing in all sixty games for Detroit without incurring a penalty. A three-time all-star when he was traded to the Bruins the following season, Quackenbush went on to win additional all-star team berths in 1951 and 1953.

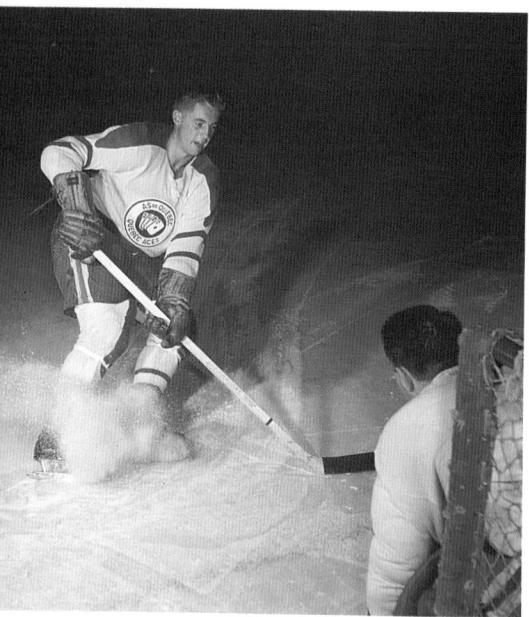

The most highly-touted prospect of his day, Jean Béliveau decided to play a season with the Quebec Aces of the Quebec Senior Hockey League instead of joining the NHL. Béliveau, who eventually signed with the Montreal Canadiens in 1953, won ten Stanley Cups with the Habs.

Cleveland Challenges for Stanley Cup

Although they had not even captured the American Hockey League championship, the Cleveland Barons filed a challenge for the Stanley Cup in March 1953. The AHL franchise issued guarantees as to gate receipts and suggested a best-of-five series. Stanley Cup trustees dismissed the challenge, citing two factors: Cleveland was not authorized to represent the AHL in such a challenge and the AHL was not considered a league of equal caliber to the NHL, a condition in the Stanley Cup charter.

The financially troubled Black Hawks were sold to former Red Wings' shareholders James D. Norris, Jr., and Arthur Wirtz prior to the start of the 1953-54 season. The Canadiens delighted their fans by signing Jean Béliveau to an NHL contract. The success he enjoyed in two earlier trials with Montreal, combined with his junior and senior hockey accomplishments in Quebec City, made him the most eagerly anticipated prospect in the history of the league. Despite the Habs' continued improvement, the Red Wings rebounded from their previous playoff setback and again dominated in 1953-54.

The Rangers seemed determined to continue their rebuilding program, adding new goaltender Johnny Bower, but they also sent Gump Worsley, the previous year's Calder Trophy winner, to the minors. (Worsley would return in 1954-55.) In mid-season, Muzz Patrick, whose brother Lynn was coaching in Boston, took over behind the Ranger bench and talked Doug Bentley out of his two-year retirement to play alongside his brother Max, who had been picked up from Toronto.

The Red Wings continued to dominate the standings, followed by the Canadiens. Although Montreal appeared capable of winning a championship, injuries to key stars such as Béliveau, Lach, and Dickie Moore dogged the team throughout the year. The Canadiens also insisted on hurting themselves with temperamental play, often involving stick-swinging and penalties. To be sure, the Red Wings' Gordie Howe and Ted Lindsay knew the way to the penalty box, but the better-balanced Red Wings were more able to withstand shorthanded situations.

For the first time in the league's history, the NHL's three top scorers each accumulated more than a hundred penalty minutes. Howe and Lindsay finished first and third, while Richard and Geoffrion finished second and fourth. Geoffrion, though he missed 16 games, still spent 87 minutes in the penalty box.

Geoffrion and the Rangers' Ron Murphy were the principals involved in a fight-filled game in Madison Square Garden on December 20, 1953. Apparently slashed by Murphy, Geoffrion retaliated with a two-handed swing at the New York winger's head which left him with a broken jaw and a concussion. After considerable review, Clarence Campbell suspended Geoffrion for the Canadiens' seven remaining games with the Rangers; Murphy was suspended from New York's next four games with the Habs.

But the suspension didn't end the controversy provoked by the incident. Maurice Richard, in a ghostwritten column that ran in the Montreal newspaper *Samedi Dimanche*, castigated Campbell for imposing the sentence, calling the league president a dictator. Richard promised to retire if his teammate wasn't reinstated by the league. Criticism of Richard's comments was almost unanimous around the league, and Campbell lost little time in reacting. The upshot of the incident was an obliged end to Richard's budding journalism career. The Rocket was forced to give up his column, apologize to the league and to Campbell, and to post a $1,000 bond to guarantee that there would be no recurrence.

On the ice, the Red Wings won their sixth consecutive league championship. Gordie Howe finished with 81 points to win his fourth consecutive Art Ross Trophy. Harry Lumley, who won the Vezina Trophy, had 13 shutouts for the Leafs, the most recorded by a goaltender since John Roach of the Rangers and Roy Worters of the Americans both had 13 in 1928-29. Another goaltender, Al Rollins of the last-place Black Hawks, won the Hart Trophy as the league's MVP. Rollins' award marked only the second occasion a player from a last-place club has won the Hart. Camille Henry was named top rookie, giving the Rangers their second consecutive Calder Trophy-winner.

The four children of the late James Norris, Sr., presented the NHL with a trophy to be awarded to the league's top defenseman. Detroit's Red Kelly was its first recipient.

In the playoffs, Detroit and Montreal had easy semi-final series wins before hooking up in what turned out to be one of the closest and most exciting Stanley Cup finals ever. The Canadiens battled back from a three-games-to-one deficit to tie the series and force a seventh game in Detroit on April 16, 1954. Regulation time ended with the score tied 1–1. But just over four minutes into overtime, Detroit's Tony Leswick cleared the puck into the Montreal end, where it deflected off the glove of Canadiens' defenseman Doug Harvey and past a startled Gerry McNeil for the Cup-winning goal. Bad feelings between the two clubs had simmered throughout the series, and the Canadiens did not shake hands with the Red Wings at the end of the finals.

(continued on p. 123)

Chairmen of the Board

In June 1953, the NHL's Board of Governors created the position of Chairman of the Board. Toronto's Conn Smythe was the first to hold this office. A list of Board Chairmen follows:

Conn Smythe, Toronto
1953-54 — 1956-57
Walter Brown, Boston
1957-58 — 1963-64
James Norris, Chicago
1964-65 — 1965-66
Bruce Norris, Detroit
1966-67 — 1967-68
1972-73 — 1973-74
William Jennings, NY Rangers
1968-69 — 1969-70
John Ziegler, Detroit
1976-77 — 1977-78
William Wirtz, Chicago
1970-71 — 1971-72
1974-75 — 1975-76
1978-79 — present

Al Rollins won the Hart Trophy in 1953–54, despite Chicago's sixth-place finish.

THE GOALTENDERS' DEMON

by Stu Hackel

In its March 4, 1966, issue, wedged between the weekly news photos and a close-up of the Harvard *Crimson*'s nineteen-year-old managing editor, *Life* magazine devoted a few pages to the exploits of National Hockey League goaltenders. The shock of America's largest mass-circulation news-feature magazine actually running a hockey piece was exceeded only by the shock of the story's opening photo, a jolting, dramatic, nine-inch-square, black-and-white portrait of the jigsawed face of Terry Sawchuk. From cheekbone to nose, from temple to scalp, from chin to lip, the scars of his merry profession had been highlighted and retouched by a make-up artist, whose rendering of Sawchuk's more pronounced gashes and gouges made them appear quite fresh.

Your first glance at the photo – the firmly stitched jaw, the crewcut scalp, the hunks of skin seemingly yanked and stapled together, the grotesquely sewn patchwork that barely deserved to be called a face – guaranteed a week's worth of Frankenstein nightmares. You could only guess how the flesh-and-blood Sawchuk reacted.

As your glance turned to gaze, something more telling emerged from the image that stared back at you from the magazine page. At the center of the embroidery were dark eyes, eyes that had seen every stick, puck, skate, and elbow that had done this damage. Surrounded by the embellishing warpaint of sutures and scar tissue, those eyes beamed undiluted anger. With his thick Ukrainian features, Sawchuk resembled a Comanche warrior, determined to avenge the wrongs done to him and his tribe.

If you saw this photo, you've never forgotten it. It hangs frozen in your memory, a memento of the time when the sticks were straight, the skaters were bareheaded, and goalies were barefaced.

Sawchuk and his tribe – Johnny Bower, Glenn Hall, Jacques Plante, and Gump Worsley – were arguably the best collection of goaltending talent ever to play in the NHL at the same time. Today, we call that time hockey's "Golden Era." We called them (and they called themselves) members of the "Goaltenders' Union," and no local ever paid more dues. They also dominated the position – and the sport – like no generation of goalies before or since.

Today, it's safe to say that centers rule hockey. Just look at the top players in the game and you'll see most of them – Gretzky, Lemieux, Yzerman, LaFontaine, Messier, Sakic, Oates, and this new kid, Lindros – are centers. The way the game is played now, center is the key position, and every general manager wants a superstar in the middle. Back in the Bobby Orr era ... well, you guessed it, defensemen – especially the rushing kind – seemed to control the play. And back in the Golden Era, it can be argued that the goalies had the biggest impact on NHL teams. Sure, there have been other times when goaltending flourished. Back at the beginnings of the NHL they had some fellows in net who should not be lost in the musty, early pages of hockey history: Vezina, Benedict, Hainsworth, Connell, Roach, Worters, and Gardiner. Nor should we forget the greats of the 1930s and 1940s: Brimsek, Thompson, Broda, Durnan, Raynor, and Lumley.

For these founding guild brothers, the shots may have packed a quieter thunder, the skaters may have burned a slower jet fuel. Yet they shared with the goaltending stars of the Golden Era that critical ingredient: they excelled in keeping at bay the demon pressure which haunts all goalies – at least during the sixty minutes of game time.

Not all goalies have that gift. Goalies are a quirky lot – eccentric, colorful, generally odd in their behavior on and off the ice. And why not? Strapping deer-hair-filled leather mattresses to your legs, a thick cloth bib on your chest, and lobster claws on your hands, then standing on ice in the path of speeding rock-hard rubber discs should produce some weird side effects. It's a strange way to make a living. The scars inflicted can be more than skin deep.

Some goalies have become legendary, if not for their play, then for the dances they have done to keep the pressure down. It's a tricky two-step, a dance of performance and survival that binds goalies in mythical, mystical union. One member of that select group, Montreal's Wilf Cude, hurled a perfectly cooked steak at his wife one Depression-era afternoon before a big game. He missed her. But "between the time that steak hit the wall, then the floor, I'd decided I'd been a touchy goalkeeper long enough," he later recalled. "By the time it landed, I'd retired."

Less striking, but no less disturbing, was the tale of Toronto's Frank McCool, who earned the nickname "Ulcers" for good reason. He doubled up in pain regularly during the 1945 playoffs, even after posting three straight shutouts against Detroit. But in the middle of game seven, he skated off the ice and tromped right into the dressing room, where he sat until Leaf coach Hap Day came after him.

"How about it then, Frank?" Day asked.

McCool didn't answer.

"There's no one else."

McCool sighed and nodded "okay," took a slug of medicine, and returned to the ice, again clutching his stomach each time play went the other way. McCool hung on for a 2–1 win and the Stanley Cup.

Colorful stories of such demonic encounters abound in hockey's ancient and recent history. "The only job worse," Worsley once said, "is a javelin catcher at a track-and-field meet."

The pressure on the Golden Era's

goalies caused each to occasionally "retire" from the NHL before their actual retirement – except for Bower, who most observers thought was old enough to have retired before ever reaching stardom. Like their predecessors, they suffered physically, psychologically, and emotionally the hazards of their job. Their mood swings were legendary. They were overworked, underpaid, and, in the words of *Life*'s John R. McDermott, "a special breed of man, half commando and half human pincushion."

With nightmarish effectiveness, a make-up artist recreates the facial scars accumulated by Terry Sawchuk before he decided to wear a facemask in 1962.

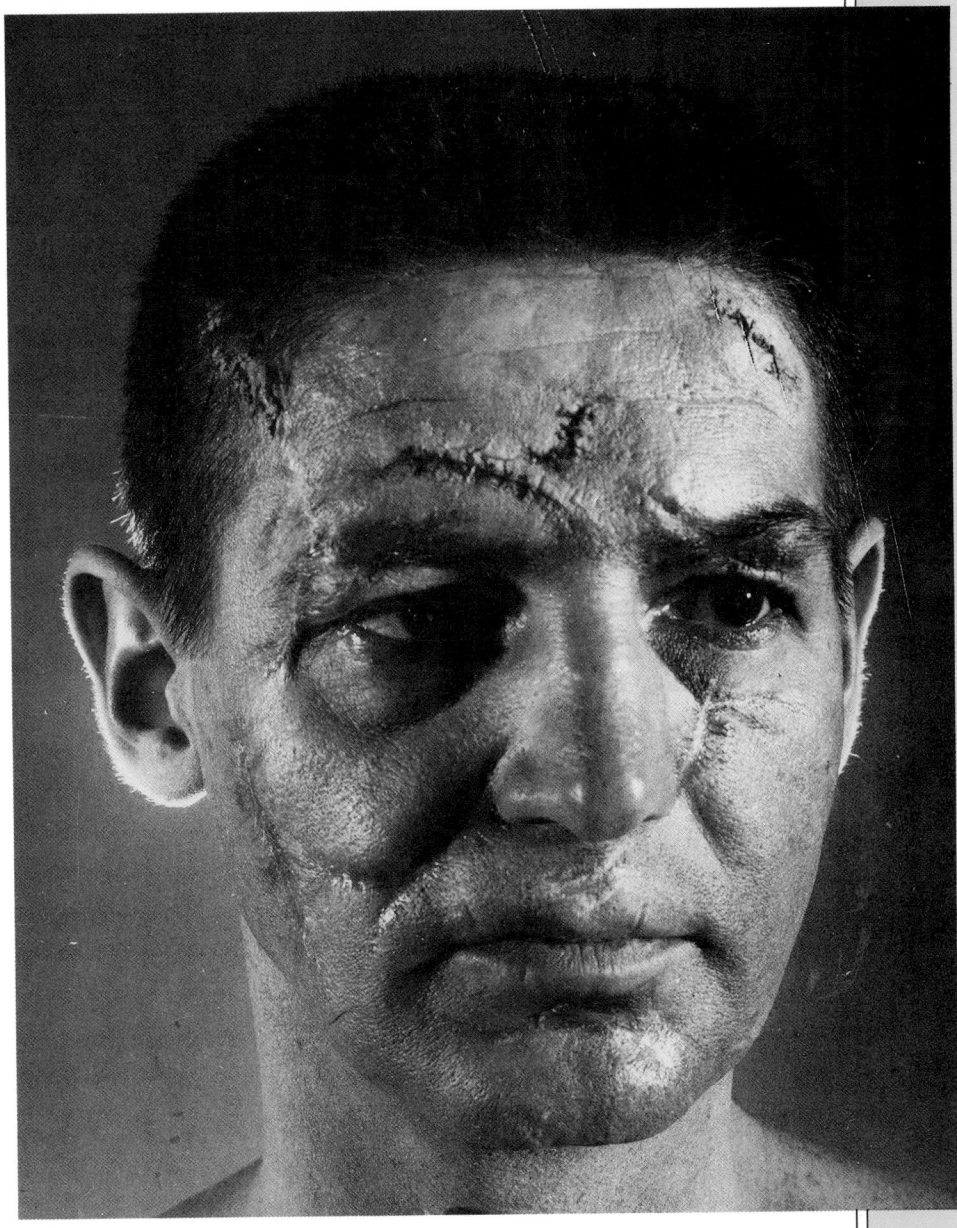

So if the occupational hazards were relatively equal, what set the goalies of the Golden Era apart from all others?

You can find part of the answer in the NHL *Official Guide and Record Book*, which exhibits their unparalleled excellence, consistency, and longevity.

All five entered the NHL in the first half of the 1950s and lasted until at least 1970. In fifteen of the sixteen seasons between 1953-54 and 1967-68, one of these fellows was (in the parlance of the day) the "regular" goalie for the Stanley Cup champion. Going one step further, at least one (and often two or three) played or backed up for one of the two Cup finalists each season between 1952 and 1970.

In nineteen out of the twenty-one seasons between 1950-51 and 1970-71, at least one, if not two, of these gentlemen appeared on the post-season All-Star teams, capturing twenty-eight out of a possible forty-two selections. Four of them were among the six all-time leaders in games won by a goaltender (Bower's long minor-league exile leaves him eighteenth). Sawchuk, Hall, and Plante are numbers one, three, and four in career shutouts.

Among them, the five won or shared the Vezina Trophy for fewest goals allowed in all but two seasons between 1951-52 and 1968-69, and one of them was (or shared) runner-up fifteen times between 1950-51 and 1971-72. Sawchuk, Worsley, and Hall each won the Calder Trophy as NHL rookie of the year. Plante was the last goalie to win the Hart Trophy as MVP in 1962. All five are, deservedly, in the Hockey Hall of Fame.

At various times, they were traded for each other, replaced each other, and, as the one-goalie system broke down, became teammates. They took turns at being the best of the lot, although the gap between one and five was never very large.

Those are the facts. But the characters behind the records and how they played the game – now there's the real story.

The NHL was a tale of six cities back then, and the *cognoscenti* referred to teams without using the definite article before the club name ("Leafs lead Rangers 4 to 1 as we get ready to start the third period"). Each of the six teams carried but one netminder (ah, yes, in those pre-TV days they'd hold up the game for a half-hour while an injured goalie was administered treatment; or if the card-playing, cigar-chomping doc couldn't stitch the poor guy up, they'd pull the "house goalie" out of the stands and slap the pads on him; yes, times have changed). With a proliferation of minor-league hockey players, dozens of hopefuls waited for the top six to falter – compounding the already immense pressure.

We who now celebrate seventy-five seasons of the NHL often think fondly of this Golden Era, not only because of our own age and memories, but also because of its quality (especially compared with the hockey played during World War II and immediately after the war), and its stability and familiarity. The top 120 players in the world played here, and the turnover was remarkably low. A team with four or five new faces in the line-up, which is probably average today, was "rebuilding" during the 1950s and 1960s. You rarely saw more than one or two rookies per team and players remained active in the NHL well into their thirties.

Yet while the faces remained the same, the game itself during the Golden Era did not. The players' knowledge of each other's strengths and weaknesses necessitated the development of new tactics by those seeking an edge. So the dangerous, even frightening, slapshot came into vogue. Geoffrion, Bathgate, Mahovlich, and, most feared of all, Bobby Hull, with their curved, whippy sticks, added the element of wild uncertainty to the hardest shots.

Starting early in the 1950s with the slickness of Doug Harvey and Red Kelly, ever-increasing through the magnificence of Bobby Orr in the late 1960s, defensemen "left home" to join the offensive army, posing a dual problem for netminders. While rushing defensemen were an added attacking threat, they were more likely to be trapped up ice, leaving goalies more vulnerable.

Skating speeds accelerated and, with them, the use of illegal tactics, resulted in more penalties. Increasingly, those wicked shots came from the point as deflections became planned rather than accidental. Creating havoc in front of the net for screen shots and rebounds further complicated the netminder's life.

Injuries mounted. No longer willing to gamble on the house goalie (who might be the other team's trainer or a moonlighting TV producer), teams began carrying their own back-up goalies. The league got involved, since it was concerned that delays caused by goalie injuries would discourage television coverage, and by the mid-1960s, spare goalies were required on each team. Among the regulars, it did little to promote job security.

Then came the most dramatic change – a doubling in size of the NHL, bringing many new skaters of, initially at least, lesser quality into the game.

The gang of five, trained to play an older game, learned and adjusted. They presided over the era and its changes for all goalies thereafter, ultimately making lasting contributions not only to the position, but to the way in which hockey is played.

Plante, of course, is heralded as the greatest of

the innovators, primarily for his adoption of the facemask in November 1959. Often erroneously credited with being the first to wear one – it was, in fact, Montreal Maroons' goaltender Clint Benedict who briefly wore a bizarre leather mask to protect his broken nose in 1930 – Plante nevertheless popularized its use and continued to perfect the device, ushering in a new epoch that would bring the barefaced netminder to extinction by 1975.

Plante introduced another novelty when he started roaming from the crease for errant pucks. His frequent slithering away from his station earned

Jacques Plante, seen here wearing the first mask that he used in game action, backstops the Canadiens in this 1959 New Year's Eve tilt against the Leafs. Plante succumbed to pressure from his coaches to abandon the mask, and played without it on March 8, 1960. The Canadiens lost 3–0, and Plante never went into the net bare-faced again.

him the nickname "Jake the Snake." Plante even took the practice a step further by passing the puck to up-ice teammates and – a ploy previously unheard of – drifting behind the net to stop the long dump shots, helping to jump-start the potent Montreal Canadiens' offense. Thrusting his arm in the air, tipping off his teammates to icing calls, was another Plante innovation. Contemporary goaltending is inconceivable without these ingredients.

But while certainly the most celebrated, Plante was not alone among his contemporaries when it came to molding the moves of the modern netminder. Sawchuk brought to the NHL a low, crouching style that saw his chin almost rest on his padded knees in order to see through the forest of legs and sticks in front of him. He earned his facial scars.

Bower, whose reflexes never seemed to slow, although he played well into his forties, used his vast experience to force the shooter to make the first move, then he would flash out his goal stick to pokecheck the puck away from the attacker.

Hall's "spread-eagle" style (today called the "but-

Glenn Hall, who was nicknamed "Mr. Goalie," is the only goaltender – and one of the only nine NHLers – to earn ten or more All-Star berths.

terfly"), in which he'd fan his knees out in an inverted "V" formation, nearly covered the area from post to post to protect against deflections, while keeping his swift glove hand free for the high shots. By digging his toes into the ice, he could quickly regain his feet, ready for the rebound.

Worsley, who would often hurl his short, plump frame in front of speeding shots, stopping them any way possible, was less an innovator when it came to the technical aspects of the game. Still, playing for the dismal New York Rangers in the 1950s and early 1960s, he was by far the best in the league on breakaways. It was a skill he most definitely did not hone in his lethargic practice sessions. "What for?" he'd ask. "I get enough practice during the games."

Gump's big contribution to the art of goaltending during his ten-year Ranger tenure might well have been his outward, carefree attitude. While others fretted after each goal allowed, taking the game home and replaying it in their sleep, Worsley's "What, me worry?" attitude was refreshing.

After winning the Calder with the last-place Rangers in 1952-53, he lounged through training camp and lost out to a more industrious Bower, who had already been a minor-league star for eight years. Gump was shipped to Vancouver of the Western Hockey League. Asked by writers what he thought of the demotion, he popped, "All I can say is that they're going to have to go a long way to present that Calder Trophy to me."

Named MVP of the WHL that year, Gump reclaimed his job the next season. Bower would languish in the American Hockey League for another three years, twice being named AHL MVP and still unable to crack the top six before Toronto acquired him in 1957-58. Meanwhile, the Gumper suffered behind timid, free-wheeling, undisciplined Ranger teams, feuding with his coach Phil Watson and firing off one-liners like Groucho Marx. The fifty-shot night became a way of life for Worsley, but it never seemed to faze him. Once after back-to-back drubbings by Montreal and Chicago, a writer asked Gump which team had given him the most trouble. "The Rangers," he replied, without a moment's hesitation.

"Don't mention backchecking in here," Gump confided in a stage whisper to a visitor in the

Gump Worsley and Johnny Bower, at the conclusion of the 1962 semi-finals. Worsley was the last Hall-of-Fame goaltender to adopt the mask, going bare-faced until 1974.

Rangers' dressing room. "It's a dirty word."

"I don't see how he stands it," said former Ranger coach Neil Colville, after watching Worsley during a New York visit. "Most goaltenders would crack up if they had to face that kind of barrage game after game. Gump just seems to have the perfect temperament for it." Worsley eventually opened a restaurant in Montreal and featured "The Ranger Special" on his menu. The Ranger Special? It was chicken salad.

In 1963, Gump packed his bags and quips for Montreal, traded to the Canadiens for Plante. Jake had been the NHL MVP a season earlier and the Canadiens' outstanding goalie for their five straight Stanley Cups. But his own reactions to the pressures of goaltending had gotten under the skin of Montreal coach Toe Blake, who believed Plante was a prima donna and a hypochondriac.

Plante knitted touques, sometimes berated his teammates, blew kisses to the crowd, and broke tradition by donning the mask, things Blake could barely tolerate. But Plante's continual string of health problems rendered him unreliable in Toe's mind. Especially irritating were Plante's asthmatic attacks, particularly during visits to Toronto, which hampered his performances in Maple Leaf Gardens.

Plante finally pinpointed the Royal York Hotel as the cause of his malady and requested boarding elsewhere. "I realize it's probably 90 per cent mental," he said, "but all I know is I couldn't breathe once I got into the lobby."

At his new lodging, however, Plante awoke wheezing. Later he explained, "I dreamed I was at the Royal York." Blake had had enough.

Plante predicted upon his arrival that the Rangers were on their way up and the Canadiens on the way down. All that went down was Plante's effectiveness, and eventually Plante himself – to Baltimore of the AHL, leading to his first retirement.

Once freed of the Ranger malaise and aided by the strong Montreal defense that had benefited Plante, Worsley sailed to four Stanley Cups and two Vezina trophies in the next six seasons. But a funny

When provoked, Terry Sawchuk would challenge anyone who raised his ire. Pressure forced him to "retire" in 1956-57, but he returned to play another thirteen seasons.

thing happened to the funny round man. The demon struck. The pressure to win in Montreal got to him. His nerves frayed, he developed digestive problems, he feuded with Blake's replacement, Claude Ruel, and, finally, his longstanding fear of flying caused him to bolt the Canadiens in 1969.

The demon pressure, growing as the game changed, had long since gotten to Gump's peers. Sawchuk's affability during his brilliant early years, when he was hailed as the best ever to play the position, gave way to a bitterness and moodiness, the product of frequent injuries and the demands on his talents. Probably most damaging was a trade from Detroit (where he had led the Red Wings to numerous championships) to an inferior Boston club. The young Hall replaced Sawchuk and was considered the Detroit goalie of the future.

Sawchuk played poorly in his first season for Boston, then returned to form. But at the midway point of the 1956-57 season, he freaked out, then walked out on the Bruins, and was eventually dealt back to Detroit. His mental decline affected everyone with whom he came into contact – fans, writers, friends, even teammates. "Ukey's a strange bird," a fellow Red Wing once said of his team's goalie. "You can be joking with him one minute in the dressing room and you'll see him on the street later and he'll just walk right by you."

If Sawchuk was known as "Ukey," Hall might have been called "Pukey," renowned as he was for his nausea attacks before, during, and after games. Almost every photo of Hall on the ice reveals a distressed expression. "I hate every minute I play," he confessed. "I'm sick to my stomach before the game, between periods, and from the start of the season to the end. I sometimes ask myself, 'What the hell am I doing out here?' But it's the only way I can support my family. If I could do it some other way, I wouldn't be playing goal."

The Wings lost faith in Hall after his mouth was shattered by a puck during the 1957 playoffs. Although he returned and played admirably, he was blamed for Detroit's elimination.

Traded to Chicago, Hall did earn a nickname – "Mr. Goalie" – as the backbone of a Black Hawk team that in 1961 won the franchise's first Stanley

Cup since 1938. Although he was probably the most consistently excellent goalie of the five, with eleven all-star selections, success brought him no happiness. "There's no such thing as an easy night for the goalie," he said, "not even if he never gets a shot on goal during the whole game."

A man who loved poetry and the wide-open Alberta spaces, Hall often needed coaxing to show up for Chicago's training camps. The rumor always had him painting his barn outside of Edmonton. He would show up, it was said, as soon as the paint dried. In fact, Hall always dreaded the prospect of another year of hell. A substantial raise usually helped the paint dry faster, and when the puck was dropped, Hall was there, playing in 552 consecutive games (502 consecutive complete games during the regular season, another 50 in the playoffs) between 1955 and 1962.

Hall finished his career with St. Louis after the NHL expanded, and he starred for the Blues as well, leading the team to three consecutive appearances in the Stanley Cup finals. In 1969, he and Plante, of all people, teamed up to win the Vezina. Hall was thirty-seven, Plante was thirty-nine.

Their teaming echoed Toronto's pairing of the aging Bower and Sawchuk a few years earlier, as that duo led the Leafs to the 1967 Stanley Cup. Although the two had been Cup heroes, they were too drained to join in their teammates' post-game dressing-room celebration, choosing instead to remain at their stalls, puffing on cigarettes while the champagne gushed around them. At the time Sawchuk was thirty-eight. Bower was suspected to be an amazing forty-four – but no one really knew for sure.

Bower had landed with the Leafs in his mid-thirties, extremely late for a professional athlete. So used had he become to minor-league life, so happy was he with his acclaim in Cleveland, that Bower actually needed persuasion to join Toronto. "I was sick of jumping around the country and I wanted to settle down with my family. Cleveland was going to be my home." Leaf boss Punch Imlach had a better idea, visiting Bower over the summer in Saskatoon to coax him into joining the Leafs. Years later, Imlach would rave about his goalie, calling him "the greatest athlete in the world. By wanting to be the best so badly, he overrode the aging process."

The oldest of Punch's veteran Leafs in the early 1960s, Bower keyed the team to three consecutive Cups and proved to be as solid a team player as he was agile in his goaltending. His coach and teammates marveled at how hard Bower pushed himself, especially in practice. Often playing through injuries without complaint, he even confounded the Leafs' doctor. "If I didn't know better," said the Doc at a mid-1960s training camp, "I'd say judging from his body, this was a twenty-five-year-old man. I've never seen a man of his reported age in such wonderful physical condition."

With his kindly face and seemingly even temper, Bower appeared unusually emotionally stable for a goalie, a hard-working happy warrior. Publicly warm and considerate, the natural choice of a CBC childrens' storyteller to record a novelty song, "Honky the Christmas Goose" ("He's the friendliest man in Canada," said Honky's creator Chip Young of the greying goalie), Bower sometimes brought those qualities to the rink, which greatly displeased Imlach.

Imlach knew Bower as a very sensitive sort, and the two had occasional run-ins. One of their blow-ups came after Canadien tough John Ferguson went flying through Bower's crease, landing in a heap in the corner. Bower skated over and inquired about Fergie's health. "I didn't like that," Imlach said. "I told him and he got sore." The next day, Bower refused to practice.

Bower also did not appreciate Imlach's occasional criticisms of his play, and let the coach know it. But at their cores, they shared a mutual respect. "He knew how much I admired him, no matter what little incident might come up between us," Imlach said.

Bower's longevity may have provided inspiration to his union brothers. He played NHL goal until he was, allegedly, forty-six in 1970. Plante (in the World Hockey Association) and Worsley, both also forty-six, lasted through the mid-1970s. Hall hung up his pads – most happily – in 1971 at age thirty-nine. Hailed as distinguished elder statesmen, acclaim accompanied their "final" retirements.

Not so with Sawchuk. The black cloud that hung over his life stalked him until the end. His ongoing miseries had driven away his wife and children and forced him to live with a divorced teammate. In the spring of 1970, after the conclusion of the season, Sawchuk and the teammate bickered, then fought outside their home. Injured during the scuffle, Sawchuk was hospitalized. Complications set in, and two weeks later, he was dead at age forty.

One might suspect that hockey had never really understood goalies. As if the pressures of the game were not enough, they were easy targets for fans and scapegoats for management, and were maligned by their coaches. With no one to take into their confidence other than each other (and they were, after all, rivals for most of their careers), they became loners among their more jovial teammates, and Sawchuk was probably the loneliest of all.

But this would begin to change for the next generation of goalies, and with some irony, the four survivors would help bring about that change. As veterans in the two-goalie era, they grew secure enough to share their burdens with their stable-mates, and, after retiring, Plante, Hall, Bower, and Worsley were among the first goaltending coaches. Ever the innovator, Plante authored a book that became a standard text for netminders.

There were certainly enough big-league goalies to receive the help. By the time the record book closed on the five, six NHL goaltending jobs had ballooned to thirty-two – with twenty-eight more in the WHA.

There were other changes as well. For starters, the money got better, as NHL owners began to see that goalies, as well as big scorers, could have marquee value.

One by one, they had donned protective face-masks: Sawchuk a few years after Plante, Hall and Bower at the end of the 1960s. Even Worsley, who held the mask in much disdain and was the last goalie of any consequence to play barefaced, conceded only in his final season. Until then, he had always said, "Anyone who wears one is chicken. My face is my mask."

With the mask becoming universal, goaltending styles changed. Where the barefaced netminder thought first of survival and moved his body to get his feet in front of shots, a new generation of masked goalies – Esposito, Dryden, Vachon, Giacomin, Parent – could dive headlong into scrambles in front of the net to clamp down loose pucks, and they could face cannonading shots with less risk of injury.

Contrast that photo of Sawchuk with the one at left, taken no more than a few years later – a photo of Boston goalie Gerry Cheevers and his famous mask, painted with stitch marks where pucks would have dented his face. Cheevers and his better-armored cronies in the next generation of the Goal-tenders' Union, a veritable Greek chorus whose flamboyantly decorated masks glamorized goaltending as never before, still faced flying steel, wood, and rubber, traveling ever faster and harder. But for them, stitches had only symbolic significance.

On Sawchuk's face, the stitches were real. The game has changed forever.

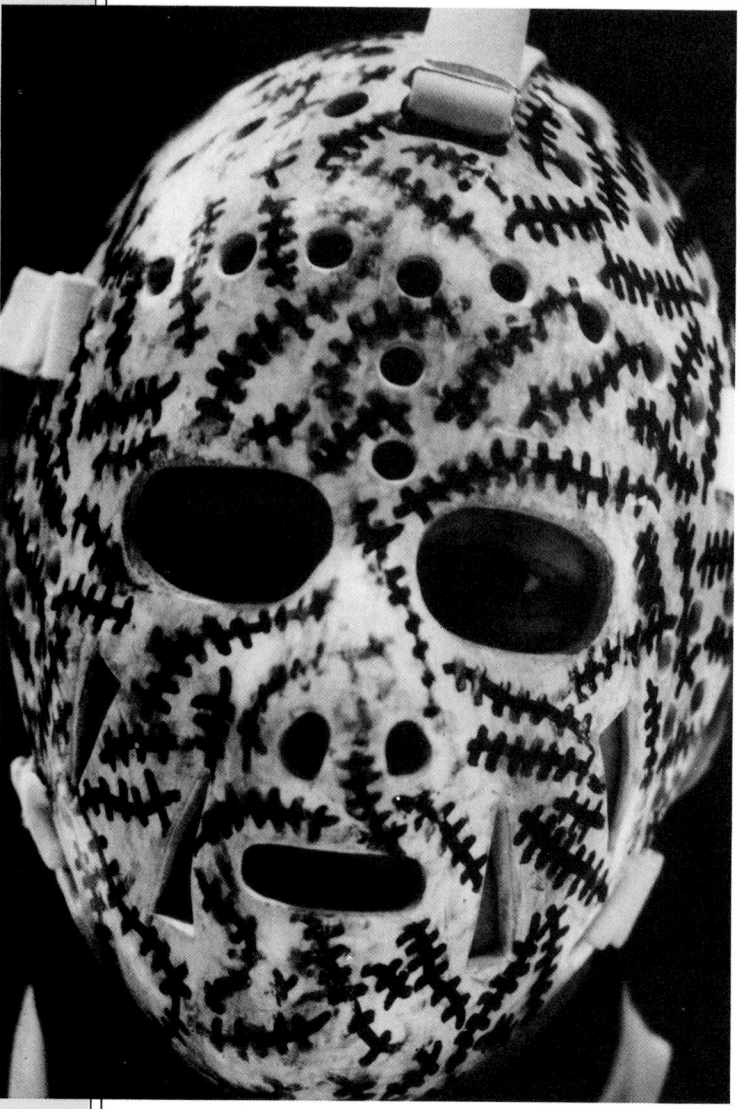

The continuing decline of the Black Hawks became a top priority for the NHL during the 1954-55 season. Despite an aid program whereby top clubs made players available to the Hawks, the team continued to draw small crowds in Chicago, forcing management to shift a number of home games to St. Louis, Omaha, and St. Paul. But attendance was equally disappointing in these markets. Nonetheless, the Hawks were an improved club, strengthened by players such as Ed Litzenberger from Montreal (who would go on to win the Calder Trophy), Metro Prystai from Detroit, and Harry Watson from Toronto. The team also got a new general manager when Tommy Ivan, who had coached the Red Wings to six first-place finishes, moved over from Detroit, where he was replaced as coach by Jimmy Skinner.

By the start of the season, Art Ross and Conn Smythe both announced their retirements, exchanging kind words about the mutual cooperation that characterized their relationship.

The Canadiens had achieved parity with Detroit. The maturing talents of Jean Béliveau, Dickie Moore, and Bernie Geoffrion combined with the explosiveness of Maurice Richard to provide Montreal with the league's best offense.

But Detroit was at least as skilled, with Earl "Dutch" Reibel, Gordie Howe, and Ted Lindsay working the forward line, and Red Kelly supplying scoring punch on defense. Toronto had adopted a defensive style that kept the team in contention, even with a line-up that didn't include the scoring firepower of a Gordie Howe or a dynamo such as Maurice Richard, who became the NHL's only 400-goal scorer in Chicago on December 18, 1954. The milestone earned the Rocket a $2,000 bonus from the Canadiens. Richard, whose temper had resulted in his being fined on numerous occasions, announced he was donating his 400-goal bonus to charity.

Richard's run-ins with NHL president Clarence Campbell were far from over. In a game on March 13, during which the Canadiens were being beaten by Boston, Richard was cut by a high stick wielded by Boston's Hal Laycoe, who drew a delayed penalty. When play stopped, Richard indicated to the referee that he had been cut, and then suddenly headed for the Boston defenseman, hitting him with his stick. Twice he was restrained and relieved of his stick by officials, only to break away, pick up another stick that had been dropped to the ice, and attack Laycoe again. Linesman Cliff Thompson was finally able to force Richard to the ice, but when he got back on his feet, the Rocket struck Thompson twice.

It was neither the first time Richard had hit an official nor the first time he had recovered a stick to use on an opponent. Taking previous conduct and warnings into account, Clarence Campbell suspended the Canadiens' star for the remainder of the season and the Stanley Cup playoffs.

In the city of Montreal, where Richard and the Canadiens were revered, the suspension was seen as a severe blow to the team's chances of dethroning the Red Wings as regular-season champions. Richard, who was also the

Out-of-Town Scoreboard

In February 1955 the use of out-of-town game scoreboards was made mandatory.

NHL's leading scorer, would now almost surely lose the league scoring championship. (The Rocket coveted this honor and would, in fact, never win it.) Although most observers agreed the penalty was just, partisan Montreal fans launched a flood of threats against the league's headquarters and Campbell himself. But Campbell, determined not to be intimidated, showed up in his regular seat for the Canadiens' next home game against Detroit.

When Detroit moved quickly into a 4–1 lead against the Canadiens, a group of hooligans moved towards Campbell. Objects were thrown, and as police and Forum staff moved to protect the NHL president, a cannister of tear gas was thrown near his seat. As crowds rushed for the exits, Montreal fire officials, fearing panic, ordered the game called off. Campbell declared the game forfeited to Detroit.

Outside the Forum, along Ste. Catherine Street, fans went on a rampage, breaking store windows and looting. By the time police quelled what became known as the "Richard Riot," more than sixty miscreants had been arrested. The following day, Richard broadcast an appeal for calm over Montreal radio stations.

Bernie Geoffrion went on to win the Art Ross Trophy as the league's top point-getter, one point ahead of the Rocket.

With Richard out of the line-up, the Red Wings defeated the Habs 6–0 in the final game of the season to take their seventh consecutive league championship – by two points over Montreal. Detroit prevailed in the playoffs as well, winning the Stanley Cup in a seven-game final series against the Canadiens. Howe set a new playoff record with 20 points in post-season play.

The Canadiens' close second-place finish and narrow loss in the finals – both accomplished during Richard's suspension – indicated that Detroit would no longer dominate as they had for several seasons. In 1954-55, Geoffrion, Richard, and Béliveau were the league's top three scorers, while Doug Harvey won the Norris Trophy as the NHL's best defenseman. Although Jacques Plante had shared his job in the playoffs, he had emerged as one of the league's top goaltenders. As history would show, it was the beginning of a dynasty.

A subplot to the continuing rivalry between Detroit and Montreal was the inevitable comparison between Gordie Howe and Maurice Richard. The Rocket, seven years older, joined the Canadiens in 1942-43 and, despite breaking a leg just sixteen games into his first season, quickly established himself as the premier right winger in hockey. His spirit was an inspiration to his teammates, and he had an almost superhuman talent for scoring when the Habs most needed a goal. He was named to the Second All-Star Team in his first full NHL season and earned a spot on the First All-Star Team for six consecutive years beginning in 1945.

Whereas Richard streaked to stardom as a pure scorer, Gordie Howe developed more slowly. He had seven goals in 1946-47, his rookie season with Detroit, and received little consideration for the Calder Trophy, which was won by Howie Meeker of the Leafs. But Howe soon earned a permanent place at right wing on the Red Wings' Production Line, playing alongside Ted Lindsay – at first with Sid Abel and later with Dutch Reibel at center – and was largely responsible for the rise of the Wings to pre-eminence in the first half of the 1950s.

Howe was neither as flashy nor as prone to tempestuous brawling as Richard, but he had enough of a mean streak to establish a reputation as one of the toughest and strongest players in the league. Howe, a more efficient checker than Richard, was also more durable than his smaller rival. And while no player of the era could lift fans from their seats as could Maurice Richard, there has been none so efficient for so long as Gordie Howe, who played big-league professional hockey for thirty-two seasons in five decades and scored a record 801 regular-season goals in NHL play.

(continued on p. 131)

Detroit's tough and gifted Production Line was the league's highest scoring forward unit in the first half of the 1950s. From left to right: Gordie Howe, Sid Abel, and Ted Lindsay.

THE HEART OF A CHAMPION

by Jean Béliveau

In 1953, after my second year with the senior Quebec Aces, I remember telling my future wife, "I'm going to be twenty-two in August, and my dream is to play for the Canadiens." I remember also telling her, "I want a decent career – I mean not just five years, but as many as fifteen. So if I want a good career in the NHL, now is the time." I ended up playing eighteen years with the Canadiens and for me they were great years. We had fun, we were winning, and when the time came to be serious, we were there. But for me, in the late 1940s and early 1950s, all of this was yet to come.

I joined the club permanently in the fall of 1953, the season after the team had won the Stanley Cup. In my first two years in Montreal – 1953-54 and 1954-55 – we lost to Detroit in the seventh game of the finals. After that we won five Cups in a row, so for a span of eight years, the team either won the Cup or was within one game of winning. In 1955-56, coincident with the start of the five Cup wins, a group of younger players joined the club, including Henri Richard, Claude Provost, Donnie Marshall, Bob Turner, and Jean-Guy Talbot. The other newcomer that year was Toe Blake, who took over as coach.

The combination of players we had between 1955-56 and 1960 was probably ideal for a coach. We always had two top offensive lines. We had Rocket and Henri Richard and Dickie Moore, who was a superb left winger. I was on another line with Bernie "Boom-Boom" Geoffrion and Bert Olmstead for the first two or three years. We also had a great defensive line – Provost, Marshall, and André Pronovost, all hard workers and terrific checkers – who on many occasions came up and scored big goals for us. We had Phil Goyette and Marcel Bonin, plus Jacques Plante in the net and Doug Harvey on defense with Tom Johnson, Dollard St. Laurent, and Talbot and all the others. Today, I know it's called "chemistry," and the chemistry of this group was perfect. There was a connection between each one of the players. Everyone was doing his job and we were all working towards a common goal, finishing first and winning the Stanley Cup.

Our coach, Toe Blake, was unique in that, even from behind the bench, he was one of our leaders, making sure that everything would go as smoothly as possible. One of the most difficult jobs Toe faced was to keep everybody content, a balance that is impossible to maintain when you have several good

The joys of winning: Canadiens' managing director Frank Selke (right) and coach Toe Blake (center) with Ralph Backstrom, Ab McDonald, and Bernie Geoffrion.

athletes on your team. But he almost managed to do it.

Toe had the respect of his players. A coach won't go very far if he doesn't have that respect. We all knew what he had accomplished as a player, and that he was a hard worker and an honest man. Toe was the type of coach who, having decided that a player was good enough to be a part of his team, would stand right behind him whatever happened, so long as the guy did his work and was playing to the best of his ability. This was well appreciated by the players and was certainly one of the ingredients in our success.

Hockey to me is a true team sport, and I believe that another of the reasons we did so well was that we had a real sense of being family, not only in the dressing room but on the train traveling to road games. To this day, that's what I miss the most: all of us helping each other. I've always felt that, when one of our key players was going through a slump, a difficult period, everybody would rally around him. We knew his coming out of a slump would help not only him but everyone else too. The team was good enough that, if everyone played his regular game, we'd be all right.

I remember coming back on those long train rides. They made us closer. Since Toe had been a player himself, he knew that every so often the team members needed a bit of a night out and a chance to relax. We'd often play on Saturday and Sunday, so we would have Monday off in Montreal, but we would make sure that we would have a great practice on Tuesday. The players were very professional in every sense of the word. Toe didn't have to sit in the lobby of the hotel and check to see who did and who didn't come in at night.

Before Toe, I played for two remarkable coaches in the first years of my career. I was fortunate to play in the Quebec Senior League under Punch Imlach when I was part of a fine organization, the Quebec Aces. High-caliber hockey was played in the Quebec

The innovative Jacques Plante was one of the first goalies to leave the crease to stop the puck for his defensemen.

Senior League, which was made up of veterans completing their careers and junior graduates not quite ready to move to the NHL.

Bernie Geoffrion, Dickie Moore, and I are the same age, and we went through junior at the same time. They went to the Canadiens in 1951-52, but I decided to stay in Quebec and play senior hockey with the Aces and Punch for two years. A few years later, after several seasons with the Canadiens, I realized I was very fortunate that the Quebec Senior League was as strong as it was. Remember, I was only twenty years old coming out of junior, and I had Punch coaching me. After almost every practice he would have somebody chase me around the ice. He said, "Jean, you could improve your quick start." I was a tall guy with a long stride. As it turned out, he was right, and my improved start really helped me in the NHL. I learned a lot in the Quebec League and I never regretted playing there.

When I joined the Canadiens, Dick Irvin, Sr., was the coach. He was one of the first great players in hockey and one of the game's first great coaches. I had come up from junior for a two-game trial with the Canadiens in 1950. I had my first NHL goal and an assist in my second game. I came up again in December of 1952 to replace the injured Elmer Lach for three games, which was the maximum number

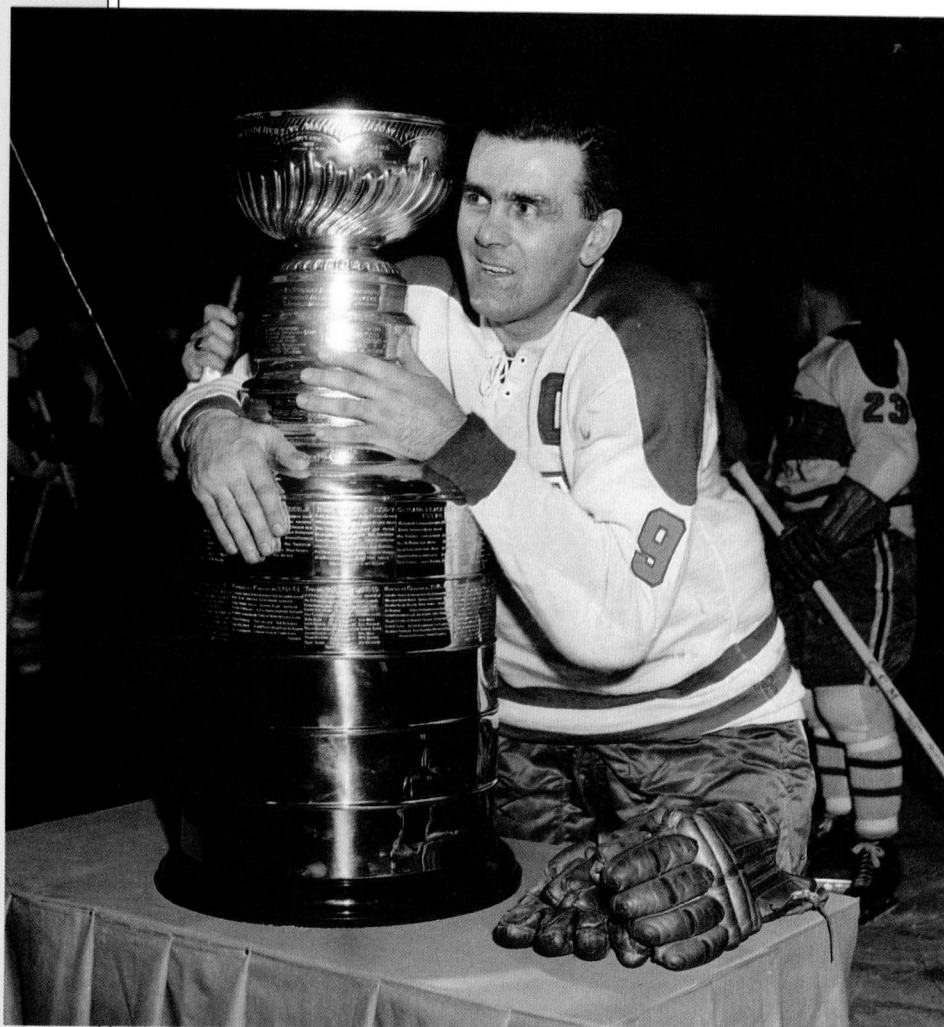

Maurice Richard, widely regarded as the NHL's greatest playoff performer, hugs his last Stanley Cup, which the Canadiens captured on April 14, 1960.

the risk of a long-term suspension if his temper got the better of him again, but Toe knew that Rocket could only help the team if he was in the line-up.

I sat beside Rocket in the dressing room for the seven years I played with him. He was an inspiration and the idol of my generation. I remembered listening to him play on *Hockey Night in Canada* on the radio in 1945 when I was fourteen years old.

On the team, we all knew he was kind of an introvert and not the greatest talker. But in his own way he was a leader, and as players, as a team, we followed him because we were inspired by his desire to win.

Even in my last ten years as captain, I was never the greatest talker in the dressing room either. I feel that when a quiet person says something, it has more weight than something said by a person who talks a lot. Even a glance or a gesture can communicate volumes. When we lost, the Rocket did not

you were allowed under the agreement of the time. In those games I scored five goals. Dick Irvin, who coached twenty-six seasons in the NHL, was an emotional man who pushed his players to succeed. Maybe he didn't use all the techniques that you hear of coaches using today, but sometimes these days I think we have to remember that the game is played on the ice, not in practice or in the classroom.

Toe Blake had played under Dick Irvin for eight years, and when he succeeded him as coach, he operated in an equally intense but more subdued manner. As a long-time former linemate of Maurice Richard, Toe could talk to the Rocket and help him keep his temper under control. Rocket, of course, had been suspended from the 1955 playoffs and ran

need to say anything to show how hard he accepted defeat. You could see it in his eyes. His silent leadership was also effective because even when he was aging, he put out a great effort, not only in the game but also in practices. He was leading in what I still think is the best way – on the ice. It's known, too, that Rocket always enjoyed scoring goals. Most of his were spectacular, especially toward the end of his career.

Rocket retired in the fall of 1960. I'll always remember that he scored four goals in the scrimmage that morning, and then announced his retirement. He was thirty-nine and had had a couple of injuries, including a torn Achilles tendon that really slowed him down in his last two seasons.

It was probably less complicated for the Canadiens to build a competitive team in the years before expansion than it is today. At that time, with spon-

sored junior clubs and leagues, each team was sort of raising its own players. Before expansion, each NHL team had a game plan or style that remained quite consistent from year to year.

Of course it was the skating game that was the Canadiens' trademark. I feel that our skating gave us a little edge on the other five teams. I enjoyed playing Detroit, New York, and Chicago, in that order, because they usually allowed for a wide-open, offensive, skating game, whereas Boston was hard-hitting, and Toronto was always known for close

checking and grabbing and clutching.

With expansion in 1967, the rules began to change, as each NHL team was given an equal chance at players from all over the world. After 1969, when we picked Réjean Houle and Marc Tardif, the Canadiens no longer had the rights to the first two French-Canadian players graduating from junior

The 1957-58 Montreal Canadiens were a powerhouse squad, which led the league in most goals scored, fewest goals against, and most wins. Thirteen members of this team have been inducted into the Hockey Hall of Fame.

each year. Now all the clubs pick from among junior, college, high-school, and European players. I have nothing against this; the NHL had to expand when it did and, to be successful, each team has to have an equal chance to acquire good players. However, it makes building an NHL club a lot more difficult with players coming from different leagues and different countries, which naturally means that they play different styles. It has become harder for coaches to blend their players into a smooth-working unit.

Before expansion, in addition to sponsoring junior teams, each NHL club operated a chain of farm clubs, the largest of which belonged to the Canadiens. Though I don't know for sure because each team kept its budget confidential, I think the Canadiens in the 1950s invested more money in their farm system than did any other NHL club. Each of us

Jean Béliveau, "Le Gros Bill," was the first winner of the Conn Smythe Trophy, winning the post-season MVP award – and the Stanley Cup – in 1965.

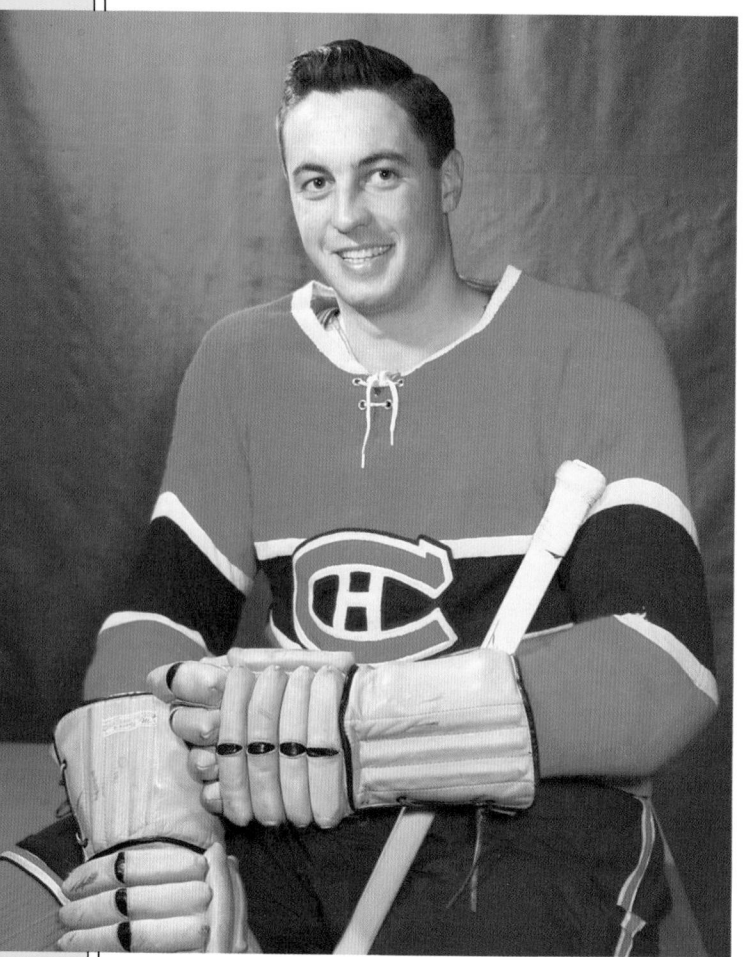

on the Canadiens knew that if we didn't perform, there certainly was somebody on one of the farm teams who could be called up. Of course, this depth also proved its worth when we needed someone because of injuries.

One thing that hasn't changed since the days before expansion is the pressure felt by younger players who join the Montreal team. But whenever I'm asked, I always tell the young guys that pressure coming from the game and from the media is part of the life of a professional athlete. I always felt that it made me play better. I knew that I had to perform because I had a responsibility as a player toward the team, my teammates, and the fans. If I wasn't performing, somebody was sure to let me know.

There's no doubt that today's player has even more pressure on his shoulders than we had – largely because sports and the media have both changed. Today there is much more coverage on television and radio and in the newspapers. In Montreal, newspapers and radio stations now have reporters whose only responsibility is to cover the Canadiens. Just like the players, there is competition among the media, which keeps reporters on edge. This means that, often, they are looking for sensation. You have young reporters who want to make their names known right away, and the fastest way to do that is to come up with something big or unusual.

As always, the simplest and best attitude, which enables a player to do well despite this pressure, is one of honesty. To thrive, an athlete must be honest with himself and his friends, honest with his employers, and honest with the fans. If he finds himself in the Canadiens' dressing room, he becomes part of the club and can look up and see pictures of players whose honest efforts and commitment earned them places in the Hockey Hall of Fame.

Each contributed to the great success of the Canadiens' organization.

When I joined in 1953, I said to myself, "Now it's up to me to keep this organization where it is and – if possible – to make it better for those who are going to follow me." I only hope that those who are there today are saying the same thing.

The 1955-56 season saw a perceptible shift in power at the top of the NHL. Despite winning the Stanley Cup the previous year, Detroit's Jack Adams decided it was time to shake up his team. His most significant trade sent goalie Terry Sawchuk, along with Marcel Bonin and Vic Stasiuk, to the Bruins for Warren Godfrey, Ed Sandford, and Réal Chevrefils. Another trade sent Glen Skov, Tony Leswick, and Johnny Wilson to Chicago for Jerry Toppazzini and Bucky Hollingworth. Adams also promoted newcomers Johnny Bucyk and Norm Ullman from the minors. The fact that he dealt Sawchuk, who was one of the top goaltenders in the league, indicated that Adams had confidence in young Glenn Hall, whom he felt was worthy of first-string status. Hall didn't disappoint him, recording a league-leading 12 shutouts en route to the Calder Trophy.

Perhaps the biggest improvement was made in New York, where Phil Watson had taken over from coach Muzz Patrick at a time when young players such as Andy Bathgate and Dean Prentice were maturing into stars. Lou Fontinato gave the somewhat undersized Rangers an on-ice policeman, and Watson brought up Andy Hebenton, Bronco Horvath, and Jean-Guy Gendron from the minors. The much-improved team would finish third, earning a spot in post-season play for the first time since 1949-50.

In Toronto, it was a rebuilding year, and the Leafs stocked their roster with youngsters such as Dick Duff, Marc Réaume, and Barry Cullen. The Leafs also added two players who had proved themselves in other sports. Gerry James was an outstanding football player with the Winnipeg Blue Bombers and would continue to divide his year between football and hockey. Jack Bionda had already established himself as one of the best lacrosse players in

Ezinicki Enters PGA Tour

"Wild" Bill Ezinicki, who spent time with the Toronto Maple Leafs, the Boston Bruins, and the New York Rangers, retired in 1955 and became a professional golfer. While on the PGA tour, he finished second at the Bob Hope Classic and fourth at the New Orleans Open.

This 1955-56 New York Rangers' "firing squad" included (left to right) Andy Bathgate, Dean Prentice, Danny Lewicki, and Wally Hergesheimer. The 1956 squad also included Gump Worsley, Harry Howell, Bill Gadsby, and Jack Evans.

Ted Lindsay (right) provides the screen as Gordie Howe, Claude Provost, and Doug Harvey struggle for position in this classic Detroit–Montreal match-up. The Wings and the Canadiens met in three consecutive Stanley Cup finals between 1954 and 1956.

the country. Although Bionda did not last with the Leafs, his arrival on the scene was in keeping with a long tradition of lacrosse players who made the jump to hockey – among them, Newsy Lalonde, Lionel Conacher, Bucko McDonald, and Ike Hildebrand.

Montreal was finally the NHL's undisputed top team. Toe Blake, a former captain of the Canadiens, took over as coach from Dick Irvin, who moved on to Chicago, while speedy center Henri Richard joined his brother on the roster, and Jacques Plante had his best season in net. The Habs captured most of the league's individual awards. Jean Béliveau's 47-goal season was a scoring record for centers and earned *le gros Bill* the Art Ross and Hart trophies. Jacques Plante won the Vezina Trophy and Doug Harvey the Norris

Trophy. The Canadiens easily captured the Prince of Wales Trophy with 100 points, 24 ahead of second-place Detroit. Not surprisingly, Montreal also won the Stanley Cup, breaking the Red Wings' two-year hold on the prize.

The Canadiens of 1955-56 had so much firepower that a two-minute power-play could result in several goals being scored. This happened in November when Jean Béliveau scored three times in 44 seconds against the Bruins. To prevent the kind of routs that this could precipitate, the NHL instituted a rule change for 1956-57 that allowed players serving minor penalties to return to the ice if a goal was scored against their team while it was short-handed.

To eliminate confusion for viewers of televised games, the NHL had revised the uniforms of its on-ice officials midway through the 1955-56 season. This revision was necessary because the officials' orange sweaters with black trim appeared entirely black when viewed on black-and-white television. The new uniform for officials featured a sweater with vertical black and white stripes, so that the television audience could more easily distinguish referees and linesmen from players. Players were also required to display their uniform numbers on the sides of their skates, so they could be more readily identified in newspaper photos and TV close-ups. Standardized hand signals for referees and linesmen were also introduced. New York-born referee Bill Chadwick, who had recently retired, was credited with introducing hand signals to the game.

In Boston, the Bruins were poised to improve, backed by the goaltending of Terry Sawchuk. In Toronto, where Howie Meeker had taken over as coach, the Leafs continued to rebuild, bringing youngsters Bob Baun, Bob Pulford, and Al MacNeil onto the roster. In addition, Meeker convinced Teeder Kennedy to come out of retirement. New York continued to rebuild, as bigger crowds turned out to watch future Hall of Famers Andy Bathgate, Harry Howell, Gump Worsley, and Bill Gadsby.

Part way through the season, the Rangers and Black Hawks were featured in a telecast game on the CBS network from Madison Square Garden. The NHL's governors welcomed interest from the American network, undoubtedly hoping that televised hockey would one day be as popular in the U.S. as it was in Canada.

The biggest surprise of the 1956-57 season was the rejuvenated play of the Boston Bruins. Despite losing Terry Sawchuk, first to mononucleosis and then to temporary retirement brought about by emotional strain, the Bruins finished a strong third, just eight points behind league-leading Detroit. Gordie Howe won the Hart and Art Ross trophies and Boston's Larry Regan won the Calder.

The Bruins continued their winning in the playoffs, upsetting the Red Wings in a five-game semi-final. Boston went on to face the Canadiens, who had defeated the fourth-place Rangers to earn their seventh consecutive berth in the finals. In game one, Maurice Richard had four goals and

Reverse-Grip Introduced

Jack Caffery of the Boston Bruins introduced the "reverse-grip" (both hands on the same side of the stick) while taking a faceoff in a game against the Toronto Maple Leafs on November 18, 1956.

The Rocket and the Man

Before a game in January 1956 between the Chicago Black Hawks and Montreal Canadiens at the St. Louis Arena, the Canadiens' great Maurice "Rocket" Richard presented one of his number 9 sweaters to St. Louis Cardinals' Stan Musial, a man Richard described as "baseball's greatest hitter."

Don Simmons, who back-stopped the Boston Bruins to consecutive appearances in the Stanley Cup finals of 1957 and 1958, was the second NHL goaltender to don a mask. Simmons, who later played for Toronto, was finally part of a Stanley Cup winner when he replaced an injured Johnny Bower in the 1962 finals. He finished his career with the New York Rangers in 1969.

Luckily, neither Gordie Howe nor Gump Worsley were seriously injured in this goal-mouth collision.

Montreal's powerful attack was too much for the hard-working Bruins. The Bruins regrouped for game two, but Jacques Plante proved unbeatable in the Canadiens' net, and the Habs won 1–0 on a goal by Jean Béliveau. The Canadiens went on to win the Stanley Cup in five games, Bernie Geoffrion leading all scorers with 11 goals in post-season play.

Heading into 1957-58, team managers juggled their line-ups, both to counter the high-octane offense of the Canadiens and to demonstrate their displeasure at the organization of the new NHL Players' Association. Detroit owner Bruce Norris traded Ted Lindsay, one of the league's best players and the president of the NHLPA, to Chicago. Jack Adams added goaltender Glenn Hall to the Lindsay deal after reacquiring Terry Sawchuk. Adams convinced Sawchuk to end his self-imposed retirement and traded John Bucyk to the Bruins to reacquire the goaltender.

The Black Hawks benefited greatly by the acquisition of Hall and Lindsay. Combined with the arrival of junior star Bobby Hull, Chicago boasted a competitive line-up. The Maple Leafs also added a highly touted junior graduate, Frank Mahovlich, who had starred for St. Michael's College in Toronto. Although he finished the season behind Bobby Hull in scoring, Mahovlich fired 20 goals and won the Calder Trophy as the league's top rookie. In Boston, the Bruins united Bronco Horvath, Johnny Bucyk, and Vic Stasiuk – three players of Ukrainian descent – to form the high-scoring "Uke Line."

The Players' Association made news throughout the season, as Ted Lindsay, a shrewd businessman away from the rink, was determined to make the organization's presence felt. In an attempt to get the NHL to raise pension benefits and increase the television revenue available to players, the NHLPA filed suit against the league and its clubs in a New York court, alleging that the defendants in the suit had monopolized the industry of professional hockey in those markets where NHL teams had operated since 1926. In Toronto, NHL players sought certification as a bargaining unit under the regulations of the Ontario Labour Relations Board. Among the players' demands was the right to free agency after five years in the league. Not all teams were four-square behind the union, and the Red Wings' players removed themselves from the NHLPA's action.

After a meeting with the NHLPA in February, club ownership refused to formally recognize the association, but made concessions to players that included a $7,000 minimum salary, increased pension and hospitalization benefits, a larger share of the playoff pool, and a limit on the number of exhibition games played. Ownership also agreed that, in the event of injury, the injured player would be the sole judge of whether he was fit to return to the line-up. Club owners remained uncomfortable with player militancy, however, and it would be a decade before ownership would formally negotiate with a reconstituted NHL Players' Association.

In the coaching ranks, Sid Abel replaced Jimmy Skinner behind the Detroit bench, and Rudy Pilous took over from Tommy Ivan in Chicago.

On the ice, not even the loss of Maurice Richard for 42 games because of a severed Achilles tendon could slow down the Canadiens. Richard's brother Henri picked up the slack, finishing second in scoring to teammate Dickie Moore. The Rangers finished in second place with 77 points, their best finish since 1941-42. New York's attack was built around two effective forward lines: Dean Prentice, Larry Popein, and Andy Bathgate, plus Camille Henry, Dave Creighton, and Andy Hebenton. The club's defense was second only to the Canadiens', and featured Bill Gadsby, Harry Howell, Jack Evans, and Lou Fontinato.

In the playoffs, the Rocket returned to the Montreal line-up and was as dominating as ever, scoring seven goals in four games as the Canadiens swept the Red Wings to earn a berth in the finals against the Bruins, who had upset New York in six games. In the finals, the Canadiens eliminated the Bruins in six games to give coach Blake his third Stanley Cup in three

The NHL's ultimate dynasty team was the Montreal Canadiens in the 1950s, winner of five consecutive Stanley Cup championships from 1956 to 1960. These half-dozen happy Habs – (left to right) Marcel Bonin, Bernie Geoffrion, Phil Goyette, Henri Richard, Dickie Moore, and Jean Béliveau – all played key roles in the Canadiens' success.

Players Permitted to Wear Facemasks

Commencing with the 1958-59 season, players were permitted to wear a plastic protective mask while recovering from facial injuries.

Jack McCartan, the hero of the U.S. Olympic Team's stunning gold-medal victory in the 1960 Winter Games, couldn't translate that success to stardom in the NHL. Although he had an impressive debut with the Rangers in 1960, McCartan's NHL career lasted only twelve games.

seasons behind the Habs' bench. Richard led all post-season goal-scorers with 11 goals in the 10 games.

The Canadiens' winning pattern continued for 1958-59 as the franchise went from strength to strength. Doug Harvey's string of Norris Trophy wins was interrupted by teammate Tom Johnson; Bert Olmstead was replaced by Ab McDonald; and Ralph Backstrom arrived from the Canadiens' junior farm club.

Boston and Chicago improved steadily to finish second and third. The Bruins' Uke Line was supported by Don McKenney, Doug Mohns, Fleming Mackell, and Leo Labine. Chicago added Dollard St. Laurent and Al Arbour to a defense corps anchored by Pierre Pilote and Elmer "Moose" Vasko. The Hawks also brought in Tod Sloan from Toronto, along with minor-leaguers Kenny Wharram and Johnny McKenzie.

In Detroit, the Red Wings were proving Jack Adams's pronouncement that good teams disintegrate every five years. Despite cleaning house, the Wings fell to sixth place, missing the playoffs for the first time since 1938.

In November, the struggling Maple Leafs made a change at the top, hiring George "Punch" Imlach as general manager. Imlach had forged his reputation in the minors, as coach and part-owner of the Quebec Aces, and had been reluctant to move to the big leagues until offered a general-manager's job. When the team floundered in the early going, Imlach fired coach Billy Reay and took over himself. On the last night of the season, the team squeezed into the playoffs by beating out the Rangers, whom the Leafs had trailed by seven points with five games to go in the season.

The Rangers' collapse began in February, shortly after a game in which New York tough guy Lou Fontinato was decisively beaten in a fight by Gordie Howe. The Rangers went on to win only three of their last 20 games. Despite the club's poor finish, Andy Bathgate, who had 78 points and was the league's third-leading scorer, won the Hart Trophy.

The improved play that got the Leafs into the playoffs continued in the semi-finals as Toronto upset the second-place Bruins in a seven-game series. In the other semi-final match-up, the Canadiens needed six games to defeat the Black Hawks in a series that ended with the resignation of veteran referee Red Storey. When an Ottawa newspaper columnist quoted Clarence Campbell as saying that Storey failed to call a penalty shot against the Canadiens at a crucial point in game six, Storey quit, citing lack of support from the league. Despite the fact that Campbell expressed his regret at the controversy, the veteran referee refused to return to the game.

In the finals, there was no stopping the Habs, who needed just five games to defeat the Leafs and become the first club since the Ottawa Silver Seven of 1903-06 to win four consecutive Stanley Cup championships.

The Canadiens' reign atop the NHL continued in the last season of the 1950s, reinforced by the addition of new players from a productive farm system stocked with talent by Sam Pollock, the organization's director of player personnel. In addition to Jean-Claude Tremblay, who made an 11-game debut with the Canadiens in 1959-60, Pollock had another Tremblay – Gilles – waiting for a chance to break into the NHL line-up.

In New York, the Rangers' Phil Watson was replaced by Alf Pike when ulcers forced him to step down as coach. In what would prove to be a long season for the Rangers, the club's leading scorer, Andy Bathgate, was fined by Clarence Campbell when a ghostwritten article under Bathgate's by-line listed the NHL players he considered most proficient at spearing. Jack McCartan, goaltender for the U.S. Olympic Team that was an upset gold-medal winner at the 1960 Winter Olympics in Squaw Valley, California, appeared in four games for the Rangers, posting an impressive goals-against average of 1.75.

The struggling Rangers sought to strengthen themselves through trades, but when the club tried to deal Eddie Shack and Bill Gadsby to Detroit for Red Kelly and Billy McNeil, the Detroit players refused to report to New York, and the deal was eventually aborted. Once it became apparent that the Red Wings were interested in trading Kelly, Punch Imlach quickly made one

Canadian Junior "A" hockey was the chief breeding ground for NHL talent during the six-team era, with every club sponsoring squads staffed with youthful prospects. This 1959-60 Ontario Hockey Association All-Star Team included future Hall-of-Famers Rod Gilbert, Jean Ratelle, and Dave Keon, as well as Vic Hadfield, Jimmy Roberts, Pat Stapleton, Eddie Westfall, and Dale Rolfe.

Four Wear Helmets in 1959-60

During the 1959-60 season, four NHL players wore helmets: Charlie Burns and Vic Stasiuk of Boston, Warren Godfrey of Detroit, and Camille Henry of New York.

of the most one-sided deals ever, obtaining the former Norris Trophy-winner for journeyman Marc Réaume. Under Imlach, Kelly would go on to give the Leafs seven solid seasons and would contribute greatly to the Toronto club's resurgence in the 1960s.

A landmark in the development of the game was Jacques Plante's decision to don a protective facemask after being cut during a game against the Rangers on November 1, 1959. The decision was made over the objections of Habs manager Frank Selke and coach Toe Blake, who, even after Plante reeled off eleven straight wins wearing the mask, remained dubious. Selke sent Plante for vision checks both with and without the mask and continued to advise against it, but Plante would not be dissuaded. New York manager Muzz Patrick soon became a believer in masks for goaltenders, making them compulsory equipment for all netminders in the Rangers' minor-league system. In Boston, the Bruins' Don Simmons soon became the second goaltender to wear a mask in NHL games. If anyone needed proof that a mask improved a goaltender's confidence, Simmons quickly provided it, racking up two consecutive shutouts with the mask on.

Plante's performance in league play earned him his fifth Vezina Trophy. But it was his performance in the Stanley Cup playoffs that eventually forced Blake and Selke to acknowledge that the mask would be a permanent piece of goaltenders' equipment. Once more, the Canadiens swept from league championship to Stanley Cup victory, this time in the minimum eight games.

Goaltenders' masks weren't the only evidence of postwar technology making its mark on the NHL in the 1950s. A marked improvement in playing conditions resulted from the widespread adoption of the Zamboni ice-finishing machine that replaced the old practice of flooding the rink between periods. Instead of merely coating the ice with water, the Zamboni scraped away a layer of the old surface first, resulting in a quicker and smoother freeze that increased the speed of play. Ice-making plants were also improved, greatly reducing problems with deteriorating ice in warm weather.

Skates also changed as new materials were employed. In 1958, manufacturers built the first molded plastic skate in an attempt to provide more support and protection to players' feet. Pads and uniforms were improved as lighter-weight plastics and fabrics became available.

Over the decades, hockey sticks had evolved from the one-piece models used in hockey's early years to two- and three-piece units with lie, weight, and flexibility modified to suit each player. The growing popularity of the slapshot, perfected by players such as Bernie Geoffrion, Andy Bathgate, and Bobby Hull, called for sticks strengthened with fiberglass tape and laminated blades.

Despite the trend to improved protective equipment, forwards and defensemen were reluctant to adopt helmets. Charlie Burns, who played for both Detroit and Boston, had suffered a fractured skull as a junior, and was

Proposal for European Tour by NHL Clubs

In February 1957 the NHL received a proposal from a Swiss group for two NHL teams to participate in a twenty-five-game tour of Europe immediately following the Stanley Cup playoffs. The league turned down the request, but two years later, the Boston Bruins and New York Rangers embarked on a twenty-three-game tour of Europe which featured games in England, Switzerland, France, Belgium, West Germany, and Austria. The tour began on April 29, 1959, and concluded May 24.

one of the few players who wore a helmet full-time in the NHL. Gordie Howe wore one for a short time in 1959 following a concussion, but he then removed it, never to wear one again.

Air travel was a major factor in improving play. Although intercity air travel had been tried from time to time by NHL clubs in previous seasons, Boston was the first club to travel regularly by airplane to road games, in 1958. Most teams followed suit soon afterwards, eschewing what had become one of the most storied aspects of life on the road: the Pullman sleeper car. Travelling by air, players were much fresher for road games, and this resulted in improved performances and faster hockey.

Between 1955 and 1960, the astonishing Montreal Canadiens won five consecutive Stanley Cup championships. In regular-season play, they scored 200 or more goals in each of five consecutive seasons and became the first team to score 250 in a single campaign. A core of ten Canadiens played on all five Stanley Cup-winning teams during these glorious years. Of those, Jean Béliveau, Doug Harvey, and Jacques Plante were selected to the First All-Star Team for each of the five seasons, while Plante won the Vezina each year and Harvey the Norris four times – his run broken only by teammate Tom Johnson in 1958-59. No team in the six-team era even approached the Canadiens' .816 winning percentage in playoff competition.

If there was a blue note in the Habs' successful 1959-60 campaign, it was the slowing of the magnificent Maurice Richard. The Rocket would score his last NHL goal during the 1960 Stanley Cup playoffs, and would announce his retirement during training camp the following autumn. While others on the Montreal roster were poised to take up much of the slack, Maurice Richard's era as the NHL's most charismatic performer had drawn to a close.

(continued on p. 147)

NHL Clubs Experiment with Orange Pucks

During their twenty-three-game exhibition tour of Europe in 1959, the Boston Bruins and New York Rangers experimented with an orange puck. The puck, designed by Clair Kinney of Toronto, did not receive rave reviews: players complained that it looked like a blur on the ice.

Montreal alternate captain Doug Harvey, wearing sweater number 2, was the NHL's dominant defenseman of the 1950s.

THE GOLDEN JET

by Bob Verdi

He came to Chicago in 1957 from an uncharted Ontario hamlet called Pointe Anne, with blond hair flowing and muscles bulging and face smiling. He looked like a star, did Robert Marvin Hull, and he was.

"When I think of Hull, I think of Gordie Howe, the all-time great I had with the Detroit Red Wings," remarked an elated general manager Tommy Ivan when "The Golden Jet" autographed his first contract with the Chicago Black Hawks.

The signature made Hull, aged eighteen, the youngest player in Black Hawk history. It was only fitting and proper, then, that he would continue to make history with the Black Hawks until he departed for another city, Winnipeg, and another league, the World Hockey Association, in 1972.

From that first goal against the Boston Bruins and Don Simmons in Chicago Stadium ("not a very artistic one, as I recall," said Hull), to the 666th and final one in Hawk spangles during the Stanley Cup playoffs at New York, Hull was the consummate athlete – an electric performer who became one of the National Hockey League's premier attractions. He was a personality, charisma's child.

"Bobby was like an evangelist, a Pied Piper," noted former Black Hawks teammate Stan Mikita, also a Hall of Famer. "Wherever he went, people followed."

The Golden Jet was the star of stars, yet he was one of the guys. He was constantly badgered for autographs, handshakes, and souvenirs, yet he always had time to oblige a youngster's request. Hull never could quite make it from the hotel lobby to the team bus without countless interruptions.

"If people think enough of me to want to shake my hand or talk to me or interview me, then time must be made for it," said Hull, who carried his fame as deftly as he jettisoned the puck. "After all, what are we but entertainers?"

And, oh, did he entertain.

"I sure am a lucky lad, aren't I?" Hull said at his rookie training camp with the Black Hawks. Sure, he had scored thirty-three goals in his first season of junior competition with the St. Catharines Tee Pees, but this was the big show. This was the NHL.

Young Bobby was not overmatched, though. He authored two modest seasons, managing 13 and 18 goals, but then he blossomed into the robust scoring machine that sent him to hockey's Hall of Fame. In 1959-60, he bagged 39 goals and 42 assists for his first of four scoring titles. He dipped to 31 goals the next winter, but more than atoned for that in 1962.

Hull surged with 35 goals in his last 31 games, and in a meaningless season finale at New York, The Golden Jet found the net at 4:58 of the first period against Gump Worsley for goal number 50. Only two players – Montreal's Rocket Richard and Boom-Boom Geoffrion – had reached that plateau. And here was The Golden Jet hitting the 50 mark, a mere youth of twenty-three.

For pure courage, hockey people will forever remember his 1963 playoffs against Detroit. In the opener, Hull scored twice on wrist shots; his shoulder, after all, was separated. In the second game, his nose was rearranged into a bloody mess. Doctors figured there was no way he could return, but Hull found a way.

Hours before game four, he walked into a Detroit hotel lobby. His eyes were black as night, his face was puffed up, and splints prevented his nose from collapsing. "I'm playing tonight," he said. And he did. And he played brilliantly throughout the rest of the series, scoring a hat trick in the final game.

Being a man of conviction, Hull had his tiffs with management. He once left training camp for three days because the front office wouldn't allow his two sons to skate at practice. Another time, he missed

Bobby Hull earned a spot in the NHL record book when he became the third NHL sniper to score 50 goals in a season, recording the historic marker on March 25, 1962, against Gump Worsley and the New York Rangers.

the first month of the season because he said management reneged on certain promises contained in his four-year contract. But being made of stern stuff, The Golden Jet was all business when he laced on his skates. And he erased record after record.

The place: Chicago Stadium. The date: March 12, 1966. On assists from Bill "Red" Hay and Lou Angotti, Hull unleashed a fifty-foot slapshot through New York Ranger goalie Cesare Maniago for his 51st goal of the campaign – another NHL milestone. He finished with 54 that season, and 52 the next, and 58 in 1968-69.

That, too, was a remarkable year. Hull broke his jaw in December but chose to return by donning a football-style helmet, with a face-protector and cushions galore guarding the injury. If that wasn't uncomfortable enough, Hull's diet for forty days consisted of a gooey mush he called "brownish ugh." Actually, the meal consisted of steak put through a blender and sipped with a straw. Hull had a partial plate in his uppers, so he took in the liquid meals where his teeth used to be. And why did he insist on playing against the desires of doctors and management? "Because," he mumbled from a mouth wired shut, "they're starting to call me Dennis's brother."

After the Black Hawks finished last in their divi-sion despite his 58 goals in 1968-69, management decreed that Hull should consider a more disciplined brand of hockey. Left wing was his alley, not the whole rink. But he adjusted. The league legislated against the curved blade he adored. But he scored anyway, with a succession of centers, many of them fameless.

So who exactly was this Robert Marvin Hull? The perfect mesomorph, he was labeled, an estimable physical specimen indeed. Hull was one of eleven children raised on a farm. He grew up raising cattle, pitching hay, shoveling snow, and building fences. Even now, Hull is still a farm boy at heart, a legend who's as comfortable around a Hereford as he is around his legion of followers. He's a man who made fans leap from their seats and goalies flinch in place. He was bigger than life, his accomplishments louder than loud. Yet Hull possessed the rare ability of imposing that inner country boy on the hurry-up of the big city where he played. He couldn't have seemed more comfortable had he been born and raised in Chicago's Loop.

Bobby Hull, wearing number 16, heads up-ice pursued closely by Detroit's Norm Ullman. Hull, who also wore number 7, finally settled on number 9, because of his respect for Rocket Richard and Gordie Howe.

"You know, you'll hear a lot of athletes say that when the game is on, they aren't aware of the crowd," Hull remarked recently. "Well, I think that's a bunch of baloney. I know it was with me. When I played in that great building, Chicago Stadium, and I picked up the puck, I could feel every voice. It was like the fans were coming up the ice behind me."

There never was, nor will there ever be, a way to determine how many children Hull visited in hospitals – in Chicago and throughout his travels – just

because he felt an urge to spread some sunshine. Some instincts can't be taught, after all. Hull was a genius on the ice, and off.

There is this little door on the west side of Chicago Stadium – gate 3½ – where players from either team enter and exit on game nights, along with referees, club officials, what have you. That was, and still is, the press gate too, and more than once an unsuspecting beat writer would finish off his final story an hour or so after the game, leave the press box, and find Hull still signing away at Gate 3½. They say the legs go first in an athlete? Maybe, but you figured Bobby Hull would retire on account of writer's cramp.

Hull could have ducked out on his admirers through any number of gates and doors, but he was always a fixture at Gate 3½. He and the security guard and hundreds of his fans, the smaller and more impressionable the better.

Where, you might wonder, did this joy ride begin?

"With hockey itself, back on the farm," Hull said. "On those cold Saturday nights when we'd turn on the radio to hear Foster Hewitt broadcasting from Maple Leaf Gardens. Nobody could do it quite like Foster, and naturally, we'd get so pumped up on Saturday nights that we couldn't wait to get up on Sunday mornings, get on the ice, and pretend we were all the heroes we'd heard about the night before on the radio."

"As for the autograph thing, well, that probably started at Maple Leaf Gardens too. Every once in a while, Mom and Dad would take me on the train down to Toronto for a game. The first one was when I was about ten years old, I would guess. Leafs versus Red Wings. We had to stand just to the west side of the main entrance on Carlton Street, a couple of hours before the last few remaining tickets would go on sale. Standing-room tickets. As soon as the doors opened, I was gone, flying up to get a spot for myself and hold a couple of spots for Mom and Dad."

"Unbelievable. Maple Leaf Gardens, a real game. Leafs versus Red Wings. And afterward, we had some time to kill before the train went back to Belleville, so Dad suggested that we wait around the lobby of the Gardens for the players. We waited under the clock. I remember. And soon, the first guys out ... none other than Gordie Howe and Ted Lindsay. Howe and Lindsay! As soon as I saw that, I ran and sort of hid behind Dad's leg. I was just grabbing onto it when Dad said, 'Hey, if you want to get an autograph like the other kids are getting, you're going to have to go up there and get it. Howe and Lindsay aren't going to come to you.'"

"I said, 'No way,' but he kept calling me a chicken. So finally I shed my fright and got the nerve to ask Dad for a piece of paper and a pen (he just happened to have both handy). I wended my way towards Howe and said, 'Uh, Mr. Howe, do you think I could please have your autograph?' He said sure. He not only didn't bite my head off, he kind of tapped me on the head and ruffled my hair and signed. I was in complete awe. Then I got real bold and went over to

Lindsay and asked for a stick. He said he was sorry, he'd given his last stick out to one of the kids before me. But he signed an autograph, and I could have flown home instead of taking the train. I never ever forgot the way Howe and Lindsay made me feel that night in Maple Leaf Gardens. And I suppose, somewhere in the back of my mind, I decided that night that if I ever realized my dream to play professional hockey, I would treat fans the same way that Gordie Howe and Ted Lindsay treated me that night in the Gardens."

Four years later, Hull was watching one of his brothers play a game in Belleville. The word of Robert Marvin was spreading then, and a youngster

Bobby Hull never forgot that it was the fans who paid the bills. He obliged thousands of autograph-seekers.

The Golden Jet relaxes on his twenty-sixth birthday with his son, who twenty-five years later would be known as "the Golden Brett." The Jet and Brett are the only father-son tandem to capture the Hart Trophy.

asked for an autograph, the very first of millions. Bobby obliged, to the delight of his mom. Don't you ever say no, son. Ever. Chances are, Bobby never did.

"All it takes to make a kid happy in that instance," Hull says, "is a little time. Athletes should never forget who pays the bills."

Hull was such a giant as a goodwill ambassador – has the National Hockey League, or any other league, ever had a better one? – that we sometimes tend to hail his attitude instead of appreciating his aptitude. Shame on us. He was an absolutely gifted virtuoso, true, but he had more than strong arms and strong legs. He had an incomparable spirit, a will, a fire within. Hull simply did not know what it was to coast through a game or a shift. There will be critics who contend that he was one-dimensional, then so be it.

Hull, we should remember, was not always a left wing, but a center. (For that matter, he wore numbers 16 and 7 before the now-retired number 9.) During the playoffs of 1959, coach Rudy Pilous switched Hull to left wing. Enough said. In ensuing seasons, it was not unusual to see members of opposing teams clinging to Hull's massive frame like so many gnats, all in the name of checking The Golden Jet. Hull himself cites Eddie Westfall of the Boston Bruins, Bob Nevin of Toronto and the Rangers, and Montreal's Claude Provost as perhaps his three most effective, and respected, "shadows." Detroit's Bryan "Bugsy" Watson? Well, Hull feels that rather enthusiastic fellow took some indecent liberties. Whatever, Black Hawks' fans shared in the triumph of good versus evil when Hull shook these defence mechanisms and continued on his mission. In Hull, after all, you weren't just talking about a point machine, but a man who also earned the Lady Byng Trophy for combining ability with sportsmanship (1964-65, 71 points and only 32 penalty minutes).

Then there was Hull's shot, often clocked at 120 miles per hour, 20 per cent faster than anybody

else's. Combined with the apprehension, the build-up, the noise that accompanied it, and the inevitability of a puck burrowing toward you with such force, the specter of Hull breaking loose to engineer one of those glorious solo forays had to raise fear and loathing in the men paid to stop him. Two of the greatest goalkeepers ever, Glenn Hall and Tony Esposito, faced Hull's blurs in practice sessions, and we should feel free to assume that neither cherished the experience. But at least their failures weren't punctuated by sirens and flashing red lights.

Toronto's Johnny Bower, whom Hull respected immensely, spoke for the brotherhood of masked men when he said that Hull's pure power, combined with that curved stick, created nothing short of havoc. Once, the puck would dip. Next time, it would sail. Next time, it would be straight and direct as a laser beam. And almost invariably, to hear Bower describe the agony, you really couldn't see the bloody thing after it left Hull's blade. You listened, you anticipated, you guessed. Also, you prayed.

"Were some of the goalies actually scared of my shot?" Hull said. "I don't know that you can play that position in the NHL and be scared. Jumpy, maybe. But not scared."

In a perfect world, Bobby Hull would have completed his career where it began, in Chicago Stadium with the Black Hawks. But such was not the case, and after 1972, nothing was quite the same, for him or them. With his NHL contract about to expire, Hull and his Chicago representative, Harvey Wineberg, asked for a "dollar more than Bobby Orr." The Black Hawks balked. Meanwhile, Winnipeg came on strong, talking $250,000 a year for five years, plus a one-million-dollar signing bonus on funds gathered from all other WHA franchises. Hull promised that, if the Jets and their new league could produce those sums, "I'm gone." The money was there, and despite a belated effort by the Black Hawks to keep The Golden Jet, Hull kept his word and became a Winnipeg Jet in June of 1972.

On adrenaline alone, it seemed, the Black Hawks of 1972-73 went to the Stanley Cup finals without him. They lost, but it was a spirited effort.

A distinct cooling-off period followed the end of the 1972-73 season, and one of the things that cooled off was hockey interest in Chicago. Attendance dipped, Black Hawk games disappeared from local free television, and disenchanted fans wondered whether the team might correct the problem by getting Hull a return ticket from Winnipeg and the WHA. There were a hundred rumors that Hull was about to reappear, but he failed to materialize. In time, the wounds healed. Hull was brought back to the Stadium in suit and tie, so that his number 9 jersey could be hoisted to the rafters. Bill Wirtz, the president of the team, said the Hull departure was the biggest mistake ever for the franchise, and Hull allowed that, well, he wished he'd never left either.

The sheer impact of Hull versus no Hull was felt by all, including Dale Tallon, a talented player acquired by the Vancouver Canucks. At his introductory press conference, Tallon was bequeathed Hull's fabled number 9. He accepted reluctantly, then turned it back after a week or so. "The only thing wrong with me wearing that number," he said, "is they forgot to put the decimal point in front of it." Case closed.

Initially, the Black Hawks went to court to try to prevent Hull from playing in Winnipeg, but after weeks of legal wrangling, he was cleared to play for his new team. Of course, this meant that he would

As the best-known member of the Winnipeg Jets, Hull scored more than 50 goals in four of the WHA's seven seasons. Note the extreme curvature of his stick.

show up in Chicago playing against the city's WHA franchise, the Cougars. On the night of his first appearance, the Amphitheater was full, and a player named Rick Morris was assigned the task of shadowing The Golden Jet. When Hull aimed an elbow at Morris, who should jump in to confront him but one of Bobby's old Black Hawk confreres, now with the Cougars, Reggie Fleming. They squared off briefly, order was restored, and the Cougars beat the Jets

The first NHL player to surpass the single-season benchmark of 50 goals, Hull was one of the Black Hawks' big chiefs through almost all of his fifteen years with the club.

3–2. Afterward, Hull repaired to an alcove for the rendering of more autographs. But alas, it was not the same.

"The World Hockey Association was great to me," Hull said, "and I hope that I did something good for the game, and good for the players. But, let's face it, I had that Black Hawks' Indian head tattooed on my chest. Every time I put on the jersey for fifteen years, it was a trip. Those were the greatest years in my life."

Hull's influence on the game of professional hockey cannot be underestimated. Had he not left for the rival WHA and campaigned tirelessly on its behalf, there may not have been a WHA. Moreover, Hull's presence in the young WHA altered the entire scope of demand versus supply. There were more jobs for more players and infinitely improved salaries.

"After all he's done for all of us," said Mikita, "all we should do is bow whenever he walks into the room and kiss his feet."

Bobby Hull was not just another great athlete with a number on his jersey and an entire league on his back. Throughout his career, he was always willing to take time with even the youngest of his many fans – a fact that one nine-year-old girl learned in Toronto. According to the well-known tale, she was one of hundreds awaiting The Golden Jet when the dressing-room door swung open after a game some years back. The team was in a hurry to catch a plane.

Hull spotted the bashful girl and asked her name.

"Catherine," she replied.

The Golden Jet smiled the famous smile, took pen in hand, and questioned her again.

"How do you spell that?" Hull inquired. "With a 'C' or a 'K'?"

The 1960-61 season proved to be Chicago's breakthrough year, and that fast-improving team finished in third place, above .500 for the first time since 1945-46. Coach Rudy Pilous put ex-Montreal Canadien Ab McDonald with second-year center Stan Mikita and veteran Ken Wharram to form what soon became known as the Scooter Line. Bobby Hull scored more than 30 goals for the second consecutive season, and the Black Hawks' defense corps helped goaltender Glenn Hall finish the season with a goals-against average of 2.57.

For some time, New York Rangers' star Andy Bathgate had observed that, if he twisted the blade of his stick, his shots would rise or dip in flight. Not too much later, during a Chicago Black Hawk practice, Stan Mikita accidentally discovered the same thing when he took shots with a stick that had a broken blade. Hull also picked up on the idea and, with a little experimentation, the two modified several new sticks, steaming the blades to give them a curve. The results were amazing. Not only could the two forwards get more velocity on their shots, but their accuracy improved – at least on the forehand. Hull and Mikita were soon ordering sticks with custom curves from manufacturers, while other NHLers were picking up on the trend and designing their own blades. Throughout the 1960s, use of the curved stick spread rapidly through all levels of hockey. Blade curvature became increasingly extreme until, in 1970, the NHL amended its rules to restrict the curve to half an inch, ending the era of the banana blade. Harder shots from curved sticks sometimes dipped en route to the net, hastening the adoption of facemasks by goaltenders.

The Canadiens' dynasty, while diminished by the retirement of Maurice Richard, was still open for business in 1960-61. The club's much-heralded

Forum Fans Get Better Protection

Before the start of the 1960-61 season, the Montreal Forum installed protective glass on top of the boards that ran along the sides of the rink. Previously, fans could lean over the boards to get a better look at the action. The move was made because of a sharp rise in the number of spectator injuries caused by pucks and sticks during the 1959-60 season.

Stan Mikita (21) and Ab McDonald search for a rebound in front of Jacques Plante in action at Chicago Stadium. McDonald and Mikita were founding members of the Hawks' "Scooter Line," one of the league's most explosive forward units, and key contributors to Chicago's Stanley Cup victory in 1961.

Topper in Goal

The Boston Bruins' right winger Jerry Toppazzini is the last regular-position player to tend goal in an NHL game. In a game against the Detroit Red Wings on October 16, 1960, "Topper" replaced an injured Don Simmons in the last minute of a 5-2 loss to Chicago.

farm system continued to develop top-rank NHL talent to the extent that Sam Pollock pronounced young Canadiens Gilles and Jean-Claude Tremblay, Ralph Backstrom, and Bobby Rousseau worth at least $100,000 each on the open market. To back-up Jacques Plante in goal, the Canadiens brought up Charlie Hodge, who got into thirty games and finished the season with a superb goals-against average of 2.50. Veterans Bernie Geoffrion and Jean Béliveau were the NHL's top scorers, Geoffrion finishing the season with 50 goals, which made him the first player to match Rocket Richard's single-season goal-scoring record. Geoffrion was awarded both the Art Ross and the Hart trophies as scoring champion and MVP, while Doug Harvey earned his seventh Norris Trophy as the NHL's top defenseman.

In New York, the Rangers remained in the doldrums, apparently unwilling to play for coach Alf Pike. The Bruins, too, played poorly despite the best efforts of coach Milt Schmidt. Boston fell to last place, finishing at the bottom of the standings for the first time since 1933-34. The Bruins would fail to make the playoffs in eight consecutive seasons.

In Toronto, Punch Imlach decided to stay behind the bench, holding down both coach and general-manager's positions. He converted Red Kelly from defense to center, playing him on a line with Frank Mahovlich, who responded with a 48-goal season. Johnny Bower won the Vezina Trophy with a goals-against average of 2.50, and Dave Keon was awarded the Calder Trophy as the league's top rookie. The team finished a strong second with 90 points. Detroit captured fourth place and the NHL's final playoff spot, while Norm Ullman had his best NHL season with 70 points. Two Red Wing rookies, right wing Bruce MacGregor and defenseman Howie Young, made their NHL debuts in 1960-61.

By the time the 1960-61 regular season wound up, Montreal led the standings for the fourth consecutive year. But while they topped the league's

The 1961 Detroit Red Wings celebrate their five-game semi-final victory over the Toronto Maple Leafs. The Wings' presence in the Stanley Cup finals marked the third time in four years that a team which finished fourth in the regular-season standings reached the championship round.

Poker-faced Chicago defenseman Jack "Tex" Evans (right) joins Bobby Hull for a photo session with the Stanley Cup after the Black Hawks' final series victory over Detroit in 1961. Evans, who scored just 21 goals in a fourteen-season NHL career, netted an unassisted marker in the third period of the sixth and deciding game against the Red Wings.

second-place club by 19, 18, and 13 points in the past three seasons, this year they finished a mere two points in front of Toronto. And Montreal's five-Cup dynasty officially ended in the semi-finals against Chicago. The Black Hawks, checking tenaciously, defeated the Canadiens four games to two, winning games five and six by consecutive 3–0 shutouts. Detroit upset Toronto in the league's other semi-final series, setting up the NHL's first all-American Stanley Cup final since 1950.

The Black Hawks defeated the Red Wings in six games to win their first Stanley Cup since 1937. The Hawks' victory also marked the first time in twenty years that a team other than Montreal, Detroit, or Toronto had won the Cup. What's more, it was only the third time since the NHL abandoned divisional play in 1938 that a team finishing in third or fourth place had won the trophy. More importantly, the Hawks' win completed the long process of franchise rebuilding begun in 1954 when the club was purchased by Arthur Wirtz and James D. Norris from the estate of Major Frederic McLaughlin.

A new Hockey Hall of Fame located on the grounds of the Canadian National Exhibition in Toronto opened its doors to the public in August of 1961. Bobby Hewitson was the curator of the new Hall.

At the beginning of the 1961-62 season, Doug Harvey left the Canadiens, moving to New York as playing coach of the Rangers. The Canadiens received Lou Fontinato as compensation.

In New York, Harvey worked newcomers Vic Hadfield and Jean Ratelle into the line-up, and continued to demonstrate his skills as the NHL's best defenseman. Despite his new responsibilities as coach, he would once again win the Norris Trophy. The Rangers' fourth-place finish earned the club its first berth in the playoffs in four seasons.

Bruins, Canadiens Use Modified Skate

In 1960 the Boston Bruins and the Montreal Canadiens began wearing an improved skate that featured an injury-reducing plastic guard fitted to the rear end of the blade.

At the NHL's annual meeting in 1961, use of the plastic CCM Pro-Guard Heel was made mandatory for all forwards and defensemen commencing with the 1961-62 season.

Andy Bathgate, here being pursued by Boston's Leo Boivin, was one of the league's great playmakers, leading the NHL in assists four times. Boivin, a stay-at-home defenseman, best known for his bruising body checks, spent nineteen years in the NHL and was inducted into the Hockey Hall of Fame in 1986.

Chicago and Detroit made few roster changes, as did Toronto's Punch Imlach, who continued as manager and coach with the security of a new three-year contract. Imlach was concerned about Johnny Bower, however, who at the time was the oldest player in the league. As insurance, he acquired Don Simmons to replace young Cesare Maniago as Bower's back-up. He also added bespectacled Al Arbour as the Leafs' fifth defenseman.

Dave Keon had 26 goals in his second season with the Leafs and was the latest in a long line of fine players groomed for the team by one of their two sponsored junior clubs, the St. Michael's College Majors and the Toronto Marlboros. A Majors' grad, Keon teamed with former St. Mike's players Dick Duff, Tim Horton, Frank Mahovlich, and Red Kelly (via Detroit). His solid performance in 1961-62 established him as one of the game's top skaters and best small players, and he followed his Calder Trophy win from the previous year with the Lady Byng Trophy.

In Boston, where the Bruins had plunged from second to last place in just two seasons, coach Milt Schmidt was replaced by Phil Watson, who had had difficulties in New York and couldn't win in Boston either. All-star defenseman Fern Flaman retired, but the Bruins' defense corps of Leo Boivin, Dallas Smith, and Ted Green, plus rookies Pat Stapleton and Ed Westfall, appeared strong. At forward, a number of new players were tried out alongside veterans John Bucyk, Don McKenney, Jerry Toppazzini, and Doug Mohns, who had been converted from defense to right wing. The departure of Bronco Horvath and Vic Stasiuk left Bucyk as the only remaining member of the Uke Line. The Bruins also signed center Tommy Williams, who, at that time, was the only American-born player in the NHL.

The 1961-62 season saw milestones reached and records set. Gordie Howe scored his 500th goal and recorded his thirteenth consecutive 20-goal year. The season also saw the emergence of Bobby Hull as the most glamorous superstar in the NHL, a status that brought on him the sort of shadow-checking that had often infuriated Rocket Richard. But despite close attention from the NHL's best checking forwards, Hull matched Richard and Geoffrion in becoming the third man to score 50 goals in a season. He finished strongly, scoring 35 goals in his last 31 games to tie Andy Bathgate for the scoring championship with 84 points. Hull was awarded the Art Ross Trophy for having scored more goals. But this performance wasn't enough to move the Black Hawks up in the standings, as Chicago again finished in third place with 75 points. The Canadiens appeared poised to recapture the Cup after winning their fifth straight league championship by a comfortable 13 points over second-place Toronto. At least part of Montreal's success was due to the performance of Jacques Plante, who won the Hart and Vezina trophies, and the play of young right winger Bobby Rousseau, the 1961-62 winner of the Calder Trophy.

In the semi-finals, Chicago overcame a two-game deficit with four straight wins to upset the Canadiens four games to two. Toronto also needed six games to get past Doug Harvey's Rangers. New York goaltender Gump Worsley, who stopped more than fifty shots, received a standing ovation from the fans in Maple Leaf Gardens at the conclusion of game five. Young Rod Gilbert scored his first and second NHL goals in this series. In the finals, the Leafs again won in six games to capture their first Cup since 1951, winning the first two and last two games of the series. Game six was scoreless, until the final period when Bobby Hull and Bob Nevin exchanged goals. Toronto's Dick Duff got the Cup-winner on a set-up from Tim Horton and George Armstrong with less than six minutes to play.

(continued on p. 159)

Dave Keon, who compiled only 117 minutes in penalties in his eighteen NHL seasons, receives the 1962 Lady Byng Trophy from NHL president Clarence Campbell. Keon, who also won the Conn Smythe Trophy in 1967, received only one five-minute major penalty in his lengthy career in professional hockey.

PUNCH AND THE LEAFS

by Charles Wilkins

The sweater-pulling war lasted 13 minutes in all. But by the time they sorted out the penalties and got the show on the road again, more than 25 minutes had elapsed. The game was scarcely under way when Imlach disagreed with the order in which referee Art Skov proposed to return the penalized players to the ice.

This little debate took another 12 minutes, during which an agitated Imlach sent to the dressing room for a pair of skates, laced them on, and prepared to skate out to debate with Skov.

"If I'd gone on the ice," said Imlach after the game, "it was going to cost me $100 and for $100 I wasn't going to go shuffling after him in street shoes."

The irascible coach stood for several minutes at the open gate of the players' bench, threatening to take to the ice, attempting to make himself heard. King Clancy stood beside him, urging him to stay put.

Eventually, Imlach called for his shoes and resumed his position behind the bench.

Toronto *Telegram*, April 15, 1966

I n a dreamier version of reality, we saw him sailing out across the rink, not quite touching it, his eyelids heavy under a weight of chicanery, ears aglow, arms pumping not with the grace of a heron's or an eagle's wings (Heaven knows, Punch was no eagle) but with the choppier mechanics of the sapsucker. We saw him circling, agitating, needling, picking up speed, his skate blades fueled by pure gall; now rising into the frenzied atmosphere above the ice, above the Sportimer, his bald head bulging with the internal pressure of his peevishness, his venom, his oceanic vengeance against the refs, against "Mahawlovich," Brewer, the Canadiens, his mouth aflap with it all. And the hat – the famous hat, the brimmed repository of his madness and metaphysics (the lot of it exquisitely honed against the dome of his skull; did he *sleep* with that hat on?) – the hat off now and tipped out above the ice, dispensing nettles, straight pins, garlic, old dogs' teeth, horseshoes, spiders, sea mists, onions, pumpernickel, Leiderkranz cheese, a hogshead of Kulmbacher beer (Punch used to say he could knock over the Rangers with his breath alone after a sandwich of Spanish onion and Leiderkranz). Out it all came, the record book, Conn Smythe's spats, the ghost of Bill Barilko and, last but not least . . . another miracle. That's what he was doing, he was on skates and he was about (we believed) to dispense a miracle. With the Leafs down 3–0 in games in their 1966 semi-final against the Habs – "facing elimination" to borrow from the broadcasters' argot – he was about to reverse the tide, surely he was, to set the team on a course that, before the month was out, would deliver another Stanley Cup, a fourth in five years, unto the expectant citizens of Hogtown.

And why not? He was, after all, a miracle-worker (just ask any Leafs fan of the late 1950s and early 1960s). Whereas Toe Blake and Milt Schmidt *coached*, Punch dealt in marvels. We had seen his handiwork first in 1958-59, shortly after he established himself behind the Leaf bench. Throughout that 1958 season, with the Leafs doing little to convince us that they had forsaken their lease on the league's crawl-space, he had promised anyone who would listen that his team would be there when the joust for the Cup began. His airy rodomontade may even have hinted at the finals or the Cup itself. "My guys are gonna rise up like Lazarus," he

announced to a caucus of reporters in early January of 1959. "In fact if Lazarus isn't under contract I might like to sign him for the stretch run." The sportswriters and fans loved it. They'd endured ten years of a team Conn Smythe had compared to jellyfish, and even the *prediction* of a playoff spot was more exciting, and made better press, than no playoffs at all. Which isn't to say they believed a word of what the coach said.

But, sure enough, during the last few weeks of that "Cinderella" year, the Maple Leafs began to stir, then to rise. So precipitous was their ascent from the dogpatch, in fact, that if you hadn't been looking you'd have sworn Punch had somehow conned the league into awarding the Leafs three or four points for a victory, while squelching the other teams' gains. The record shows that between March 14 and March 22, they won four games in a row, climbing from seven points back of the last playoff spot to within a point of the swooning fourth-place Rangers. On the last night of the season, still one point out of

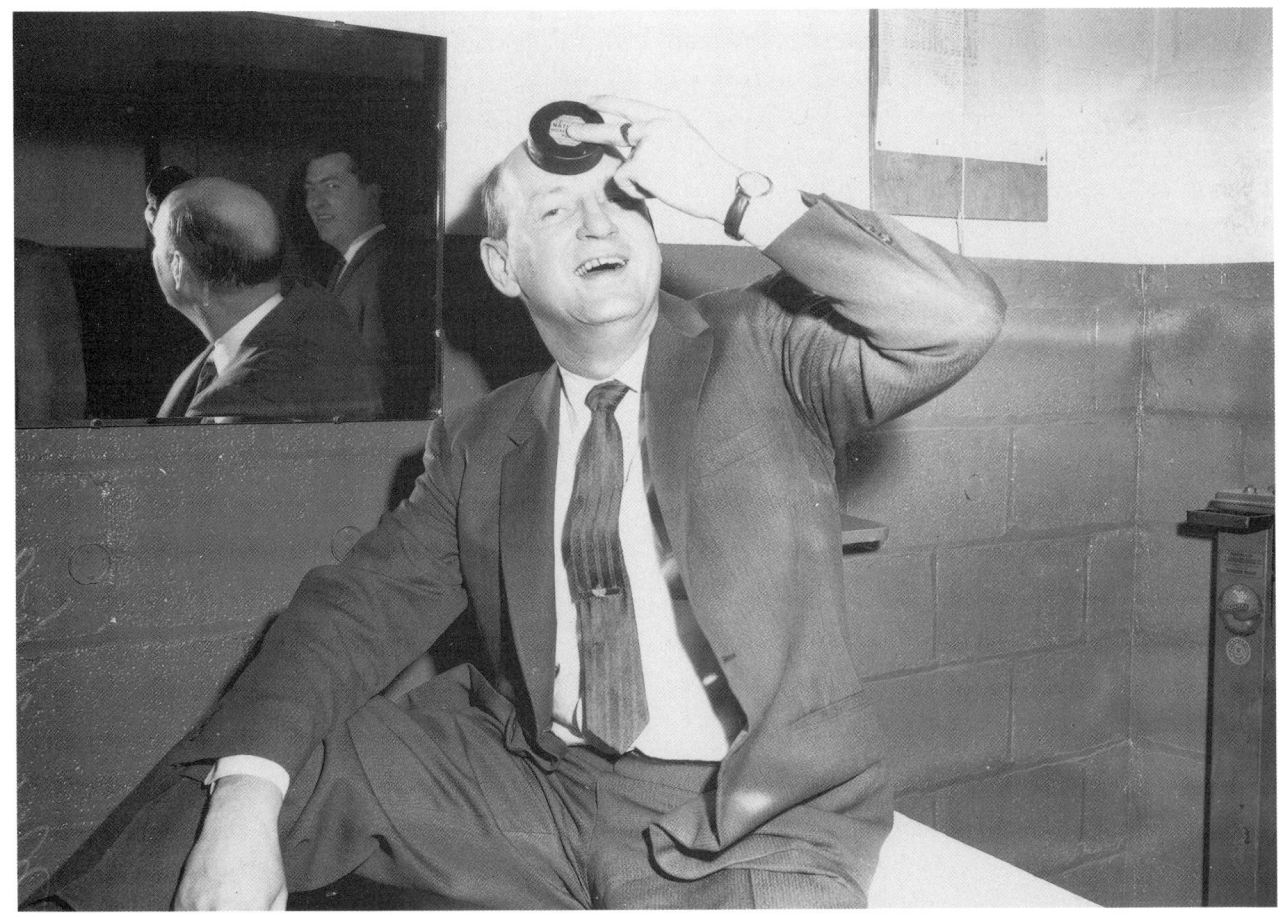

a playoff position, the team wheeled into Detroit for a fateful appointment with the Red Wings, who had recently replaced the Leafs at the bottom of the league food chain. Behind 2–0 at the end of the first period, and with owner Stafford Smythe gloomily allowing that the season was over (between periods, he went so far as to congratulate Punch on "a pretty good year"), the team quickened to prophetic impulse. By the end of the second period they had tied the game 4–4.

By the time they left Motown that night, Punch's pudgy foot was firmly lodged in a glass slipper. The Leafs had made the playoffs, as promised.

Ten days later they finished off the Bruins in the semi-final before conceding the final to the Canadiens, who at the time were impervious even to miracles.

An even headier marvel occurred in '62, when the Leafs, who had finished the schedule thirteen points behind the first-place Habs, responded to Punch's playoff abracadabra and took the Cup, returning it to Toronto for the first time in eleven years. For Leaf fans, it was as if some once-great aristocracy, some long-deposed embodiment of our pride and well-being, had been rightfully, triumphally, restored. We were delirious. Toronto paraded its heroes through the city's main streets under a rain of streamers and ticker-tape. Along King Street and up Bay to City Hall they came: Duff ... Armstrong ... Frank ... the lot of them grinning like gleeful children, and somewhere down the line, Punch himself, his halo indistinguishable from the pearly glow that emanated from his hairless pate.

They repeated in 1963, then again in 1964 after a desultory season of thirty-three wins and a third-place finish. Employing an art somewhere between that of Atilla and Tinkerbell, Punch rallied them when it mattered, confirming to our ever-willing brains that he was the man we believed he was – a miracle-worker.

But now it was 1966, and, skates or no skates, Leiderkranz or no, Punch and his team were about to crash land for the second year in a row. And when

Bobby Baun (right) watches as his shot rocks, rattles, and rolls past Terry Sawchuk, giving the leafs a 4-3 overtime win in game six of the 1964 Stanley Cup finals.

they did, we thought it was the end for Punch, that the Power had deserted him, never suspecting that Elmer Fudd, the Mad Hatter, the Old Bald Muledriver, was saving one last miracle for our delectation. It came in the spring of 1967, and, oh, it was sweet in that last campaign, the grand finale of the old six-cylinder league. All year the Leafs had limped along, their youngsters (Pappin, Stemkowski, Walton, Ellis) not yet ready to assume a full share of the load, the vets looking increasingly like outpatients from the waxworks (a couple of years hence, comedian Johnny Wayne would observe that they were the only team in the history of pro sport to have had their dynasty ended by prostate problems). They had finished the season in third place, nearly twenty points behind first-place Chicago. Had it not been for a stretch late in the winter when Punch booked off sick and his Paddy lieutenant, King Clancy, coaxed the old gang to a string of successive victories, they might not have been in the playoffs at all. But here they were, not just in the prelims but in the finals against their old rivals from *la belle province*. In the semis, where all but the feeble-minded had expected they'd be cooked to within a molecule or two of pure carbon – with goaltender Terry Sawchuk balancing by turns on his ear, his nostril, his armpit, his baby finger, his brush-cut, his brisket – they had upturned Hull, Mikita, and the most compelling version of the Black Hawks ever loosed on the league.

And now, after five games of the championship series, they were within a victory of the Cup and were returning to Toronto for their finest hour. No Leaf fan of the era will forget that last tremulous minute of game six, the Leafs leading 2–1, Montreal's net empty, faceoff to Sawchuk's left. *"Imlach is making his stand with an all-veteran line-up!"* crowed Foster Hewitt above the bawling of the crowd. *"Stanley, Horton, Kelly, Pulford, and Armstrong. Sawchuk, of course, is in goal."* Allan Stanley went noggin to noggin with Jean Béliveau in the faceoff circle, and referee John Ashley dropped the puck. Stanley pulled it to Kelly, who kicked it to Pulford, who passed it to Armstrong heading up the wing. In his brittle, slow-motion style, Army guided the puck toward center-ice and across the red line

Frank Mahovlich (left), with four Stanley Cup wins to his credit, and Red Kelly, who had just captured his record-tying eighth, celebrate the Leafs' 1967 championship.

before wrenching loose that rheumatic-looking shot of his. Clocks stopped, muscles stiffened, blood froze as the thing skipped across the Canadiens' blue line, the inside edge of the circle, the goal crease, and on into history. The Maple Leafs were champs.

The Leafs of 1967, what a combination of cubs and old lions they were: one great skater, Dave Keon; one great pillar of stone, Tim Horton; one great clown, Eddie Shack; one great-grandfather, Johnny Bower; and one extraterrestrial, Frank Mahovlich. When Frank entered the league in 1957, King Clancy declared that the M in his name stood for Moses and that he was going to lead the Leafs out of the Wilderness. And, indirectly, he did (if it is possible to say a team can be led from the rear, or from a distant planet such as the one Frank lived on). The facts need little interpretation; the team won four Cups during Frank's years in Toronto and have not won again since he was traded to Detroit in 1968.

If Clancy was mistaken in his assessment of Frank, it was in likening him to the wrong prophet,

for he was less a Moses than an Ezekiel, a man of visions, depressions, mystic melancholy, a man who, like his biblical soulmate, saw wheels within wheels and heard voices from Beyond. At times, Frank would go for a month or more without seeming to fully inhabit his uniform; part of him was back home on Zorag. During his latter years with the club, he suffered two nervous breakdowns. But, oh, he could play when the Spirit was upon him – or, more accurately, when it left him alone. He once said, "There were times it seemed I could just bull my way through the opposition." At other times he played as if he were protecting a teddy bear, or some delicate missive from the Firmament, beneath his jersey.

It has been postulated (by, among others, Frank himself) that Punch drove Frank nuts. It has also been postulated that Punch was one of the few people who understood Frank (it stands to reason that one extraterrestrial – one, albeit, from the opposite end of the galaxy – should understand another). He certainly understood him to the point where, in 1960, he perceived not only the need for a catalyst to convert Frank's enormous potential to some sort of dynamic but perceived exactly what form that catalyst should take. Who but Punch could have divined that Leonard "Red" Kelly, an aging,

sweet-tempered defenseman (the ugliest word in Red's vocabulary was "heck"), could be brought from Detroit, shifted to center-ice after thirteen years on the blue line, and could so successfully light Frank's fire? In Kelly's first full season with the team, Frank scored 48 goals, with Kelly assisting on just about every one of them. Frank finished third in league scoring that year (he would be the Leafs' leading scorer for the next six years), while his red-headed benefactor finished sixth, accumulating seventy points, just two fewer than Gordie Howe.

Red's success with Frank lay in his reassuring disposition, which balanced Imlach's abrasiveness, and in his ability to dish an impeccable backhand pass as his larger-than-life winger dieseled down the left side of the rink. The case might even be made that, in his catalytic role, Kelly, as much as Frank, Punch, or anyone else, made a winner of the Leafs. His years with the team, 1960-67, coincide all too neatly with the Cup's tenure at Maple Leaf Gardens. To put too much emphasis on Kelly's role, however, would unfairly shadow the contributions of Dave

The Leafs were often on edge during the coaching reign of Punch Imlach, but regardless of his methods, no one could argue with the results: four Cup victories and six final-series appearances.

Keon (whose Duracell skating earned him the Conn Smythe Trophy in the 1967 playoffs), of Johnny Bower, Bob Baun, Bob Pulford, Tim Horton, Carl Brewer, Eddie Shack, Billy Harris, and any, or all, of a brace of reclamation projects – Stanley, Bathgate, Litzenberger, Pronovost, Olmstead, Arbour, Don McKenney, Sawchuk – that were perhaps the true glory of Punch's championship years. Conn Smythe's comment that Punch was "the best coach and the worst general manager in hockey" was grossly unfair. It wasn't his managing but his coaching – his insistence on sublimating the individuality of his stars to the greater good of the team, plus the relentless "motivational" hectoring for which he was famous – that drove the febrile and talented Carl Brewer into premature retirement in 1965 and eventually reduced Frank to an emotional stickpin.

The curious thing about Punch's relationship with Brewer – they were truly the Punch and Judy of the Maple Leaf Side Show – is that they were so uncannily similar in temperament (was it beyond coincidence that Carl eventually went bald like his old antagonist?) Both could be cunning and egotistical; both could be brilliant; both could be wilful and neurotic. Punch's skate caper in 1966 was the sort of stunt that might well have been lifted from Carl's own book of Nettlesome Attention Grabbers.

Both Brewer and Imlach could also be downright pests – and not just toward one another. Brewer managed to alienate half the league's forwards with his needling and baiting, his out-and-out mischief. He played, for instance, with the palms cut out of his gloves, the better to clutch an opponent's sweater undetected. He would goad an opponent to anger but would invariably be gone from the scene if a dust-up ensued.

When Carl held out for more pay in 1963, he not only went AWOL from training camp but, in a move calculated to infuriate Imlach, enrolled at McMaster University in Hamilton and went out for the football team. On the day that a photo of Carl in his football uniform appeared in a Toronto newspaper, Imlach dispatched King Clancy to the scene, and Brewer was signed within hours. But a toll had been exacted in disaffection, and Brewer eventually worried his career into decline, while Punch lost his all-star

defenseman, one of the most talented ever to wear the Maple Leaf.

Whatever the warts and cankers of his coaching style – the views of Conn Smythe notwithstanding – Punch could be a brilliant general manager, all but infallible in his instinct for acquiring other teams' overripe all-stars, or even journeymen, and wringing good seasons out of them. It is worthy of Ripley that, between 1958 and 1968, he brought no fewer than ten future Hall-of-Famers to the Leafs – count 'em: Bower, Stanley, Kelly, Bathgate, Pronovost, Sawchuk, Olmstead, Pilote, Ullman, and Dickie Moore – while relinquishing only two in return: Bathgate and Frank. And all but three of Punch's blue-chip acquisitions (Pilote, Ullman, and Moore) contributed substantially to Leaf championships. More remarkable yet is that, in most cases, Punch gave up little or nothing to get them. In 1958, he traded the soon-forgotten Jim Morrison to acquire Allan Stanley, who would give him ten sterling years and play on three all-star teams while with the Leafs. He put Red Kelly in a Leaf uniform for the bargain price of Marc Réaume, and it insults reason to consider that he got Bower, Sawchuk, and Olmstead for *no players at all* through the intraleague draft.

The truth about Punch is that he wanted players who were as unlike himself as possible – no neurotics, no eccentrics, no hard cases. No self-styled mystics or magicians. He wanted trenchmen, soldiers, men whose feet were firmly in contact with the planet. "What I want," he once said, "is a guy who will *play* for me" – in other words a guy who would accept without question the stingy, defensive conformity that defined Punch's brilliance. The true Imlach players were the likes of Baun, Bower, Olmstead, Keon, Armstrong, and of course the ultimate Imlach archetype, Tim Horton.

Was there ever another player with the stable valences, both physical and mental, of Tim Horton? Everything about him bespoke calm invincibility – the brush-cut, the serene boyish face, the bullish head and neck, the slowness to anger, the selfless devotion to the Leafs and to Imlach. It was that seeming invincibility, that inarguable, silent strength of Horton's, that made his death a few years later all the more shocking and improbable.

Tim Horton, the defensive backbone of the Leafs for twenty years, escapes the grasp of Jean Béliveau during the 1967 Stanley Cup finals.

Bob Pulford was another Imlach ideal – a hard-headed, defensive centerman who could score and who never voiced a bad word about his coach.

There were exceptions too. Eddie Shack, for example, was hockey's version of a (barely) guided missile – reckless speed, fiery enthusiasm, explosion on contact. But Punch *understood* Ed's recklessness. He could control it and deploy it to his advantage. That made the difference.

If he'd had options, Imlach would never have picked Frank and Brewer for his team. Nor would they have picked him for theirs. But no one had any choice in the matter; Carl and Frank were already with the team when Imlach arrived in 1958. To be fair to Punch, he stuck with Frank for ten years, and might well have stuck with Brewer if Brewer had stuck with him. Punch was not without heart. And to be fair to Carl and Frank, they contributed as much as, or more than, anyone to the Leafs' success.

Asked once if he *liked* his players, Punch responded, "The team comes first, but that's not to say the guys aren't special. In fact, I like them a lot," then in typical Imlach fashion, "I even like the guys I don't like. They're a terrific buncha bums."

And did the players like Punch?

"I had some fun with him," says Eddie Shack. "Some of the guys weren't too keen." Some, in fact, detested him.

But it didn't matter. They *played* for him, and that's what Punch cared about. And that's what *we* cared about.

Asked at the beginning of the 1967 playoffs what chance his team had of bringing home the Cup, Punch smiled his cryptic, world-weary smile (had he somehow foreseen the miracle that was to come?) and said, "With the guys I've got, it isn't going to take any miracles."

With the guys I've got: the infirm, the retreads, the rookies – guys who would *play* for Punch.

As it turned out, it did take a miracle – mostly of goaltending, but also of aging savvy and of the bounce and brilliance of Dave Keon.

And of coaching too. "Punch can be a hard man to work for," Tim Horton once said. "But if you do things his way you're going to win the Stanley Cup once in a while."

The 1967 Cup marked the end of the old league and the end of the old Leafs. By the time training camp opened the next summer, five regulars – Baun, Kelly, Shack, Sawchuk, and Douglas – had moved on. Within a year, five more were gone, Stanley and Mahovlich among them. Two years hence, Punch himself would be history (he would return in 1979 after more than a decade in Buffalo, but by that time the Age of Marvels would be long past).

By 1971, only Dave Keon and Ron Ellis would still be wearing the old uniform – in fact, the old uniform itself would be transformed, updated. By 1974, Terry Sawchuk, Stafford Smythe, and Tim Horton would be in their graves.

But in that glorious spring of 1967, we were content to live briefly in the present. (For some of us, the team's epochal achievements of the 1960s have become our fairest fix on that memorable decade.) Canada was celebrating her one hundredth birthday, and Expo '67 was about to open in the city of Montreal. An era had ended, a new one was about to begin. And the Toronto Maple Leafs had the Stanley Cup.

Despite the Black Hawks' improvement, and the modest success of the Rangers, NHL governors remained concerned about the disparity between the league's top three teams and the last-place Boston Bruins, who had finished 60 points behind first-place Montreal in 1961-62. Early in the 1962-63 season, the league introduced procedures designed to enrich the league's weaker teams. Under the new rules, teams were allowed to draft any seventeen-year-old player who was not on a junior team sponsored by an NHL club. Twenty-one juniors were drafted under this scheme. The Canadiens retained their right of first refusal on top French-Canadian prospects.

Before the 1962-63 season began, a spectacular but unconsummated "deal" set the hockey world on its ear. During a party before the annual All-Star Game, Chicago owner James D. Norris cooked up an agreement with Toronto's Stafford Smythe – son of recently retired Leaf president Conn Smythe – to pay the Leafs one million dollars for Frank Mahovlich. The story was reported by the media and was accorded some credibility, since the big left winger was frequently at loggerheads with manager-coach Punch Imlach. Under closer scrutiny, it appeared that Norris and Smythe had worked out the deal in decidedly social circumstances. As well, Stafford Smythe didn't have authority to approve the sale of Mahovlich on his own; he needed the go-ahead from the other six members of the Leafs' "Silver Seven" management committee. So, in the cold light of morning, the deal was squelched. But the fact that it was even considered gave an indication of the value being attached to the biggest NHL stars.

Maple Leaf Gardens Innovations

Maple Leaf Gardens was the first arena to have glass surrounding the boards (1948), escalators (1955), and separate penalty boxes (1963). Prior to the separation of the "sin-bins," the penalized players sat — and served their penalties — together.

The 1962-63 All-Star Team, after dropping a 4–1 decision to the defending Stanley Cup champion Toronto Maple Leafs. Front row, left to right: Provost, Backstrom, Worsley, Pilote, Ullman, Boivin, and Harvey. Back row: Plante, Geoffrion, Bathgate, Talbot, Delvecchio, Howe, Evans, McKenney, Mohns, Hull, Hall, and coach Rudy Pilous.

Hall's Streak Ends after 33,135 Minutes

Chicago Black Hawks' goaltender Glenn Hall's record consecutive-games-played streak of 552 came to an end on November 7, 1962. The streak, which covered 33,135 minutes and included both regular-season and playoff games, ended when Hall took himself out of a game against Boston at 10:21 of the first period with a back injury. The sacroiliac condition in his lower back was caused by the stiffness of new pads that Hall had tried out in a practice the day before.

Boston, coming off two last-place finishes, replaced coach Phil Watson with Milt Schmidt fourteen games into the season. The Bruins would finish with their best point total since 1960, but still found themselves in sixth place, 22 points out of a playoff spot. The Rangers, too, switched coaches, beginning the 1962-63 season with manager Muzz Patrick behind the bench as Doug Harvey relinquished the coach's portfolio to play full-time again. Halfway through the season, Patrick appointed Red Sullivan to the coaching job. The Rangers, though strengthened by the addition of Jim Neilson and flashy Guelph junior graduate Rod Gilbert, finished well out of the playoffs in fifth place.

At the top of the standings, the NHL's elite engaged in one of the closest races in years. Just five points separated fourth-place Detroit from first-place Toronto. The Wings were led, as usual, by Gordie Howe, who won his sixth Art Ross Trophy as the league's leading scorer and his sixth Hart Trophy as league MVP. Howe's sixth Hart set him in a class by himself. No other player had won the award five times, and only Eddie Shore had won it on four occasions. The Wings' roster yielded another record-setting performance, as defenseman Howie Young established a single-season high of 273 penalty minutes.

The Canadiens, who had not finished lower than second place since 1951, ended the season in third, albeit just four points out of top spot. Chicago finished only a point behind Toronto, despite Hull's decline from 50 to 31 goals. The Hawks were led by Stan Mikita, who finished third in scoring to Howe and Bathgate. Early in the season, a back injury forced Chicago goaltender Glenn Hall to sit out a game, ending his record-setting consecutive-games-played streak for goaltenders at 552. Hall had appeared in every game his team had played since 1955. If any mark in the *NHL Official Guide & Record Book* is unbreakable, it may be this one.

The biggest success story of 1962-63 was the team-oriented play of the Maple Leafs. Imlach had built a team that stressed strong defense and a balanced attack. Frank Mahovlich finished fourth in league scoring with 36 goals and 73 points; and, although no other Leaf finished among the NHL's top ten scorers (only Mahovlich, Red Kelly, and Dave Keon surpassed the 20-goal mark), Toronto finished second in team scoring with 221 goals, only four behind the Canadiens.

The ability to spread scoring throughout the roster proved to be Toronto's strength in the 1963 playoffs. In both rounds, the Leafs' opponents contained Frank Mahovlich, but Toronto got enough scoring from the rest of the line-up to polish off both Montreal and Detroit in five games each to win their second straight Stanley Cup.

Three consecutive last-place finishes dictated that the Boston Bruins' rebuilding job continue into the 1963-64 season. In a major overhaul, general manager Lynn Patrick demoted or traded seven players from the 1962-63 roster. He promoted center Orland Kurtenbach from San Francisco of the Western League and acquired two veterans, defenseman Tom Johnson from Montreal and right winger Andy Hebenton from the Rangers. Johnson and Hebenton were available to the Bruins, having been left unprotected in the NHL's annual intra-league draft. Three graduates of Leighton "Hap" Emms's Niagara Falls Flyers junior club – Don Awrey, Ron Schock, and Gary Dornhoefer – also played their first NHL games with the Bruins in 1963-64. But these wholesale changes brought no immediate improvement in the Bruins' performance on the ice or at the gate. On one occasion, disgruntled fans began singing the 1960s anthem "We Shall Overcome" in response to the team's poor play.

Montreal signed John Ferguson, a tough right winger from the Cleveland Barons of the AHL and a first-class lacrosse player in hockey's off-season. In June of 1963, the Habs and Rangers had participated in a major trade that sent Jacques Plante, Phil Goyette, and Don Marshall to New York in exchange for Gump Worsley, Dave Balon, and Leon Rochefort. Unfortunately for the Canadiens, Worsley played only eight games before an injury sidelined him for the rest of the season. The Habs also promoted top defense prospect Jacques Laperrière to their NHL roster.

In Detroit, veteran superstar Gordie Howe whisked past Maurice Richard's record of 544 regular-season goals, scoring number 545 short-handed in a 3–0 shutout of the Canadiens in November. And while Terry Sawchuk wasn't always healthy (Roger Crozier got into 15 games as his back-up), he still managed to register his 95th shutout, surpassing George Hainsworth's record of 94 set between 1926 and 1937. To augment a maturing forward corps, the Red Wings called on the services of center Pit Martin and right winger Paul Henderson, both of whom were graduates of the Red Wings' junior franchise in Hamilton, Ontario, and of the club's AHL farm team in Pittsburgh.

The Maple Leafs added right winger Jim Pappin to 1963's Cup-winning line-up, but by mid-season it was apparent to Punch Imlach that his veteran roster could not keep pace with the superior offenses of the Black Hawks and the Canadiens. Injuries to Bower, Mahovlich, and Baun placed further pressure on Imlach to make a move. He responded by making a five-for-two trade with the Rangers in February of 1964, sending Dick Duff, Bob Nevin, Arnie Brown, Bill Collins, and the rights to Rod Seiling to New York in exchange for veteran forwards Andy Bathgate and Don McKenney.

Even with the trade, the Leafs could not rise above a third-place finish behind the Canadiens and Black Hawks. The front-running clubs dominated the NHL's individual awards, Mikita winning the Art Ross Trophy by two points over Bobby Hull, Pierre Pilote winning the Norris, and Kenny Wharram the Lady Byng. Montreal's Charlie Hodge won the Vezina Trophy. Hodge was an injury replacement for Gump Worsley in the Montreal nets, but played so well that he retained the starting job. Jacques Laperrière won the

Detroit–Boston Game Postponed

The Detroit Red Wings–Boston Bruins contest on November 24, 1963, was postponed to honor the memory of U.S. President John Kennedy, who was assassinated on November 22.

Talented right winger Rod Gilbert scored 24 goals in 1963-64, his second season as an NHL regular. That same campaign saw Chicago's Pierre Pilote win the second of what would prove to be three consecutive Norris trophies as the NHL's best defenseman.

NHLers in Parliament

Four players in NHL history have served terms as members of Parliament — Lionel Conacher (Liberal, Toronto-Trinity), Bucko McDonald (Liberal, Parry Sound-Muskoka), Howie Meeker (Progressive Conservative, Waterloo-South), and Red Kelly (Liberal, York West).

In 1963 Kelly defeated Alan Eagleson, who was a candidate for the Progressive Conservative Party.

Calder, and Jean Béliveau, who finished third in scoring, won the Hart.

In the 1964 playoffs, Imlach's trade for Bathgate and McKenney paid off as both former Rangers performed to their coach's expectations. The Leafs defeated the Canadiens in the semi-finals and then faced the Red Wings, who advanced by upsetting Chicago. After six games in which the two teams alternated victories, the Leafs prevailed with a 4–0 shutout in game seven to take their third consecutive Stanley Cup.

(continued on p. 168)

Bobby Baun takes a congratulatory sip of champagne after helping the Leafs defeat the Wings 4–0 in game seven of the 1964 Stanley Cup finals. Baun, who scored the overtime winner in game six while playing on a fractured ankle, provided the Leafs with an emotional lift when he played a regular shift in the deciding game of the finals.

LIFE ON THE OFF-RAMP: CHARACTERS AND FLAKES IN THE NHL

by Frank Orr

Character: a person who attracts attention for being different or eccentric.
Flake: a small, light mass; a soft, loose bit.

The late Fred Shero heard the suggestion that, as coach of the Philadelphia Flyers, Stanley Cup champions in 1974 and 1975, he lived in the fast lane. Shero disagreed with that viewpoint. "I don't live in the fast lane," he said. "I live on the off-ramp."

While the National Hockey League has always had citizens who drove in all lanes on the highway of life – fast, slow, and passing – the chaps who were on the off-ramps, on the shoulders, or in the ditch, have supplied the game with much of its appeal. Characters, flakes, different personalities, loonies, just plain old filberts, call them what you want, are entrenched deeply in the history and folklore of the game.

"Half the game is mental; the other half is being mental," said Jim McKenny, the resident wit and philosopher of the Toronto Maple Leafs in the 1970s, quoting a widely used line.

"You don't have to be crazy to play hockey, but it helps," said Bob Plager, a defenseman, scout, and minor-league coach for the St. Louis Blues and a busy dispenser of good humor. "Being a hockey player meant that my boyhood lasted a long time and I often asked myself what I was going to be when I grew up. If you take the game seriously, you go crazy anyway, so it helps if you're a bit nuts to start with, because you don't waste time getting that way."

From the day the NHL was founded in 1917, the nuts were prominent. The league motto – at least from the perspective of the game's early players – seemed to be: "We didn't make much money but we had a lot of fun." The finest historian of the game's nonsense, its patron saint of fun, Francis Michael "King" Clancy, was the confidant of every cashew in hockey history and had a tale to tell on each one.

From his first game in 1921 with the Ottawa Senators to his death in 1986, Clancy, who played defense at 135 pounds, brought joy to the NHL as a player, referee, coach, and executive. He spent his last fifteen years as buddy of the chairman of the board of the NHL "off-ramp" society, the late Harold Ballard, owner of the Maple Leafs.

As a referee, Clancy was legendary, although he admitted he never really learned all the rules, ruling more by good humor and banter than by the rule book. If a player swore at him, Clancy swore back.

He was renowned for his verbal exchanges with fans. A Toronto doctor in a rinkside seat often gave Clancy a rough ride, and finally King gave it back: "Maybe I'm not perfect, Doc, but I don't bury my mistakes like you do."

Clancy's yarns about some of the NHL's earliest stars embellish the game's history. He had his own version of poetic license in the telling of the yarns, but who cares? If King's stories were even reasonably accurate, meeting Sprague Cleghorn – was there ever a better name – would have been fun. The same goes for Bill Dwyer, the number-one bootlegger in New York during prohibition, who owned the New York Americans. Or Major Frederic McLaughlin, who gave Chicago the Black Hawks and who once hired a man he met on a train to coach his team.

While no accurate tabulation of flake-by-position is available, a strong claim can be made that a higher percentage of goaltenders have qualified for the designation than practitioners at any other position.

"Being a goaltender is not a job that would attract any normal, straight-thinking human," said Gump Worsley, a splendid goaltender through two decades. "People don't even know what we are," he lamented launching into one of his regular complaints. "The rule book only says that each team is allowed to dress seventeen men – plus two goalies."

Georges Vezina, called the Chicoutimi Cucumber because of his unflappable approach, was the first glamor goaltender and a member of the Canadiens from 1917 to 1926.

"Cripes, Georges probably figured that playing goal in an NHL game was the quietest spot in his life," King Clancy said. "After all, he was the father of twenty-two children."

Walter "Turk" Broda was another loose object, who often forgot to pay his bills, which meant the light and heat in his house were occasionally turned off. But among oldtimers, Turk is regarded as the best "money" goalie ever – at his best in the pres-

Turk Broda's famous "Battle of the Bulge" prompted hundreds of fans to send diet tips to the rotund Leaf netminder.

sure of the playoffs when, it was said, "Broda could catch lint in a hurricane."

Broda had a simple explanation for his playoff efforts. "The bonus money for winning wasn't much but I always needed it," he said. "Or maybe I was just too dumb to know the situation was serious."

A common theory is that because goaltending isn't a job that attracts chaps who fit the parameters of the so-called "normal" anyway, they can't be called nuts.

Johnny Bower was normal, except that he played in the NHL until he was forty-five. "Mr. Goalie," Glenn Hall, was normal except that he threw up before most games and often between periods and insisted he liked everything about hockey except the games. Jacques Plante was normal, too, except for 2,456 idiosyncrasies. "Goaltending a normal job?" Plante said. "Sure! How would you like it in your job if every time you made a mistake, a red light went on over your desk and fifteen thousand people stood up and yelled at you?"

Goaltenders from the six-team era didn't have a monopoly on being different. John Garrett, who played goal for several NHL teams, studied college Latin via correspondence. "It's a good language to have, because if I meet an ancient Roman, just think of the great conversation I can have with him." Garrett also studied Hebrew, which he said was very handy when his net partner was a born-again Christian who felt that prayer was a fine goaltending aid. "We work well together," Garrett said. "He can contact biblical figures and I can translate what they say for him."

Gilles Gratton will be an early inductee in any Hall of Fame for flakes and nuts. He was big on reincarnation, streaking, and meditation. He once claimed that he suffered a leg wound when he was a soldier in the Franco-Prussian war in a previous life and that it bothered him during games.

Then there are the head coaches. Most of them last fewer than three seasons behind the bench for any one NHL team. Each season, at least a couple of coaches are fired because they can't turn base metal into gold. When general managers tie the can to the man behind the bench (team owners avoid participation in the nasty job of sacking the coach), they often say they can't fire the team so they have to fire the coach. "Just think how refreshing it would be if that were reversed just once," said Roger Neilson, who had head or co-coaching stints with six NHL teams. "Wouldn't it be a shock if a general manager said that they were keeping the coach and getting rid of the whole team because no one on earth could extract a decent performance from such a terrible collection of players?"

The late Punch Imlach, who was general manager of the Leafs twice and Buffalo Sabres once, doubling as head coach much of the time, said it best: "As a coach – or general manager for that matter – you must always remember that when you're on your way in, you're on your way out. It all depends on how fast your old wheel is turning because your only end is the boot into the street."

While coaching turned many happy men bitter, Don Cherry and Harry Neale were coaches who retained their sense of humor through the ups and downs of NHL coaching stints. They were two of the most engaging flakes ever, very popular with the media, and both went on to be very successful as broadcasters on *Hockey Night in Canada* telecasts.

"When I was a kid, I prayed for enough talent to be a pro hockey player, but I forgot to say NHL because they only gave me enough to make the minors," said Cherry, who played only one NHL game in an eighteen-year career.

Cherry had five stormy, very successful years as coach of the Bruins in the 1970s, when his outrageous pronouncements made him the most quoted man in hockey. He made a celebrity out of his bull terrier Blue, claiming that he consulted the dog on hockey matters and that Blue ignored him when he came home after a loss. In his dazzling wardrobe, Cherry continues to be outrageous as a TV commentator. He strongly opposes the presence of European players in the NHL and Swedes are his main target. In the days before *glasnost*, the Soviets stirred things up by moving their submarines into Stockholm harbor, inspiring a fabled Cherry line: "It was easy for the Commies to hide," Cherry said. "They just put the subs in the corner of the harbor because everyone knows Swedes don't go in the corners."

The "Master of the Mouth," Don Cherry played only one NHL game, appearing with the Bruins in the final game of the 1955 semi-finals.

Neale had coaching stints with the Vancouver Canucks (he was also general manager) and the Detroit Red Wings and was a serious, intelligent coach who just happened to be a very funny man. His most famous line came during a prolonged Canuck losing streak. "We're losing at home; we can't win on the road," he said. "My failure as a coach is that I can't figure out any place else to play."

A few other Neale dandies:

"Our best system of forechecking is to shoot the puck in and leave it there."

"We have too many guys who are small but slow."

"We have a couple of defensemen who can rush once a game – and then we have to replace the puck."

After Curt Ridley, a Canuck goalie, injured both knees on one play, Neale was asked if he had ever seen such a happening before. "No, I never have," he said. "It's pretty good, too, because the NHL record is three."

"Clear the track! Here comes Shack!" Eddie the Entertainer posted at least one twenty-goal season for five different NHL teams.

Because no definitive list of hockey's leading eccentrics is available, how about a random look at a few fellows who skated and marched to a different drummer?

Eddie Shack never learned to read and write, but he proved that not everything a chap needs to know is picked up from books. Shack, who was selling poultry in his hometown of Sudbury, Ontario, when he was twelve years old, became a very wealthy man via land speculation and assorted business efforts such as selling Christmas trees. "Maybe I couldn't read books, but I sure learned to listen to guys who did," Shack said.

As a hockey player with several teams, notably the Maple Leafs, Shack was the flywheel come loose from the shaft, the closest thing to a whirling dervish the NHL has had, a winger of whom Imlach once said: "Shackie can play all three forward positions, but his trouble is that he tries to do it at the same time."

"Clear the track, here comes Shack" was the first line of a country song about Fast Eddie, who had several nicknames, the most whimsical of which was "Sugar," inspired by the pop song "Sugar Shack."

Fans everywhere loved Shack and the helter-skelter way he played the game.

"I think when people watched him and the sheer fun he had playing, they realized it was a little boys' game and that Shackie was one guy who never forgot it," said Bob Baun, the rock 'em defenseman on the great Leaf teams in the 1960s.

Wayne Cashman combined hard work, fun, and mayhem in a long NHL career with the Bruins. He was a superb cornerman, at his best at combat in the pits, producing many of the passes on which Phil Esposito scored his record-setting goals. Cash claimed corners were a large influence in his life. "I have to live in a house on a corner lot, and when I die, I hope they bury me in the corner plot of the cemetery, because if I'm in a corner, I'll be able to rest in peace forever."

There was Howie Young, who had a bad temper, considerable ability, and a serious problem with alcohol that often took him into unusual situations. Young quit hockey as a junior, saying he wanted to try "the real world," but quickly returned, claiming the real world wasn't as easy as he thought it would be.

The Red Wings gave Young assorted chances to make it as an NHL defenseman, but his short fuse kept him in constant on-ice trouble – his trademark red face in times of stress indicated a destructive tantrum on the way – and he simply could not avoid problems off the ice. On one occasion, when he hadn't come home from a night out, management received a call from the police. Howie had met a milkman during his nocturnal meanderings and gone home with him. The chap was unable to deliver his milk, so Howie took over his route for him, but lost the list of customers. Young simply left a quart on every front step on one street early one morning, then rang the doorbell to inform the occupants of the delivery. One customer called the police to complain; the cops recognized Howie and informed the team of his largesse with the dairy's products.

Then there was the Plager family – Barclay, Bob, and Bill – hockey's "royal family" of mayhem and fun. Bob's considerable ability as a storyteller is one big reason for the brothers' secure spot in puck folklore. He spun dandy whimsical yarns about their boyhood in Kirkland Lake, Ontario, and the many scraps he had with his brothers.

"Barc would beat me up, I would beat up Billy, and Billy would go across the street and pound the crap out of our cousin, who never could figure out why he was always getting clobbered," Bob said.

Barc (Peterborough Petes) and Bob (Guelph Royals) had a fabled fight in one junior hockey game – on the ice with sticks and in the arena corridors with fists. That prompted Bill to say: "I wish I'd been there. I would have slapped them both silly for making such asses of themselves."

Barclay, who died in 1988 after a valiant fight against cancer, stated what has become the tough players' credo: "It's not how many you win that's important; it's how many you show up for."

No list of hockey characters, the guys who were different, would be complete minus Bryan "Bugsy" Watson, a great pest and outstanding citizen – he was a devoted worker for worthy causes, notably the Special Olympics for the mentally handicapped. He also parlayed a modest bit of ability into a seventeen-season career.

Watson first gained notoriety with the Red Wings when he "shadowed" Bobby Hull, the NHL's best scorer, in a playoff series.

"Geez, did I get sick of that – going on the ice and

Howie Young, who always marched to the beat of a different drummer, makes his living today as an actor and movie stuntman.

the Black Hawks had Bobby Hull, who wasn't even a good checker, covering me!" Bugsy said.

Watson supplied perhaps the most creative explanation ever for missing on a breakaway. While a Washington Capital, Watson went in alone from center and missed the net by at least forty feet. When he returned to the bench, Tommy McVie, the Caps' coach at the time, asked, "Bugsy, what the hell happened?"

"Coach," Watson replied, "I couldn't get my stick out of cross-check."

Hockey is high-speed excitement and tension, and the NHL version of the sport is the finest in the world, so it is a tribute to the league and its players that – amidst the pressure, the precision, and the toughness – characters, flakes, rebels, oddballs, and iconoclasts have flourished for seventy-five years.

Imlach continued to alter the make-up of the Leafs by acquiring talented veterans. For the 1964-65 season, he convinced former Canadiens' scoring star Dickie Moore to return to the NHL after a season in retirement because of recurring knee problems. Imlach also grabbed veteran goaltender Terry Sawchuk, left unprotected by the Red Wings, who believed that Roger Crozier was ready to be their club's number-one netminder.

The Red Wings reactivated a veteran player of their own, bringing back left winger Ted Lindsay, who had been out of hockey for four seasons. The Bruins traded Doug Mohns to Chicago for Reg Fleming, Murray Balfour, and Ab McDonald. The Black Hawks also added Fred Stanfield and Dennis Hull, a pair of left wingers from their junior club in St. Catharines, Ontario. Phil Esposito, who had played in 27 NHL games in 1963-64, scored 23 goals in his first full season with Chicago. The Canadiens inserted speedy Yvan Cournoyer into the line-up for 55 games, while Jacques Laperrière established himself as one of the league's finest defensemen. In a mid-season deal, the club acquired Dick Duff from the Rangers in exchange for Billy Hicke.

In New York, general manager Emile Francis released Doug Harvey and gave regular ice time to defensemen Arnie Brown and Rod Seiling, who had come to the Rangers from Toronto in the McKenney–Bathgate deal. Boston was led by Johnny Bucyk, who would finish the season with 26 goals. The Leafs added center Pete Stemkowski and right winger Ron Ellis, both of whom were former members of the Toronto Marlboros junior club.

Early in the season, the Leafs lost Frank Mahovlich, when the high-scoring winger was hospitalized suffering from stress. In Detroit, Gordie Howe continued his assault on the NHL record book, scoring his 627th combined regular-season and playoff goal to eclipse the mark established by Maurice Richard. Ted Lindsay's four-year sabbatical didn't appear to have cooled down the left winger's notorious temper. When he was fined for disputing a penalty call with a referee, he refused to pay, giving in only when president Campbell threatened to suspend him.

By mid-season, the Rangers and Bruins again seemed likely to miss the playoffs, and Toronto's hopes were dimming as the Cup champions languished in fourth place. Imlach shuffled his line-up, moving Tim Horton to right wing on a line with Dave Keon and Eddie Shack. Don McKenney and Billy Harris were sent down to the Leafs' American Hockey League farm club in Rochester, New York, though McKenney would return in time for the playoffs. Despite these and other maneuvers, the Leafs finished the season in fourth place, 13 points behind first-place Detroit.

Toronto's veteran goaltending duo of Johnny Bower and Terry Sawchuk shared the Vezina Trophy, while another goaltender, Detroit's Roger Crozier, won the Calder as top rookie. The rest of the NHL's individual awards went to members of the Black Hawks – Bobby Hull won the Hart and Lady Byng, Stan Mikita edged out Detroit's Norm Ullman for the Art Ross, and Pierre Pilote won the Norris.

Roger Crozier puts his best foot forward to silence this Chicago attack while Bill Gadsby and Stan Mikita jockey for position near the Detroit crease. Crozier became the first goaltender and first member of a losing team to be awarded the Conn Smythe Trophy in 1966.

The Black Hawks, led by Hull's eight goals, eliminated the first-place Red Wings in a seven-game semi-final. The Canadiens earned the right to face Chicago by defeating the Maple Leafs on Claude Provost's overtime goal in game six in Toronto. In the finals, the Canadiens effectively shackled Bobby Hull, holding the stellar left winger to just two goals, both scored in Chicago's 5–1 win in game four. Gump Worsley and Charlie Hodge split the goaltending duties for the Canadiens, Worsley recording two shutouts, Hodge one. Worsley's 4–0 win in game seven brought the Stanley Cup back to Montreal and gave the Gumper his first Cup triumph in twelve NHL seasons. The new Conn Smythe Trophy was awarded for the first time to the top playoff performer, Jean Béliveau.

Having won the Cup the previous year, Toe Blake felt little urgency to tinker with his roster for the 1965-66 season. Chicago, the other finalist for the Stanley Cup in the spring of 1965, added Pat Stapleton and Ken Hodge.

The New York Rangers signed goaltender Eddie Giacomin, while the Bruins added Bernie Parent and Gerry Cheevers. All three would eventually be inducted into the Hockey Hall of Fame. Boston also acquired Johnny McKenzie, Ron Stewart, and Gilles Marotte, and, though the club improved, manager Hap Emms was already dreaming of the day when Boston's sensational junior prospect, Bobby Orr, would wear the Bruins' jersey.

The Leafs and the Red Wings, both eliminated in the semi-finals, engineered an eight-man trade in May of 1965. Andy Bathgate, Billy Harris, and Gary Jarrett went to Detroit in exchange for Marcel Pronovost, Larry Jeffrey, and three other players. Detroit also picked up Don McKenney on waivers from the Leafs.

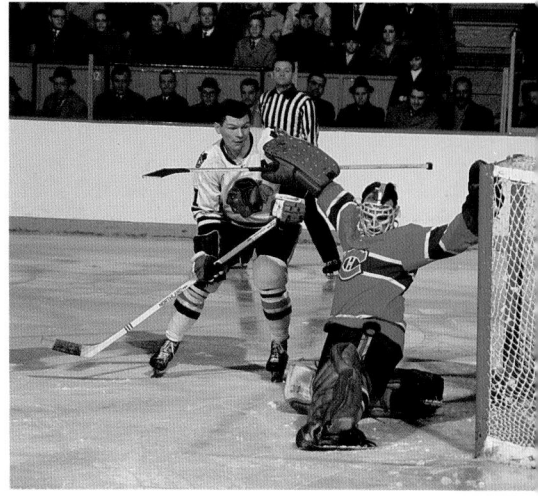

Stan Mikita watches as Montreal's Charlie Hodge kicks away a shot from the slot. Mikita, who led the league in penalty minutes in 1963-64, won the Lady Byng Trophy in 1967 when he spent only twelve minutes in the penalty box.

Goaltender Eddie Giacomin recorded nine shutouts and was selected to the First All-Star Team in 1966-67, his second season with the Rangers.

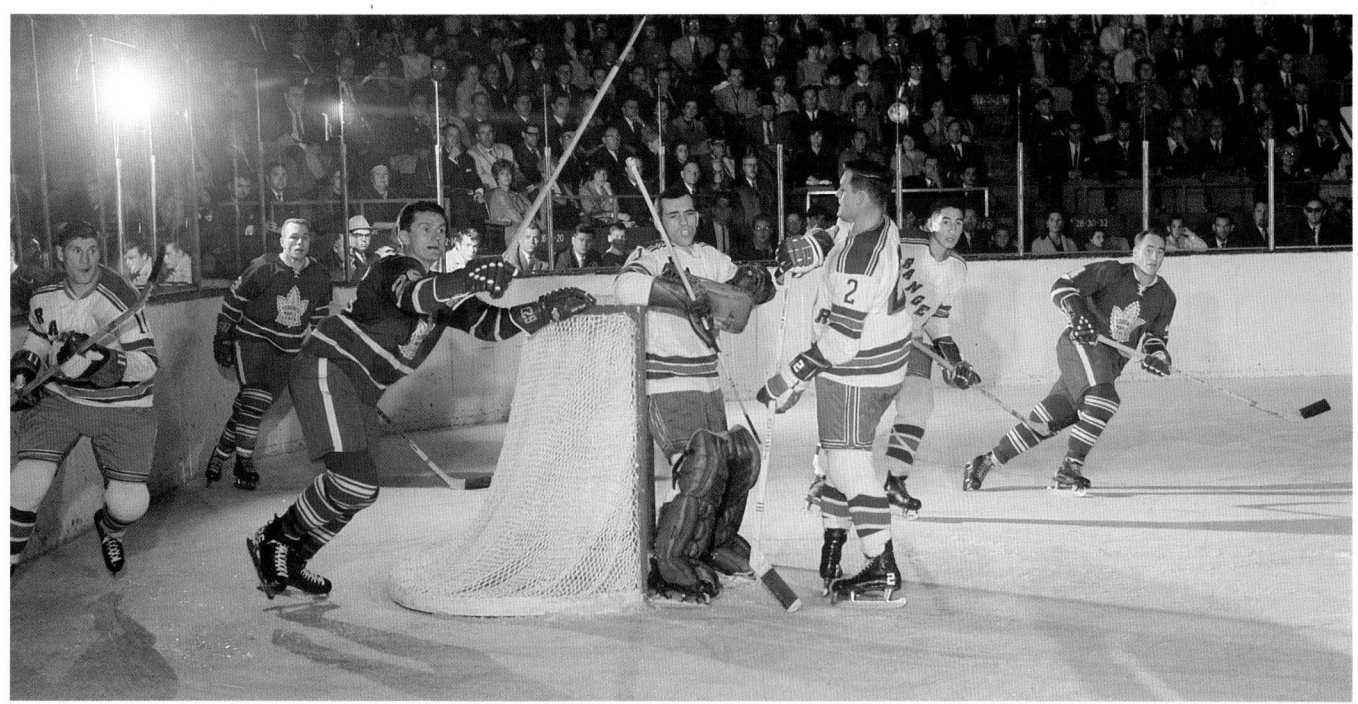

Toronto added size up front, acquiring Orland Kurtenbach in an off-season deal with the Bruins. Punch Imlach faced difficult contract negotiations with defensemen Bob Baun and Carl Brewer, both of whom wanted more money. Baun eventually signed, but Brewer announced his retirement. The Leafs also signed forward Brian Conacher, who came to pro hockey with an impeccable pedigree: his father, Lionel, and his uncle, Charlie, had been NHL stars in the 1920s and 1930s. Conacher, who had played with the Canadian National Team that competed in the IIHF World Championships, demanded a contract that guaranteed he would not play in the minors. Imlach flatly refused, and Conacher spent all but two games of the 1965-66 season with the Leafs' Rochester farm club. He would, however, become a regular on left wing with the Leafs the following season.

Gordie Howe reached yet another milestone when he scored his 600th NHL regular-season goal against Gump Worsley in Montreal on November 27, 1965. Howe's achievement, coming in his twentieth NHL campaign, was felt to be beyond the reach of other players. The only active player who had a chance to come even close to Howe's career marks was felt to be Bobby Hull, who, in 1965-66, broke through the magic 50-goal barrier with 54. Hull scored his 51st on March 12 against Cesare Maniago of the Rangers. He also set a new single-season point-scoring record with 97, one better than Dickie Moore's mark of 96 set in 1958-59.

Expansion of the NHL had been under discussion since air travel had begun to provide easier intercity connections across the continent. In February of 1966, Clarence Campbell announced that the NHL had awarded conditional expansion franchises to Los Angeles, Minneapolis–St. Paul, Philadelphia, Pittsburgh, St. Louis, and San Francisco. These new clubs would begin play in the 1967-68 season in a twelve-team NHL. The concern that doubling the size of the league would result in reduced quality of play was partially offset by the belief that many talented players existed, but had left pro hockey because of the scarcity of big-league jobs in the six-team NHL.

At the end of the regular season, it was clear that the defending Cup-champion Canadiens were still the class of the NHL, as they finished in first place with 90 points. Chicago, Toronto, and Detroit followed, while Boston and New York were once more out of the playoffs. The Bruins' fifth-place finish marked the first time the club had ended the season out of the league basement since 1959-60. Hull's record-breaking season earned him the Art Ross and Hart trophies, and Montreal goaltenders Charlie Hodge and Gump Worsley shared the Vezina. Third-year defenseman Jacques Laperrière won the Norris, while Toronto's Brit Selby won the Calder Trophy, scoring 14 goals in his rookie campaign.

The Canadiens proved to be unstoppable in the playoffs. Defenseman J. C. Tremblay's two goals and nine assists led the Habs to a semi-final sweep of the Leafs and a six-game triumph over the Red Wings in the finals. Game six was decided on a disputed overtime goal, as the puck found the net after

Allan Stanley (center), Claude Provost (right), and Dave Balon (left) battle for a loose puck during the 1964 semi-finals. Stanley played on four of the "original six" teams, finally winning the Stanley Cup after he joined the Leafs in 1959. Provost, who won nine Stanley Cups in his career, is the only player to have played on that many championship teams without being a member of the Hockey Hall of Fame.

colliding with a sliding Henri Richard. Detroit goaltender Roger Crozier won the Conn Smythe Trophy. For Toe Blake, Jean Béliveau, Henri Richard, Jean-Guy Talbot, and Claude Provost, the Cup victory was their seventh in eleven seasons.

The New York Rangers presented the NHL with the Lester Patrick Trophy, to be awarded for outstanding service to hockey in the United States. Former Detroit manager Jack Adams was its first winner.

With an Expansion Draft scheduled for June of 1967, most of the NHL's "original" six clubs made only modest roster changes for 1966-67. The Boston Bruins welcomed brilliant rookie defenseman Bobby Orr to their line-up, as well as Harry Sinden, who, at thirty-four, was the youngest head coach in the NHL.

Bobby Orr takes flight during an exhibition game prior to the 1966-67 campaign. Orr, who is wearing number 27 in this rare photo, transformed the Bruins from perennial cellar-dwellers to Stanley Cup champions in four years.

The Canadiens dealt Red Berenson to the Rangers. Berenson, who first appeared in the Canadiens' line-up in 1962, was the first player to jump directly from U.S. college hockey to the NHL. The Habs also brought up defenseman Carol Vadnais and goaltender Rogie Vachon. Chicago added rookie Ed Van Impe on defense, while Denis DeJordy joined the club as a back-up to goaltender Glenn Hall. In Detroit, the Red Wings lost two starting defensemen; Bill Gadsby retired, and an eye injury forced Doug Barkley to end his promising career. The Rangers reacquired Orland Kurtenbach and also coaxed Bernie Geoffrion out of a two-year retirement. Rod Gilbert, who injured his back in February, made a successful return from major surgery. In Toronto, the Leafs soldiered on with a veteran line-up at least five of whose members were in their late thirties or early forties.

The Black Hawks won seven of their first ten games, but at the season's halfway point, the Rangers sat alone in first place, two points ahead of Chicago. New York's fine play had been drawing sellout crowds to Madison Square Garden. This attendance increase enabled hockey to take precedence when scheduling conflicts with the circus threatened to disrupt the Rangers' playoff schedule in April. The team's success was due, in part, to all-star seasons by goaltender Ed Giacomin and by veteran defenseman Harry Howell, who won the Norris Trophy for 1967.

Both Toronto and Montreal experienced difficulties during the regular season. The Canadiens seemed to lose their scoring touch, a problem that Toe Blake blamed on the number of players who had been experimenting with pronounced curves in their sticks. The Leafs' poor performance resulted partly from injuries to Red Kelly, Frank Mahovlich, and Terry Sawchuk, but Imlach also accused the rest of his team of underachieving, and he became so distraught at a lengthy losing streak in February that he entered hospital suffering from exhaustion. With Imlach temporarily replaced by easygoing King Clancy, the Leafs loosened up considerably, going ten games without a loss, as Bower and Sawchuk took turns shutting down the opposition. Sawchuk posted his hundredth shutout against the Black Hawks on March 4.

The biggest story of the year was the play of Bobby Orr in Boston. Despite a knee injury that forced him out for three weeks, he was easily the most exciting new performer in the NHL and an instant favorite with Boston fans, who repeatedly packed Boston Garden to see him in action. Orr was not the first defenseman to direct his team's attack. Doug Harvey had done so for years in Montreal, and Pierre Pilote continued to run the show for the Black Hawks in Chicago. Orr, though, not only choreographed the Boston offense, but was its spearhead with his whirling rushes and accurate passing and shooting. At the end of the regular season he was awarded the Calder Trophy, finishing with 13 goals and 41 points, second only to Pilote among defensemen.

Chicago was clearly the NHL's top team in the last regular season of the six-team NHL. The Black Hawks captured their first league championship in forty years, breaking what had become known as the "Curse of Muldoon." (Pete Muldoon was the Hawks' first coach who, upon being fired, vowed that the team would never finish in first place. Muldoon, in fact, said no such thing; the "Curse" was invented by a sportswriter in 1941.) Cursed or not, the Hawks finished 17 points ahead of the second-place Canadiens, who were followed closely by Toronto and New York. Chicago's 264 goals set a new single-season record, surpassing the 259 goals scored by Montreal in 1961-62. Three of the league's top four scorers were members of the Black Hawks. Stan Mikita tied Bobby Hull's single-season individual scoring record with 97 points. Hull, despite a late-season injury, scored 52 goals, and Kenny Wharram was the league's fourth-highest scorer with 31 goals and 65 points. Chicago was sound defensively as well: Denis DeJordy and Glenn Hall shared the Vezina Trophy, and Pierre Pilote was runner-up for the Norris.

The 1966-67 season witnessed a remarkable turnaround in the career of Stan Mikita, who had long been one of the league's most penalized players. Through intense self-discipline, he cut his penalty time to a mere twelve minutes and became the first player to win three individual awards – the Art Ross, the Hart, and the Lady Byng trophies – in a single season.

The Red Wings fell from a place in the Stanley Cup finals in 1966 to fifth place in 1966-67. Norm Ullman was the club's top scorer, and Gordie Howe became the NHL's longest-serving player by completing his twenty-first season. Howe scored 25 goals, giving him a record eighteen consecutive 20-goal seasons. To bolster the club's depleted defense, Howie Young was reacquired from Chicago and Doug Harvey was called up from the AHL to play two games.

The Hawks were heavily favored to win their second Stanley Cup of the 1960s. But a dogged and inspired Toronto team, with brilliant goalkeeping from Sawchuk and Bower, shut down Chicago's high-scoring attack and led the Leafs to a six-game upset win in the semi-finals. In the other semi-final series, the Rangers' first playoff appearance in five years was a flop; they were defeated in four straight games by the Canadiens. The resulting all-Canadian final was the first such match-up since 1960 and was a highlight of the nation's 1967 Centennial celebrations. The series again served as a showcase for the Leafs' goaltending duo, and Toronto's veteran line-up closed out the six-team era with a six-game final series victory over the Canadiens. Dave Keon, whose tireless skating and checking paced the Leafs, was awarded the Conn Smythe Trophy.

(continued on p. 179)

Multiple Cup-Winners

Only three players in the history of the NHL have won multiple Stanley Cups with more than one team. Frank Mahovlich won two Cups with the Montreal Canadiens and four with the Toronto Maple Leafs. Dick Duff played on two Cup winners in Toronto and four in Montreal. Red Kelly, who won four Cups with Detroit and four with Toronto, is the only player to win at least six Stanley Cup rings and not play for Montreal.

Yvan Cournoyer prepares to fire a backhand shot at the Toronto Maple Leafs' net during the 1967 Stanley Cup playoffs. Cournoyer, known as "the Roadrunner" during his sixteen years in the NHL, won the Conn Smythe Trophy in 1973 when he set a playoff record with 25 post-season points.

CLARENCE CAMPBELL AND EXPANSION '67

by Brian O'Neill

I f any one person could be singled out as the driving force of the 1967 expansion, it would be William Jennings of the New York Rangers, who submitted a memo to his fellow governors in September 1963 about the possibility of expanding to the West Coast, starting with two clubs that would

William Jennings of the New York Rangers lobbied for the NHL to expand to the West Coast of the United States.

begin play in the 1964-65 season. At the time, he was concerned that the Western Hockey League would compete as a "major" hockey league and, in fact, that league did indicate the following year that it did not plan to renew its agreement to act as part of the minor-pro farm system that fed the NHL.

Jennings's concern about the WHL was, of course, not his sole motivation in recommending an expansion of the NHL. He hoped, rather, that additional teams on the West Coast would give the league a truly national status and a better opportunity for access to network television in the United States. His memo was discussed at the October 1963 meeting of the NHL Board of Governors and, following that rendezvous, the topic of expansion was included at every Governors' meeting until the franchises were awarded in 1966.

In a matter as radical as this there were, of course, divergent views about the number of teams to be admitted and the plan for allocation of players. It appeared, however, that the governors arrived at the asking fee of $2,000,000 with very little debate. But, after the fact, several of them decided that the asking price had been too low.

Bill Jennings later acknowledged that he had changed the views he expressed in his original 1963 memo, and had come to believe that the NHL's best approach to expansion was the creation of a second division of six teams, to begin play in 1967-68.

The hottest issue of all in the 1967 expansion was the matter of allocation of players to the new franchises. It was reported that Clarence Campbell fought fiercely for a plan that would allow the new teams to be competitive from the outset. He proposed that each established club should be allowed to exempt only nine players from the Expansion Draft, whereas several clubs favored a protected list of fourteen. It was politely pointed out to Mr. Campbell that, although he was president of the league, the owners were the ones who had to relinquish their assets, and the decision would, of necessity, rest with them. Mr. Campbell did not entirely lose out, since the eventual protected list ended up at eleven. The plan, which was credited primarily to Montreal Canadiens' manager Sam Pollock, was obviously a compromise between the strong teams that had much to lose and the weaker established teams that viewed expansion as an opportunity to restore the balance of competition. However, even though the protected list ended up at eleven, the procedure of "claim-and-fill" helped ease the pain for teams that were concerned with the loss of quality players. "Claim-and-fill" allowed a team that had had a player claimed by an expansion club to add one more player to its protected list.

Once the decision to add six teams was made in 1965, the question arose as to how much interest there would be from potential franchise owners in Canada and the United States. As it turned out, the response was encouraging. Fourteen applications were received, four of which were for the Los Angeles area. The only other city that had competing bids was Pittsburgh, where two groups sought a franchise.

At the February 1966 meeting of the Board of Governors, all applications were reviewed and applicants interviewed. It was decided to award franchises to Philadelphia, Pittsburgh, Minnesota, San Francisco, and Los Angeles; the unsuccessful bidders were Baltimore, Buffalo, and Vancouver.

The governors also decided at that meeting that, even though St. Louis did not submit an application at the time, the city would be granted a franchise, providing an acceptable application was received by April 5, 1966. This decision was influenced by the Wirtz and Norris families, who owned the St. Louis Arena. If no suitable candidate had come forward for St. Louis, the sixth franchise would have been granted to Baltimore.

The applicants that were not successful were disappointed, but in two cases this disappointment was short-lived, as Buffalo and Vancouver were accepted two years later.

Some very prominent names were among the applicants for these franchises. Bing Crosby, Jack Kent Cooke, Dan Reeves, Senator Jack McGregor, Douglas Fairbanks, Jr., Bill Putnam, and Senator Stuart Symington were either major shareholders or provided support for a local bid. Although the applicants were largely successful businessmen, they were prepared to put up money without full knowledge of what they were buying. Unlike the NHL's

Terry Sawchuk, along with Glenn Hall and Charlie Hodge, was one of three former Vezina Trophy-winners tending goal for new expansion clubs in 1967-68.

current procedure, the applicants did not have precise knowledge of the plan of expansion before they put in their entries. In fact, it was only at the same February meeting at which franchises were granted that the assignment to prepare a plan of player draft and allocation was given to Sam Pollock.

It has been suggested that Clarence Campbell did not support expansion to twelve teams. His concern, of course, focused on the ultimate quality of play that would result. He did not feel that the supply of amateur players would be forthcoming, and to some extent his misgivings were well founded, since the top amateur players were tied up by the six teams already operating, through the process of sponsorship. But as might have been expected, expansion was the catalyst that spurred amateur hockey to greater heights. More players realized their goals of playing hockey at the NHL level, which reverberated in a substantial increase in registrations in the Canadian Amateur Hockey Association and the Amateur Hockey Association of the United States.

This is not to say that hockey in the immediate post-expansion period did not suffer in quality as a result of dilution. A lapse was anticipated, but it was expected that a new level of quality would eventually be established because of additional opportunities for careers in the NHL. This expectation was fulfilled.

The 1968 Cup finals pitted the Canadiens against the St. Louis Blues, a veteran squad that featured Glenn Hall (right) in goal and Doug Harvey (center) on defense.

There was a general feeling at the time of expansion that minor professional teams would be able to supply a sufficient number of players in the expansion draft to allow the new clubs to be competitive. Of course, the creation of a new division made up exclusively of the expansion teams reduced the necessity for the new to be on a par with the old six. Four of the new six were guaranteed a position in the playoffs, and it was only in the finals where they had to meet head on with the stronger, established division.

The stated objectives of the NHL at the time of expansion are worthy of note:

1. Through the establishment of the new division, the NHL will become the only major professional league operating coast-to-coast in the United States and Canada.

2. The quality of NHL hockey will not be affected in any material way during the establishment of the new division. In the opinion of the Board of Governors, this is a most realistic objective. There are numerous players today in the minor professional leagues who could play effectively in the NHL. With the acquisition by the new franchises of top caliber players through the New Division

Player Purchase Plan, these other players will help provide the additional talent for competitive teams. Further, with twice the number of NHL jobs available, many more of the fine Canadian junior players will continue their hockey careers than is now the case. An additional factor will be the potential introduction to NHL ranks of a substantial number of young United States players.

When the Governors were considering what cities would be granted franchises, the first announcement indicated that Los Angeles and St. Louis had acceptable arenas and therefore were prime candidates. In a subsequent news release in October 1965, the Board of Governors stated that it had approved San Francisco–Oakland and Vancouver as acceptable cities for the league's new division, and that, together with Los Angeles and St. Louis, potential sites for four out of the six teams were now established. As events unfolded, however, Vancouver was to wait for the second phase of expansion before entry into the league.

It was a source of concern for Clarence Campbell when Vancouver was not admitted in the 1967 expansion, especially since the city had been approved as a suitable candidate for a team. He certainly was instrumental in the decision to guarantee Vancouver a franchise in the next phase of expansion. It was typical of the man that he felt personally that he had let the city of Vancouver down and he was determined to make amends.

This entire period of expansion was traumatic for Campbell. He was faced with the task of adjusting the league's operation to administer the affairs of not six but twelve teams. This presented a scheduling problem, increased activity in the Central Registry Department, because of the need to keep track of upwards of two to three hundred more players, and meant that the Finance Department now had to employ computers to maintain league accounts.

The new look of the league also made necessary increased public relations and marketing, which were practically nonexistent at the time, and higher staffing levels – a switch for Clarence Campbell, who had always boasted that the success of his operation was based on a small, highly competent staff. He was, however, persuaded primarily by Bill

Jennings and David Molson of Montreal that additional staff were required, particularly at the senior level. To this end the league governors hired a search company to fill one senior position in Montreal and another in New York, where a new league office was to be established. Campbell was not keen on "babysitting" a new executive in the Montreal office, but nevertheless acquiesced to the wishes of the owners and undertook to work with the successful applicant.

He was somewhat surprised at the number of candidates interested in these openings, and in particular those interested in the one in Montreal. Over 125 applications were reviewed, and after this number was reduced to six, Campbell made the decision about the successful candidate, even though all the individuals on the short list were interviewed by Jennings and Molson.

President Clarence Campbell, who served as the NHL's chief executive for thirty-one years, oversaw the league's growth from six teams in 1946 to eighteen in 1977.

With established stars like Bobby Baun and Charlie Hodge, the California Seals were favored to win both on the ice and at the box-office. However, they missed the playoffs in seven of their nine seasons in Oakland and were transferred to Cleveland in 1976.

Having acquiesced to the new wave, Campbell took advantage of the situation. I was the Montreal appointee and, on my first day in the office, was immediately given responsibility for the league schedule. Campbell took an hour to explain the intricacies, and then, with a great sigh of relief, retired to his office. From there on in, he retained only a cursory interest in that phase of the operation.

Clarence Campbell may have been slow in accepting the new look of the league, but to his credit he was quick to adjust and faced the changes with enthusiasm. He made a special effort to work with the new owners and shared with them the expertise he had acquired over his thirty-odd years of association with the league. He was particularly helpful in lining up staff for the new clubs.

Although he ruled the league for only ten more years after the 1967 expansion, it is almost certain that those were the years that challenged him the most. His contribution to the growth and stability of the National Hockey League and to hockey wherever it was played was immense.

Expansion Time

A S THE NHL HEADED INTO ITS EXPANSION SEASON OF 1967-68, THE league's popularity in its "original" six cities had never been higher. In Chicago, the Black Hawks were at the peak of their game and were playing in front of sellout crowds. The Rangers had rekindled hockey interest in New York with a competitive club, and even Boston, the weakest team of the 1960s, was enjoying full houses attracted by the remarkable skills of Bobby Orr. The Bruins had become a bigger draw than basketball's Celtics in Boston Garden. Throughout the 1960s, 93 per cent of the tickets available for NHL games were sold.

Expansion meant dramatic changes in the business of hockey – including ownership's absolute control over player salaries. It was Bobby Orr who ushered in hockey's new age, retaining Toronto lawyer Alan Eagleson to act as his agent in the negotiation of his first contract with the Boston Bruins in 1966. Bruins' general manager Hap Emms had offered Orr a standard rookie contract: an annual salary of $8,000, plus a $5,000 bonus. At first, Emms refused to deal with Eagleson, but when Orr stood firm, he eventually sat down with the young star's representative. In the end, Orr signed a two-year contract worth $75,000. Word of Eagleson's coup quickly spread, leading to the reconstitution of the NHL Players' Association, which hired Eagleson to negotiate with the NHL on behalf of its members. Eagleson coordinated the NHLPA'S effort to be recognized by the league's board of governors as the players' official bargaining agent. Early negotiations between the league and the NHLPA were tense, but agreements were reached which raised the minimum NHL salary from $7,500 to $10,000, increased the players' share of playoff revenues to $567,000 beginning in 1967-68, and provided players with increased opportunities to earn money from endorsements.

Many of the new franchise owners had sports experience. San Francisco's Barry Van Gerbig, for instance, was a former goaltender for the Princeton University Tigers. He led a group that was associated with the Ice Follies and

Opposite: Buffalo's Rick Martin, checked here by Serge Savard of the Canadiens, played left wing on the Sabres' successful French Connection Line in the early- to mid-1970s. The Sabres eliminated the Canadiens in the 1975 semi-finals to become the first expansion club to defeat Montreal in a post-season series. Buffalo then went on to face Philadelphia in the NHL's first all-expansion final.

Below: With eight goals and seven assists in fourteen games, Minnesota's Bill Goldsworthy was the NHL's leading playoff scorer in the league's first expansion season.

The 1967-68 Los Angeles Kings were coached by Red Kelly and finished second in the West Division, one point behind the Flyers.

Front row (left to right): Norm Mackie (trainer), Howie Hughes, Howie Menard, Red Kelly (coach), Jack Kent Cooke (owner), Larry Regan (general manager), Bob Wall, Réal Lemieux, Danny Wood (assistant trainer).

Second row (left to right): Wayne Rutledge, Paul Popiel, Eddie Joyal, Bryan Campbell, Terry Gray, Brent Hughes, Lowell Mac-Donald, Terry Sawchuk.

Third row (left to right): Bill Flett, Jim Murray, Dale Rolfe, Jacques Lemieux, Gordon Labossiere, Brian Smith, Ted Irvine.

Back row (left to right): Dave Amadio, Bill White, Mike Corbett, Doug Robinson, Jacques Caron.

the Western Hockey League's San Francisco Seals, whose name the NHL team adopted. Hoping to attract fans from both sides of San Francisco Bay, the club began play in the NHL as the "California" Seals, but changed to the "Oakland" Seals in November when early-season crowds proved disappointing. Van Gerbig had hired former Black Hawk coach Rudy Pilous as general manager and coach of the WHL Seals (Pilous turned down a job with the Boston Bruins to move to California, leaving the Bruins' job to Harry Sinden), but replaced him with former Montreal Canadien and Toronto Maple Leaf Bert Olmstead a month before the team joined the NHL.

California's other NHL franchise, the Los Angeles Kings, went to Jack Kent Cooke, a transplanted Canadian, who already owned the city's National Basketball Association Lakers and had once owned Toronto's only professional baseball team, the Triple A Maple Leafs. Cooke, who beat out Dan Reeves, owner of the National Football League's Rams, for ownership of the NHL franchise, showed his good faith by promising to build the 16,000-seat Forum in which the Kings and Lakers play to this day. Until the Forum opened in December 1967, however, the Kings played in the Long Beach Arena and the Los Angeles Sports Arena. Cooke hired former NHL player Larry Regan as general manager and then scooped Red Kelly from the Toronto Maple Leafs as coach, only a year after Kelly had helped the Leafs win the Stanley Cup in the last year of the six-team league. In fact, Cooke would soon prove the equal of any of the existing teams' management and ownership when it came to maneuvering behind the scenes.

In Minnesota, where hockey had long been popular at the minor-league, high-school, and collegiate levels, ownership of the new NHL franchise, the North Stars, was granted to Gordon Ritz, Bob McNulty, and former college player Walter Bush, Jr. Together, the trio had operated the Central Hockey League's Minnesota Bruins in the twin cities of Minneapolis–St. Paul. For their NHL venture, they built a new rink in Bloomington, close to the two cities, and hired Wren Blair as coach and general manager. Blair, a veteran junior and minor pro coach and manager, had considerable NHL experience as a scout and director of minor-league personnel for the Boston Bruins. Blair also had a background in international hockey, having managed the Whitby (Ontario) Dunlops, IIHF world amateur champions in 1958.

Pittsburgh had previously been the home of an NHL club, the Pirates, who played from 1925-26 to 1929-30. Like Minnesota, the city also had a successful minor professional hockey franchise. Indeed, a year before local businessman Peter Black and Pennsylvania Senator Jack McGregor led a local group to buy the NHL franchise, the city's Hornets had won the American Hockey League championship. In addition, the city already had a suitable arena, the dome-roofed Civic Arena, dubbed "The Igloo" by locals. This gave rise to the NHL team's name, the Penguins. The team was managed by Jack Riley and coached by former New York Ranger Red Sullivan.

Philadelphia was no stranger to the NHL, having been home to the short-lived Quakers in 1930-31. The new Philadelphia ownership was put together by Ed Snider, who had been involved in the NFL Eagles franchise, and Joe Scott, after Snider bought out two other initial partners. The Flyers, named (as were many other new franchises) following a local contest, hired Norman "Bud" Poile as general manager and Keith Allen as coach, and planned to play in a new arena named the Spectrum.

Like Philadelphia, St. Louis had been the home of a one-season NHL team, the Eagles of 1934-35. But in the era of train travel, the city was felt to be too far away from the other clubs in the league, and the team folded. The expansion of 1967, however, placed St. Louis in the center of the NHL map. Sid Salomon, Jr., and his son Sid Salomon III, acquired the St. Louis franchise and promptly paid $6 million to buy and renovate the St. Louis Arena, where the St. Louis Blues would play. Lynn Patrick, whose lineage in hockey went back to his father's and uncle's roles as pioneer players and executives, was hired as general manager. Patrick also coached the team for their first sixteen games and then hired coach Scotty Bowman, a thirty-four-year-old player-development specialist from the Montreal system.

Once the decision to expand was made, NHL administrators devoted considerable discussion to devising a system to stock the new teams. Clarence Campbell was forced into a balancing act: the owners of established teams wanted to protect as much talent as possible, while the owners of new clubs, each of whom had paid $2 million to join the league, wanted recognizable, good-quality players, who would score goals and sell tickets.

Six-Team Player

Bronco Horvath was the only NHL player to have signed for all "original" six teams. Horvath signed with Detroit, but was traded to the New York Rangers before he had a chance to play for the Wings. From there, Horvath went to Montreal, Boston, Chicago, and Toronto, before finishing his NHL career with the Minnesota North Stars.

NATIONAL HOCKEY LEAGUE EXPANSION DRAFT
Montreal, June 6, 1967
EAST DIVISION PROTECTED PLAYERS AND FILLS
(Names in boldface type indicate players in original protected lists of one goaltender and 11 forwards and defencemen for each team.)

BOSTON BRUINS

Goaltenders
Gerry Cheevers
Ed Johnston

Forwards & Defencemen
John Bucyk
Ted Green
Ed Westfall
Tom Williams
John McKenzie
Don Awrey
Ken Hodge
Phil Esposito
Eddie Shack
Fred Stanfield
Gary Doak
Dallas Smith
Phillip Krake
Ron Buchanan
Wayne Cashman
Jean Pronovost
Bob Heaney
Ted Hodgson
Ron Murphy
John Arbour
Glen Sather
David Woodley
Brian Bradley
Ted Snell
Wayne Maxner
Bob Leiter

CHICAGO BLACK HAWKS

Goaltenders
Denis DeJordy
Dave Dryden

Forwards & Defencemen
Dennis Hull
Bobby Hull
Doug Jarrett
Chico Maki
Gilles Marotte
Pit Martin
Stan Mikita
Doug Mohns
Pierre Pilote
Pat Stapleton
Ken Wharram
Eric Nesterenko
Wayne Maki
Matt Ravlich
Paul Terbenche
Geoffrey Powis
Doug Shelton
Wayne Smith
Mike Chernoff
Roger Bellerive
Albert LeBrun
Oscar Gaudet
Jack Stanfield
Brian McDonald
Dick Meissner
Ross Eichler

DETROIT RED WINGS

Goaltenders
Roger Crozier
George Gardner

Forwards & Defencemen
Gary Bergman
Bert Marshall
Bob McCord
Alex Delvecchio
Gordie Howe
Norm Ullman
Paul Henderson
Bruce MacGregor
Dean Prentice
Ted Hampson
Doug Roberts
Howie Young
Floyd Smith
Gary Jarrett
Bob Falkenberg
Nick Libett
Ron Anderson
Craig Cameron
Jim Watson
George Harris
Irv Spencer
Jim Peters
Fred Hilts
Gary Marsh
Rick McCann
Larry Billows

MONTREAL CANADIENS

Goaltenders
Lorne Worsley
Rogatien Vachon

Forwards & Defencemen
Jean Claude Tremblay
Jacques Laperriere
Terry Harper
Ted Harris
Jean Beliveau
Ralph Backstrom
Henri Richard
Gilles Tremblay
John Ferguson
Yvan Cournoyer
Bobby Rousseau
Claude Larose
Claude Provost
Dick Duff
Carol Vadnais
Serge Savard
Danny Grant
Jacques Lemaire
Andre Boudrias
Mike McMahon
Bob Charlebois
Don Johns
Bill McCreary
Bill Plager
Leo Thiffault
Jim Paterson

NEW YORK RANGERS

Goaltenders
Ed Giacomin
Gilles Villemure

Forwards & Defencemen
Arnie Brown
Rod Gilbert
Phil Goyette
Vic Hadfield
Wayne Hillman
Harry Howell
Orland Kurtenbach
Don Marshall
Jim Neilson
Bob Nevin
Jean Ratelle
Reg Fleming
Gord Berenson
Larry Mickey
Bob Plager
Paul Andrea
George Konik
Gary Sabourin
Dunc McCallum
Bob Jones
Bob Blackburn
Bob Ash
Bill Knibbs
Ron Ingram
Gord Vejprava
Wayne Hall

TORONTO MAPLE LEAFS

Goaltenders
Johnny Bower
Al Smith

Forwards & Defencemen
Tim Horton
Larry Hillman
Marcel Pronovost
Mike Walton
Jim Pappin
Pete Stemkowski
Bob Pulford
Frank Mahovlich
Dave Keon
Ron Ellis
Brian Conacher
Murray Oliver
Allan Stanley
George Armstrong
Duane Rupp
Darryl Sly
Red Kelly
Gerry Ehman
Dick Gamble
Don Cherry
Norm Armstrong
Bronco Horvath
Les Duff
Barry Watson
Stan Smrke
Milan Marcetta

NATIONAL HOCKEY LEAGUE EXPANSION DRAFT
Montreal, June 6, 1967
WEST DIVISION PLAYER SELECTIONS
(Abbreviations in brackets indicate East Division team from which player was selected. Legend: Bos—Boston Bruins; Chi—Chicago Black Hawks; Det—Detroit Red Wings; Mtl—Montreal Canadiens; NY—New York Rangers; Tor—Toronto Maple Leafs).

CALIFORNIA SEALS

Goaltenders
Charlie Hodge (Mtl)
Gary Smith (Tor)

Forwards & Defencemen
Bob Baun (Tor)
Kent Douglas (Tor)
Bill Hicke (NY)
Billy Harris (Det)
Larry Cahan (NY)
Wally Boyer (Chi)
Joe Szura (Mtl)
Bob Lemieux (Mtl)
Jean-Paul Parise (Bos)
Ron Harris (Bos)
Terry Clancy (Tor)
Tracy Pratt (Chi)
Aut Erickson (Tor)
Ron Boehm (NY)
Alain Caron (Chi)
Mike Laughton (Tor)
Bryan Hextall (NY)
Gary Kilpatrick (Chi)

LOS ANGELES KINGS

Goaltenders
Terry Sawchuk (TBR)
Wayne Rutledge (NY)

Forwards & Defencemen
Gord Labossiere (Mtl)
Bob Wall (Det)
Ed Joyal (Tor)
Real Lemieux (Det)
Poul Popiel (Bos)
Terry Gray (Det)
Bryan Campbell (NY)
Ted Irvine (Bos)
Howard Hughes (Mtl)
Bill Inglis (Mtl)
Doug Robinson (NY)
Mike Corrigan (Tor)
Jacques Lemieux (Mtl)
Lowell MacDonald (Tor)
Ken Block (NY)
Bill Flett (Tor)
Brent Hughes (Det)
Marc Dufour (NY)

MINNESOTA NORTH STARS

Goaltenders
Cesare Maniago (NY)
Gary Bauman (Mtl)

Forwards & Defencemen
Dave Balon (Mtl)
Ray Cullen (Det)
Bob Woytowich (Bos)
Jean-Guy Talbot (Mtl)
Wayne Connelly (Bos)
Ted Taylor (Det)
Pete Goegan (Det)
Len Lunde (Chi)
Bill Goldsworthy (Bos)
Andre Pronovost (Det)
Elmer Vasko (Chi)
Murray Hall (Chi)
Bryan Watson (Det)
Bill Collins (NY)
Sandy Fitzpatrick (NY)
Parker MacDonald (Det)
Billy Taylor (Chi)
Dave Richardson (Chi)

PHILADELPHIA FLYERS

Goaltenders
Bernie Parent (Bos)
Doug Favell (Bos)

Forwards & Defencemen
Ed Van Impe (Chi)
Joe Watson (Bos)
Brit Selby (Tor)
Lou Angotti (Chi)
Leon Rochefort (Mtl)
Don Blackburn (Tor)
John Miszuk (Chi)
Garry Peters (Mtl)
Dick Cherry (Bos)
Jean Gauthier (Mtl)
Jim Johnson (NY)
Gary Dornhoefer (Bos)
Forbes Kennedy (Bos)
Pat Hannigan (Chi)
Dwight Carruthers (Det)
Bob Courcy (Mtl)
Keith Wright (Bos)
Terry Ball (NY)

PITTSBURGH PENGUINS

Goaltenders
Joe Daley (Det)
Roy Edwards (Chi)

Forwards & Defencemen
Earl Ingarfield (NY)
Al MacNeil (NY)
Larry Jeffrey (Tor)
Ab McDonald (Det)
Leo Boivin (Det)
Noel Price (Mtl)
Keith McCreary (Mtl)
Ken Schinkel (NY)
Bob Dillabough (Bos)
Art Stratton (Chi)
Val Fonteyne (Det)
Jeannot Gilbert (Bos)
Tom McCarthy (Mtl)
Bill Dea (Chi)
Bob Rivard (Mtl)
Mel Pearson (Chi)
Andy Bathgate (Det)
Les Hunt (NY)

ST. LOUIS BLUES

Goaltenders
Glenn Hall (Chi)
Don Caley (Det)

Forwards & Defencemen
Jim Roberts (Mtl)
Noel Picard (Mtl)
Al Arbour (Tor)
Rod Seiling (NY)
Ron Schock (Bos)
Terry Crisp (Bos)
Don McKenney (Bos)
Wayne Rivers (Bos)
Bill Hay (Chi)
Darryl Edestrand (Tor)
Norm Beaudin (Det)
Larry Keenan (Tor)
Ron Stewart (Bos)
Fred Hucul (Tor)
John Brenneman (Tor)
Gerry Melnyk (Chi)
Gary Veneruzzo (Tor)
Max Mestinsek (NY)

The protected lists and the expansion-team draft lists from the NHL Expansion Draft, which took place on June 6, 1967.

The Expansion Draft, which consisted of twenty rounds, took place on June 6, 1967. Each of the established teams was permitted to protect eleven skaters, one goaltender, and any junior-aged players signed the previous season. The first two rounds were devoted to goaltenders. Once an established team lost a goaltender, it was permitted to protect another. In effect, this made available the second- and fourth-string goaltenders from each of the "original" teams.

The second stage of the draft began with round three, and consisted of eighteen rounds, in which the expansion teams selected forwards and defensemen from players left unprotected by the established teams. With the exception of rounds five through seven, the established teams were permitted to protect one additional player for every player selected by an expansion club.

For the first two seasons after expansion, all teams were permitted to protect two goaltenders and fourteen skaters in the annual intra-league draft. This relatively small protected list was adopted to accelerate the improvement of the expansion teams by making available middle-rank players from the deeper talent pools of the established clubs.

The ingenuity of owners and managers of both established and expansion teams was demonstrated in their efforts to outflank the Expansion Draft. Managers of established clubs were willing to part with cash, players, and future draft choices to induce their expansion counterparts to pass over the best unprotected players on their lists. The Canadiens, for example, traded three players from their talent-rich farm system (André Boudrias, Bob Charlebois, and Bernard Coté) to Minnesota for the North Stars' first choice in the 1971 amateur draft. What didn't appear in the official trade record was the North Stars' agreement to select someone other than the Habs' Claude Larose with the first overall pick in round three of the 1967 Expansion Draft.

Originally the property of the Boston Bruins, Gary Dornhoefer was selected by the Philadelphia Flyers in the Expansion Draft, finishing as the second leading scorer on the club during the 1967-68 season with 43 points.

Minnesota used its pick to select Dave Balon from the Montreal roster, enabling the Habs to keep Larose.

Jack Kent Cooke, the owner of the Los Angeles Kings, bought an instant farm system when he acquired the Springfield Indians of the AHL from former Boston star Eddie Shore. Cooke announced his purchase the night before the Expansion Draft, prompting Philadelphia's Ed Snider to buy the AHL'S Quebec Aces in order to keep pace with Los Angeles.

The twelve-team NHL was split into an East and a West Division for the 1967-68 season, with the expansion clubs all playing in the West. The regular-season schedule consisted of 74 games, 50 within a team's division and 24 outside of it. The first four teams in each division qualified for the playoffs, which now consisted of three best-of-seven rounds. The quarter-finals and semi-finals would determine the champion of each division, with the two division winners meeting in the Stanley Cup finals. This guaranteed that an expansion club would meet an established team in the final round. The Prince of Wales Trophy, formerly awarded to the league's regular-season champion, would be awarded to the regular-season winner of the East Division. A new trophy, the Clarence S. Campbell Bowl, would be awarded to the regular-season winner in the West.

Average annual salaries reflected the more experienced make-up of the East Division, whose clubs paid an average of $21,000 per player. West Division clubs paid $18,000. The league also expanded its statistics-keeping in 1967-68, and began to track individual player's plus/minus totals, as well as power-play and shorthanded scoring.

Player transactions continued both before and after the Expansion Draft. Chicago and Boston engineered a six-player swap that sent Phil Esposito, Ken Hodge, and Fred Stanfield to the Bruins in exchange for Gilles Marotte, Pit Martin, and goaltender Jack Norris. The next decade of play in the NHL would reveal that Boston got the better of this exchange. In Toronto, Punch Imlach dealt Frank Mahovlich, Pete Stemkowski, Garry Unger, and rights to the retired Carl Brewer to Detroit for Norm Ullman, Paul Henderson, and Floyd Smith.

The first year of expansion forced even the established teams to make changes. At the season's halfway point, Montreal was in last place in the East as young players, promoted to fill the holes left by the Expansion Draft, took needed time to adapt to the NHL. By the end of the season, however, the Habs' overall depth and the maturing of a young defense vaulted the team into first place. The Rangers, who moved into a new Madison Square Garden in February, were the runners-up in the East, while Boston climbed from sixth to third place, qualifying for the playoffs for the first time since 1958-59. New Bruin Phil Esposito finished second in scoring with 84 points, three behind Chicago's Stan Mikita. Bobby Orr won the Norris Trophy in only his second NHL season, while Derek Sanderson of the Bruins was named rookie of the year. Chicago finished fourth in a season that saw

Bobby Hull score his 400th career goal and Mikita repeat his triple-award sweep of the previous season, once again winning the Art Ross, Hart, and Lady Byng trophies.

Neither Detroit nor Toronto fared well, both finishing out of the playoffs despite their off-season trade. For 1967-68, it appeared that the Leafs had got the better of the deal, as Norm Ullman finished in the top ten in scoring, well ahead of Mahovlich.

Games tended to be wide open in the West, where five of the six new teams proved to be evenly matched, finishing just below .500. Philadelphia ended the season on top with 73 points, one ahead of Los Angeles, three ahead of St. Louis, and four up on Minnesota. Just six points separated the Flyers from the fifth-place Pittsburgh Penguins. The Flyers' good showing was achieved in spite of having to shift seven late-season home games to New York, Toronto, and Quebec when high winds damaged the roof of the Philadelphia Spectrum. Solid goaltending by Doug Favell and Bernie Parent left the Flyers with the third-lowest goals-against total in the NHL. The West Division's top scorer was Minnesota's Wayne Connelly, who had 35 goals, including a league-leading 14 scored on the power-play.

The sixth-place Oakland Seals performed poorly both on the ice and at the gate, finishing with just 15 wins and 47 points, and having to borrow nearly a million dollars to survive. At the end of the season, coach Bert Olmstead resigned.

In the playoffs, the St. Louis Blues proved there was no substitute for experience – and a few ex-Canadiens in the line-up. Veterans Red Berenson and Dickie Moore, along with Doug Harvey, who signed as a free agent in April, contributed to the Blues' success. The quarter-finals proved to be a graveyard for the first- and second-place teams, as St. Louis defeated Philadelphia and Minnesota eliminated Los Angeles. The Blues then defeated the North Stars to become the first playoff champion of the West Division. Notably, all three series went seven games, and four games of the St. Louis–Minnesota semi-final series were decided in overtime. Ron Schock scored the series winner for the Blues at 2:50 of the second overtime period in game seven.

In the East, Chicago and Montreal advanced to the semi-final, which was won by the Canadiens in five games. Montreal was heavily favored over St. Louis in the first post-expansion final, and though the Canadiens won the Cup in four straight games, each was decided by one goal. Goaltender Glenn Hall played spectacularly for the Blues, earning the Conn Smythe Trophy as playoff MVP.

The first year of expansion brought with it the NHL's first on-ice fatality when, in January, center Bill Masterton of Minnesota hit his head on the ice after being checked. Masterton died in hospital two days later, without regaining consciousness. His accident prompted many players, most notably scoring champion Stan Mikita, to don helmets. Later that season, the NHL

Toe Blake and Gump Worsley celebrate the Canadiens' four-game sweep of the St. Louis Blues in the 1968 Stanley Cup finals. Worsley, who was undefeated in 11 games during the 1968 playoffs, was sold to the Minnesota North Stars on February 27, 1970.

Stan Mikita, the Chicago Black Hawks' career leader in games, seasons, assists, and points, was the first NHL player to win the Art Ross, Hart, and Lady Byng trophies in consecutive seasons.

Writers' Association presented the league with the Bill Masterton Memorial Trophy, to be awarded annually to the NHL player who best exemplifies the qualities of perseverance, sportsmanship, and dedication to hockey. Montreal's hard-working right winger Claude Provost was its first recipient in 1968.

Management of West Division teams successfully lobbied for more games with East Division clubs in 1968-69. The regular-season schedule was extended to seventy-six games and arranged so that each team would play the clubs in its own division eight times and those in the other division six times. This new schedule guaranteed each team in the West three home games with each of the crowd-pleasing, high-profile teams from the East.

Danny Grant started his career with the Montreal Canadiens, playing 23 games over two seasons and earning a Stanley Cup ring in 1968. Traded to Minnesota in June 1968, Grant won the Calder Trophy in 1969 when he recorded 34 goals and 31 assists for the North Stars.

A new owners' group, led by Potter Palmer, took charge in Oakland (the same group also owned the Harlem Globetrotters). Immediate steps were taken to improve the team. In addition to wholesale player changes, Bill Torrey was hired as executive vice-president, Freddie Glover became the Seals' new coach, and Frank Selke, Jr., was promoted to general manager.

In Los Angeles, Red Kelly traded Terry Sawchuk to Detroit for center Jimmy Peters. The St. Louis Blues, whose hot goaltending had taken them to the Stanley Cup finals the previous season, enticed Jacques Plante out of retirement to split the goaltending job with Glenn Hall. The Blues' two-goalie system paid dividends, and the veterans shared the Vezina Trophy, combining to record 13 shutouts. Again, the Blues were led offensively by Red Berenson, who scored six goals in one regular-season game and promptly found himself on the cover of *Sports Illustrated*.

The Blues were the top team in the second season of the West Division and, with 88 points, became the first of the 1967 expansion clubs to finish above .500. Parity no longer ruled in the West: Oakland was a surprising second, but finished 19 points behind St. Louis. Philadelphia and Los Angeles qualified for the playoffs by finishing third and fourth. Two West Division rookies, Norm Ferguson of Oakland and Danny Grant of Minnesota, equaled the league's forty-two-year-old rookie scoring record of 34 goals. Grant also set a new rookie mark for points with 65.

In Montreal, Claude Ruel, a respected minor-league coach and instructor in the Canadiens' farm system, replaced the retired Toe Blake behind the Habs' bench. Because he had helped develop many of Montreal's young players, the Canadiens felt that Ruel, who at twenty-nine was now the youngest head coach in the NHL, would extract a good performance from the Habs.

Two general managers relieved themselves of their coaching duties, signing new coaches for 1968-69. Sid Abel hired Bill Gadsby in Detroit, and Emile Francis hired Bernie Geoffrion in New York. But the biggest change in the East Division was the emergence of the Boston Bruins as one of the NHL's best teams. Phil Esposito, in his second year with Boston, became the first

NHL player to break the 100-point barrier, finishing the season with 49 goals and 77 assists for a record 126 points. His performance earned him both the scoring title and the league MVP award. His linemate Ken Hodge had 45 goals and 90 points. Bobby Orr set single-season goal- and point-scoring records for defensemen, with 21 goals and 64 points. Boston set NHL records for goals (303), assists (497), and penalty minutes (1,297), and finished in second place with 100 points.

Chicago began the season by signing Bobby Hull to a three-year contract that made him the first NHL player to earn $100,000 a season. Hull delivered value-for-dollar, scoring a record 58 goals, breaking 100 points, and finishing second in scoring to Esposito. Stan Mikita had 97 points, the fourth-best total in the NHL, and young Pat Stapleton contributed 50 assists, a league record for defensemen. Despite these strong performances, the Black Hawks slid out of the playoffs, finishing in last place for the first time since 1956-57.

Bill Gadsby's Red Wings also missed the playoffs, despite Gordie Howe finishing with 44 goals, including his 700th, and 103 points on the season. The line of Howe, Frank Mahovlich, and Alex Delvecchio combined for a league-record 118 goals, Mahovlich contributing 49 and Delvecchio 25.

The Canadiens showed admirable balance; five of their scorers registered 29 goals or more. They finished with 103 points, to top the Bruins and the

Gordie Howe slips his 700th career goal through the pads of Pittsburgh goaltender Les Binkley on December 4, 1968. Linemates Alex Delvecchio and Frank Mahovlich drew assists on the historic marker.

Red Berenson, whose seventeen-year NHL career included stops in Montreal, New York, Detroit, and St. Louis, set an NHL record for goals in a single road game when he scored six against Doug Favell and the Philadelphia Flyers on November 7, 1968.

East Division by three points. New York finished third, led by the G-A-G (Goal-A-Game) Line of Jean Ratelle, Vic Hadfield, and Rod Gilbert. Emile Francis replaced coach Bernie Geoffrion in mid-season. Rookies Brad Park and Walt Tkaczuk added spark to the offense. Toronto finished fourth, 18 points behind first-place Montreal and six behind the Rangers.

The increased number of games between teams of the two divisions dramatized the talent gap between East and West. Of all West Division teams, only St. Louis's 88 points surpassed the point total of Chicago, the last-place team in the East. The results of the playoffs further emphasized the disparity between divisions.

In the East Division, Montreal beat New York in the first round, while Boston beat Toronto in a series that cost Punch Imlach his job. Montreal then narrowly defeated Boston in a six-game semi-final that featured three overtime wins by the Canadiens.

In the West, St. Louis, led by Jacques Plante's two shutouts, defeated Philadelphia. Throughout the other quarter-final series, an all-California affair in which Los Angeles beat the Seals, crowds were ominously sparse. St. Louis ended the prospect of a California team playing in the Stanley Cup finals by beating the Kings. In the finals, Montreal swept the Blues with relative ease. Defenseman Serge Savard had 10 points in post-season play and earned the Conn Smythe Trophy as playoff MVP.

The 1968-69 season saw scoring records topple as expansion fostered a more open style of play. Throughout the league, defensemen, led by Bobby Orr, became increasingly involved in their teams' attack.

In June of 1969, the league staged its first universal amateur draft. The draft established an order of selection whereby NHL clubs picked the best available twenty-year-old players. (Draft eligibility would later be amended to allow eighteen-year-olds to be selected in the first three rounds.) The order of selection at the draft was from "worst-to-first," based on the final standings of the 1968-69 season, but draft choices could be sold or traded.

The new draft changed the function of scouts in the NHL. Under the old sponsorship system, a scout would scour his territory for promising teenaged players who, after signing a letter of intent, were tied to the scout's NHL organization. Players would then be assigned to junior clubs sponsored by the NHL organization and would endeavor to work their way up to the NHL through a farm system that included junior and minor pro teams.

In the era of the universal draft, players could not be signed until they reached draft age. Scouts would evaluate all players eligible to be drafted, and then help their team's general manager select the best player available when their club's turn came up during each round of the draft.

Established teams, all of which had prospects at the junior level, were reluctant to give up players they felt they had raised "in the family" under the old system. Montreal's Sam Pollock swapped journeyman players from the

Tony Esposito, who played a minor role in the Canadiens' 1969 Stanley Cup championship, joined Chicago for 1969-70. With the Black Hawks, he won the Calder Trophy in 1970, setting an NHL rookie record with 15 shutouts.

Canadiens' organization to obtain the first two choices in the 1969 amateur draft, picking Réjean Houle and Marc Tardif, two highly prized scorers from the Montreal Junior Canadiens who would almost certainly have been drafted by other clubs before the Canadiens' would have had an opportunity to select them.

With twelve NHL organizations competing for talent, more effort was made to scout U.S. college hockey. Chicago signed three prospects from the University of Denver: defenseman Keith Magnuson, right wing Cliff Koroll, and goaltender Tony Esposito (brother of Bruin star Phil), who came to the team via the Canadiens' organization. In his first season with the Black Hawks, Esposito recorded 15 shutouts, gaining the nickname "Tony O." No goaltender had had 15 shutouts in a single season since George Hainsworth's league record 22 in the ultra-low-scoring NHL of 1928-29. His excellent play earned Esposito the Vezina and Calder trophies. Magnuson and Koroll also played with the Black Hawks for the entire season.

These collegiate players were part of a Chicago team that climbed from sixth to first place in one season, even though the early weeks of 1969-70

Frank Mahovlich's career was reborn in Detroit, where he teamed with Gordie Howe and Alex Delvecchio to set a record for points by a forward line when the trio accumulated 264 in 1968-69.

were disrupted by the absence of two important players: Bobby Hull held out for an improved contract until November of 1969, and veteran Kenny Wharram was forced to retire after encountering heart problems at training camp. Despite these setbacks, the Hawks played winning defensive hockey and finished in first place with 99 points. Hull played 61 games and scored 38 goals, including his 500th. At the time, only two other NHL players, Gordie Howe and Maurice Richard, had reached the 500 plateau.

Detroit finished third, four points behind Boston, aided by former-Leaf Garry Unger's 42 goals. Gordie Howe scored his 800th career goal, including playoff markers. The Rangers and the Canadiens finished tied with 92 points and identical won-lost records, but the Rangers, who had scored more goals on the season, were awarded fourth place. Montreal finished out of the playoffs for the first time in 22 seasons. Joining them on the sidelines was sixth-place Toronto, 21 points out of the last playoff spot. For the first time in the history of the NHL, no Canadian team qualified for post-season play.

In the West, St. Louis continued to be the best expansion club, finishing with 86 points, 22 ahead of second-place Pittsburgh. Minnesota and Oakland were the West's other playoff teams. The Flyers, who had to settle for fifth place, set an NHL record for games tied, with 24. Rookie center Bobby Clarke scored 15 goals for Philadelphia. Phil Goyette, who was traded to St. Louis by the Rangers, became the first player with a West Division club to finish among the NHL's top-five scorers.

The lead story of the 1969-70 season, though, was in Boston, where the combination of Phil Esposito and Bobby Orr had transformed the Bruins into the hottest ticket in the league. Orr smashed NHL records, scoring 33 goals and 87 assists, to become the first defenseman to win the Art Ross Trophy as the league's leading scorer and the fourth player to top 100 points in a season. Orr added the Norris and the Hart to his trophy case as well. Esposito scored 43 goals and finished second to Orr's 120 points with 99.

A semi-final playoff match-up between the Bruins and Black Hawks – Orr and Phil Esposito versus Hull, Mikita, and Tony Esposito – created great expectations when both clubs won their quarter-final series, but the Bruins stormed past the Hawks in a four-game sweep.

Veteran Johnny Bucyk, who endured eight consecutive seasons out of the playoffs, accepts the Stanley Cup after the Bruins swept St. Louis in 1970. The other Boston players pictured are Eddie Westfall and Phil Esposito.

St. Louis's Noel Picard successfully upended Bobby Orr in overtime of game four of the 1970 Stanley Cup finals, but not before Orr took the shot that beat Glenn Hall and brought the Stanley Cup to Boston.

St. Louis earned its third consecutive berth in the Stanley Cup finals, with series wins over Minnesota and Pittsburgh in the West Division playoffs. The Blues again failed to win a game in the final, and the Bruins captured their first Stanley Cup since 1941 on Bobby Orr's overtime goal in game four. The image of Orr, airborne after scoring, already celebrating the Cup, has endured among the NHL's most cherished photographic icons: superb action, showing a master of the game at one of the finest moments of his career. Though coach Harry Sinden would resign to pursue business interests outside of hockey two days after the Bruins' Cup triumph, the club's strong line-up established Boston as the NHL's top team heading into the 1970s.

(continued on p. 199)

It Doesn't Get Any Better Than This: The Big Bad Bruins

by Francis Rosa

Not long after two human beings from planet Earth walked on the moon, the Bruins of the early 1970s took a trip of their own. And they took Boston, the Commonwealth of Massachusetts, and sure, most of the hockey world, along with them.

They have not let go of their place in hockey history – nor have they been allowed to let it go.

Forever Boston's team. And after that trip, hockey would be forever different. They were the agent of change, part of the refinement of the game that comes with each succeeding decade.

They spawned the Bruins' Lunch Pail Athletic Club of the late 1970s and the greybeards who still come to the Boston Garden will tell you they were there on Mother's Day in 1970 when the Bruins won the Stanley Cup, when Bobby Orr won the Cup with an overtime goal. They were the fun-loving, swashbuckling Bruins of the "Bobby and Phil and Them" era. No need to add last names. "You don't have a team," coach Harry Sinden was once told, "you have a gang."

Sinden recalls, "They were hockey's Gas House Gang. There was incredible confidence and togeth-

Coach Harry Sinden's ability to combine role-players and superstars into a cohesive squad resulted in a decisive Stanley Cup victory for the Bruins in 1970.

erness on and off the ice. I've never quite figured out which comes first, if winning comes from togetherness or togetherness comes from winning." Said Tom Johnson, who ascended to coach the team after Sinden defected to the world of industry, "It comes from winning. The players were so together they never called a team meeting that I can recall." Whatever, the togetherness has never vanished. Not even the passage of time could destroy that. Has any other championship team in any sport ever had a four-day twentieth reunion? With 100-per-cent attendance? They did. And Phil Esposito said, "I think we had more fun at the reunion than we had at the championship party."

Orr, of course, was the prime mover of the reunion – just as any recollection of the Bruins of the era is dominated by endless images of Orr, "Bobby Hockey," and his exquisite artistry. And Esposito too.

A young Bobby Orr beats the Rangers' Phil Goyette to the puck during action in the 1966-67 season.

In the 1972 finals, a seasoned hockey writer from the *New York Times* asked a veteran writer from the *Boston Globe*, "I counted six things Orr did tonight that I've never seen in a hockey game. Is that about right?" The reply was, "I really couldn't say. We stopped counting about four years ago." Orr, naturally and instinctively, had gone where no defenseman before him had ever gone, carrying the role of the defenseman to a new dimension – a dimension that today makes an offensive defenseman a team necessity.

There was no programming of his moves when the puck was on his stick. His genius was reaction in sportdom's ultimate reaction sport. Anyone who ever saw him play will recognize one image, captured in slo-mo frames in the mind's eye: Orr, circling the enemy net with four Black Hawks following him in single file and four Bruins hurrying to the front of the goal, waving their sticks for a pass. And another scene: Orr, in a game against the Atlanta Flames, holding the puck for twenty-one seconds while killing a penalty and ending up scoring. Countless images – even off the ice. Such as being the first to arrive in the dressing room on game nights, playing gin with trainer John Forristal and working on his sticks.

The Bruins of the 1970s belong to Bobby Orr. No player before him or since has been able to control the tempo of a game as he did. They were his Bruins and he shared them with everyone. He owned Boston. Nay, he still owns the place. Said a coach of a girls' youth team, who previously had coached a boys' youth team during the halcyon days, "It was bad enough when every father thought his son was another Bobby Orr. Now every mother thinks her daughter is another Bobby Orr." That's how Orr took Boston. He was theirs and they loved him no matter what. An oft-told incident: one night he accidentally put the puck into his own net. Dead silence engulfed the Garden – until a voice bellowed out of the second balcony, up there from the gallery gods' Mount Olympus, "It's all right, Bobby. We still love you."

Love? When Orr was inducted into the Hockey Hall of Fame in 1979, he chose Mrs. Weston Adams, widow of the owner, to give his induction speech. The first woman so honored, she concluded by saying, "I give you Bobby Orr, number 4 in your program, number 1 in our hearts." Wayne Gretzky recalls his father taking him to a game in Maple Leaf Gardens when the crowd booed Orr and he wondered why. "It's because he's so good," Walter Gretzky told him.

Not long ago, Larry Bird, the basketball superstar of today's Boston Celtics, attended a Boston Garden unveiling of a larger-than-life wooden sculpture of himself. When asked what he was thinking as he gazed at all the banners overhead, he said, "I wasn't looking at the Celtics' championship banners. I was looking at the Bruins' number 4 banner . . . and hoping that when I'm finished playing, Boston will hold me in the same esteem as Bobby Orr." It won't likely happen, for Orr was, is, and forever will be Boston's Bobby.

Sure, it was Orr's team. It was also Phil Esposito's team. No team would have two such magnificently talented and explosive players until Wayne Gretzky and Paul Coffey got together in Edmonton. Esposito was an absolute marvel. His 76–76–152 season of 1970-71 stood as a record for ten years – until Gretzky broke it. Esposito virtually invented the slot, a triangle of ice from the crease to the hashmark, where he established position and shot endlessly. It wasn't the only area of the ice from which he scored. Still, Esposito in the slot, being grabbed and hooked, and shooting and shooting, brought this remark from goalie Ken Dryden of Montreal: "I see him taking all those shots and I wonder why his arms don't fall off."

Orr and Esposito gave Boston a menacing power-play, but Johnny Bucyk's role is not to be discounted either. He'd back his fat butt into the left corner and thread incredibly accurate passes to Orr at the right point, or play give-and-go with Fred Stanfield at the left point. "Bucyk," Sinden has said, "was one of the greatest passing wings of all time."

After the dramatic and historic 1972 series with the Soviets – when time stood still on two continents – the late Harold Ballard of Toronto said: "Give me Phil Esposito, and I'll put him and the Stanley Cup in my station wagon and we'll go on an exhibition tour around the league." For those eight games, Esposito was the greatest player who ever

Phil Esposito, parked near the slot, is guarded by Brad Park. In one of the decade's biggest trades, Esposito was swapped for the Rangers' all-star defenseman in 1975.

lived. As the late Punch Imlach, then with Buffalo, said, "I'd buy Phil Esposito with my own money if I could, and I'd rent him to the Sabres."

The Bruins of the 1970s were crazy. Crazy enough to be called Bobby Orr and the Big, Bad Bruins. If "bad" was a misnomer, it was only a matter of connotation. They were big, maybe the biggest team in the league then. But bad? "We always took it as a term we were proud of . . . to mean we were a very rugged team, a good hockey club with highly skilled players, a combination that is hard to find," said Sinden. "We wanted to be as tough as there was in the league. The greatest thing about them was how seriously they took their hockey. When it came time to play there was no question they'd play. They were very serious about playing and winning. And that's maybe the only thing they were serious about."

Crazy? "We might have done some crazy things," said defenseman Gary Doak, "but it was all in fun, and we never hurt anyone." Things such as Johnny McKenzie standing alongside Mayor Kevin White on the platform at the civic celebration for the 1970 Cup, and pouring a pitcher of beer on the mayor's head. "There were so many people around the Garden that day," said Sinden, "it took us three

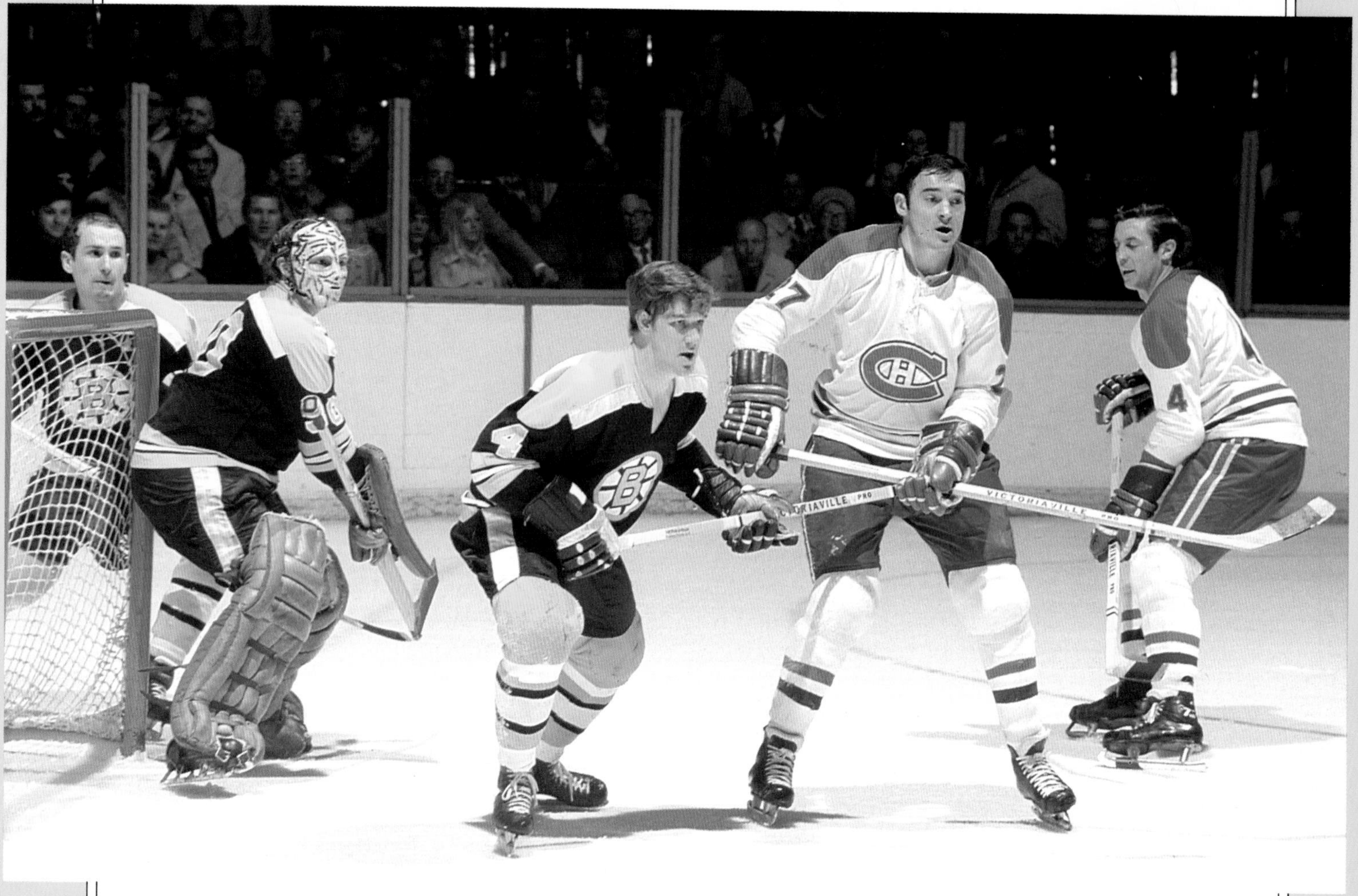

The Montreal Canadiens, led by Jean Béliveau (4) and Frank Mahovlich (27), upset Orr, Cheevers, and the big, bad Bruins in the 1971 quarter-finals.

hours ... well more than an hour ... to go the half-mile to City Hall Plaza." McKenzie says, "We were a bunch of misfits nobody else wanted, but when we got together, all of a sudden it worked." Close, but not quite true. There were enough superstars and the right players in the right roles, and they weren't really misfits: four of them and Sinden are in hockey's Hall of Fame.

Somehow there was no distinction between them – no elite and no lower class. They had an intangible quality that infected the team and made them brothers; not their brothers' keepers, but their brothers' brothers. Love me, love my brothers; hate me, hate my brothers. Sinden's togetherness. It lives among them to this day.

They did everything together, most of it unscheduled, as spontaneous as the game they played. Not always by design, they'd wind up at the same pizza place after practice, the same Chinese restaurant after a game. They laughed together, they won together. They lost together, they cried together. They won two Stanley Cups, 1970 and 1972, when they should have won four, missing in 1971 and 1974, and everybody in Boston cursed the damn Habs and the Broad Street Bullies. Those were the days when the scoreboard at the Garden seemed frozen in an eternity of the present tense at Boston 5, Visitors 2.

They had wonderful nicknames. Johnny Pie and Cheesie and E.J., and Chief and Turk and Half-ton, and Espie and Hodgie and Cash, and Buggsy and Swoop and Acer. That's McKenzie and Gerry Cheevers and Eddie Johnston, and Johnny Bucyk and Derek Sanderson and Dallas Smith, and Phil Esposito and Ken Hodge and Wayne Cashman, and Don Awrey and Wayne Carleton and Garnet Bailey.

The days of the crewcuts and then sideburns. The days of Sinden pulling Sanderson into his office between periods of a game against Montreal and telling him, "Turk, you've taken three dumb penalties; one more and I'll bury you so deep *The Hockey News* won't be able to find you." A couple of years after his second Stanley Cup in 1972, Sanderson buried himself in the WHA. Cheevers, too, left for the WHA, to return and become one of the links, along with Bucyk and Cashman, to the Lunch Pail Athletic Club of the late 1970s. That, too, was a bit of a misnomer, for they were not a no-talent team.

Beyond the esteem for Orr, there were other things that put the Bruins into a special relationship with the community. Sinden put it this way: "We were a clone of the city – good and rugged. People had an identification with that team, the Bruins of the late 1960s and early 1970s." Some of the craziness of the team was contagious. It rubbed off on their fans.

There was the notorious case of the Phantom of the Garden in 1970. In those days banners of every team in the league hung from the Garden roof, huge banners about six feet by ten feet. So it was decided, said the Phantom, "We'd break into the Garden through the old Hotel Madison, climb up into the rafters, and steal the flags of the Rangers, the Black Hawks, and the Bruins. We'd return the New York and Chicago banners when they were eliminated, and the Bruins' when they won the Cup." It became an amusing and almost death-defying stunt, with all the overtones of a Damon Runyon short story.

The Phantom's story made the front page of the *Boston Globe*. True to his word, he returned the Rangers' and Black Hawks' banners when those teams were defeated, but saved the Bruins' banner for the championship game. He planned to sneak down onto the ice and drape it over Orr or Bucyk or Cheevers. But he made a mistake. Before the historic game started, he draped it over the facing of the second balcony, and the sellout crowd gave him a standing ovation. It also brought the Garden security force rushing up to the second balcony to collect it.

The 1972 Cup became part of the legend this team was writing. After it was won in Madison Square Garden, thousands of fans headed for Logan Airport to welcome the champions home. "The problem," coach Tom Johnson recalled, "was created by people trying to get to the airport. Sumner Tunnel was clogged with cars, so the people left their cars there and got out and walked to the terminal. They created a massive traffic jam. Nothing could get through the tunnel. I don't know how many people were there, but they damaged the terminal and there was such a crush of people that one guy snatched my briefcase out of my hands. It had $3,500 in it, and I chased him and got it back. He wasn't stealing the money; he was just looking for a souvenir and anything would do."

Coaching the Bruins wasn't easy. "I had to turn the other cheek a lot," Sinden said. "I had to work their butts off in practice because all the training was done on the ice then." The Bruins wiped out the league the following season with four 100-point scorers, then broke everyone's heart by losing to Montreal in the playoffs. They came back in 1972 to win another Cup. The next season, they fell out of the playoffs when Phil Esposito's knee was wrecked in a collision with Ron Harris. That merely created the setting for another crazy stunt: they decided to party, and Phil, still in the hospital after surgery, had to be present – so they wheeled him in his hospital bed down the street to Orr's Branding Iron restaurant, a couple of blocks away. Hodge and Smith still owe Esposito $750 for the hospital door they removed to wheel him out.

In 1974, the Bruins lost to Philadelphia in the finals in spite of another Orr–Esposito class act. The Flyers loved to bring out Kate Smith to sing "God Bless America" before a crucial game. When she came on the ice, Orr and Esposito skated up to her and presented her with flowers.

Even the people around the Bruins were characters. After the Black Hawks eliminated the Bruins in the first round in 1975 in Chicago, a team physician chided the Boston writers: "Why don't you write what you see? The referee took the game away from us." The late Tom Fitzgerald of the *Globe* replied, "Doctor, I would never presume to tell you how to practice medicine ... please don't tell me how to write." The doctor responded, "It's because of writers like you that some players on this team need psychiatric help." Fitz replied, "Really? Which ones?"

Then Esposito was traded and Brad Park became a Bruin to play ten unforgettable games alongside Orr on the power-play. The trade stunned Boston. In 1976 Orr had gone to Chicago, and Boston went into mourning. "Our season ticket sales tumbled from thirteen thousand to six thousand," said Sinden, who was by then the general manager, "and the fans didn't even wait to see what kind of team we had."

Wayne Cashman (left), seen here battling with the Flyers' Joe Watson, was the last pre-expansion player to retire, finally ending his on-ice career after the Bruins lost to the Islanders in the 1983 semi-finals.

The Bruins of the early 1970s passed the torch to Don Cherry's Lunch Pail Gang of the late 1970s, a band of overachievers led by Terry O'Reilly, who captivated Boston in their own way. They, too, carried marvelous nicknames. The coach was Grapes; the starry right winger was Magic or Nifty (Rick Middleton); the smooth center was Ratty (Jean Ratelle); Cheesie was back in the goal; Cash was still there; so was Chief; Taz (O'Reilly) was the talented hard worker; and on defense they had Dooner (Mike Milbury), who has become their coach. The tradition lived.

Bucyk doubled as sort of a traveling secretary for the Cherry-coached teams, and one of his chores was to handle the players' tickets for road games. One day at practice in Boston, O'Reilly asked him, "Do I still owe you any money for the game in Toronto last week?" Bucyk replied, "Yes, thirty-five dollars." O'Reilly said, "Will you take a check?" The answer was, "Sure." The word was hardly out of his mouth when Bucyk was picking himself up off the ice, where an O'Reilly check had landed him.

Five times the Bruins reached the Stanley Cup finals during the decade they shared with Montreal. In 1979, they lost the seventh game of the semifinals in Montreal, the infamous too-many-men-on-the-ice penalty that cost them the game and probably another Stanley Cup. They wept. Boston wept with them. Never had a team won so much in defeat.

It matters not that the Bruins won only two Stanley Cups in the 1970s. A Cup win is not the only definition of success in hockey. What matters is that they won so many more games than they lost in the decade. (They averaged 48 wins and 108 points per season in the 1970s.) What matters is that they provided so much entertainment for so many people. What matters is that they gave themselves to the game and spent the best years of their lives believing, "It doesn't get any better than this."

Buffalo and Vancouver, two cities that had narrowly missed being awarded franchises in the 1967 expansion, paid franchise fees of $6 million to join the NHL in 1970-71, making a fourteen-team league. The Buffalo Sabres, owned by Seymour and Northrup Knox, would play out of the city's War Memorial Auditorium, which had been upgraded to hold 15,000 fans. The Vancouver franchise was awarded to Medicor, a Minneapolis-based company that already owned the Western Hockey League's Vancouver Canucks, a minor-pro team whose name would be given to the NHL club. The NHL Canucks would play out of Vancouver's Pacific Coliseum.

Both franchises chose veteran hockey executives to build their organizations. Buffalo hired Punch Imlach as coach and general manager, while Vancouver appointed Bud Poile as general manager, a job he had held with the Philadelphia Flyers when they entered the league. Hal Laycoe, a former NHL defenseman and one-time coach of the Los Angeles Kings, became the Canucks' first coach.

Both the Canucks and Sabres joined the NHL's East Division, despite Vancouver's location on Canada's West Coast. To equalize the number of teams in each division, the Chicago Black Hawks, the league's top team in 1969-70, was switched to the West. These divisional assignments were designed to reduce the competitive gap between East and West. The regular-season schedule was extended to seventy-eight games. For the first time since the two divisions were established in 1967-68, the schedule was balanced. Each team would play six games against each of its thirteen opponents. Uniform regulations were also altered for 1970-71. Teams would wear white uniforms at home and colored uniforms on the road.

The playoff structure was also revamped in response to criticism that the East-versus-West format of the Stanley Cup finals had resulted in one-sided championship-round match-ups. In the new playoff structure, teams from the two divisions would cross over to play each other in the semi-finals. This preserved the possibility that the NHL's two best teams could meet in the finals, even if both those teams played in the same division.

The two newcomers of 1970-71 were awarded the first two picks in the 1970 amateur draft, affording them a better opportunity to build than had been granted the expansion teams of 1967-68. The Sabres, who had won the right to pick first over the Canucks on the spin of a wheel, took Gilbert Perreault, a star center with the Montreal Junior Canadiens. To backstop the offense expected from Perreault, Imlach made a deal with Detroit to get goaltender Roger Crozier and put together a team that included Phil Goyette (fourth in scoring the previous year with St. Louis), Donnie Marshall, Eddie Shack, and tough Reg Fleming. In fact, the Sabres' employment of veterans was reminiscent of Imlach's successful methods with the Leafs.

The Canucks followed the model of the Boston Bruins, choosing to build their club around Dale Tallon, a mobile, high-scoring defenseman whom some had labeled another Orr when he played junior hockey with the

The first player selected by the Buffalo Sabres in the 1970 Amateur Draft, Gilbert Perreault holds or shares ten Sabres' team records. Perreault retired in 1987 with 512 goals and 1,326 points.

Toronto Marlboros. The Canucks selected Orland Kurtenbach from the Rangers with their first pick in the expansion draft and also acquired goaltender Charlie Hodge and right winger Rosaire Paiement, who would lead the club with 34 goals in its first season. The Canucks played to near-sellout crowds, thanks to a season ticket base of twelve thousand.

Further down the West Coast, the Oakland Seals continued to draw small crowds. Charlie Finley, the colorful Chicago insurance magnate who owned the American League baseball team in Oakland, bought the Seals for $4.5 million, confident that the same kind of promotion that had long been a part of baseball could be used to sell hockey. Finley had put his baseball players in white shoes, and figured colored skates would liven up the Seals' uniforms as well. He also tried to broaden the franchise's market by renaming the team the California Seals. In a later attempt to jazz-up the team's image, he would modify its name again, changing it to the California Golden Seals.

The Pittsburgh Penguins lost Michel Brière when the young center was severely injured in an automobile accident during the off-season. Brière, who had a promising rookie debut with the Pittsburgh Penguins in 1969-70, would remain in a coma for almost a year before passing away.

The Penguins also experienced financial difficulties. Owner Donald

Vancouver's Orland Kurtenbach, who is surrounded by the Toronto trio of (left to right) Norm Ullman, Jim Dorey, and Ron Ellis, later coached the Canucks in 1977-78.

Promising Pittsburgh rookie Michel Brière, who was killed in an off-season car accident in 1970, is the only Penguin to have had his number (21) retired. The pursuing Canadien is Claude Provost.

Parsons's unwillingness to sustain further losses forced the NHL to take over operation of the franchise. This was the first time the league had been involved in the day-to-day running of a club since the war years, when the New York/Brooklyn Americans ran into money problems.

Cash-flow issues of a different sort prompted many NHL veterans to hold out for bigger contracts at the start of the 1970-71 season. The large amounts offered to unproven newcomers such as Perreault and Tallon were cited by established stars as a basis for increased salaries. Four of the New York Rangers' top players – Brad Park, Jean Ratelle, Vic Hadfield, and Walt Tkaczuk – sat out during training camp in attempts to get better contracts.

Pre-season trading activity saw the Maple Leafs acquire Jacques Plante from St. Louis as a replacement for the retired Johnny Bower. The Leafs later traded Plante's back-up, Bruce Gamble, to Philadelphia as part of a larger deal in which the Leafs acquired goaltender Bernie Parent from the Flyers.

The Detroit Red Wings, en route to a seventh-place finish, would drastically retool their club over the course of the 1970-71 season. The changes began with the hiring of successful college coach Ned Harkness from Cornell University. Harkness soon clashed with Detroit general manager Sid Abel, who resolved the dispute by resigning from the club. Promoted to general manager, Harkness dismantled the team that Abel had been

Bobby Orr, here attempting to get around Henri Richard, was the first player to win two Conn Smythe trophies, capturing the post-season MVP award in 1970 and 1972.

building. Garry Unger and Wayne Connelly were sent to St. Louis for Red Berenson and Tim Ecclestone. Bruce MacGregor went to the Rangers as part of a deal that brought Arnie Brown to Detroit. In January, Frank Mahovlich was shipped to Montreal for Mickey Redmond, Guy Charron, and Bill Collins, a trade that seemed to benefit both organizations. Mahovlich would play well for three more seasons in Montreal, while Redmond would became Detroit's first 50-goal scorer in 1972-73.

The 1970-71 season proved to be a showcase for the offensive firepower of the Boston Bruins. The club shattered numerous league records, winning 57 games to finish in first place with 121 points. They raised the team single-season goal-scoring record from 303 to 399 and added 695 assists. The club's boisterous style earned them the name "Big Bad Bruins," and allowed the team's busy penalty-killers to score 25 goals shorthanded. Esposito, Orr, Johnny Bucyk, and Ken Hodge each finished with more than 100 points, which put them atop league scoring. The line of Esposito, Hodge, and Wayne Cashman potted a record 140 goals, of which Esposito scored 76. Previously, no player in the NHL had scored more than 58 goals in a season. Esposito matched his goal-scoring output with 76 assists, to finish with 152 points. Bobby Orr added 37 goals and a record 102 assists to finish with 139 points.

Gilbert Perreault, who justified the Sabres' decision to draft him first overall, set a new scoring record for rookies with 38 goals and was an easy winner of the Calder Trophy. Another rookie, Ken Dryden, a former college goaltender at Cornell, also made his mark on the NHL in 1970-71. Dryden was brought up from the Canadiens' AHL farm club late in the season. He was undefeated in the Habs' last six starts and continued his fine play into a quarter-final series in which the third-place Canadiens played the heavily favored Bruins. Dryden was brilliant against Boston's superb offense, and the Canadiens' engineered a seven-game upset. In the series' second game, Montreal came back from a 5–1 deficit to hand the Bruins a stunning 7–5 defeat. Jean Béliveau scored twice in the third period for the Habs. In the other East Division quarter-final, New York needed six games to eliminate Toronto.

In the West, the transplanted Black Hawks finished with 107 points, 20 points ahead of runner-up St. Louis. Al Arbour made his coaching debut with the Blues, but resigned after fifty games to return to the playing ranks as a defenseman. In the quarter-finals, the Hawks defeated Philadelphia, while Minnesota upset the Blues. Under the revised playoff format, East and West division quarter-final winners opposed each other in a second round that saw Montreal eliminate the surprisingly stubborn North Stars in six games, and Chicago sideline the Rangers in seven. Three games in the Chicago–New York series were decided in overtime, with New York winning two on goals by Pete Stemkowski. In game six, he scored after forty-one minutes of extra time.

The resulting Chicago–Montreal series was the first final since expansion in which one team was not the overwhelming favorite. Chicago, led by Tony Esposito, and Montreal, with the rookie Dryden in net, both had outstanding stoppers. The series went seven games, the Canadiens winning the final contest 3–2. Henri Richard, who had feuded with coach Al MacNeil earlier in the series, scored the final two goals of the game, including one on a long shot that skipped past Tony Esposito. Frank Mahovlich set playoff records with 14 goals and 27 points, and Ken Dryden was awarded the Conn Smythe Trophy as 1971 playoff MVP.

Two of the game's greats retired after the 1970-71 season. Forty-three-year-old Gordie Howe finished his twenty-fifth NHL season with 23 goals for the last-place Red Wings. Jean Béliveau, who finished with 507 regular-season goals and 79 in the playoffs, retired after eighteen NHL seasons and

Conn Smythe Trophy Voting

Until 1971, voting for the Conn Smythe Trophy, awarded to the MVP in each year's playoffs, was conducted by the NHL's Board of Governors. Since that time, members of the Professional Hockey Writers' Association have handled the balloting.

Ken Dryden relaxes in the familiar pose that became almost as famous as his heroics in the 1971 Stanley Cup playoffs. Dryden, who won the Vezina Trophy in five of his eight NHL campaigns, never lost more than ten games in a season and led the league in victories four times.

Minnesota defenseman Barry Gibbs wheels away from St. Louis defender Barclay Plager during action in the 1972-73 season. The North Stars, despite having seven 20-goal scorers, were eliminated in the 1973 quarterfinals by the Philadelphia Flyers.

ten Stanley Cups. The Hockey Hall of Fame acknowledged the contributions of the two by waiving the customary five-year waiting period between a player's retirement and his induction.

The Canadiens and Red Wings took the first steps toward filling the gaps left by their retired superstars by selecting two superb junior graduates in the 1971 amateur draft. The Habs, who had constructed an elaborate network of deals to acquire California's first overall selection, chose Quebec Remparts' superstar Guy Lafleur. Detroit, selecting second overall, took Marcel Dionne of the St. Catharines Black Hawks of the Ontario Hockey Association. Both would be NHL stars by the mid-1970s.

The playoff system was modified once more, so that quarter-finals in 1972 would match the first-place club against the fourth, and the second-place club against the third. This replaced the old system of one versus three and two versus four, instituted in 1943. The intent of the new system was to increase the competitive reward for finishing atop the division by providing the first-place finisher with a weaker quarter-final opponent.

The Canadiens hired Scotty Bowman as coach for the 1971-72 season. Bowman, who had coached and later served as general manager in St. Louis, had previously been an assistant to Montreal manager Sam Pollock. The Canadiens traded goaltender Rogie Vachon to Los Angeles, as playoff hero Ken Dryden was slated to be the club's starting goaltender. They also reacquired Jim Roberts from St. Louis. The defensive forward had played four seasons for the Habs in the mid-1960s.

Buffalo, drafting fifth overall in 1971, chose another high-scoring Quebec junior, Rick Martin of the Montreal Junior Canadiens, to play alongside Gil Perreault. Martin set a new NHL rookie scoring record with 44 goals in 1971-72.

Boston and New York again finished first and second in the East Division. Although Boston's big line of Esposito, Cashman, and Hodge scored more goals, New York's so-called G-A-G Line – Ratelle, Hadfield, and Gilbert – was better balanced and became the NHL's first forward unit to have all three members score more than 40 goals in a season. On defense, Bobby Orr, who had signed a new multi-year contract, had become hockey's first $1-million player, but New York's Brad Park had also established himself as a highly skilled offensive defenseman. Park's 73 points in 1971-72 were second only to Orr's total among defensemen.

As in the last years of the six-team NHL, the 1971-72 season ended with the league clearly still divided into "have" and "have-not" teams. In the East, Boston, New York, and Montreal were knotted near the top of the standings with Toronto 28 points out of third place and Detroit four points back in fifth. Buffalo and Vancouver lagged well behind the Maple Leafs and Red Wings. In the West, Chicago, a transplanted East Division club, finished 21 points ahead of second-place Minnesota and 40 points in front of third-place St. Louis. The North Stars finished above .500 for the first time in the franchise's five-year history and had the league's second-best defensive record. Doug Mohns, Barry Gibbs, Tom Reid, and Ted Harris led the Stars' defense corps in front of Cesare Maniago and Gump Worsley.

The league's scoring leaders mirrored the standings; Bobby Clarke of the Flyers was the only player from an expansion club in the top ten.

In the playoffs, Boston and New York advanced to the Stanley Cup finals as the Bruins defeated the Leafs and Blues and the Rangers eliminated the Canadiens and Black Hawks. The Rangers' appearance in the finals was the club's first since 1950. The championship series was the first to feature the NHL's top two regular-season teams since the Canadiens defeated the Leafs

Jean Béliveau became the fourth NHL player to score 500 goals by firing this Frank Mahovlich pass past Gilles Gilbert of the Minnesota North Stars on February 11, 1971.

Jean Ratelle (center) relaxes with linemates Vic Hadfield (left) and Rod Gilbert. The Rangers dealt Ratelle to the Bruins in 1975.

Derek Sanderson, who brashly predicted his Calder Trophy win in 1968, was one of the first NHL stars to jump to the WHA. Sanderson played only eight games in the new league and eventually returned to the NHL with the Bruins.

to win the Cup in 1960. In a series that received wide exposure in the United States, Orr led the Bruins to a six-game triumph. It was the club's second Cup of the 1970s, and Orr earned his second Conn Smythe Trophy. His 19 assists established a new playoff record.

In June, Orr underwent surgery on his left knee to repair ligament damage. The extent to which the game's top player would recover was one of many questions that would be answered in 1972-73.

The ascendancy of the Bruins and Rangers to the top of the standings represented a complete reversal of the NHL standings of the early and mid-1960s, but this change seems insignificant in light of the upheaval that swept the sport beginning in 1972-73. Two landmark events – the formation of a rival league and a showdown series with the national team of the Soviet Union – would forever change the NHL.

The World Hockey Association was incorporated in July of 1971 and was promoted by two California entrepreneurs, Dennis Murphy and Gary Davidson, both of whom were involved in the American Basketball Association, which, like the WHA, was set up to compete with its sport's established major league. The WHA began signing NHL players in February of 1972 when goaltender Bernie Parent inked a contract. Early signings involved players in the minors and on the fringes of the NHL, but in June the new league landed its first superstar when the Winnipeg Jets signed Bobby Hull to a ten-year deal worth $2.75 million. The signing of Hull established the WHA as an alternative for many players, and its ability to sign quality NHL talent increased. Ted Green, J. C. Tremblay, Gerry Cheevers, and Derek Sanderson also joined WHA clubs for the new league's inaugural season, and other players would follow.

But before the WHA and NHL began their 1972-73 schedules, hockey fans throughout the world focused on an eight-game exhibition series that marked the first meeting between the NHL's top players (Team Canada) and the Soviet Nationals. The Soviets were the defending Olympic champions and had won nine IIHF World Amateur Championships since 1963. The IIHF prohibited the use of professional players, and Canada had withdrawn from international competition after 1969, feeling that its amateur national team could not compete with the hockey team produced by the Soviets' year-round program of intensive coaching and training.

The 1972 NHL-Soviet series resulted from complicated negotiations headed up by NHLPA executive director Alan Eagleson. Four games were set for four Canadian cities, to be followed by four in Moscow. Although there was some dissent, the consensus in the North American hockey community was that Team Canada, despite the absence of Orr (knee surgery) and Hull (now playing in the WHA), would derail the Soviets' swarming attack and handily win the series.

The result of this first match-up between the Soviets and the NHL has

become the stuff of legend: the Soviets stunned Team Canada in the Canadian portion of the series and returned to the Soviet Union with two wins and a tie in four games. In Moscow, the Soviets took control of the series by winning game five, but Team Canada rallied for three consecutive late-game wins to capture the series four games to three with one game tied. Paul Henderson scored the winning goal in each of the last three games. Phil Esposito played brilliantly and emerged as Team Canada's leader.

The impact of what came to be known as the "super series" was felt at many levels. It established international hockey that involved the NHL and the Soviet Union as a first-rank attraction and made negotiator Alan Eagleson one of the most influential men in the game. It also demonstrated that the best hockey played in Europe was on a par with that of the NHL and that precision passing and high-speed play executed by superbly conditioned athletes were tough to beat. These lessons weren't lost on NHL general managers.

(continued on p. 215)

Alan Eagleson (center), whose vision of a hockey superpower showdown resulted in the 1972 Summit Series, reviews Team Canada's victory with (left to right) Ken Dryden, Paul Henderson, and Phil Esposito.

THE BOYS OF SUMMIT: THE 1972 NHL–SOVIET SERIES

by Red Fisher

"Liapkin rolled one to Savard ... "

Was it a generation ago, or was it only yesterday that Foster Hewitt started firing those words into a microphone in Moscow? They were words which, seconds later, would make everybody in Canada feel good about themselves.

It was, after all, THE goal. There was none like it before – there has been none like it since. It came with only thirty-four seconds remaining in this wildly emotional eight-game series between the best from the National Hockey League and the Soviet Union. Finally, after twenty-seven days and eight games less thirty-four seconds: Paul Henderson had scored THE goal.

"Savard cleared the pass to Stapleton ... "

Gorky Street on a summer night in Moscow in July 1972 is small cars careening at breakneck speed on a six-lane thoroughfare. It is the nonstop chatter of strollers, the bemused look of a first-time visitor, and the Muscovites' stares at the tourist. Gorky Street, even in early evening, is heat that clings like young lovers. It is wave after wave of people. One group no sooner disappears than another appears, as if on signal. Where do they all come from?

Alexandr Grinberg is twenty-eight. He drives a truck in Moscow. He is broad-shouldered, with thick, black hair that is slicked down. His eyes are dark. He wears a grey, checked shirt that goes well with his black trousers. Ah yes, he says, he had heard about the Canada – Soviet hockey series, even though its start was more than six weeks away. The first four games would be played in Canada, the last four in Moscow.

"I think the chances of the teams are exactly the same," he says. "I am a fan of my team, and I hope our fellows will play well. I would hope that out of the eight games, our fellows would win a good three, even though the Canadians are a very serious team. They have very strong players. I am told the professionals are something special and that is why we shall suffer," he says.

Sasha Petrosyan is twenty-five. He is an artist. He is not, like truck-driver Grinberg, a man of the outdoors, so his face is pale. His hair is sandy-colored. He smiles easily. "I think the chances of the Canadians are a great deal better than the Soviet team," he says. "They are substantially greater. Naturally, professionals are stronger than amateurs. Our boys are strong as amateurs."

Iosif Green is a lawyer from Baku on the Caspian Sea. He walks alone on Gorky Street, his white shirt open at the collar, his blue trousers baggy at the knees. He is a stocky man with a five-o'clock shadow on his chin. "I understand a little English very well," he says.

"How do you think the Soviets will do against the Canadians?" he is asked.

"The match will show," he replies. "I would like to talk of chess."

Victor Nikolayevich Kostykov has chosen this night to walk along Gorky Street with his co-worker, Vyacheslav Segeyevich Smirnov. Factory-worker Victor Nikolayevich is pale, like the artist, Sasha Petrosyan. His face is strong. His eyes shine in the gathering dusk. He wears an orange shirt and grey trousers. His belt is pinched tightly around his waist. "We are Soviet fans," he says, "and naturally, we cheer for our team. The series should end 5–5."

"There are only eight games in the series," he is told.

"In that case," he laughs, "it should end 4–4."

"I don't agree," says his friend, Vyacheslav. "I think we should win six out of the eight games. We are good ... very good."

"The team that will play the Soviets are professionals," Victor and Vyacheslav are told.

Kostyukov and Smirnov look at each other quickly. Then both throw up their hands in mock horror.

"Ah," says Kostyukov, "that is a different story."

"Of course, in that case," says Smirnov, "the games will be complicated."

"He cleared to the open wing to Cournoyer..."

Victor Ivanovich Gulyayev, a mathematics student, walks briskly along Gorky Street, glancing to neither the left nor the right. He has the look of someone who is late for class. He is nineteen. There is a briefcase under his arm and he is wearing a rose-colored shirt and black trousers. There is a peach fuzz of a beard on his thin, pinched face. "You have lots of soloists," he says. "You can be very successful with that. Still, I think we can win. Not all. Just part." He looks up into the lights of a nearby build-

Phil Esposito raises his arms in celebration after scoring the first goal of the 1972 Summit Series between Canada and the Soviet Union. The Soviets stormed back with seven goals to capture the first match of the eight-game set by a 7–3 score.

ing, and then sighs heavily. "With hockey," he says, "it is a business with the professionals. You cannot afford to lose. If you lose, you lose your prestige, too."

"What would be your reaction," he is asked, "if the Soviets lost all of the games to the Canadians?"

"If that happens," he smiles, "then we will have to learn from the Canadians."

"Cournoyer took a shot..."

Andrei Starovoitov is the General Secretary of the U.S.S.R. Hockey Federation this day in 1972. He is a severe-looking man, who appears to regard a smile as sign of weakness. He is one of the twenty Soviet officials sitting around a table. "Martin," he says, "is he of your team?"

Gary Bergman (2) watches as a loose puck slides wide of the post. Never flashy players in the NHL, Bergman and fellow Team Canada defenseman Bill White played the finest hockey of their careers in the Summit Series.

Seth Martin is a goaltender who played a total of twenty-six games in the National Hockey League. Before playing those games with the St. Louis Blues in 1967-68, the first year of expansion, his time was divided between senior-hockey assignments and international competition. His record at the international level left an impression on the Soviets.

"Your [Ken] Dryden, is he as good as Martin?" Starovoitov asks.

"I'm sure Martin was a very good international goaltender," he is told, "but he wasn't good enough to play in the National Hockey League. Dryden is a championship-caliber goaltender. That's how much better Dryden is," the Soviet official is told.

Starovoitov looks bewildered. Then he asks: "How do you think the series will go?"

"Eight straight," he is told.

"The defenseman fell over, Liapkin ... "

The Montreal Forum had put on its best face for the start of the first-ever game between the professionals of the NHL and the Soviet Union's "amateurs." Red, white, and blue bunting was draped on the faces of the choice seats. Canadian Prime Minister Pierre Trudeau was there for the ceremonial faceoff. So was the Soviet ambassador. The floors had been scrubbed to a high sheen. The ice on which hockey's greatest players had performed was a flat table of shimmering white.

The NHL versus the Soviets: Team Canada, hockey's greatest names, against a passel of no-names – to Canadians, at least: Tretiak, Kharlamov, Yakushev, Maltsev, Petrov, Mikhailov. *Who*, for heaven's sake?

Thirty seconds into the game, Phil Esposito scored. Six minutes and two seconds later, it was Henderson. Easy. Eight straight.

By period's end, the Soviets had tied the score. Valery Kharlamov scored twice in the second period before Bobby Clarke scored in the ninth minute of the third. Then, three more by the Soviets. Team Canada, 3. Team Soviets, 7. Thud!

How could this happen? How could this be allowed to happen? What went wrong? And why? They were questions hundreds of stunned reporters and Canadians across the country asked themselves over and over again in the moments after the game. What? How? Why?

The reporters had congregated for the post-game press conference in the Forum's garage. Their questions were not so much aimed at seeking answers as they were directed at themselves. It was one thing for the team and its coaches to be taken in, so to speak, but how could they have allowed themselves to be fooled so completely. Who *were* these Soviets?

Starovoitov worked his way through the crowd with a few questions of his own. "Do you remember me from Moscow, Mr. Fisher?" he asked.

"Yes, Mr. Starovoitov."

"Do you remember you said the series would go in eight straight?"

"Yes, Mr. Starovoitov."

"You could be right," he snapped. Then he swung on his heel and disappeared into the stunned crowd. He was smiling.

"Cournoyer has it on that wing ... "

Two nights and nine player changes later, Team Canada showed up in Toronto. Tony Esposito was in nets instead of Dryden. The Jean Ratelle–Rod Gilbert–Vic Hadfield line, which had played in game one, was benched. Serge Savard was in the line-up. He, better than anyone, put his team's 4–1 victory in perspective.

"All through training camp, I don't think we really put enough emphasis on defense. All the time, it was goals ... goals ... how many goals are we going to beat them by! Score! Score! But in this game," he said, "we brought some defense back into the game. Everybody was coming back, and it made it a lot easier for the defensemen. If we skate ... did you see Cournoyer go around Ragulin? ... we can beat them. We can't beat them eight straight now, but we can come close."

"There's a shot!"

There is a point in a game or series when it's time to say, "Whoa! What have we here?"

Team Canada was on another level awaiting game three in Winnipeg. Their victory in Toronto two nights earlier was vintage professional. Excellent goaltending. Good defense. Goals when they needed them.

They started the Winnipeg game the way they finished in Toronto. High. In command. Fewer than two minutes into the game, Jean-Paul Parise beat Tretiak, and even though the Soviets snapped a short-handed goal beyond Esposito less than two minutes later, Team Canada re-established its one-goal margin with a goal by Ratelle late in the period. Esposito added another early in the second, then it was Kharlamov with another short-handed goal.

Canada led this game 3–1 and 4–2, yet the Soviets came out of it with a tie, the tying goal coming with less than two minutes remaining in the second period. The Soviets were outshot 38–25, yet earned a tie. Whoa!

Teams just don't lose two-goal leads twice at the NHL level – and leave the game satisfied. Yet this was coach Harry Sinden after the game: "Aren't we all glad to be alive to watch that kind of hockey?" he asked.

And this was goaltender Dryden: "That's the way things always turn out in games against the Russian team. People leave the rink feeling we gave the game away, but that's the way they play. They keep coming and coming. They'll never outshoot you, but every time they shoot, either the goalie has to make a good save or it's a goal."

Whoa! This was supposed to be easy, so why is it so hard?

"Henderson makes a wild stab for it and fell ..."

It wasn't any easier in Vancouver, the next stop in this international cold war at the hockey summit.

It started with high hopes after Team Canada's victory in Toronto and tie in Winnipeg. It ended with Team Canada trailing 2–0 and 4–1 before falling 5–3, with the braying of Canadian fans in their ears.

Losing the series' first game was embarrassing, but Vancouver hurt desperately. It left the players empty. It left Esposito angry. "We're doing our best," he told a national TV audience immediately after the game. "If the fans in Moscow boo their players, I'll come back here and personally apologize to every-

Before the 1972 series between Team Canada and the Soviet Nationals, goaltending was believed to be a Soviet weak spot. Vladislav Tretiak debunked this theory by playing superbly. His goaltending anchored the Soviet team throughout his career before he retired in 1984. He later became the first Soviet-trained player inducted into the Hockey Hall of Fame in 1989.

body, but I don't think that's going to happen. I really don't," said Esposito. His pained monologue sounded less like a complaint than a scream for help.

"Here's another shot!"

Team Canada had looked empty during two mid-series exhibition games in Sweden, but now it was time to see what the players could do about the series they were trailing 1–2–1. The first of the final four games was just ahead in Moscow, and if that wasn't bad enough, a major problem from within had erupted.

Defections.

Rangers left winger Hadfield, who hadn't played much – and not that well when he did–decided to go home. So did rookies Jocelyn Guevremont and Rick Martin, who hadn't played at all in the series.

The day before game five, Hadfield wasn't on a regular line in practice. His reaction was to sit on the bench during the skating drills. Assistant coach John Ferguson skated over to him. "Get out there, do some skating," he snarled.

"Aw, anybody can see I won't be playing," said Hadfield. "What's the point?"

"At least loosen your legs," Ferguson insisted. Hadfield remained on the bench.

Sinden came over to the bench and ordered Hadfield onto the ice. Hadfield shook his head. "If you don't want to skate," said Sinden, "get your stuff off." It may have been at that exact moment that

Phil Esposito added an air of levity to the pressure-packed proceedings of the Summit Series when he took a tumble during the player introductions prior to game five in Moscow.

Hadfield decided to quit the team. Perhaps he had already made up his mind. Either way, it wasn't right.

"That's what I tried to tell him," Ferguson said. "It's a bad move. What are the people back home going to think? How's he gonna get people to forget he left the team when the series was only half over?"

They didn't forget. Throughout the regular season that followed, Hadfield was reminded of his defection wherever he played. Fans still remember. What they also remember was that Team Canada came out for game five higher than they had ever been in the series. After two periods, they led 3–0 on goals by Parise, Clarke, and Henderson. With fewer than eleven minutes remaining in the game, they led 4–1. From his heavily guarded private box, a Soviet fan named Leonid Brezhnev sat glowering.

Then the wheels fell off.

The Soviets scored twice in eight seconds. A little more than two minutes later, the game was tied. Even as Hadfield was airborne for home, the Soviets won, 5–4. That meant that a Soviet victory in one of the three remaining games in Moscow would assure them of the series victory. Team Canada had no room to breathe.

In his private box, Brezhnev smiled broadly. So did Nikolai Podgorny, the president of the Soviet Union. So did prime minister Alexi Kosygin and the first deputy minister, Dmitri Polyanski. Smiles everywhere.

"Right in front . . . "

Three games left. Five had been played, and Team Canada was trailing 1–3–1. Our system against theirs. Team Canada was on The Brink.

There was no scoring in the first period of game six. There was a lot of it (five goals) in the second. Dennis Hull, Cournoyer, and Henderson scored for Team Canada, despite being shorthanded for seventeen minutes, including two minutes with the team short two men. Canada's three-goal outburst in one minute and twenty-three seconds did all the offensive damage, and then it was up to the defensive players to exert control on the Soviets.

Somehow, they held the Soviets to only two goals. Still alive, after six games. Somehow.

And, miraculously, very much alive two nights

later after a 4–3 victory in game seven, one in which Team Canada led 1–0, trailed 2–1, led 3–2 early in the third period and, finally, won on a Henderson (there's that man again) goal with fewer than three minutes remaining.

"Of all the goals I've ever scored," Henderson said after his second consecutive winning goal, "this one gave me the most satisfaction."

Back from The Brink. Seven games had been played, and now it was 3–3–1. Is it any wonder coach Sinden was saying about the series finale: "It could be the greatest game ever played."

A triumphant group of Team Canada skaters surround Paul Henderson after another key goal. Henderson would score the winning goal in each of the last three games of the series.

Emotionally, there was nothing to match it before, nor has there been since. Not even close. Maybe that's why the most frequently used phrase in the moments after this 6–5 classic was "off the floor."

"We came off the floor," said assistant coach Ferguson.

"Off the floor," said Alan Eagleson, the executive director of the NHL Players' Association, who had put the series together.

Off the floor ... after Team Canada matched the Soviets goal for goal in the first half of the game, only to fall behind 5–3 in the last half of the second period.

Off the floor ... when goals came from Esposito and Cournoyer in the first thirteen minutes of the third period. Ah, yes, the Cournoyer goal. He beats Tretiak at 12:56 of the period. The puck is in the net, but there's a problem: the red light doesn't go on. The referee has his arm raised to signal the goal, but not everybody sees it. Among them is Eagleson.

He is sitting in a front-row seat at center-ice. When the red light doesn't go on, he stands, leaps from his seat onto the floor five feet below. He bumps into several Soviet police when he lands. One of them turns and shoves Eagleson. The players' man shoves back. Hard. In an instant, Eagleson is grasped firmly by a half-dozen policemen and is half-pushed, half-dragged to the nearest exit. Even while the Canadian players are flinging their arms around each other over the goal, a buzz of fear sweeps over the people who are watching helplessly as Eagleson is being dragged away. Peter Mahovlich is the first player to notice the problem. He races to the boards. Gary Bergman joins him there, flailing at the police.

The remaining players on the ice dash to the struggling group, and now all the players race from the bench. Ferguson ... Sinden ... all of them straining to get at the police in their attempt to free Eagleson.

Eventually, Eagleson is shaken loose and brought across the ice, finger raised skyward, to the Team Canada bench. Once there, he shakes his fist at the goal judge in a final gesture of defiance. Seven minutes and four seconds remain.

Does a team that has struggled from behind three times in a hockey game settle for a tie after heading into the final period with a two-goal deficit? Most do. Not this one. But have you any idea how difficult it is for a team to outshoot the Soviets 14–5 in the final period of an eight-game series, with everything riding on the outcome? Relentlessly they come. Skate ... shoot ... hit ... skate harder ... hit harder. Now there are six minutes left ... three ... two ... one – the seconds and the series are ticking away. Skate ... hit ... pressing and pressing. Esposito is there and then Henderson ... a rebound ... another shot and now Hewitt is screaming joyously ...

"They score!!! Henderson has scored for Canada!"

THE goal!

Only thirty-four seconds remained before victory in this greatest of all international hockey series could be claimed. THE goal!

Ken Dryden describes it this way:

I was less than 200 feet away. I remember things from just before and just after, but not then. I remember feeling no fear of losing, no desperation as the clock blinked down to the series' end, no resignation over the all-but-certain tie. A year before, from the same distance away, I had seen Henri Richard's Stanley Cup-winning goal seconds before it happened. Clearly, absolutely. From where Esposito and Henderson, Liapkin and Tretiak were standing, from the position of the puck, I remember feeling no sudden rush of hope, no pattern that made me know what would happen next.

Sprinting, tripping in bulky leg pads, my own whoops shouting in my ears – I remember being somewhere in the middle of Luzhniki's vacant ice dashing to catch the scrum of celebration near the Soviet net. Memory goes away before I reach the pile. It comes back again several seconds later, in the midst of the joyous pummeling. Stop, I hear myself say. Get a hold of yourself. There's still thirty-four seconds to go!

THE Goal. Henderson's last-minute game- and series-clincher came on his second stab at a rebound from a shot taken by Phil Esposito.

My next memory comes after the game is over. Finding a corner deep inside myself, grinning, burning with twenty-seven days of pleasure, disaster, and relief, I think to myself – wouldn't this have been great to watch at home! Can you believe what it must've been like. I mean, I would've gone crazy.*

Sure, he would've. All of us went crazy on the last of those twenty-seven days in September 1972. Wonderful, marvelous, chest-out-to-here, soul-stirring crazy!

Eight hockey games: 480 minutes of the wildest, most emotional roller-coaster ride we and hockey have ever experienced. Our best against their best.

Highs. Lows. Pure and soaring joy. Depression. Pride. Humility. And then, THE goal!

*Quotation from Home Game *(p. 192) courtesy of McClelland & Stewart.*

For the 1972-73 season, the NHL added franchises in Atlanta and Long Island, two markets that were also of interest to the WHA. The Atlanta club was owned by a syndicate headed by Tom Cousins, who had developed the Omni hotel-and-arena complex where the team would play its home games. Bill Putnam, formerly of the Philadelphia Flyers, was hired as club president. Cliff Fletcher, who had been assistant general manager in St. Louis, became the Atlanta Flames' first general manager. Bernie Geoffrion, who rapidly became an adopted "favorite son" in Atlanta, was hired as coach. The Flames were assigned to the West Division.

The other new expansion franchise was granted to Roy Boe and a group of New York investors. Based in Long Island's Nassau Veterans' Memorial Coliseum, the team, which would play in the East, was named the New York Islanders. Boe hired Bill Torrey from the California Golden Seals as general manager, and Torrey hired Phil Goyette as the team's first coach.

The Flames and Islanders each paid $6 million in franchise fees to join the NHL. The Islanders also paid a reported $5 million to the New York Rangers as indemnification for overlapping their market area. The Islanders were hard hit by WHA signings, losing seven of their first twenty draft choices. The new club would be built around defensive specialist Ed Westfall from Boston and goaltender Gerry Desjardins from Chicago. To sign their number-one choice, Billy Harris, a star with the Toronto Marlboros, the Islanders had to pay $100,000 a year for three years. Only a few seasons earlier, this

Oldest Rookie

The oldest rookie ever to play in the NHL is Connie Madigan, who didn't arrive in the league until he was thirty-eight years old. Madigan played over seven hundred professional games before getting a call to join the St. Louis Blues on February 6, 1973. He played in twenty regular-season games and another five in the playoffs before finishing his career back in the WHL.

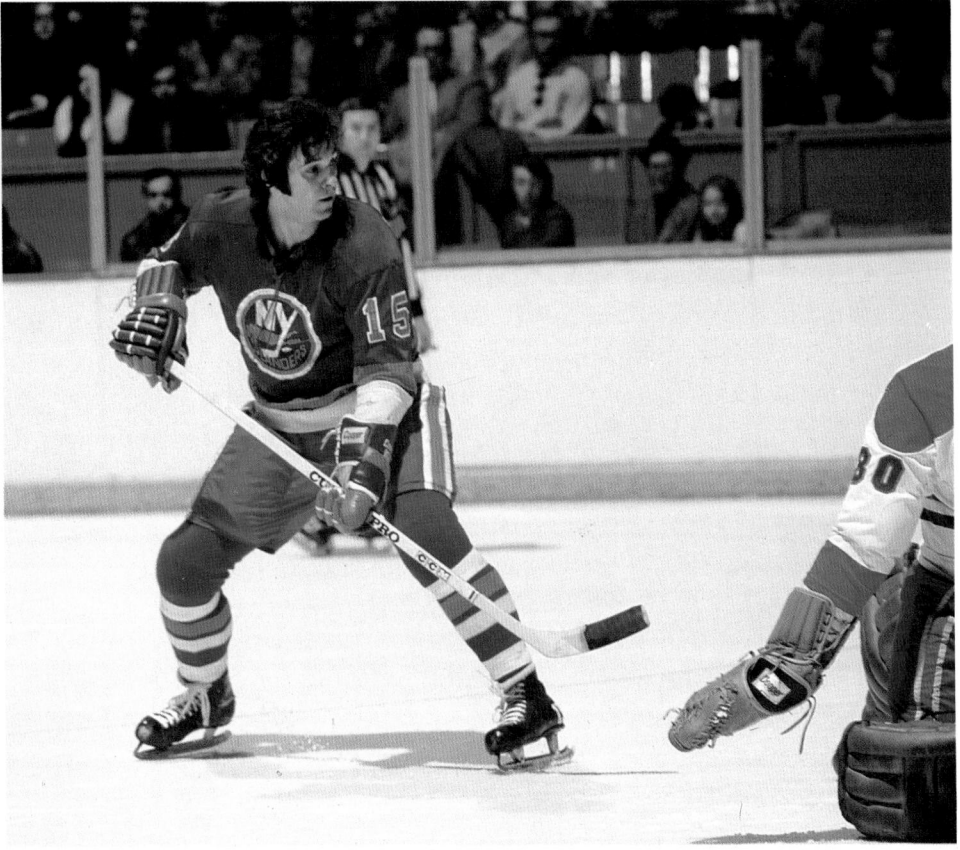

Billy Harris, the first player selected in the 1972 Entry Draft by the expansion New York Islanders, scored at least 22 goals in each of his first six seasons in the NHL.

Wings' captain Alex Delvec-chio (center) stands poised near the California Seals' crease, creating a distraction for Seals' goaltender Gilles Meloche. Delvecchio is second only to former teammate Gordie Howe in career games played in the NHL, suiting up 1,549 times for the Detroit Red Wings.

Last Maskless Goaltender

Journeyman goaltender Andy Brown — who played for Detroit and Pittsburgh in the early 1970s — played his last NHL game on March 31, 1973, against the St. Louis Blues. Brown's appearance marked the last time an NHL goalie appeared in a game without a facemask.

kind of money was paid only to the game's top stars such as Bobby Hull – and then only after Hull held out during the pre-season. Atlanta anchored its new team with goaltenders Phil Myre from Montreal and Daniel Bouchard from Boston. In the universal draft, the club selected Jacques Richard, who had replaced Guy Lafleur as the high-scoring star of the junior Quebec Remparts.

The Montreal Canadiens proved to be the elite team of 1972-73, losing just ten games en route to a 120-point first-place finish. The Habs received a 44-goal performance from Jacques Lemaire and 93 points from Frank Mahovlich. Ken Dryden won the Vezina Trophy. Other players in the East Division reached career milestones: Boston's Johnny Bucyk got his 400th goal, the Leafs' Dave Keon his 300th, and Montreal's Mahovlich became the sixth man in league history to score 500. Detroit's Alex Delvecchio moved into second place on the NHL's all-time point-scoring list behind former linemate Gordie Howe. Bobby Orr, bad knee and all, topped 100 points for the fourth straight year and won the Norris Trophy yet again. The status quo remained intact in the East Division, as Boston and the Rangers shared the top spots with the Canadiens. All three teams finished with more than 100 points.

The surprise team of 1972-73 was the Buffalo Sabres, fourth-place finishers in only their third NHL season. The success of the French Connection, a forward line made up of Gilbert Perreault, Rick Martin, and René Robert, propelled the Sabres past Detroit, Toronto, and the expansion Islanders and Canucks, into the last playoff spot in the East. The Islanders set an NHL record, losing 60 games, and accumulated just 30 points, the lowest total for an NHL team since the Rangers logged 17 in the 50-game 1943-44 season. The Islanders used their last-place finish to claim defenseman Denis Potvin with the first pick in the 1973 amateur draft.

Philadelphia made a significant move up the standings of the West Division. Eliminated from a playoff spot when they allowed a goal with four seconds left to lose 3–2 to Buffalo in the last game of the 1971-72 season, the Flyers posted a 19-point improvement to finish second in 1972-73. Bobby Clarke, the NHL's youngest team captain, had 37 goals and was runner-up to Phil Esposito in scoring. Clarke became the first expansion-team player to break 100 points in a season and was the first player from the West Division to be named league MVP. Rick MacLeish, who finished with 100 points, gave the Flyers the scoring punch they had lacked, and became the first expansion-team player to score 50 goals. The Black Hawks finished first in the West, with the North Stars and Blues earning the remaining playoff berths.

In the quarter-finals, Montreal, the Rangers, Chicago, and Philadelphia advanced. Phil Esposito of the Bruins sustained a knee injury in Boston's quarter-final match-up with the Rangers, contributing to New York's upset win. In the semi-finals, the Flyers and Rangers both won the first games of their respective series against the Canadiens and the Black Hawks before being eliminated in five games. The Flyers were impressive in defeat against the Canadiens, playing well in every game. The Canadiens handled the Black Hawks in a six-game final to win their eighteenth Stanley Cup. Yvan Cournoyer, who scored a record 15 goals in the playoffs, was awarded the Conn Smythe Trophy. Henri Richard, who had ten points in the post-season, was a part of his eleventh Stanley Cup-winning team. This is an NHL record for Cup wins by a player.

The WHA had survived its first season, and, in preparation for the 1973-74 campaign, continued to sign NHL players and top draft choices. It scored a public relations coup by announcing that Gordie Howe would end his two-year retirement to join his sons Mark and Marty with the Houston Aeros. Others who jumped to the WHA included Ralph Backstrom, Réjean Houle, and Marc Tardif. The Philadelphia Flyers reversed the trend, signing Bernie Parent after the former Leaf and Flyer spent one season in the WHA. The Canadiens lost goaltender Ken Dryden, not to the rival league, but to the practice of law. After reaching an impasse in contract negotiations with the Canadiens, Dryden chose to article with a law firm in Toronto, taking a one-year sabbatical from the NHL. On the ice, European players began to make an impression in the NHL. Swedish national-team players Inge Hammarstrom and, particularly, Borje Salming played well for the Leafs.

The Philadelphia Flyers had become an imposing physical team, dedicated to protecting offensive stars Bobby Clarke, Rick MacLeish, and Bill

Borje Salming was the first European-trained player to make an impact in the NHL, playing seventeen seasons with Toronto and Detroit. A six-time NHL All-Star, Salming is the Leafs' all-time assists leader.

Barber. Coached by Fred Shero, the Flyers escalated the use of strategic intimidation – an early-1970s trademark of the "Big Bad (Boston) Bruins" – and acquired a nickname of their own: the "Broad Street Bullies," after one of Philadelphia's main thoroughfares. The club enjoyed its best season, winning 50 games and finishing first in the West with 112 points. Several of the league's penalty-minute leaders were Flyers, among them Dave Schultz and Andre "Moose" Dupont, who finished first and second.

The Flyers' success relegated Chicago to second place in the West for the first time since the club joined the division in 1970-71. The Los Angeles Kings, who were led by fifth-year center Butch Goring's 28 goals, finished third, reaching the playoffs for the first time in five seasons. Atlanta, in only its second NHL season, placed fourth. The Flames' goaltending tandem of Daniel Bouchard and Phil Myre was one of the club's strengths. The fifth-place Pittsburgh Penguins had two 40-goal scorers as Lowell McDonald and Jean Pronovost reached this plateau playing on a line centered by Syl Apps, Jr.

In the East Division, the sophomore New York Islanders, led by Calder Trophy-winning Denis Potvin, improved by 26 points, but still finished in last place. The Buffalo Sabres lost veteran defenseman Tim Horton, who was killed in a car accident. Star center Gil Perreault, who had 88 points the previous season, broke his leg 55 games into the season. The Sabres slumped to 76 points and a fifth-place finish. The Toronto Maple Leafs, who had acquired goaltender Doug Favell from Philadelphia, replaced Buffalo in fourth, posting 86 points, the franchise's best mark since the 1960-61 season. Fourth-year player Darryl Sittler led the Leafs with 38 goals.

Bobby Clarke and Phil Esposito follow the flight of the puck after a key draw in the Boston zone. The Philadelphia Flyers, who upset the Bruins in the 1974 Stanley Cup finals, were the first 1967 expansion team to defeat an "original six" squad in the championship round.

The powerful Bruins, with Harry Sinden back as general manager, regained first place in the East with 113 points. The Canadiens and Rangers finished second and third. The Bruins' Esposito scored his 400th goal and 1,000th point, while Bobby Orr, after only seven seasons in the NHL, broke Doug Harvey's record for assists by a defenseman. Esposito, Orr, Hodge, and Cashman finished in order atop the league's scoring list.

In the playoffs, Philadelphia and Boston advanced to the semi-finals by sweeping Atlanta and Toronto. In the second round, the Bruins needed six games to eliminate the Black Hawks, while the Flyers hooked up with the Rangers in a seven-game thriller. Philadelphia won the final game of the series 4–3 behind Bernie Parent's superb goaltending. Flyers' defenseman Barry Ashbee sustained a career-ending eye injury in this series.

The championship series between the Flyers and Bruins was a showdown between the NHL's toughest teams. The Flyers won in six games, clinching the Cup with a 1–0 win at home in game six. Seven seasons after joining the NHL, the Flyers' combination of skill and rugged play had closed the gap between "original" and expansion teams.

The Flyers didn't play classic offensive hockey, but they were the darlings of their fans and furthered the exposure that Esposito and Orr had given the NHL in the United States. High-school and prep-school hockey flourished, while competition for talent between the NHL and WHA provided American-born players with increased opportunities to be scouted and drafted by professional organizations.

This same competition for players between the two leagues was causing financial hardship for some clubs, however. Teams not attracting sellout crowds still had to pay the greatly increased salaries that resulted from the bidding war for players. Against this backdrop of rising costs, secret talks between the rival leagues took place as early as 1973, but reticence from owners on both sides would delay the reaching of an accommodation until 1979.

(*continued on p. 226*)

BOBBY CLARKE AND THE FLYERS

by Jay Greenberg

When the Broad Street Bullies ruled hockey, they were not only too tough to get what was coming to them, but also too good. They eluded justice not only with their talent, which was considerable, but also with their zeal, which even their legions of detractors found admirable. The Philadelphia Flyers were decried as goons and outlaws, prosecuted by tough players and even tougher power-plays, but they proved themselves so clearly the best team in the NHL in winning consecutive Stanley Cups in 1974 and 1975 that nobody laid a hand, clenched or otherwise, on them.

Only now, as they get meaner in every retelling with each passing year, are the Bullies doing time for their transgressions. In the view, spiteful or otherwise, of almost anyone ever beaten to a puck or a pulp by the Flyers, they are justly serving the longest misconduct penalty in NHL history: an image they can't cleanse.

Three members of the Hockey Hall of Fame played on those championship teams, and still they are largely remembered as a bunch of thugs. The Flyers were impressively organized, totally driven, and as worthy a champion team as the NHL has ever produced; yet they behaved so badly, so often, that outside of Philadelphia, any credit they receive is largely begrudged.

The line that has separated an acceptable level of NHL aggression from the unacceptable has always been a dotted one. But unquestionably, when those Flyers crossed it, they never felt compelled to apologize. The Boston Bruins, who, by consensus, preceded the Flyers as the best team in the NHL, were celebrated as Big and Bad, and in fact, were at least part of the role model upon which the Bullies patterned themselves. But punch-for-punch, slash-for-slash, sneer-for-sneer, the Flyers set new standards of rowdiness. They established records for penalty minutes, cleared their bench with great enthusiasm, and even found themselves answering formal charges in Vancouver and Toronto courtrooms.

Through it all, they were unrepentant. In fact, they even credited the Vancouver incident, which occurred in December 1972, as a

It was this thumping body-check by Ed Van Impe on Valery Kharlamov in a 1976 exhibition game with Moscow's Central Red Army that solidified the Flyers' position as the league's toughest competitors.

turning point in their ascendency from a nonde-script expansion team to contenders. In an attempt to loosen a chokehold that Flyer winger Don Saleski had placed on Vancouver defenseman Barry Wilkins, a fan pulled Saleski's hair. Flyer back-up goaltender Bobby Taylor, seated nearby on the bench, climbed into the stands after the fan, and the Flyers followed to make sure Taylor was not outnumbered.

As in most of the incidents that would follow over the next few years, the spectacle created was con-siderably worse than the actual damage. A few punches were thrown, but most of the Flyers did nothing worse than bang their sticks on chairs vacated by frightened spectators. However, on the team's next visit to Vancouver two months later, several of the players had to appear in court to answer charges ranging from obscene language to common assault. The case was postponed until sum-mer, when six players were fined and Taylor received a suspended thirty-day sentence for pushing a policeman. Still, the shame of being hauled before civil authorities the day of a game should have meant that the Flyers would be on their best behav-ior that night.

Not these guys, though. In the second minute of play, defenseman Andre "Moose" Dupont high-sticked Vancouver's Bobby Schmautz, drawing a bar-rage of eggs and outrage. But the Flyers killed off Dupont's major penalty by scoring twice short-handed and led 4–0 after only ten minutes. The third period culminated in Saleski, having already twice thrashed the diminutive Richard Lemieux, trying to climb into the penalty box to attack Lemieux again.

After the Flyers' 10–5 victory, a Vancouver writer approached Dupont in the locker room. The defenseman wore only his helmet, and held a ciga-rette in one hand and a beer in the other. "It was a good day for us," Dupont said. "We didn't go to jail, we beat up their chicken forwards, we scored goals, and we won. Now, The Moose drinks beer."

That pretty well summed up the Flyer philosophy. One could sense that this was a team beginning to call attention to itself. Until that season, the Flyers' sixth in the league, they had not only been nonde-script, but also seemingly cursed. In their first

Dave Burrows (3) and Flyers' career goal-scoring leader Bill Barber meet in the 1976 All-Star Game in Philadelphia.

season, the roof blew off their new home, the Spec-trum, forcing them to play their final fourteen regu-lar-season games on the road. Twice, in 1969-70 and 1971-72, the Flyers were eliminated from a playoff spot on the final day of the regular season by bizarre goals. In 1969-70 they needed only one point in their last six games to clinch a playoff spot. They lost them all, including the last one, 1–0, when goalie Bernie Parent lost sight of Minnesota defenseman Barry Gibbs's lob from center-ice. In 1971-72 the Flyers, requiring only a tie on the final night in Buffalo to make the playoffs, were four seconds away from getting one when the Sabres' Gerry Meehan beat goalie Doug Favell from the blue line.

In the aftermath of that nightmare, it would have taken either extraordinary foresight or incredible faith to predict a Stanley Cup only two years away. Eleven players whose names wound up on the Cup joined the Flyers in the fifteen months following the bitter 1972 finish. Gamebreaking center Rick MacLeish, a 1971 addition in a trade with Boston, had spent the 1971-72 season in the minors after floundering in his first Flyer trial. Bill Barber, a consummately talented left wing, was the team's first-round pick in 1972. Parent, traded away by the Flyers to Toronto in 1971, was reacquired before the beginning of the 1973-74 season. And Dave Schultz, the tough-guy left wing who gave the Flyers courage – and the NHL authorities some of their biggest headaches in history – became a regular with the team on opening day of 1972-73.

Still, while critical pieces of the nucleus came together relatively suddenly, the essence of the Flyers had already been in place for three seasons. In the midst of all the bad luck that cursed the Flyers in their growing years had come an extraordinary stroke of fortune. In the 1969 draft, twelve teams passed over the best player in junior hockey, Bobby Clarke, because he had diabetes. The Flyers, not bold enough to take Clarke in the first round, were smart enough to take him in the second.

Clarke scored a modest 15 goals and 31 assists in his rookie season. Nevertheless, general manager Keith Allen, who had wisely steered away from the ruinous path that most of the expansion teams had taken – trading away draft choices for veterans and instant respectablity – was already convinced that

Bernie Parent's superstar goaltending played a major role in the Flyers' championship season of 1973-74. He was the league leader in minutes, wins, average, save percentage, and shutouts.

painfully shy but ferociously driven kid from the copper-and-zinc-mining town of Flin Flon, Manitoba, was a player he could build around. Off the ice, Clarke, bespectacled, polite, and shy, looked like an altarboy. But when the puck dropped, he would do anything to win. "He's the kind of player who eventually will carry the Flyers to the Stanley Cup," Allen said.

However, even when the Flyers were ordinary, Clarke did not joust alone against their mediocrity. Three original Flyers, all taken in the 1967 expansion draft – defensemen Joe Watson and Ed Van Impe and right wing Gary Dornhoefer – all proved strong of character, and improved as players as the seasons went by. Defenseman Barry Ashbee, stereotyped as a career minor-leaguer when he was rescued by Allen from Hershey of the American League in 1970, added more of the singlemindedness that would become the team's trademark.

In 1972-73 Clarke announced his arrival as a dominating player with his first 100-point season. MacLeish suddenly exploded for 50 goals and 50 assists. Rookies Schultz and Saleski fought everybody, every time, everywhere. The Flyers recorded their initial winning season, beat Minnesota for their first-ever playoff-series victory, and then stunned heavily favored Montreal at the Forum with an overtime victory in game one of the semi-finals. The Flyers then lost four consecutive close games to the Canadiens, but, as they dressed to go home, the pervading feeling was that their season had ended with a beginning. "We were anxious to start training camp right then," said Barber.

The last piece in the puzzle – Parent, a goalie about to perform what may be the two best-goaltended seasons in NHL history – was fitted over the summer, and the Flyers gleefully set out to meet their destiny. They won fifty games and the heart of a city whose other professional teams were decided losers. As their penalty minutes crested, so did their status as the league's top road draw. And the more they were decried, the more willing they became to give the fans exactly what they had paid to see. The Flyers would gather regularly in their locker room to read their press reviews and giggle about how they were being portrayed. As the chip on their shoulder grew bigger, their confidence level soared. The effect on their opponents was hardly subtle.

"Whenever I walked through that big, black door leading into the visiting locker room at the Spectrum," said former Buffalo and Vancouver defenseman Mike Robitaille, "I thought I was walking through the gates of hell." A new strain of twenty-four-hour virus, commonly known as the Philadelphia flu, ravaged teams on visits to the City of Brotherly Love, leaving them short of key (albeit meek) players. There were a lot of nights when the Flyers had to do little more than growl on the first few shifts to establish complete control of the game. There were also plenty of nights when they didn't even have to get ugly at all. Still, most teams were far more intimidated by the Flyers' work habits than by their fists and butt ends. They forechecked rabidly and backchecked devastatingly. Their execution of the simple, effective system Fred Shero had drilled into them was almost flawless.

This is why it is so unfortunate that their reign as champions is remembered as a dark age for hockey. The Flyers were an excellent team. They overcame a general lack of speed – MacLeish was their only true gamebreaker – with nearly flawless execution of Shero's dump-and-chase system. Not gifted with a game-controlling, puck-carrying defenseman, the Flyers nevertheless controlled games defensively. The seventeen games they won by one goal on the way to their first Cup did not come by being stronger of fist, but by being stronger of mind.

The seven-game semi-final victory over the Rangers in that first-Cup season, 1973-74, was filled with penalties – and bitterness. Many felt the New York defeat was sealed when Schultz bloodied defenseman Dale Rolfe without drawing retaliation. But the finals against Boston were relatively cleanly played. Only the fifth game, a 5–1 Bruin victory, got out of control, and it was the least consequential game of the six. The series, and the home-ice advantage, turned on Clarke's overtime goal in Boston in game two and was decided by Rick MacLeish's tip-in goal that gave the Flyers the game-six clincher, 1–0. But the championship was really won by Parent's game-in, game-out excellence.

The most memorable fistic encounter of the drive to their second Cup saw young Islander winger Clark

Center Rick MacLeish scored 50 goals in his first full season with the Flyers. He was the NHL's leading playoff scorer in both of the Flyers' Cup-winning years.

Gillies beat Schultz badly in a game-five fight. The Islanders, who had climbed out of a 3–0 series deficit to beat Pittsburgh the previous round, again won three straight after losing the first three games of the Flyers series, but Philadelphia blew open game seven early and smothered the young Islanders the rest of the way. The six-game Cup-clinching victory over Buffalo that followed did not contain a single fight.

Certainly there have been more dazzling teams in NHL history than the Flyers, but none that has been any better drilled. The drilling came from Fred Shero, their introspective and sometimes bizarre coach. When Shero, sneaking out for a quick cigarette after the first exhibition game he ever coached with the Flyers, managed to lock himself out of the arena, his nickname, "Freddie the Fog," was born. Shero moved furtively around hotels and arenas, always leaving the impression he would rather be alone. Yet he could turn the simplest question into a monologue on hockey theory and his philosophy of life. "Sometimes I don't think he knows the difference between Tuesday and Wednesday," said Scotty Bowman, then the Montreal coach. "And sometimes

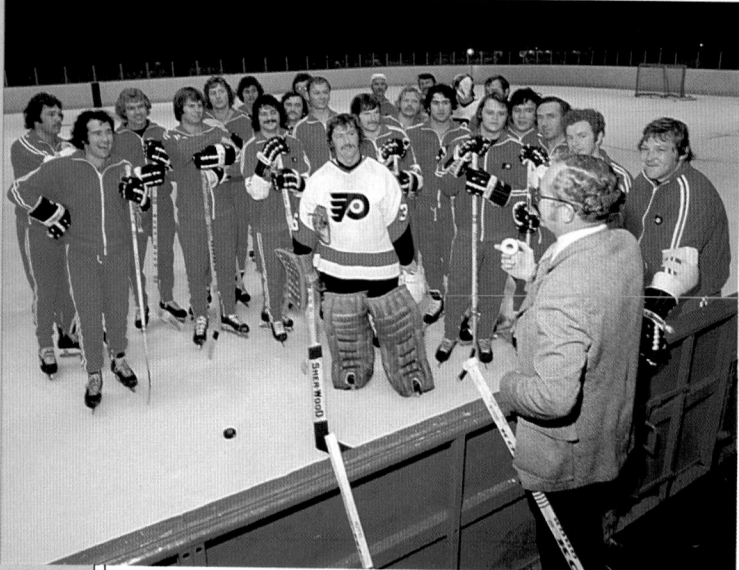

Fred Shero, the Flyers' coach in their Cup-winning seasons of 1974 and 1975, addresses the troops before the start of another practice session.

I think he's a genius who has us all fooled." There was truth in both assessments, and once Shero acquired the image of the bumbling genius, he was not reluctant to embellish it.

He practised the Flyers with tennis balls, repeatedly expressed his admiration for the fluid, graceful, Soviet style of play, and regularly consulted Bartlett's quotations for inspirational messages that he placed on the locker-room blackboard. Yet the Flyers succeeded with methods that were anything but European, and they were almost never addressed in one-on-one conversation by their coach. If they read the quotations, or understood them, it was only because they had come to believe in Shero's system. It gained credibility the first time a Flyer defenseman, under heavy forechecking pressure, looked up to find the Flyer right-wing along the boards waiting for an outlet pass. *Voilà*. Just as Freddie had been patiently diagramming it. MacLeish and Barber added talent, Schultz added bravado, and Reg Leach, who arrived in 1974-75, a sniper's touch around the net. From then on, nothing succeeded like success.

The motivation was left largely to Clarke, who may have been the greatest leader in the history of the game. "He gives more of himself than anybody I've ever seen," said Punch Imlach, the late Toronto

and Buffalo coach. The example Clarke set was the essence of Clarke's effect on the Flyers. "He has no outstanding talents," said Ed Snider, the Flyer owner. "[Players] see somebody like Bobby Orr or Guy Lafleur, they know they could never be like them no matter how hard they tried. But when they see Bobby, they think, 'I can do that.' They feel they can do everything he can do if they just put out the same effort."

They couldn't, of course. It only looked like they could. Clarke didn't retire in 1984, after fifteen Flyers seasons, as the NHL's tenth all-time leading scorer and fourth-best all-time assist-maker simply on the force of his work habits. His drive was extraordinary, but as he gained recognition for his steely-eyed determination, his skills were underrated. They never should have been. Clarke was hardly fast, but he did get a better jump from a standing start than most players, and he was exceptionally strong on his skates. His corner and faceoff work offered a primer in body leverage. He regularly, uncannily, gained control of the puck from players who outweighed him by twenty or thirty pounds.

Clarke had a less-than-average shot, but until Wayne Gretzky, nobody ever passed the puck in a more inventive way or had a better sense of the location of the other eleven players on the ice. And there simply has never been a better defensive forward in the game's history.

His instincts and drive came naturally; his skills were developed during hours and hours of work on a hockey rink. Clarke wouldn't call the time he spent work, though. He believed it to be bliss. "Every kid in Flin Flon played hockey," Clarke said. "Some played three nights a week, some played four. I played every night. All I ever wanted to do was play hockey and I just played it the way I thought it had to be played." Which, simply, was as if his entire being depended on his next turn on the ice.

Losing is dying only in the allegorical sense, but the way Clarke played suggested he was skating for his very life. Problems associated with diabetes often portend a short lifespan, and Clarke attacked hockey as if he was compelled to enjoy it as much as he could. He always denied that, though. His eyes, though myopic, were otherwise healthy. His cuts

healed quickly. He took his insulin every day, just like he brushed his teeth. Clarke was a diabetic, yes, but he believed himself to be one of the lucky ones.

All the same, he undoubtedly overcompensated for an affliction that had become a cross for him to bear when he was diagnosed as diabetic at age thirteen. Clarke was so fearful of people's perception of diabetes that he refused to even discuss it in his early years in Philadelphia. In time, as it became obvious that the condition was not debilitating, he dealt with it more easily and openly. Of course, when Clarke turned thirty and the inevitable erosion of his game began, he had something else to deny: the aging process. He refused to give in to it. To the end of his fifteen seasons, nothing was more important to him than his next shift. Clarke retired as one of the ten best players in the game's history because he was absolutely relentless in blocking everything out. He was an excellent player, but human. It was his will that bordered on the supernatural.

Bobby Clarke, who was the spiritual and offensive leader of the Flyers for fifteen years, was the first skater from an expansion team to win the Hart Trophy.

The Flyers, diminished during the 1975-76 season by injuries to Parent and MacLeish, lost the Cup to a powerful Montreal team in four straight close games. Though they remained one of the league's better teams, they reached the finals only one more time – in 1980 – during the Clarke era. Throughout his career, he was every bit as valorous in defeat as he was in victory.

To any opposing player who ever felt his pitchfork or ever found swallowing difficult as he opened that black Spectrum locker-room door, Clarke impersonated the devil himself. To a tough town that had turned cynical on itself, he materialized as an angel. And took the Flyers to heaven.

Expansion Fees

The expansion franchise fee for the six clubs that were part of the league's first expansion in 1967-68 was $2 million. The cost per franchise for each of the next four expansions — 1970-71, 1972-73, 1974-75, and 1979-80 — was $6 million.

Tom Lysiak, the Atlanta Flames' best performer in their early years, was involved in a late-season trade of club scoring leaders in 1978-79 when he was exchanged for Ivan Boldirev of the Chicago Black Hawks.

The NHL undertook its fourth expansion in 1974-75, adding the Kansas City Scouts and Washington Capitals to create an eighteen-team NHL. Each new franchise paid $6 million to join the league. The Washington franchise, which would play its home games in the Capital Centre in Landover, Maryland, was owned by Abe Pollin, who hired veteran general manager Milt Schmidt to put together the team. In Kansas City, the new franchise, owned by Edward Thompson, was to be assembled by former Detroit general manager Sid Abel and would play in the 16,500-seat Kemper Arena.

With thirty-eight teams in the NHL and WHA combined, talent was thinly spread and expensive to obtain. The Capitals, who drafted defenseman Greg Joly first overall in the 1974 universal draft, spent $2.5 million to sign their first five amateur draft choices. The Scouts were forced to pay untried junior star Wilf Paiement $500,000 over three years to prevent his signing with a WHA club. Contracts such as these exceeded the amounts paid to even the league's most accomplished superstars only a few seasons before.

The addition of the Scouts and Capitals led to a realignment of the NHL's divisions and the creation of a new playoff system. The East and West divisions that had been devised to accommodate the expansion of 1967 were replaced by two conferences, each of which was made up of a four- and a five-team division. The conferences were named to match the trophies that would be awarded to their regular-season champions, while the four divisions were named after pioneer builders of the game. The Clarence Campbell Conference consisted of the Lester Patrick Division (Atlanta, New York Islanders, New York Rangers, Philadelphia) and the Conn Smythe Division (Chicago, Kansas City, Minnesota, St. Louis, Vancouver). The Prince of Wales Conference was made up of the Charles Adams Division (Boston, Buffalo, California, Toronto) and the James Norris Division (Detroit, Los Angeles, Montreal, Pittsburgh, Washington). The regular-season schedule was increased to eighty games, with each team playing its divisional rivals six times and those in other divisions either four or five times each.

Twelve teams would now qualify for the playoffs, with each of the four division winners receiving a bye to the second round. The eight clubs finishing in second or third place in the four divisions would be ranked from first to eighth, based on points in the regular season's final standings. Four three-game preliminary-round series would be played, the match-ups to be determined by this one-to-eight ranking. The team ranked first would play the team ranked eighth, second would play seventh, third would play sixth, and fourth would play fifth. The four preliminary-round winners would then join the four division champions in the seven-game quarter-final round, the eight clubs again being ranked and paired by regular-season final standings. The four semi-finalists would also be ranked and paired in the same way. This revised system rewarded a strong regular-season performance by matching successful teams against weaker playoff opponents.

During the 1974-75 season, Marcel Dionne and Guy Lafleur, the top two

draft picks in 1971, began to fulfill their promise as NHL superstars. Bobby Orr and Phil Esposito topped the scoring, but Dionne and Lafleur were close behind. The two young stars, who had been so closely compared during their junior careers, were separated by just two points, Dionne totaling 43 goals and 74 assists for 121 points, Lafleur, 53 goals and 66 assists for 119. Peter Mahovlich, younger brother of Frank and a linemate of Lafleur, finished fifth at 117, and all three members of Buffalo's French Connection made the top ten. Seven players reached 100 points, three more than had done so in any previous season.

Although only in its first year, the revised divisional alignment yielded a surprisingly balanced result, since expansion teams had closed the talent gap between themselves and the "original" six clubs. Philadelphia, Montreal, and Buffalo ended the season with identical 113-point totals to lead their divisions, while upstart Vancouver, twelfth in the NHL in 1973-74, finished

The New York Islanders cele-brate Jean-Paul Parisé's over-time goal that gave the Isles a 4–3 win over their cross-town rivals, the New York Rangers, in the 1975 playoffs. Parisé's marker was the first series-clinching goal and the first overtime winner in Islanders' franchise history.

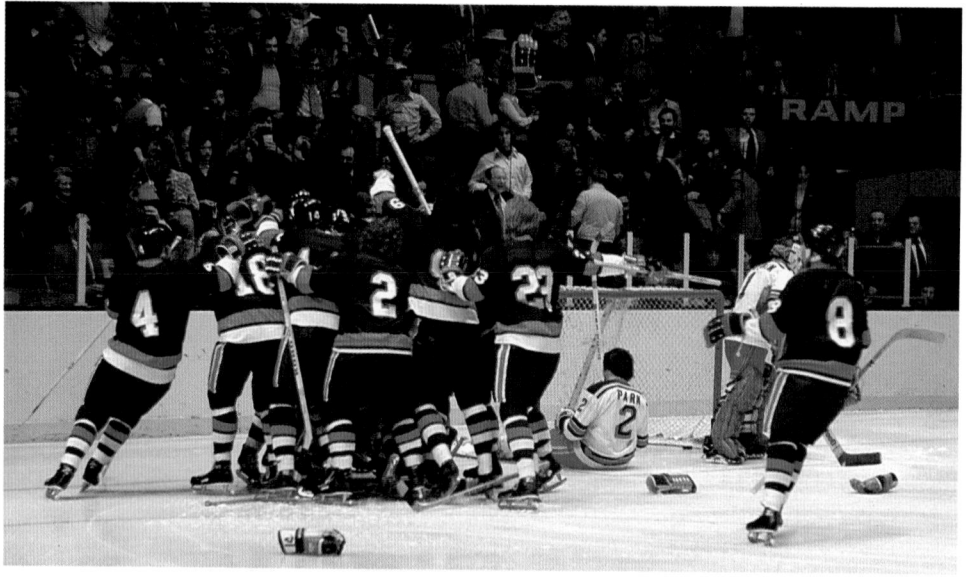

first in the Smythe Division. The Canucks' offense was led by Don Lever, who had 38 goals, and John Gould, who had 34. The Los Angeles Kings finished second to Montreal in the Norris, with a team-record 105 points. The Kings received brilliant goaltending from Rogie Vachon and featured a balanced attack: seven Kings had more than 20 goals. The Boston Bruins, having promoted former AHL coach-of-the-year Don Cherry from Rochester, had 94 points for the league's fifth-best record.

At the bottom of the standings, talent-poor Washington gave up a league-record 446 goals-against and won just eight times all season and only once on the road. Kansas City had 15 wins and California 19. The Atlanta Flames, with 83 points, were the strongest fourth-place team in the league, and would have made the playoffs in two of the other three divisions. The Flames' rookie left winger Eric Vail scored 39 goals and won the Calder Trophy.

The preliminary round saw Toronto upset Los Angeles to advance, along with Chicago, Pittsburgh, and the Islanders. In the quarter-finals, Philadel-phia, Montreal, Buffalo, and the Islanders won, the Isles becoming the first team since the Leafs in 1942 to come back from a three-game deficit to win a seven-game series. The Islanders almost accomplished the feat again in the semi-finals as well, falling behind three-games-to-none to the Flyers and then tying the series at three apiece before losing game seven by a score of 4–1. The Islanders, who received strong goaltending from Glenn "Chico" Resch, won seven of eight games in which they faced elimination.

Kate Smith sang "God Bless America" to a cheering sellout crowd in the Spectrum before the final game. She had become the Flyers' good luck charm and would be invited to sing the unofficial anthem before other important games in Philadelphia.

The Stanley Cup final was the NHL's first all-expansion affair, as the defending-champion Flyers faced the Buffalo Sabres, who had eliminated

the Canadiens in six games. Despite acrobatic goaltending by Buffalo netminders Gerry Desjardins and Roger Crozier, the Flyers won their second consecutive Cup in six games. During some games in Buffalo, warm spring weather caused white fog to rise from the ice surface, forcing play to stop while the players skated slowly around the ice holding up large towels in an attempt to disperse the mist. Bernie Parent, who for the second year in a row gained a shutout in the final match, was again playoff MVP.

The Flyers' second Cup overshadowed the emergence of the New York Islanders as a playoff contender. Denis Potvin had become one of the game's top defensemen on a team stocked with talented pluggers who adhered to coach Al Arbour's disciplined style. Their success in just their third season was a tribute to general manager Bill Torrey's skill at assessing talent.

Successful expansion teams, such as the Flyers and Sabres, were winning on the ice and selling out at the ticket window. But at the bottom of the standings, several expansion clubs were losing games and playing in front of small crowds. California, Kansas City, and Washington were all losing money. Attendance slumped by more than 600 fans per game to 13,224 in 1974-75, a drop that would continue for the rest of the decade, falling to

Philadelphia's Bob Kelly (9) is closely checked during the first final series match-up between two expansion clubs – the Flyers and the Buffalo Sabres – in 1975.

Marcel Dionne, who began his career in Detroit and later signed with the Los Angeles Kings, fired 731 goals in his eighteen-year NHL career. Dionne retired in 1989 as the league's second leading goal-scorer, trailing only Gordie Howe.

12,644 in 1975-76 and 11,408 by 1978-79. At the same time, costs continued to rise. The average player salary jumped $11,000 to reach $85,000 in 1975-76.

Two clubs made ownership changes. Mel Swig purchased the California Golden Seals, and former Minnesota executive Wren Blair and two partners bought the Pittsburgh Penguins for $4.4 million. The Penguins' selling price was indicative of tough times in the NHL; just a year before, the Scouts and Capitals each joined the league for $6 million.

Marcel Dionne, the league's third-highest scorer in 1974-75, had played out his option in Detroit, choosing instead to sign as a free agent with Los Angeles. Dionne took advantage of the new regulations governing free agency that were part of a five-year collective bargaining agreement between the NHL and the NHLPA signed in 1975. The new rules acknowledged the right of a player to change clubs if his contract was fulfilled, but stipulated that clubs losing players to free agency were entitled to compensation. The Red Wings and the Kings constructed a deal that saw Bart Crashley and the rights to Dionne dealt to Los Angeles in exchange for Dan Maloney, Terry Harper, and a draft choice.

Bobby Orr, who had won the scoring championship the previous year, was forced to undergo two additional operations on his left knee and would play just ten games in 1975-76. The loss of Orr was a devastating blow to the Bruins. He had had six consecutive 100-point seasons and had won the Norris Trophy as the NHL's top defenseman every season since 1967-68, his second in the NHL.

But Orr wasn't the only focus of attention for Bruins' fans in 1975. In November, general manager Harry Sinden astounded the hockey world by trading Phil Esposito and Carol Vadnais to the Rangers in exchange for Jean Ratelle, Brad Park, and Joe Zanussi. Along with Orr, Esposito had probably done more than any other player to sell hockey to American fans, particularly in the northeastern United States. But Sinden knew his club was aging. With Orr's career in jeopardy, he had to look ahead. In Brad Park, he obtained a gifted offensive defenseman, and in Jean Ratelle, a superb center who would have many productive years for the Bruins. Another productive Bruin, Johnny Bucyk, scored his 500th goal during the 1975-76 season, and later moved past Alex Delvecchio into second spot on the all-time scoring list.

In December and January, two top teams from the Soviet National League – Central Red Army and Soviet Wings – each played four games in NHL arenas. The Soviet clubs won five, lost two, and tied one. Red Army, which boasted many of the top players from the Soviet Nationals of 1972, hooked up with the Montreal Canadiens on New Year's Eve, 1975, in a 3–3 tie that many consider one of the finest games ever played. The final game of Red Army's tour, against Philadelphia, wasn't nearly as elegant, as the Flyers treated the Soviets to the kind of on-ice rumbling that had won two Stanley Cups. Like some NHL teams in the Philadelphia Spectrum, Red Army was intimidated, eventually losing 4–1. When Philadelphia defenseman Ed Van Impe decked and pummeled Soviet star Valery Kharlamov in the first period, Red Army's coaches pulled their players off the ice. Threats by Alan Eagleson to withhold payment from the Soviets if they didn't return resulted in the eventual resumption of play.

In the regular schedule, the Flyers again finished first in the Patrick Division with a franchise-high 118 points. Reggie Leach, who had been acquired from California before the start of the 1974-75 season, scored 61 goals. Wayne Stephenson became the Flyers' starting goaltender, as Bernie Parent missed most of the season due to injury.

It was the improvement of the second-place Islanders that attracted comment. Led by the 98-point season of defenseman Denis Potvin, 34 goals from Clark Gillies, and the fine play of Calder Trophy-winning center Bryan Trottier, the Islanders finished with 42 wins and 101 points. Potvin became the first Norris Trophy-winner other than Bobby Orr since Harry Howell won the award in 1967.

The Bruins, without Esposito or Orr, finished first in the Adams Division with 113 points. But they were victimized by Toronto's Darryl Sittler on February 7, 1976, when the Maple Leafs' star centerman scored a single-game record ten points on six goals and four assists in an 11–4 Toronto win. In New York, the Rangers missed the playoffs for the first time since 1965-66, despite replacing general manager Emile Francis with former Montreal Canadiens' left winger John Ferguson in January. Esposito finished with 29 goals in New York, a drop of 32 from his total in 1974-75. In Pittsburgh, youth was on the rise, as twenty-year-old Pierre Larouche became the NHL's youngest-ever 50-goal scorer.

The Montreal Canadiens were the NHL's top team, finishing the regular season with a record 58 wins and 127 points. Although Henri Richard had retired, the Canadiens received plenty of offensive production from their top line of Lafleur, Pete Mahovlich, and Steve Shutt. Yvon Lambert and Yvan Cournoyer both scored 32 goals, and two young defensive forwards, Bob Gainey and Doug Jarvis, established themselves as two of the NHL's finest checkers and penalty-killers.

The Toronto Maple Leafs' career leader in goals and points, Darryl Sittler, set an NHL single-game points record when he recorded six goals and four assists against Boston on February 7, 1976. The victim of Sittler's onslaught, Bruins' goaltender Dave Reece, never played another NHL game.

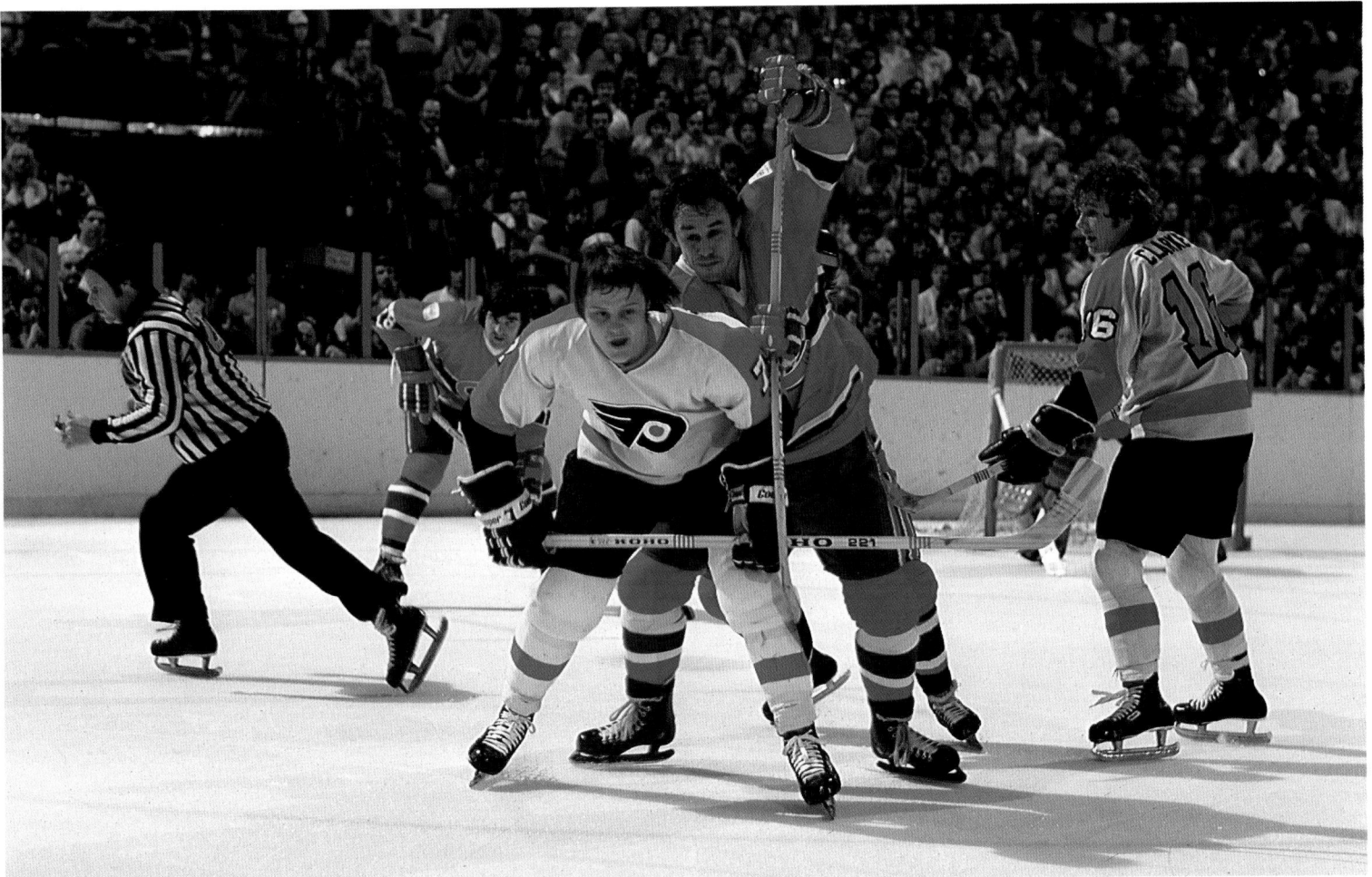

In the playoffs, Los Angeles, the Islanders, Toronto, and Buffalo advanced after wins in the preliminary round. In the quarter-finals, Montreal swept Chicago in four straight, while the Islanders took Buffalo in six. The series between Toronto and Philadelphia went seven games before Philadelphia prevailed. Darryl Sittler had a five-goal game in this series, tying Maurice Richard's single-playoff-game record. Boston needed seven games to defeat the Kings, setting up a Boston–Philadelphia semi-final that the Flyers took in five games. The star of the series was Reggie Leach who, in the final game, scored five goals, equaling the mark shared by Sittler and Richard.

In the other semi-final series, the Canadiens defeated the Islanders in five games, three of which Montreal won by one-goal margins. The resulting Montreal–Philadelphia Stanley Cup final was seen as a clash of hockey cultures – the Canadiens' high-speed, skill game against the Flyers' grinding intimidation hockey. The result was an anticlimax. Although Leach's 19 goals in 16 playoff games earned him the Conn Smythe Trophy, Montreal swept the Flyers in four close games.

The absence of both Bobby Orr and Phil Esposito from 1975-76's top-ten scoring leaders signified a changing of the guard atop the NHL. No event more dramatically exemplified the change than the signing of Bobby Orr as a

Montreal's Jimmy Roberts ties up Philadelphia's Bill Barber during the 1976 Stanley Cup finals. Although he never scored more than 14 goals in a season, Roberts defensive expertise played an important role in five Montreal Stanley Cup victories.

When Bobby Orr signed as a free agent with the Chicago Black Hawks on June 24, 1976, it was evident that repeated knee surgery had virtually ended his great career. After only 26 games with Chicago over three seasons, Orr retired in November 1978. In September, he was inducted into the Hockey Hall of Fame, the last player to be so honored without having to serve the customary three-year waiting period.

free agent by the Chicago Black Hawks in June of 1976. The move indicated that Boston management was convinced Orr could not return from his most recent knee surgery. But Orr's remarkable play for Team Canada at the six-nation Canada Cup tournament that preceded the 1976-77 NHL season called the Bruins' conclusion into question.

This open round-robin tournament featured the best amateur and professional players from Canada, the United States, the Soviet Union, Czechoslovakia, Sweden, and Finland. This time, the WHA's Bobby Hull, who had not been invited to join the all-NHL squad in 1972, was part of Team Canada. The tournament featured wonderful hockey, especially from Orr, who dominated play, despite limited mobility. He was selected Canada's outstanding player in three games and was named tournament MVP. Sadly, this would prove to be the last hurrah for the player who, in the previous ten years, had done more than any other to change the game. Since he established a new standard, the gifted, offense-generating, rushing type of defenseman has become a required element for elite NHL clubs.

Orr's knee would allow him to play just twenty games for Chicago in 1976-77. He would not play the following season, and then would attempt to come back in 1978-79. He played six games for the Black Hawks that season, but his knee simply could not withstand the the rigors of NHL play. He announced his retirement in November of 1978 and was inducted into the Hockey Hall of Fame the following September. He was 1979's recipient of the Lester Patrick Trophy for service to hockey in the United States.

Before the start of the 1976-77 season, two of the league's weakest franchises relocated. The Kansas City Scouts moved to Denver to become the Colorado Rockies, while the California Golden Seals moved to Cleveland and adopted the name previously used by the city's AHL entry, the Barons. This double shift represented the first time NHL clubs had relocated since the Ottawa Senators became the St. Louis Eagles in 1934-35. While Colorado

improved by 18 points over the previous season, neither team escaped last place in its division. Wilf Paiement scored 41 goals for the Rockies. Only the Detroit Red Wings, who had crashed to 41 points and last place in the Norris Division, prevented the two city-jumping franchises from being the worst teams in the NHL.

At the top of the standings, the Montreal Canadiens established new NHL team records, finishing with 60 wins and 132 points. The Habs were led by Art Ross Trophy-winner Guy Lafleur with 56 goals, and Steve Shutt with 60. Canadiens' defenseman Larry Robinson won the Norris Trophy, recording

Guy Lafleur, who had six consecutive seasons with at least 50 goals and 100 points for the Montreal Canadiens, played three NHL seasons after being inducted into the Hockey Hall of Fame in 1988.

66 assists. The Philadelphia Flyers also continued their strong play, winning the Patrick Division with 112 points. The New York Islanders were second in the Patrick, right behind the Flyers with 106 points.

In the Adams Division, the Bruins finished first with 106 points, just ahead of the Sabres, who had 104. In the off-season, Boston had traded veteran Ken Hodge to the Rangers for Rick Middleton, a twenty-two-year-old right winger who would go on to have five 40-goal seasons for the Bruins. The Smythe had become the NHL's weakest division, led by St. Louis with only 73 points. Emile Francis took over the general manager's job in St. Louis in April of 1976 and promptly used the Blues' first draft choices to select Bernie Federko and Brian Sutter, two players who would become team leaders.

In the preliminary round of the playoffs, the Islanders, Buffalo, Toronto, and Los Angeles advanced to the quarter-finals. In the second playoff round, Montreal defeated St. Louis, the Islanders beat Buffalo, Boston eliminated Los Angeles, and Philadelphia again sidelined Toronto in an emotional series. Trailing two games to none, the Flyers rallied with late goals to force overtime in games three and four, which they eventually won. Rick Mac-Leish, Bobby Clarke, and Reggie Leach scored the crucial goals for the Flyers in these two games, and the team went on to win the series in six.

In the semi-finals, Boston swept Philadelphia, winning consecutive over-time contests in games one and two. The Canadiens needed six games to eliminate the Islanders, defensive specialist Bob Gainey getting the series-clinching goal in game six. As in 1976, the Canadiens swept the Stanley Cup finals. Boston pushed the Habs into overtime in game four, but Conn Smythe Trophy-winner Guy Lafleur's sweet pass to linemate Jacques Lemaire gave the Canadiens their second straight championship.

The success of the Canadiens and the support enjoyed by the NHL's top clubs didn't mask the fact that regular-season attendance had dipped by nearly 540,000 fans, and weak franchises were on the verge of going broke. In 1976-77, the league and the NHL Players' Association had to lend money to the Cleveland Barons to ensure that players would be paid. In Atlanta, where the Flames were playoff contenders, fan apathy obliged the players to buy $25,000 worth of tickets to help the franchise survive.

In September of 1977, John A. Ziegler, Jr., succeeded Clarence Campbell as president of the NHL. Ziegler, who had served as chairman of the league's board of governors and as legal counsel for the Detroit Red Wings, became the NHL's fourth president, following Frank Calder, Red Dutton, and Campbell, who had held the job for thirty-one years.

The 1977 amateur draft yielded a rich bounty of NHL players. First-round choices included Dale McCourt (selected first overall by Detroit), Barry Beck (second, Colorado), Robert Picard (third, Washington), Doug Wilson (sixth, Chicago), Mark Napier (tenth, Montreal), and Ron Duguay (thir-teenth, Rangers). Mike Bossy, who would prove to be the top player

Four League Presidents since 1917

The NHL has had only four presidents in its seventy-five-year history. Frank Calder served from 1917 until 1943; Mervyn "Red" Dutton from 1943 until 1946; Clarence Campbell from 1946 until 1977; and John A. Ziegler, Jr., from 1977 to date. Mr. Ziegler holds the distinction of being the only man in league history to hold the dual positions of Chairman of the Board and League President, which he held during the 1977-78 season.

available in 1977, was passed over fourteen times before being selected fifteenth by the New York Islanders – clear evidence of how difficult it is to pick the best player in any draft. The Islanders also took John Tonelli thirty-third, while Montreal used the thirty-sixth pick to take Rod Langway from the University of New Hampshire. Napier, Tonelli, and Langway played for WHA clubs in 1977-78, joining the NHL clubs that drafted them the following season.

A further modification to the league's playoff format removed automatic playoff berths for teams finishing third in each division. Instead, the four teams with the most points not finishing in first or second place would advance to the playoffs. This change would open the playoffs to fourth-place teams in strong divisions. With the new rule in place, the fourth-place Rangers (73 points in the Patrick) would make the 1977-78 playoffs; the third-place Canucks (57 points in the Smythe) would not.

Franchise closures reduced the WHA from twelve to eight teams for 1977-78, resulting in players with WHA experience finding their way into the NHL. Vaclav Nedomansky, a former star with the Czechoslovakian national team, who had played with the WHA's Toronto Toros and Birmingham Bulls, signed as a free agent with Detroit in November of 1977, playing 63 NHL games in 1977-78. A 50-goal scorer in the WHA, Nedomansky would go on to 38- and 35-goal seasons with the Red Wings. Detroit also hired coach Bobby Kromm from the WHA's Winnipeg Jets. Aided by 33 goals from first-draft pick Dale McCourt and a strong season by rookie defenseman Reed Larson, the Red Wings improved from last place to second place in the Norris Division.

In Chicago, Bob Pulford was hired as coach and general manager of the Black Hawks. Pulford replaced coach Billy Reay and Tommy Ivan, who was the league's longest-serving general manager, having held the post since 1954-55. Under Pulford, the Hawks enjoyed a 20-point improvement to finish in first place in the Smythe Division. Ivan Boldirev centered Darcy Rota and J. P. Bordeleau on the club's top line.

No rookie in the history of the NHL ever performed as Mike Bossy did for the Islanders. Bossy, who had been a prolific scorer with the Laval Nationales of the Quebec Junior Hockey League, rewarded general manager Bill Torrey with 53 goals, a record for rookies. Only one other first-year player – Rick Martin of the Sabres, who had 44 goals in 1971-72 – had even broken the 40-goal plateau. Playing on a line with Bryan Trottier and Clark Gillies, Bossy finished sixth in scoring and was an easy winner of the Calder Trophy. Trottier's 123 points placed him second in scoring, and Denis Potvin, who won his second Norris Trophy, gathered 94 points to finish fifth.

The Toronto Maple Leafs promoted Roger Neilson from their Dallas farm club to coach the Leafs. Neilson, who had been a highly successful junior coach with the Peterborough Petes of the OHA, installed a defensive system that reduced the Leafs' goals-against from 285 to 237. Linemates Lanny McDonald with 47 goals and Darryl Sittler with 45 led the Leafs to 41 wins, 92 points, and third place in the Adams Division.

Player's Name on Stanley Cup

Before the 1976-77 season, only those players who competed in the Stanley Cup playoffs were eligible to have their names engraved on the Cup. In January 1977, however, the NHL changed the criteria to allow players competing in forty regular-season or one final series game to have their names on the Cup.

Denis Potvin was a key contributor to the Islanders' success. He was a leader on offense and a three-time winner of the Norris Trophy on defense. The second rearguard to record 100 points in a season, Potvin was inducted into the Hockey Hall of Fame in 1991.

Colorado's stay in the NHL was a Rockie one, as the team finished in last place in four of six seasons. Although it featured fine talent like Paul Gardner (left) and John Van Boxmeer, the club's best youngsters were often traded in an attempt to realize immediate improvement.

Player Names on Sweaters

At their August 1970 meeting, the NHL's Board of Governors passed a resolution allowing the home team to put names on the back of player sweaters. Visiting teams could do the same only with consent of the home club.

Beginning with the 1977-78 season, it became mandatory for all players to have names on the backs of their sweaters.

The Colorado Rockies qualified for the playoffs for the first time in franchise history. Led by right wing Wilf Paiement's 87 points and Barry Beck's record-setting 22 goals by a rookie defenseman, the Rockies finished in second place in the Smythe Division, albeit with only 59 points.

Defending Cup-champion Montreal remained the NHL's top club, losing just ten games, while accumulating 129 points. The Habs were led by the spectacular play of Guy Lafleur, who netted 60 goals en route to his third consecutive scoring title, and by a steady defense anchored by Larry Robinson, Guy Lapointe, and Serge Savard. Ken Dryden and Michel Larocque shared the Vezina Trophy, allowing 27 fewer goals than the league's second-best goaltending duo, Glenn "Chico" Resch and Billy Smith of the New York Islanders.

The Habs' defensive prowess extended to their forwards as well. Left winger Bob Gainey was awarded the newly created Frank Selke Trophy as the league's top defensive forward. In November, the Canadiens acquired former 50-goal man Pierre Larouche from Pittsburgh in a deal that sent Peter Mahovlich to the Penguins.

The hardworking Boston Bruins under coach Don Cherry won 51 games to finish first in the Adams Division and second overall with 113 points. Though lacking superstar talent to match the Canadiens and Islanders, Boston's grinders and diggers combined to score 333 goals, the third-highest total in the league. Terry O'Reilly epitomized the Bruins' abrasive style. He spent 211 minutes in the penalty box and recorded 90 points, becoming the only player in league history to earn 200-or-more penalty minutes and finish as a top-ten scorer in the same season. The Buffalo Sabres finished second in the Adams with 105 points as second-year goaltender Don Edwards led the NHL with 38 wins.

In the playoffs, Philadelphia, Detroit, Buffalo, and Toronto won their preliminary round series. In the quarter-finals, three series were one-sided; Boston swept Chicago, Montreal eliminated Detroit, and Philadelphia handled Buffalo.

The quarter-final series between the Islanders and Leafs is remembered as a playoff classic. Despite the Islanders' 19-point superiority over the regular season, in many respects, the teams' strengths offset one another. Up front, Trottier and Bossy were countered by Sittler and McDonald. On the blue

The Boston Bruins of the late 1970s featured hard-nosed grinders like (left to right) Peter McNab, Terry O'Reilly, and Mike Milbury. Both O'Reilly and Milbury would later coach the Bruins to an appearance in the Stanley Cup finals.

line, the Islanders' Denis Potvin, acknowledged as the NHL's finest defenseman, was all but equaled by the Leafs' Borje Salming, a four-time all-star and one of the best skaters in the game. As well, coaches Al Arbour and Roger Neilson were also both sound tacticians.

As the low-scoring series wore on, injuries depleted the benches of both teams. The Islanders won the first two games in New York, including a 3–2 overtime thriller in game two. The Leafs rebounded to tie the series at home, despite losing Salming to an eye injury, before the Islanders won another overtime contest, with a 2–1 win in game five. In game six, both Bossy and Trottier were hurt, and the Leafs won 5–2 to force a seventh game. The series finale also went into overtime before Lanny McDonald batted down a knee-high pass to split the Islanders' defense and go in and score on Chico Resch. The Leafs' 2–1 win put the club into the semi-finals for the first time since 1967.

The rest of the post-season was less dramatic. The Leafs were swept by Montreal, while Boston ousted Philadelphia in five games. In the finals, the Bruins tied the Canadiens at two games apiece on Bobby Schmautz's overtime winner in game four, but back-to-back 4–1 wins by the Canadiens earned Montreal and coach Scotty Bowman their third straight Stanley Cup.

Pro hockey was still a money-losing proposition for many NHL and WHA clubs heading into the 1978-79 season. The WHA, now involved in discussions with the NHL to unify big-league hockey, started with seven teams and dropped back to six when the Indianapolis Racers folded after just twenty-five games. Prior to going out of business, the Racers sold the contract of seventeen-year-old Wayne Gretzky to the Edmonton Oilers. In the NHL, two problem franchises, Cleveland and Minnesota, were merged to create one superior organization that would continue in the NHL as the North Stars, taking Cleveland's place in the Adams Division. The Smythe Division was reduced to four teams. The renewed North Stars signed 1978's first overall draft choice, Bobby Smith, who had played for the Ottawa 67s of the OHA.

The Rangers set out to remake their club in 1978-79, signing Swedish WHA superstars Ulf Nilsson and Anders Hedberg to $1-million two-year contracts. Nilsson and Hedberg had each recorded four consecutive 100-point seasons, playing on a line with Bobby Hull in Winnipeg. The Rangers also hired former Philadelphia Flyer coach Fred Shero to fill the dual job of coach and general manager. Phil Esposito led the team with 42 goals and finished the season on a line with Don Murdoch and Don Maloney. Murdoch missed the first forty games of the season while serving a suspension for cocaine possession. The Rangers finished fourth in the Patrick Division.

Other WHA players jumped to the NHL as the seven-year-old circuit continued to have financial difficulties. Cam Connor, Ken Linseman, and John Tonelli, who had signed with WHA clubs as teenagers, signed with the NHL clubs that held their draft rights.

Hall-of-Famer's Return

Frank Udvari became the first Hall-of-Fame member to return to active duty when he was forced to referee a game thirteen years after retiring. On December 30, 1978, Udvari, who was working as an administrator for the league at the time, replaced injured official Dave Newell in a game between the New York Islanders and the Atlanta Flames.

In Toronto, owner Harold Ballard continued to make headlines. The previous season, he had protested a league edict that required teams to display players' names on the backs of their sweaters by having the Leafs wear blue jerseys with their names sewn on the back in blue letters that were unreadable. The Leafs played one game so attired, before complying with the league's rule. In 1978-79, Ballard used a post-game interview to announce that he had fired coach Roger Neilson–only to rehire him two days later. On the ice, the Leafs held on to third place in the Adams, but dropped 11 points from their finish of a year earlier.

The Atlanta Flames had their best season in 1978-79, fueled by Bob MacMillan and 50-goal shooter Guy Chouinard, both of whom finished with more than 100 points. The Flames finished with the NHL's sixth-best record, accumulating 90 points, but still found themselves in last place in the strong Patrick Division.

Detroit signed former Los Angeles goaltender Rogie Vachon as a free agent. The Kings, who were entitled to compensation for the loss of Vachon, were awarded Dale McCourt, the first player selected in the 1977 draft. The Kings included him in their media guidebook for 1978-79, but McCourt, who wanted to remain in Detroit, refused to report to Los Angeles and challenged the legality of his assignment in the courts. He won a preliminary injunction barring the move, but this was later overturned by the Sixth U.S. Circuit Court of Appeals in Cincinnati. McCourt then appealed the case to the U.S. Supreme Court, but dropped the appeal when the Red Wings reacquired his rights by trading André St. Laurent and two draft choices to the Kings in August of 1979.

Team NHL and the Soviet National Team exchange handshakes at the conclusion of the 1979 Challenge Cup series, a three-game set won by the Soviet Union two games to one.

The NHL Challenge Cup was presented to the winner of the best-of-three series between the NHL and the Soviet Union that replaced the NHL All-Star Game in 1979.

Bryan Trottier (left) and Bobby Clarke battle along the boards during the 1980 Stanley Cup finals. Trottier, who won his fifth Stanley Cup in 1991, was the last man to lead the NHL in assists before Wayne Gretzky entered the league in 1980.

The 1978-79 season also saw the Soviet Union's top players face the NHL's all-stars in a best-of-three mid-season exhibition series called the Challenge Cup. This one-time event replaced the annual NHL All-Star Game and ended in a Soviet victory. The NHLers dominated game one and led game two by a 4–2 score until the Soviets seemed to shift gears, taking over to win 5–4. In game three, the NHL's defenses cracked, and the Soviets skated to a 6–0 victory.

Meanwhile, in regular-season play, the Islanders finally dethroned Montreal as the top club, earning 116 points compared to the Canadiens' 115. Bryan Trottier dislodged Lafleur as the league's top scorer, winning both the Art Ross and the Hart trophies. Linemate Mike Bossy remained the league's premier sniper with 69 goals, a single-season mark second only to Phil Esposito's 76 in 1970-71. Clark Gillies, the third member of the Islanders' top line, contributed 35 goals and finished with 91 points. Denis Potvin won his third Norris Trophy as the league's top defenseman and had his first 100-point season.

In the playoffs, the Rangers were the surprise team of 1979. Led by Phil Esposito and Don Maloney, they advanced to the semi-finals by eliminating Los Angeles and Philadelphia. They then faced off against the Islanders in the first seven-game series to be played between these "cross-town" rivals. The Islanders' ultra-potent attack made them prohibitive favorites, but the Rangers, backstopped by goaltender John Davidson, engineered a six-game upset, despite losing twice in overtime, and advanced to the finals for the first time since 1972. Despite four consecutive 100-point seasons, the Islanders continued to struggle in post-season play.

The Canadiens' attempt to win a fourth consecutive Cup appeared to be in jeopardy in game seven of their semi-final with the Bruins. Guy Lafleur set up two goals as the Habs battled back from 3–1 to tie the score, but Rick Middleton gave the Bruins the lead with less than four minutes to play. In the tense action that followed, a poorly executed line change resulted in Boston being penalized for having too many men on the ice. During the Montreal power-play that followed, Guy Lafleur sent the game into overtime, scoring on a hard, low drive past goaltender Gilles Gilbert. The Canadiens poured on the pressure in extra time, and eliminated the Bruins on a goal by Yvon Lambert. Boston's string of playoff-series losses to the Canadiens extended back to 1931 and had become one of the most notable "hexes" in the NHL.

In the finals, Ken Dryden did not play well in goal for the Canadiens as the Rangers won game one. Habs' coach Scotty Bowman elected to start back-up goaltender Michel Larocque in game two, but when Larocque was injured in the pre-game skate, Dryden replaced his replacement and played well as the Canadiens won four straight games to win the Cup. Bob Gainey was awarded the Conn Smythe Trophy.

In the season to come, the biggest news in hockey was made not on the ice but in the league offices of the NHL and the WHA. The two leagues had struck

Bob Gainey is hoisted on his teammates' shoulders after the Canadiens captured their fourth consecutive Stanley Cup in 1979. Gainey's excellent defensive play during the series was rewarded when he won the Conn Smythe Trophy as playoff MVP.

a deal. The WHA would cease operations following its 1979 playoffs, after which the NHL would expand to 21 teams, granting franchises to four former WHA clubs: the Edmonton Oilers, the Hartford (New England) Whalers, the Quebec Nordiques, and the Winnipeg Jets. The off-ice war that had turned hockey upside down for seven seasons was over.

The NHL's newest clubs would begin play in 1979-80. One player whose arrival in the NHL would be closely watched was a slim eighteen-year-old who had scored 46 goals and 110 points with Indianapolis and Edmonton in his only WHA season. In the decade ahead, Wayne Gretzky would come to dominate his sport in a way unmatched by any other athlete.

(*continued on p. 251*)

THE DYNASTY-MAKERS: GUY LAFLEUR AND MIKE BOSSY

by Dick Irvin

Dynasty. The dictionary defines the word as a "sequence of rulers from the same family or group."

Hockey fans define it as a team that has won the Stanley Cup more than three years in succession. Which applies to only two teams in the NHL's postwar era: the Montreal Canadiens, who did it twice, and the New York Islanders, who did it once.

Close calls don't count. The Toronto Maple Leafs twice were Stanley Cup winners three straight years. A fourth straight eluded them, first in 1950 then again in 1965. Not good enough.

In the 1980s the Edmonton Oilers won two in a row, didn't win the following year, then were champions again the two years after that. Still not good enough.

The Montreal Canadiens of the late 1950s won a record five straight Stanley Cups, beginning in 1956. Indeed, they were only a few goals short of winning eight straight. Following their Cup win in 1953, the Canadiens lost in the finals to the Detroit Red Wings the next two years. In 1954 the series was decided in overtime in game seven. In 1955 the Red Wings also won in a seventh game, by a score of 3–1. After that, the Canadiens didn't lose another playoff series until 1961.

The second Montreal dynasty began with the first of four straight Stanley Cups in 1976. Between 1960 and 1976 the Canadiens had won the Cup six times, but never more than twice in a row. Their Cup triumph in 1973 came after a season in which they had been beaten only ten times. But they had to watch the Philadelphia Flyers win the following two years before the second Montreal dynasty began.

When the Montreal Canadiens' first dynasty was overpowering the rest of the six-team NHL, I was a paying customer for their home games at the Forum. When the 1976 team was winning the Stanley Cup, I was broadcasting their games on radio and television for *Hockey Night in Canada*. I had a great view of a great team, and it was something to behold.

Statistics can be overdone, but in this case they reveal a remarkable story. In the three seasons starting with 1975-76, the figures in the Canadiens' loss column were eleven, eight, and ten. Twenty-nine defeats in 240 games. Add the playoffs and you come up with 213 wins, 34 ties, and just 34 losses in 281 games, a three-year standard of excellence that likely will never be equaled.

Guy Lafleur unleashes the shot that rocketed him into the Hockey Hall of Fame and enabled him to capture three league scoring titles.

The last season of the Canadiens' second dynasty was 1979-80. The team lost seventeen regular-season games and finished second to the fast-improving New York Islanders in the overall standings. On the streets of hockey-mad Montreal this prompted the question, "What's wrong with the Canadiens?" But the team got its act together in the playoffs and won a fourth straight Stanley Cup.

Sam Pollock was the general manager whose skilful handling of draft choices and trades put the team together. Scotty Bowman was the coach who orchestrated the players' talents on the ice. Together they produced a true hockey dynasty.

As the Montreal Canadiens were losing only ten times during the 1972-73 season, the New York Islanders were losing sixty times.

The Islanders had joined the NHL that season, along with the Atlanta Flames, raising the number of league teams to sixteen. Nobody expected them to perform miracles, but nobody thought they would be so bad as to lose sixty games. And certainly nobody who watched them struggle pitifully through that first season would have dreamed that, in just eight years, the Islanders would be winning the first of four straight Stanley Cup championships.

The Islanders' precipitous rise from the NHL's basement is another remarkable statistical story. The figures in their loss column went from sixty to forty-one to twenty-five in three seasons. Their victory totals climbed from twelve to nineteen to thirty-three. They made the playoffs in their third season. In their seventh season they won fifty-one games, finishing first over all.

The Islanders entered the Stanley Cup record book in 1975, the first year they made the playoffs. In a series against the Pittsburgh Penguins they lost the first three games, then came back to win the next four and the series. That feat had been accomplished just once before, by the Toronto Maple Leafs in the 1942 Stanley Cup finals against Detroit.

The Islanders then got everyone excited all over again when they almost did the same thing against the defending Cup champions from Philadelphia in the next playoff round. The Flyers won the first three games, then the Islanders took the next three.

Mike Bossy, the first player to score 50 goals as an NHL rookie, became the second player to score 50 goals in 50 games on January 24, 1981.

A second miracle wasn't to be, however, and the Flyers escaped with a win in game seven.

While the Montreal dynasty of the late 1970s had been built and nurtured by Sam Pollock and Scotty Bowman, on Long Island the men doing that job were general manager Bill Torrey and coach Al Arbour. Their team in 1978-79 had finished first, yet fell to the New York Rangers early in the playoffs. Perhaps it was a case of a rising club still not quite ready to win. The next year they were.

Not all Stanley Cup-winning goals are indelibly etched in the minds of hockey fans, but a few do fall into that category. Bobby Orr's famed flying leap when the Bruins beat the Blues in 1970 is one. And so is Bob Nystrom's goal for the Islanders – at 7:11 of overtime in game six of the 1980 finals against Philadelphia, to give them their first Stanley Cup championship. In this age of television, that dramatic goal has been replayed countless times.

The Islanders won the Stanley Cup three consecutive years after that. While the mighty Canadiens of

Although his career was cut short by a back injury, Bossy still scored 573 career goals and was inducted into the Hockey Hall of Fame in 1991.

the late 1950s won five straight Cups in ten playoff rounds, today's teams have to work at it a lot longer. During the reign that stamped them as one of hockey's true dynasties, the New York Islanders won sixteen straight series.

You have to wonder if that feat will ever be equaled, or surpassed.

During their four straight Stanley-Cup-winning years, the New York Islanders played seventy-eight playoff games, winning sixty and losing eighteen. In the four years before that, the Montreal Canadiens played fifty-eight playoff games, losing only ten.

Teams with records like that have much in common. Montreal's Ken Dryden and New York's Billy Smith provided the caliber of goaltending needed to win Stanley Cups. Both clubs had the dominant defensemen of the era. Montreal had Larry Robinson, the Islanders, Denis Potvin. The Canadiens' Jacques Lemaire and New York's Bryan Trottier were all-round productive leaders at center-ice. And both teams had a hard-working, hard-checking supporting cast, the "grinders," as the current phrase has it: players such as Risebrough, Lambert, Gainey, Nystrom, Gillies, and a couple of Sutters.

There was another area of great similarity. Both the Canadiens of the late 1970s and the Islanders of the early 1980s had a high-scoring, game-breaking right-wing player whose mighty talents gave their teams the decisive edge over all the others. In Montreal it was Guy Lafleur. In New York it was Michael Bossy.

There were many similar patterns in the careers of these two dominant goal-scorers of their eras. Both played junior hockey in Quebec. In his final two years with the Quebec Remparts, Lafleur scored 103 and 130 goals. Bossy played four years with the Laval Nationales, starting at the age of sixteen, and never scored fewer than seventy goals a season.

Lafleur became eligible for the NHL draft in 1971. The Canadiens had won the Stanley Cup that season after finishing fourth in the overall standings and would normally have been picking well down in the draft order. They desperately wanted the Quebec-born prodigy, however, and thanks to a series of trading machinations orchestrated by the team's shrewd general manager, Sam Pollock, Montreal owned the number-one pick on drafting day. Pollock, normally a dour type, drew a laugh by playfully requesting "Time" when NHL president Clarence Campbell asked him for the name of his team's first choice. As if there was any doubt.

Jean Béliveau had retired that same week. Now a new French-Canadian hero had arrived to replace a legend, and all was right again in the pressure-packed hockey world in and around Montreal.

Six years later, Pollock and a few other NHL general managers didn't appear very shrewd when Mike Bossy became eligible. Despite his remarkable goal-scoring record as a junior, Bossy wasn't at the top of anyone's list of draft prospects because scouts questioned his ability to withstand the rigors of rough play in the NHL. Dale McCourt, Mike Crombeen, Brad Maxwell, and Scott Campbell were among the players chosen in the top ten. The Canadiens drafted next, and Pollock selected another right winger, Mark Napier.

Three picks later, Bossy was still not chosen. The New York Islanders had the fifteenth choice, and it was only then that the name "Mike Bossy" was heard. The Islanders' arch rival, the Rangers, had owned two choices in the first fourteen and had selected Lucien DeBlois and Ron Duguay.

By the time Mike Bossy became a New York Islander, Guy Lafleur was being called the best player in all of hockey. In 1977, Lafleur had won his second straight scoring championship, and the Canadiens, following a remarkable season in which the team lost only eight games, had just won their second straight Stanley Cup.

Before the start of the following season, Bossy struggled through an uninspired performance at the Islanders' training camp, but still managed to make the team. Had he been drafted by Montreal, he would likely have begun his professional career on the Habs' farm club in the American Hockey League. Ahead of him at right wing would have been established stars such as Lafleur, Yvan Cournoyer, and Mario Tremblay.

Mike Bossy's first year with the Islanders was the team's seventh in the NHL. There was little in the way of tradition for him to follow. It was a far different story for Lafleur in Montreal. He was expected to carry on in the skate marks of previous high-scoring Canadien right wingers, like Maurice Richard and Bernie Geoffrion.

During his first three seasons, "The Flower" wilted badly and was a major disappointment. He scored 29 times as a rookie, 28 in his second season, and only 21 in his third. Sam Pollock and coach Scotty Bowman felt they had a decision to make. Should they keep Lafleur and hope he improved, or should they try to trade him? Fortunately for the Canadiens, they decided to keep him.

Mike Bossy's start with the Islanders was a far different story. After his shaky training camp, he became an almost instant scoring sensation in the NHL. He set a rookie record by scoring 53 times in his first season. While Lafleur managed just 78 goals in his first three years with Montreal, Bossy scored 173 goals in his first three in New York.

Regular-season statistics are remembered more from individual standpoints, while team perform-ances stand out at playoff time. But a look at how Guy Lafleur and Mike Bossy performed during the playoffs, when their teams were winning four straight Stanley Cups, provides another interesting comparison of their great careers.

During the Canadiens' four straight Cup-winning years, beginning in 1976, the team played 58 playoff games. Lafleur scored 36 goals and added 51 assists for 87 points, an average of a point and a half per game.

During their four straight Cup-winning years, beginning in 1980, the Islanders played seventy-eight playoff games. Bossy scored 61 goals and

In 1974-75, Guy Lafleur became the first member of the Montreal Canadiens to score 50 goals in a season since Bernie Geoffrion accomplished the feat in 1960-61. Ten seasons later, when Lafleur retired from the Canadiens, he was the franchise's all-time leading point-scorer.

added 50 assists for 111 points. On a per-game basis, Bossy had the edge in goals, Lafleur had the upper-hand in assists, and they were almost dead even in points.

From 1976 through 1979, Lafleur led the playoffs in goals once, assists twice, and points twice. In the following four years, Bossy led in playoff goals three times, assists once, and points once.

In 1979, when the Canadiens finished their run of four straight Stanley Cups, Lafleur's post-season record stood at 10 goals and 13 assists. When the Islanders won their first of four straight the following year, Bossy's playoff record was an identical 10 goals and 13 assists.

Lafleur was chosen winner of the Conn Smythe Trophy as the playoff MVP once, in 1977. Bossy won it once, in 1982.

The two men were remarkable performers to watch and, for me, to describe in action from the

Three of the greatest marksmen to ever fire the puck pose prior to the start of the 1981 Canada Cup tournament. From left to right: Lafleur, Bossy, and Gretzky.

broadcast booth. I was present for all of the Canadiens' playoff games during their run of four straight Cups, and for many of the Islanders' playoff games during the following four years. Guy Lafleur and Mike Bossy were the type of players who gave everyone a lot to remember.

Lafleur's greatest goal came in the semi-finals in 1979, against Boston, when he tied the game on a Montreal power-play with just a few minutes remaining in regulation time. The Bruins had iced the puck, killing the penalty. Lafleur picked it up deep in his own zone and quickly moved up-ice. When he crossed the blue line, he passed the puck ahead to Jacques Lemaire, who had just jumped onto the ice on a line change.

Lemaire was barely onside when he took the pass right at the Boston blue line. Lemaire carried the puck into Boston territory, taking four quick strides, then dropped it back to a flying Flower, who by then was streaking into the Bruins' zone.

When you study the TV replay, Lafleur is lost from camera range for a few seconds after he passes the puck to Lemaire. It is amazing how quickly he catches up to the play.

Lemaire's pass reached Lafleur two feet outside the faceoff circle, on the right wing. Lafleur didn't handle the puck at all. He had his stick drawn back in a shooting position before the puck reached him. When it did, he fired it home immediately, "one-timed it" as announcers say, low to the far side. Boston goaltender Gilles Gilbert didn't have a chance.

The Canadiens went on to win the game and, eventually, their fourth straight Stanley Cup. Night after night, game after game, Lafleur performed in a manner which earned him, at the time, the unofficial title as the world's best player.

Two of Mike Bossy's most remembered goals came in the 1982 Stanley Cup finals against the Vancouver Canucks. One was at 19:58 of the first overtime period, when an errant Canuck pass in Vancouver territory was quickly intercepted by Bossy and just as quickly turned into the game-winning goal. Bossy scored this goal because of something all great goal-scorers possess – anticipation. Vancouver defenseman Harold Snepsts had control of the puck along the back boards in his own zone. With time running out in the period, Snepsts didn't play it safe. Instead, he elected to pass the puck ahead, towards the blue line. Bossy was cruising on right wing, inside the faceoff circle. The instant Snepsts began to pass the puck, Bossy darted to his left. Snepsts followed through with the pass, and Bossy was in a perfect position to intercept it. He snared the puck on his backhand, swung to his forehand, and drilled it at the net from the near rim of the circle. Goaltender Richard Brodeur had no time to react. The puck was past him like a rocket, top corner, short side. It was pure Bossy.

A few nights later, in Vancouver, he scored a game-winner while flying through the air, both skates off the ice. This was another case of typical Bossy anticipation. The puck seemed lost in a tangle of bodies in front of the Canucks' goal crease. Suddenly, it popped loose, and so did Bossy, who left his feet to reach it. Both of his skates were off the ice when his stick made contact with the puck. Again the element of surprise worked for Mike Bossy, another example of why he was referred to as a "pure goal-scorer." This goal is Mike's personal favorite among the 61 goals he scored during the Islanders' reign of four straight Stanley Cup triumphs.

Guy Lafleur retired early in the 1984-85 season. In 1987 Mike Bossy's career was ended by a chronic back injury. Neither man played in 1987-88, but the following autumn, Guy Lafleur made one of the most talked-about comebacks in NHL history. Lafleur had been retired for almost four seasons and had been voted into the Hockey Hall of Fame. Then, at the age of thirty-seven, he came back to play for the New York Rangers and, later, for the Quebec Nordiques.

Memories. The stuff Stanley Cups are made of for fans as they look back on what used to be. From 1976 until 1983 there were two great Stanley-Cup-winning teams, the Montreal Canadiens and the New York Islanders. And those teams gave us two superstars: "The Flower" in Montreal and "The Boss" on Long Island, goal-scoring dynamos for two separate dynasties.

The 99 Era

THE NHL'S EXPANSION TO FOUR FORMER WHA CITIES INAUGURATED A period of stability in which the league would keep its twenty-one-team configuration for twelve seasons. Under the new entrants' terms of admission to the NHL, each ex-WHA club was allowed to protect two skaters and one goaltender from its 1978-79 roster. Apart from those protected players, the rights to players previously drafted by NHL clubs reverted to the NHL organization that had originally selected each player. The four new franchises participated in an expansion draft, acquiring up to fifteen skaters and two goaltenders from the established clubs. Each of the seventeen incumbent franchises relinquished four players in the draft.

Several talented players shifted from the former WHA clubs to NHL teams under these rules. Kent Nilsson was reclaimed by Atlanta after two 107-point seasons with the Winnipeg Jets. Goaltender Mike Liut joined the St. Louis Blues after two seasons with Cincinnati. Defenseman Dave Langevin joined the New York Islanders from Edmonton, and Terry Ruskowski, a five-year WHA veteran with Houston and Winnipeg, joined the Chicago Black Hawks. The four expansion teams also participated in the amateur draft, which, that year, was renamed the "entry draft" because of the availability of players with professional (WHA) experience in the draft pool. Former WHA players who had turned pro while still below the NHL's minimum draft age of eighteen – including Rob Ramage, Mike Gartner, Rick Vaive, Craig Hartsburg, Michel Goulet, and Mark Messier – were among the top players available in what proved to be a strong draft year.

To accommodate twenty-one teams, the NHL adopted a balanced eighty-game schedule that saw each team play four games against twenty opponents. The new clubs were assigned to three of the league's four divisions: Quebec was placed in the Adams, Winnipeg and Edmonton in the Smythe, and Hartford – the renamed New England franchise – in the Norris. The Patrick Division remained unchanged. All divisions consisted of five

The results of the 1979 Expansion Draft, when the NHL added four teams from the defunct WHA. Doug Favell, a goaltender selected by Edmonton, had previously been selected in the league's first expansion draft, held in 1967.

NATIONAL HOCKEY LEAGUE EXPANSION DRAFT
Montreal, June 13, 1979
EXPANSION TEAMS' PLAYER SELECTIONS

		EDMONTON	HARTFORD
GOAL KEEPERS PRIORITY	1	DRYDEN, Dave	GARRETT, John
	2	MIO, Ed	
	1	GRETZKY, Wayne	DOUGLAS, Jordy
	2	GUSTAFSSON, Bengt	HOWE, Mark
	1	LoPRESTI, Pete (Minn.)	LAPOINTE, Normand (Van.)
	2	FAVELL, Doug (Col.)	
PLAYERS	1	CONNOR, Cam (Mtl.)	HANGSLEBEN, Alan (Mtl.)
	2	FOGOLIN, Lee (Buff.)	FOTIU, Nick (N.Y. R.)
	3	PRICE, Pat (N.Y. I.)	LEY, Rick (Tor.)
	4	CAMPBELL, Colin (Pitt.)	SIMS, Al (Bos.)
	5	BROWN, Larry (L.A.)	SAVARD, Jean (Chi.)
	6	ARESHENKOFF, Ron (Buff.)	KLASSEN, Ralph (Col.)
	7	HAMMARSTROM, Inge (S.L.)	HODGSON, Rick (Atl.)
	8	GOULD, John (Atl.)	KEMP, Kevin (Tor.)
	9	HICKS, Doug (Chi.)	BENNETT, Bill (Bos.)
	10	EDUR, Tom (Pitt.)	JOHNSTON, Bernie (Phil.)
	11	BIANCHIN, Wayne (Pitt.)	HILL, Brian (Atl.)
	12	FORBES, Mike (Bos.)	GIVEN, Dave (Buff.)
	13	PATEY, Doug (Wash.)	SCHURMAN, Maynard (Phil.)
	14	KELLY, Bob (Chi.)	BEVERLEY, Nick (Co.)
	15		KOZAK, Don (Van.)

NATIONAL HOCKEY LEAGUE EXPANSION DRAFT
Montreal, June 13, 1979
EXPANSION TEAMS' PLAYER SELECTIONS

		QUEBEC	WINNIPEG
GOAL KEEPERS PRIORITY	1	BRODEUR, Richard	MATTSON, Markus
	2		
	1	BAXTER, Paul	CAMPBELL, Scott
	2	LARIVIERE, Gary	LUKOWICH, Morris
	1	LOW, Ron (Det.)	MIDDLEBROOK, Lindsay (N.Y. R.)
	2	PARRO, Dave (Bos.)	HAMEL, Pierre (Tor.)
PLAYERS	1	FARRISH, Dave (N.Y. R.)	MARSH, Peter (Mtl.)
	2	HART, Gerry (N.Y. I.)	HULL, Bobby (Chi.)
	3	PLANTE, Pierre (N.Y. R.)	CAMERON, Al (Det.)
	4	STEWART, Blair (Wash.)	HOYDA, Dave (Phil.)
	5	BABY, John (Minn.)	ROBERTS, Jim (Minn.)
	6	SMRKE, John (S.L.)	STAMLER, Lorne (Tor.)
	7	KUZYK, Ken (Minn.)	HEASLIP, Mark (L.A.)
	8	CLOUTIER, Roland (Det.)	McTAVISH, Gord (S.L.)
	9	MARTIN, Terry (Buff.)	SMITH, Gord (Wash.)
	10	MASTERS, Jamie (S.L.)	HAMILTON, Clark (Det.)
	11	MONAHAN, Hartland (L.A.)	CUNNINGHAM, Jim (Phil.)
	12	ANDRUFF, Ron (Col.)	ABGRALL, Dennis (L.A.)
	13	COTE, Alain (Mtl.)	RILEY, Bill (Wash.)
	14	ZETTERSTROM, Lars (Van.)	CARR, Gene (Atl.)
	15		GRAVES, Hilliard (Van.)

The 1979-80 Edmonton Oilers won nine of their last ten games to finish the club's first season with a respectable 69 points, good for fourth place in the Smythe Division. Two players in this photo remained with the Oilers throughout the 1980s: Mark Messier (second row, sixth from left) and Kevin Lowe (second row, fifth from right). Wayne Gretzky is at top row, center. Coach Glen Sather is in the front row, second from right.

clubs, except for the Smythe, which now had six.

The playoffs were modified to eliminate the first-round exemption for division winners. Under the new format, teams would be ranked on the basis of points. The top sixteen clubs would advance to a best-of-five preliminary round, the team that finished first facing the team finishing sixteenth, second facing fifteenth, and so on. As before, ranking and pairing would be used to determine match-ups in all playoff rounds.

In Montreal, the Canadiens were faced with an unusual number of changes. Scotty Bowman resigned as coach to take on the combined job of coach and general manager in Buffalo. Al MacNeil, who had coached the Canadiens to the Cup in 1971, and had recently served as the club's director of player personnel, jumped to Atlanta to coach the Flames. First-line center Jacques Lemaire left the NHL to coach and play in Switzerland, and Ken Dryden retired. The Canadiens hired former star Bernie Geoffrion as coach, but before the end of the season, he would be succeeded by Claude Ruel.

Taking over in Buffalo, Scotty Bowman hired Roger Neilson – who, along with general manager Jim Gregory, had been fired by the Leafs – as an associate coach. In Toronto, Harold Ballard rehired former Leaf coach and general manager Punch Imlach – who had been fired by the Sabres – as the club's new general manager. Imlach gave the Leafs' coaching job to ex-Buffalo scout Floyd Smith.

In Boston, Don Cherry demanded a raise, didn't get what he wanted, and ended up coaching the Rockies in Colorado. To replace Cherry, Harry Sinden hired Fred Creighton, who had previously coached in Atlanta. One of Sinden's main concerns was rebuilding an aging Bruins' roster. The team still had Brad Park, Wayne Cashman, Terry O'Reilly, and Bobby Schmautz from the "lunch pail" teams of the late 1970s, but the future belonged to players such as Ray Bourque and Brad McCrimmon, two promising rookie defensemen obtained in the 1979 entry draft. Bourque would win the Calder Trophy.

The Flyers, still built around veterans Bobby Clarke, Bill Barber, Rick MacLeish, and Reggie Leach, added Ken Linseman and Brian Propp, as coach Pat Quinn tried to revitalize the Philadelphia attack.

Improved team defense was Scotty Bowman's top priority in Buffalo. Danny Gare would emerge as a scoring star, with 56 goals in 1979-80, but it was the addition of defenseman John Van Boxmeer, acquired from Colorado for former French Connection winger René Robert, that made the Sabres' defense click. Buffalo cut its goals-against by 62 to 201, winning the Vezina Trophy for goaltenders Bob Sauvé and Don Edwards.

The New York Rangers acquired third-year defenseman Barry Beck in a November deal that saw the Rangers send five players to Colorado. Beck, who set an NHL record for goals by a rookie defenseman with 22 in 1977-78, had impressed the Rangers' general manager Fred Shero with his play during February's three-game Challenge Cup series with the Soviets in Madison Square Garden. The Washington Capitals made an early-season coaching change, replacing Danny Belisle with Gary Green, who had coached Peterborough to the Memorial Cup Canadian major junior championship in May. Green, just twenty-six, became the youngest head coach in NHL history.

The Atlanta Flames acquired veteran Garry Unger from St. Louis prior to the start of the season. Unger had eight consecutive 30-goal seasons and had been the NHL's "Iron Man" since 1975, when he surpassed Andy Hebenton's record of 630 consecutive games. Unger had played more than eleven seasons without missing a game when he joined the Flames, but his streak ended on December 21 at 914 games.

The Minnesota North Stars finished in third place in the Adams Division behind Boston and Buffalo, and recorded a franchise-high 88 points. Al MacAdam and Steve Payne both had 40-goal seasons for the Stars. Gilles Meloche and Gary Edwards split the goaltending duties.

The Los Angeles Kings' "Triple Crown Line." From left to right, Dave Taylor, Marcel Dionne, and Charlie Simmer, who holds the modern-day record for goals scored in consecutive games, potting at least one in thirteen consecutive games during the 1979-80 season.

At the age of fifty-one, Gordie Howe returned to the NHL with the Hartford Whalers when the league expanded to include four WHA cities. Near the conclusion of the 1979-80 season, Howe realized the NHL version of the dream that had first come true for him with Houston of the WHA – playing on an all-Howe forward line with his sons, Mark and Marty.

The Los Angeles Kings, purchased by Jerry Buss, who also owned the NBA Lakers and the Forum in Inglewood, California, were led by the Triple Crown Line of Marcel Dionne, Dave Taylor, and Charlie Simmer. The line combined for 328 points, and Dionne finished tied for the league's scoring lead. Simmer scored in twelve consecutive games, the longest goal-scoring streak since Harry "Punch" Broadbent of the Ottawa Senators scored in sixteen straight games in 1921-22.

Of the NHL's four expansion clubs, the Hartford Whalers remained most like the team that had played in the WHA, since they had relinquished fewer players than their expansion counterparts. The Whalers' line-up featured Gordie Howe, who, at fifty-two, would score his 800th career NHL goal. (Howe and his two sons joined the Whalers in 1977-78 after four seasons in

Houston.) Hartford also employed forty-year-old Dave Keon and acquired Bobby Hull, forty-one, who played nine games in the 1979-80 season.

The Whalers also received fine performances from three younger players who had performed in the WHA. Mark Howe, already in his seventh professional season at the age of twenty-four, had 80 points. Center Mike Rogers had 44 goals and 61 assists for 105 points, adding 33 points to his previous season's totals, and right winger Blaine Stoughton, a former Leaf and Penguin, tied Charlie Simmer and Buffalo's Danny Gare for the NHL's goal-scoring lead with 56. Rogers and Stoughton were joined on a forward line by Pat Boutette, who came to the Whalers in a mid-season trade with the Leafs.

But nothing in 1979-80 compared with the performance of Wayne Gretzky of the Edmonton Oilers. Gretzky, whose hockey skills had earned him cross-Canada attention before he was ten, had outshone every other player through minor and junior hockey and in the WHA. In the NHL, success followed upon success. During that first year, he had seven assists in a game against Washington, scored 51 goals, and finished tied with Marcel Dionne for the scoring lead with 137 points. (This marked the second occasion in league history that two players tied for the scoring lead; Bobby Hull and Andy Bathgate both finished with 84 points in 1961-62.) Dionne was awarded the Art Ross Trophy by virtue of having scored more goals, but Gretzky won the Hart and Lady Byng trophies, capturing the imagination of the entire sports world.

Far from appealing to Toronto fans' imagination, Punch Imlach inflamed the hometown crowd when he attempted to shake up the Leafs by trading the popular Lanny McDonald and Joel Quenneville to Colorado for Wilf Paiement and Pat Hickey. At the time, this was not a bad trade for either club, but it so disturbed Leaf captain Darryl Sittler, a close friend of McDonald's, that he temporarily abdicated his captaincy in protest. In other deals, Vancouver acquired Dave "Tiger" Williams and Jerry Butler from Toronto for Bill Derlago and ex-Birmingham Bull Rick Vaive in a mid-season trade. Vaive would go on to record three consecutive 50-goal seasons for the Leafs and score more than 400 goals in the NHL. Late in the season, the Islanders sent Dave Lewis and former number-one draft pick Billy Harris to Los Angeles for veteran center Butch Goring, who would prove to be the missing ingredient general manager Bill Torrey and coach Al Arbour had been seeking for the playoffs.

In February, interest and enthusiasm for hockey in the United States was supercharged by the U.S. Olympic team's upset gold-medal victory at the Winter Olympics in Lake Placid, New York. The U.S. squad was made up of collegiate players, nine of whom joined NHL clubs after the Games, boosting the total of Americans in the league to a high of 66. In addition to goaltender Jim Craig, who had been the star of the Lake Placid Olympics, Steve Christoff, Mike Ramsey, Mark Johnson, Ken Morrow, and Dave Christian were among the gold medalists to finish the season in the NHL. Neal Broten,

Lanny McDonald, seen here with the Colorado Rockies, began his NHL career with the Toronto Maple Leafs and became one of the most popular players ever to skate in Maple Leaf Gardens. He went from Toronto to Colorado and, in 1981, to Calgary, where he gained a new following by scoring 66 goals in 1982-83.

who would become the first American-born player to score 100 points in the NHL, entered the league with Minnesota in 1980-81.

As much as the gold-medal win at the 1980 Olympics was a victory for the players on the American team and for U.S. college hockey, it was also a breakthrough for the NHL. It provided a final convincing argument that college hockey was developing players who could compete with the world's best, and signified that American-born players had now become an important part of the talent pool that sustained the NHL. The Lake Placid win also glamorized the game throughout the United States, and attracted an increased number of young players to the sport. By the end of the 1980s, American college and high-school players would account for approximately 40 per cent of the players chosen in each year's entry draft.

During the 1979-80 season, the Philadelphia Flyers topped the standings for the first time since 1974-75, finishing with 116 points. From October through January, the Flyers set a league record, playing 35 games without a loss, winning 25, and tying 10. Scotty Bowman's Sabres were second with 110 points, followed by the Canadiens with 107 and the Bruins with 105. Surprisingly, the Islanders, who had finished with more than 100 points in each of the previous four seasons, slumped 25 points to finish with 91, fifth overall and second to the Flyers in the Patrick Division. Two former WHA clubs – Hartford and Edmonton – qualified for post-season play.

In the preliminary round of the playoffs, only one series – Boston over Pittsburgh – went to the new five-game limit. The first-place Flyers swept the sixteenth-place Oilers, but needed two overtime wins to do so. The Canadiens swept Hartford, but the Whalers' Gordie Howe scored the 1,071st and final goal of his thirty-two-year NHL and WHA career in game three of the series.

In the quarter-finals, the Minnesota North Stars engineered a major upset, defeating the Canadiens in seven games to end Montreal's bid to establish an unprecedented second five-Cup dynasty. The North Stars trailed three to two in games, but came back with wins in games six and seven. The Canadiens' attack was hampered by injuries to 50-goal scorers Guy Lafleur and Pierre Larouche. Minnesota was stopped in five games by the Flyers in the semi-finals, and the Islanders defeated the Sabres in six to earn their first berth in the finals.

The Islanders had proven to be the wizards of overtime thus far in the 1980 playoffs, winning four games in extra time and extending this number to five in game one of the finals. The Flyers and Islanders battled to a sixth game in the Nassau Coliseum, where two third-period goals by the Flyers forced overtime. But a goal by Bob Nystrom on a set-up from John Tonelli brought the Stanley Cup to Long Island and ended the Islanders' four-year string of playoff disappointments. Bryan Trottier won the Conn Smythe Trophy and was the leading point-scorer in the playoffs with 12 goals and 17 assists. However, it was the hard work, character, and 19-point playoff effort of late-

season acquisition Butch Goring that was credited with pushing the Islanders to the top. The victory rewarded management's patience, and it was confirmation of the team's policy of building through good scouting and draft selection.

Back in September of 1976, the Montreal Canadiens had sent two players who did not fit into their long-term plans to the Colorado Rockies. In return, the Canadiens and the Rockies agreed to switch first-round selections in the 1980 entry draft. Colorado's nineteen-win season and last-place finish in 1979-80 cost coach Don Cherry his job, and meant that Montreal's acquired pick would be first overall. With their elimination in the quarter-finals by a big, young team from Minnesota very much in mind, the Canadiens chose to draft size over finesse. Two superb offensive players were available, and

Bob Nystrom and Lorne Henning celebrate Nystrom's overtime goal in game six of the 1980 Stanley Cup finals. The decisive marker gave the New York Islanders their first Stanley Cup championship. Nystrom scored four overtime goals in his career, including two in the 1980 playoffs.

Montreal used its pick to select Doug Wickenheiser, a big center from Regina, Saskatchewan, who had been selected Canadian Major Junior Player of the Year for 1979-80. The player the Canadiens did not take was Denis Savard, a high-scoring Montreal junior, who was taken third overall by Chicago. Savard would give Chicago ten strong seasons and score more than 1,000 points, while Wickenheiser would never hit stride in Montreal, scoring just 49 goals in parts of four seasons before being traded in 1983.

The Winnipeg Jets, picking second, opted for another western junior, defenseman Dave Babych. Edmonton, drafting sixth, selected Paul Coffey from the Kitchener Rangers of the OHA.

The 1980-81 season would prove to be a long one for the Winnipeg Jets. The team finished with just 32 points – the lowest total since the Washington Capitals had 32 in 1975-76 – and set an NHL record by going thirty games without a win. Washington finished with a franchise-high 70 points in 1980-81. Dennis Maruk scored 50 goals, and Mike Gartner added 48, but the Capitals finished four points behind the Rangers, who captured the final playoff spot in the Patrick Division.

The Quebec Nordiques did much to close the gap between themselves and the rest of the Adams Division by signing Peter and Anton Stastny, brothers and scoring stars with the Czechoslovakian national team. Anton had been drafted by the Nordiques eighty-third overall in 1979, and Peter signed as a free agent after both had defected to Canada. The Stastnys immediately became front-line players for the Nordiques, Peter setting a rookie points-scoring record with 109 and winning the Calder Trophy. The Nordiques also got a 52-goal season from Jacques Richard and improved 17 points in the standings under rookie head coach Michel Bergeron.

The Atlanta Flames relocated to Calgary for 1980-81. Five consecutive seasons in the playoffs and 50-goal scorers notwithstanding, the franchise had never established a strong season-ticket base in Georgia. In Calgary, the Flames opened for business with an instant rival just up the highway in Edmonton. The club's first president was former WHA team owner Nelson Skalbania, but before the start of the 1981-82 season, Skalbania would sell his shares in the club to six Calgary business executives, including former Canadian Football League all-star Normie Kwong.

The Flames won the "Battle of Alberta" in 1980-81, finishing with 92 points to Edmonton's 74, but the Oilers were not without honors as Gretzky set a new single-season scoring record with 164 points. The Flames' Kent Nilsson came third in scoring with 131, behind the Kings' Marcel Dionne, who scored 58 goals and finished with 135 points. Dionne, Lafleur, and Bobby Clarke reached career milestones, topping the 1,000-point mark during the season.

The league's goal-scoring crown, however, belonged to Islander sharp-shooter Mike Bossy, who scored 68 goals and equaled Rocket Richard's record-setting pace of 50 goals in 50 games. The Islanders topped the standings with 110 points. Over the course of the season, Billy Smith

Although Mike Bossy was best known for his ability to put the puck in the net, he was equally adept at setting up goals. On January 6, 1981, he set an Islanders' team record by assisting on all six goals in a 6–3 win over the Toronto Maple Leafs.

Mike Liut, the Bowling Green State University graduate who backstopped the St. Louis Blues to a 107-point season in 1980-81, finished second in voting for the Hart Trophy, and won the Lester B. Pearson Award as the league's top player – as selected by the members of the NHL Players' Association during his sophomore season.

emerged as the team's top goaltender, and, in March, Chico Resch was dealt to Colorado.

The St. Louis Blues improved by 27 points in the standings to finish with 107. The Blues hired Red Berenson as coach and received superb goaltending from Mike Liut, who would finish a close second to Wayne Gretzky in voting for the Hart Trophy. Center Bernie Federko had his first 100-point season, right wing Wayne Babych scored 54 goals, and left wing Brent Sutter added 35 more. Montreal was the league's third-best club with 103 points, followed by Buffalo and Los Angeles with 99. All three members of the Kings' Triple Crown Line topped 100 points. Boston, with 87 points, finished second to Buffalo in the Adams Division. Right winger Rick Middleton scored 44 goals and finished with 103 points. Rogie Vachon was the Bruins' number-one goaltender, backed up by Jim Craig.

The New York Rangers won only four of their first twenty games and made a mid-season management change. Craig Patrick, who had joined the club as director of hockey operations in July, replaced Fred Shero as coach and general manager. Patrick had an impeccable hockey pedigree: his grandfather, Lester, built the Rangers, and his father, Lynn, and his uncle, Muzz,

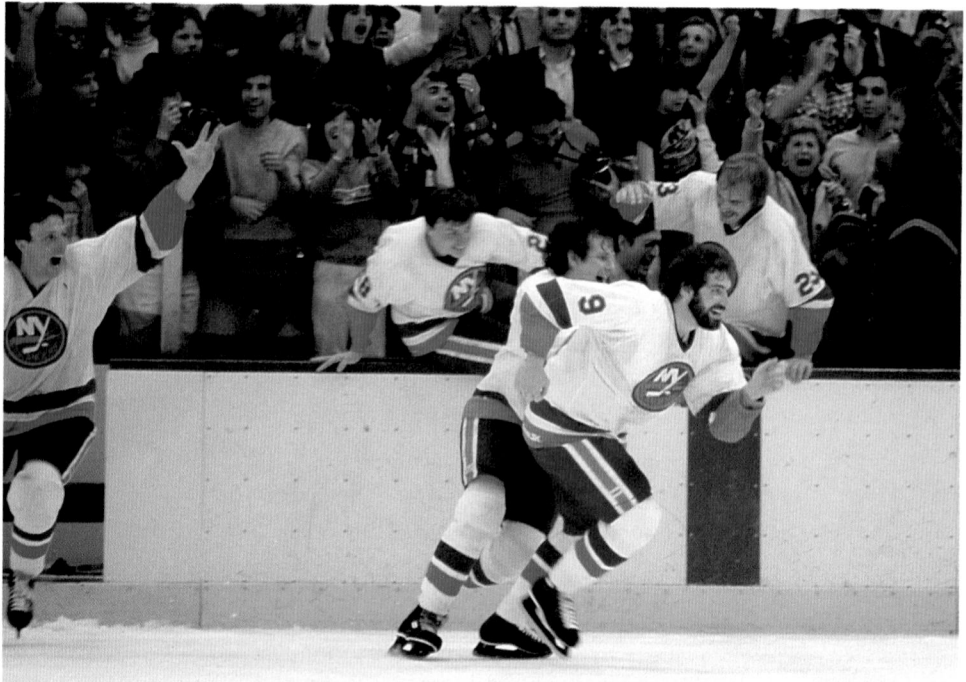

Clark Gillies leads the Islanders' charge off the bench as they celebrate their second consecutive Stanley Cup title. The Islanders dismissed the upstart Minnesota North Stars in five games to capture the 1981 championship.

played for and coached the team. Craig had been the assistant coach and assistant manager of the 1980 U.S. Olympic hockey team.

In the playoffs, the powerful Canadiens were upset by Edmonton in a three-game preliminary-round sweep in which Gretzky proved to be unstoppable. The defeat was clearly symbolic of the league's new order. The Canadiens were the established team, with a glorious playoff history; the Oilers were a scrappy young outfit led by Gretzky, the game's pre-eminent point-producer. But in the quarter-finals, the magic ended for the Oilers as the Islanders eliminated them in six games. The New York Rangers needed six games to upset heavily favored St. Louis in their quarter-final series, but in the semis, the Islanders swept the Rangers to advance to the finals for the second consecutive season.

The Minnesota North Stars would prove to be the Islanders' final-series opponent, defeating Adams Division rivals Boston and Buffalo before eliminating Calgary, who had upset the Flyers, in a six-game semi-final. Bobby Smith, Steve Payne, and Dino Ciccarelli provided most of the North Stars' offensive power, while Craig Hartsburg and Curt Giles anchored the defense. The Islanders, however, were too strong for Minnesota in the final series, winning the Stanley Cup in five games. Bossy, Trottier, and Potvin were the Isles' leading scorers, but it was the determined hustle of Butch Goring that was rewarded with the Conn Smythe Trophy. Ciccarelli set rookie point- and goal-scoring records for one playoff year with 14 goals and 21 points.

Two more of the game's all-time greats, Jean Ratelle and Phil Esposito, retired after the 1980-81 season. This, coupled with the retirements of

Gordie Howe, Bobby Hull, and Stan Mikita the previous season, left Dave Keon as the only active player who had starred in the six-team era.

The league's governors and general managers realigned the NHL's four divisions and adopted an unbalanced schedule that saw clubs play more games against teams in their own division. With few exceptions, clubs were placed in divisions made up of teams from neighboring cities. This reduced travel costs and fostered regional rivalries. The Campbell Conference contained the NHL's western teams, plus Toronto, and was now made up of the Norris and Smythe divisions. The six-team Norris was based in the Midwest, and included Chicago, Detroit, Minnesota, St. Louis, Toronto, and Winnipeg. The western Smythe Division comprised Calgary, Colorado, Edmonton, Los Angeles, and Vancouver. The Prince of Wales Conference was based in the East and contained the Adams and Patrick divisions. The northeastern Adams Division was home to Boston, Buffalo, Hartford, Montreal, and Quebec, while the Patrick, running south from New York City, included both New York teams, Philadelphia, Pittsburgh, and Washington.

To take advantage of these geographical groupings and build divisional rivalries, each team in the Adams, Patrick, and Smythe played clubs in its own division eight times a season. Teams in the larger six-team Norris played one another seven times. Just three games would be played against each club in the other divisions.

The format for the playoffs was similarly revised; the one-to-sixteen ranking, in place since 1979-80, was scrapped in favor of a system by which the first four finishers in each division qualified for post-season play. In each division, two rounds would be played to determine a divisional winner. In round one, a five-game division semi-final, the first-place finisher would play the fourth and the second-place team the third. The two winners would then play a seven-game division-final series. The two division champions in each conference would then meet in a seven-game conference final. The winner of the series between the Norris and the Smythe victors would receive the Clarence Campbell Bowl as champion of the Campbell Conference; the winner of the Adams and Patrick would be awarded the Prince of Wales Trophy as champions of the Prince of Wales Conference. Previously, these trophies were awarded to the club in each conference with the best regular-season record. The two conference champions would meet in a seven-game Stanley Cup final series.

On the ice, a second edition of the six-nation Canada Cup was played in September, concluding with the Soviets defeating Team Canada 8–1 in the final game. The 1981 Canada Cup marked the first North American appearance of a five-man unit that would become the Soviets' top forward line and defense pair of the 1980s. These five players – forwards Sergei Makarov, Igor Larionov, and Vladimir Krutov, and defensemen Viacheslav Fetisov and Alexei Kasatonov – came to be known as the "Green Unit," after the color of the jerseys they wore in practice. Though the possibility of Soviet players

Aluminum Sticks

In December 1981 the NHL's Board of Governors gave its approval for the use of aluminum-shaft sticks in league play.

Dino Ciccarelli, who joined the North Stars midway through the 1980-81 season and recorded 30 points in 32 games, set an NHL record for goals (14) and points (21) by a rookie in one playoff year as the North Stars reached the Stanley Cup finals.

joining NHL clubs was remote, all five members of the Green Unit were selected in the NHL entry draft between 1983 and 1988.

The top story of the 1981-82 season, however, was Wayne Gretzky, who shattered all previous single-season scoring records with 212 points. Before his twenty-first birthday in January, Gretzky had 50 goals in just 39 games, 11 fewer than the 50-in-50 milestone shared by Richard and Bossy. He kept right on scoring to finish with an astonishing 92 goals (no player other than Phil Esposito had scored even 70). Gretzky also had a record-setting 120 assists, leading the Oilers to a record 417-goal season and first place in the Smythe Division with 111 points. Edmonton had cracked the 100-point plateau in just its third NHL season. Gretzky was ably supported by Glenn Anderson, Paul Coffey, Jari Kurri, and Mark Messier – four young players whose names would be mentioned frequently throughout the 1980s.

The Islanders' balanced combination of firepower and defense led to the league's best record of 54 wins and 118 points, and first place in the Patrick. Mike Bossy scored 64 goals and had 83 assists for 147 points, finishing second to Gretzky in scoring. The 250 goals given up by the Islanders were the league's second-fewest, 27 more than the total surrendered by Montreal's Rick Wamsley and Denis Herron, who shared the newly created William Jennings Trophy for fewest goals-against. The Vezina Trophy was now awarded to the goaltender judged to be most valuable to his team by the league's twenty-one general managers. Billy Smith of the Islanders was the first recipient of the newly defined award.

The New York Rangers finished second in the Patrick with 92 points. Before the start of the 1981-82 season, coach and general manager Craig Patrick relinquished the head coaching job, hiring Herb Brooks, who had coached the University of Minnesota Golden Gophers and the 1980 U.S. Olympic team. Brooks instituted a crowd-pleasing, European-style offensive system that was built around weaving, criss-crossing, and circling. Mike Rogers led the Rangers with 103 points, and Ron Duguay contributed 40 goals. Barry Beck and Finnish rookie Reijo Ruotsalainen led a defense corps that was very much involved in the Rangers' attack.

The defensive-minded Canadiens finished first in the Adams with 109 points, while Minnesota, powered by 114 points from Bobby Smith and 55 goals from Dino Ciccarelli, won the Norris Division title. The order of finish from first to fifth in the Norris – Minnesota, Winnipeg, Chicago, Toronto, and Detroit – provided strong evidence that any distinction between the "original" six teams and expansion clubs had disappeared. The Leafs, who dropped from 71 to 56 points, dealt Darryl Sittler, their all-time leading scorer, to Philadelphia in January. Sittler's former linemate, right winger Lanny McDonald, had already been traded for the second time in his career, going from Colorado to Calgary in November. One bright light among the "original" Norris teams was Chicago defenseman Doug Wilson, who won the Norris Trophy scoring 39 goals, the second-highest number ever scored by a

defenseman, surpassed only by Bobby Orr's record 46 in 1974-75.

Two second-year centers had superb seasons. Quebec's Peter Stastny improved on his record-setting rookie campaign with 46 goals and 93 assists for 139 points and third spot on the list of leading scorers. A third Stastny brother, Marian, joined the Nordiques for 1981-82. In Chicago, Denis Savard exhibited dazzling puck-handling skills to finish sixth in scoring with 87 assists and 119 points.

In Winnipeg, the Jets made the greatest gain of any team in 1981-82. After a last-place finish the previous season, the Jets used 1981's first overall draft selection to pick high-scoring Dale Hawerchuk from the Cornwall Royals of the Quebec Junior Hockey League. Hawerchuk lived up to his junior billing, scoring 45 goals and winning the Calder Trophy. Morris Lukowich contributed 43 goals, and the team won 33 games to finish second in its division with 80 points. The club's 48-point improvement earned former

Left: Doug Wilson had his finest season in 1981-82, winning the Norris Trophy and earning a berth on the NHL's First All-Star Team. Top, right: Quebec's Peter Stastny established an NHL rookie point-scoring record in 1980-81. Bottom, right: Dale Hawerchuk reflects on his first career hat-trick, three of 45 goals he would score in his Calder Trophy-winning rookie season with the Winnipeg Jets in 1981-82.

University of Toronto coach Tom Watt the Jack Adams Award as the NHL's coach of the year. The Jets' rejuvenation ended in the first round of the playoffs, however, when the St. Louis Blues eliminated Winnipeg in four games. Chicago then defeated St. Louis to become the Norris Division champions.

In the division semi-finals, two first-place clubs were upset by fourth-place finishers. In the Smythe, Los Angeles and Edmonton played a high-scoring five-game thriller that was won by the Kings. In game three in Los Angeles, the Kings came back from 5–0, forcing overtime on a goal by Steve Bozek at 19:55 of the third period. Rookie left winger Daryl Evans got the winner for the Kings at 2:15 of extra time. This comeback became known as the "Miracle on Manchester" after the location of the Kings' rink on West Manchester Boulevard in Inglewood.

In the Adams, Quebec needed five games to eliminate their provincial rivals from Montreal. The *coup de grâce* was a goal by Dale Hunter just 22 seconds into overtime of the final game. The Nordiques then won the championship of the Adams Division by upending the Bruins in seven games. Meanwhile, the Los Angeles Kings bowed to a surprising Vancouver club in a five-game series that featured strong goaltending by the Canucks' Richard Brodeur.

Quebec's visit to the conference finals ended in a four-game sweep by the Islanders, who reached the third round of the playoffs by eliminating Pittsburgh and the Rangers. The Penguins had given the Isles a scare in the division semi-finals, stretching the defending champions to overtime in the fifth game before being eliminated on a goal by John Tonelli, who had also tied the game with a goal in the last minute of the third period. By defeating Quebec, the Islanders reached the finals for the third consecutive season.

The Vancouver Canucks needed five games to eliminate Chicago and claim the Campbell Conference championship in a series between two sub-.500 teams. Led by Swedish center Thomas Gradin, right winger Stan Smyl, and Brodeur in goal, the Canucks' win gave the city of Vancouver its first chance to witness a Stanley Cup final game since the Ottawa Senators defeated the Vancouver Maroons and the Edmonton Eskimos in that city in March of 1923. In game two in Chicago, exasperated Vancouver coach Roger Neilson and Canucks' forwards Tiger Williams and Gerry Minor were ejected from the game after waving white towels at the referee to protest a penalty call that led to a goal by Denis Savard. These "terrible towels" immediately became a badge of honor for Canucks' fans, and, beginning with game three in Vancouver, more and more whirling white squares of terrycloth appeared in the seats of the Pacific Coliseum.

The Canucks' Cinderella season fell apart in the finals against the scoring punch and savvy of the Islanders, who swept the Campbell Conference champions in spite of Richard Brodeur's fine goaltending. Mike Bossy's seven goals in the finals – including a game-winner in overtime in game one – helped move the Islanders into some select company: since the NHL was established in 1917, only the Canadiens and the Leafs had won the Stanley Cup in three consecutive years.

Soon after the playoffs, Bruce Norris sold the Detroit Red Wings to Mike Ilitch, ending fifty years of involvement with the NHL by the Norris family. In addition, John McMullen, who owned baseball's Houston Astros, led a group of New Jersey investors who purchased the financially troubled Colorado Rockies franchise, transferred it to the Brendan Byrne Meadowlands Arena just outside New York City, and renamed the club the New Jersey Devils. McMullen's group negotiated territorial indemnification payments with the Devils' three closest neighbors – the Rangers, the Islanders, and the Flyers – whose markets the team would share. The move from Denver to the Meadowlands resulted in two clubs shifting divisions. The Devils moved from the Smythe to the Patrick, and Winnipeg moved from the Norris to the Smythe. These changes made the Patrick the NHL's one six-team division.

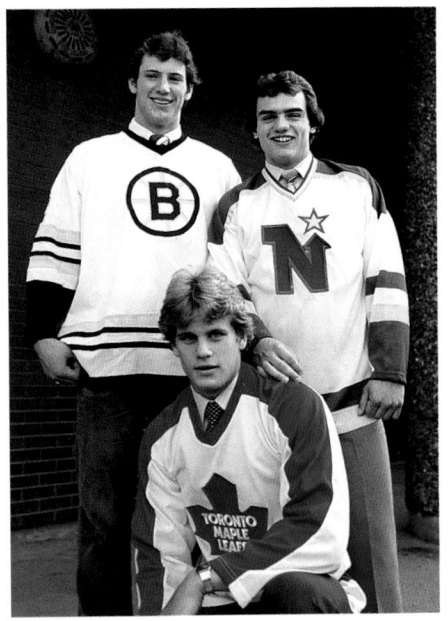

The top three picks in the 1982 Entry Draft: Gord Kluzak (Bruins), Gary Nylund (Leafs), and Brian Bellows (North Stars). Almost a decade later, Nylund is with his third NHL club, the New York Islanders, Kluzak was forced to retire after eleven knee operations, and Bellows remains a team leader for the North Stars.

Defense was the prized commodity at the 1982 entry draft. Top picks included Gord Kluzak (Boston), Gary Nylund (Toronto), Scott Stevens (Washington), and Phil Housley (Buffalo). A pair of twin brothers from Western Canada, Ron and Rich Sutter, were drafted in the first round by Philadelphia and Pittsburgh, respectively, bringing the number of Sutters in the NHL to six. Brian Sutter had entered the league in 1976 with St. Louis; Darryl had followed in 1979 with Chicago, the same year Duane joined the Islanders. Brent joined Duane and the Islanders in 1980. All six played with the same tenacious, hard-nosed style.

The Bruins, who never seemed to be out of a season's race for top spot, finished first in the Adams Division and the NHL with 110 points. The team, led by Rick Middleton, who had 49 goals, and Barry Pedersen, with 46, got sound goaltending from Pete Peeters, who won 40 games and had a league-leading goals-against average of 2.36. Peeters also posted eight shutouts, which would prove to be the highest single-season total for a goaltender in the 1980s. Ray Bourque continued to stand out on defense, earning his fourth consecutive all-star selection. The Canadiens finished second in the Adams with 98 points, the club's first finish out of top spot and below 100 points since 1974-75.

Normand Leveillé, a promising second-year Boston forward, drafted fourteenth overall in 1981, suffered a brain hemorrhage between periods of an early-season game in Vancouver. Leveillé survived and returned home after a lengthy stay in hospital, but was unable to resume his hockey career.

In September, the Habs and the Washington Capitals completed a four-for-two player transaction that sent Brian Engblom, Rod Langway, Doug Jarvis, and Craig Laughlin to Washington for defenseman Rick Green and forward Ryan Walter. The Capitals appeared to gain the early advantage in this deal, as Langway became the wheelhorse of the Washington defense and won the

Norris Trophy. The Caps enjoyed a 29-point improvement in the standings, finishing third in the Patrick Division to qualify for post-season play for the first time in franchise history.

The Islanders started the season slowly, but began to win consistently in the second half of the schedule. They finished second in the Patrick, ten points back of the Philadelphia Flyers. The Flyers had improved their defense in the off-season, trading for Mark Howe of Hartford in a three-cornered deal that sent Ken Linseman to Edmonton, and Risto Siltanen to the Whalers. The Flyers' goaltending duties were split between two rookies, Pelle Lindbergh and Bob Froese. The Pittsburgh Penguins, who came within a last-minute goal of upsetting the defending-champion Islanders in the 1982 playoffs, plunged 30 points in the standings to finish in last place in the Patrick.

The Black Hawks surged from fourth to first in the Norris. In addition to 121 points from Denis Savard, the Hawks got 54 goals from Al Secord and another 43 from Steve Larmer, the year's Calder Trophy winner. Larmer was a first-year bargain for the Hawks, who selected him 120th overall in the 1980 entry draft.

In the Smythe, Calgary's Lanny McDonald scored 66 goals, and Kent

Denis Savard, in only his second NHL campaign, recorded 119 points for Chicago, establishing a team record for points that he would eventually eclipse twice in his ten years with the Black Hawks.

Nilsson had 104 points, as the Flames finished in second place. Vancouver and Winnipeg finished third and fourth, leaving Los Angeles out of the playoffs. The Kings' Marcel Dionne scored his 500th goal and had his fifth consecutive 100-point season. Dionne was the NHL's unknown superstar, toiling for a distantly located team that had never reached the third round of the playoffs.

The team that attracted the most notice continued to be the Edmonton Oilers. Again, Gretzky soared above the league's top scorers, leading Art Ross runner-up Peter Stastny by a record 72 points. Glenn Anderson and Mark Messier each scored 48 goals, and Jarri Kurri had 45. These three forwards combined with Gretzky to give the Oilers four 100-point scorers, equaling a team mark set by the 1970-71 Bruins. Defenseman Paul Coffey finished with 97 points as the Oilers again set a team single-season scoring record, rapping in 424 goals.

In the Campbell Conference playoffs, the Oilers continued to roll, needing just one game over the minimum to defeat Winnipeg, Calgary, and Chicago as they headed for the Cup finals. The Oilers' one loss was to the Flames in the first playoff match-up between the two Alberta rivals. In the Wales Conference, Montreal was ousted from the Adams Division semi-finals with surprising ease by Buffalo, who swept the Canadiens after shutting them out in the first two games of the series. The Canadiens had not won a playoff series since 1980. The Sabres were defeated in seven games by Boston in the Adams Division finals, with Brad Park scoring for the Bruins in overtime in the final game. In the Patrick, the fourth-place Rangers eliminated the Flyers, but were defeated by the Islanders in a six-game division final series. This set up a Wales Conference championship series between the Bruins and Islanders, which the Isles won in six games.

The Stanley Cup match-up between the defending champions and the potent young scoring machine from the West proved to be more exciting on paper than it was on the ice. The Islanders held Edmonton to six goals, four of which were scored on assists from Gretzky, and swept the Oilers in four straight games. Islander goaltender Billy Smith was awarded the Conn Smythe Trophy.

At the end of the 1982-83 season, the Islanders remained the only team to win the Stanley Cup in the 1980s.

After a forty-one year absence, regular-season overtime returned to the NHL for the 1983-84 season. In the event of a tie in regulation time, both teams would take a two-minute break before playing a five-minute sudden-death overtime period. Unlike during playoff overtime, the ice would not be resurfaced, and play would resume following a two-minute rest period.

Two high-school players from the United States were taken first and fifth overall in the 1983 entry draft. Brian Lawton, selected by the Minnesota North Stars, and goaltender Tom Barrasso, chosen by the Buffalo Sabres,

Only One Unanimous Hart Trophy Winner

In 1982-83 Wayne Gretzky became the only player in NHL history to capture the Hart Memorial Trophy by a unanimous vote. Gretzky received all sixty-three first-place votes from the Professional Hockey Writers' Association.

Battling Billy Smith watches as Denis Potvin (right) attempts to remove another feisty competitor, Terry O'Reilly, from the Islanders' crease. Smith's fiery temperament was the perfect match for the Islanders' confident style, and the combination resulted in four consecutive Stanley Cups in the early 1980s.

Harold Ballard, the colorful and almost always controversial owner of the Toronto Maple Leafs, left his mark at center ice in Maple Leaf Gardens on the night before his eightieth birthday. Originally, Ballard's hand- and footprints were part of the "sculpture," but have since been filled in because they affected the quality of the ice at the center face-off dot in the Gardens.

became the second and third players to jump directly from high-school hockey to the NHL. The first player to do so was Bobby Carpenter, who scored 32 goals for Washington after being picked third overall in 1981.

In Buffalo, the Sabres' sixth draft choice from 1982, Phil Housley, would combine with Barrasso to boost the Sabres to a second-place 103-point finish in the Adams Division, one point behind Boston. Barrasso appeared in 42 games, winning both the Calder and the Vezina trophies.

The St. Louis Blues, who had previously traded away their first- and second-round picks, declined to participate in the entry draft which took place on June 8, 1983. Citing alleged financial losses, Ralston Purina, the Blues' corporate owner since 1977, had tried to move the club to Saskatoon, Saskatchewan. When the NHL prevented the move, Ralston Purina closed the Blues' front office and announced that it would no longer operate the club. Despite the league's urging it to participate in the entry draft, the company refused to do so. Beverly Hills businessman Harry Ornest bought the Blues at the end of July, hiring Ron Caron as his general manager. Caron had been the director of scouting and player personnel in Montreal and would need all

After four seasons with the Canadiens, Rod Langway was both a First Team All-Star and the winner of the Norris Trophy with the Washington Capitals in 1982-83 and 1983-84.

his talents as a dealmaker to make up for St. Louis' lost draft choices.

The New York Islanders, who had signed defenseman Ken Morrow after the 1980 Olympics, drafted two 1984 Olympians, both of whom would join the club after the Games in Sarajevo. Pat LaFontaine was a member of the U.S. Olympic team; Pat Flatley was part of the Canadian squad. The Islanders returned to top spot in the Patrick Division in 1983-84, winning 50 games despite injuries to Trottier and Bossy during the season. The Isles scored 357 goals and allowed just 269, finishing with the league's second-best offense and fourth-best defense. Bossy, despite missing 13 games, scored 51 goals and had 67 assists for 118 points and his fourth consecutive 100-point season.

Washington finished with a franchise-high 101 points and was a strong second behind the Islanders in the Patrick. During the off-season, the Caps traded for former U.S. Olympian Dave Christian, who became the club's second-highest scorer with 81 points. Washington's tight defensive style helped netminders Al Jensen and Pat Riggin to win the Jennings Trophy for fewest goals-against. Rod Langway won his second Norris Trophy, as his former club, the Montreal Canadiens, skidded to fourth place and the team's first sub-.500 record since 1948-49. The Canadiens had undertaken a rebuilding program, hiring former star defenseman Serge Savard as managing director. Savard traded Keith Acton, Mark Napier, and a draft choice to Minnesota for center Bobby Smith. With Smith's acquisition, the Canadiens now employed three former first-overall draft selections: Guy Lafleur (1971), Rick Green (1976), and Smith (1978). Lafleur scored his 500th goal in February and went on to dislodge Jean Béliveau in second place behind Rocket Richard on the Canadiens' all-time goal-scoring list. Despite Lafleur's milestone, goals eluded the Canadiens all season; they scored just 286, the fewest of any team to make the playoffs.

Third place in the Adams went to the improved Nordiques with 94 points. Michel Goulet, with 56 goals and 121 points, and Peter Stastny, with 46 and 119, were the league's third- and fourth-highest scorers. Quebec's defense, led by Mario Marois and goaltender Daniel Bouchard, allowed 58 fewer goals-against than in 1982-83.

The Norris had become the NHL's weakest division; none of its teams won 40 games. First-place Minnesota finished with 88 points and was led in scoring by Neal Broten and Brian Bellows. Steve Yzerman was the division's most promising rookie, scoring 39 goals in his first season with Detroit. The Red Wings finished in third place behind St. Louis, qualifying for the playoffs for the first time since 1977-78. Other rookies who brought hope to Norris clubs in 1983-84 included Claude Loiselle and Kelly Kisio of the Red Wings, Russ Courtnall and Gary Leeman of the Maple Leafs, and Doug Gilmour and Greg Paslawski of the Blues.

In the Smythe, Edmonton's offensive power made the Oilers very difficult to beat. The club's 119 points would prove to be the highest total recorded by

Bill Barber became the NHL's nineteenth 400-goal scorer in a game against Pittsburgh on October 9, 1983. Barber underwent reconstructive knee surgery after the 1983-84 season, but, despite a year off for rehabilitation, was forced to retire. He is the Flyers' all-time leading goal-scorer.

any team in the 1980s. Gretzky won an unprecedented fourth consecutive Art Ross and fifth consecutive Hart Trophy, leading the league with 87 goals and 205 points in 74 games. He produced 153 of those points during a record 51-game scoring streak that began at the start of the season. Gretzky and teammate Paul Coffey formed a scoring duo reminiscent of Esposito and Orr, Coffey finished second in league scoring, with 40 goals and 86 assists for 126 points, joining Orr as just the second defenseman to score 40 goals in a season. Jari Kurri added 52 goals, and Glenn Anderson again topped the 50-goal mark, as the Oilers scored 446 goals, averaging 5.58 per game, a record that would also remain unmatched into the next decade.

In the division semi-finals, Montreal swept first-place Boston in three games. To revitalize the Canadiens for the playoffs, Serge Savard brought up minor-pro goaltender Steve Penney, who, as Ken Dryden had done in 1971, stonewalled the favored Bruins. Washington eliminated Philadelphia in three straight games, giving the Caps their first playoff-series victory in the ten-year history of the franchise. Two other division semi-final series went the five-game limit. Minnesota edged Chicago, and the Islanders needed an overtime goal from Ken Morrow in game five to eliminate the Rangers, who received superb goaltending from Glen Hanlon in what many consider to have been one of the most exciting series of the 1980s.

The NHL's provincial rivals met in the Adams and Smythe division finals. The Canadiens eliminated the Nordiques in six games, while the Oilers needed seven to subdue the Flames after Calgary won games five and six by identical 5–4 scores. In the Norris, Minnesota needed an overtime goal from Steve Payne in game seven to eliminate St. Louis. The Islanders had an easier time, winning the Patrick in five games over Washington.

The Edmonton Oilers' scoring machine, led by (left to right) Mark Messier, Wayne Gretzky, and Paul Coffey, hit top gear in the 1983-84 season and, exploded for an NHL-record 446 goals.

In the Wales Conference championship, Steve Penney's miraculous goal-tending staked the Canadiens to a two-game lead, before the Islanders rebounded with four straight wins. In the Campbell championship, the Oilers' path to the finals was assured by a four-game sweep of the North Stars.

The second final-series meeting of the Oilers and Islanders was a convincing reversal of the first. In game one, Kevin McClelland got the game's only goal, as the Oilers, with Grant Fuhr in net, shut out the Islanders 1–0. The Islanders won the next meeting, but beginning in game three, the Oilers' sharpshooters found the target, outscoring the Islanders 19–6 as Edmonton won the next three games, denying the Islanders a fifth consecutive Stanley Cup championship. Gretzky led all playoff scorers with 35 points, but it was the skill and power of Mark Messier that earned the Conn Smythe Trophy and invited comparisons to a young Gordie Howe.

It had taken coach and general manager Glen Sather just five seasons to take the Oilers from expansion draft to Stanley Cup. Gretzky and his teammates, hoisting the Cup in celebration, would prove to be the enduring image of NHL hockey in the 1980s.

(continued on p. 281)

GRETZKY – DOUBT DISPELLED

by Jay Teitel

The first time I saw Wayne Gretzky play, in a packed Junior A arena in Sault Ste. Marie in the late winter of 1978, I was filled with doubt. I'd gone to the Soo to write a story about Gretzky, carrying the same set of expectations I might have toted along to a meeting with a family in the Ozarks who had spent a week on board an alien spacecraft. I was more than skeptical; I was *consumed* with skepticism. It was a complex sort of doubt, built of nostalgia for the six-team NHL of the past, a leeriness about hockey's future, and a cynicism based paradoxically on pure romance. It was the same doubt that would ironically follow Wayne Gretzky for the next decade and a half of his career, and it belonged not just to me, but to a whole generation of hockey fans who in a way would come to define themselves by that doubt. Like so much else in sport that approaches the mystical, the doubt revolved around numbers.

These were the numbers. In the winter of 1978 Wayne Gretzky had just turned seventeen. Eleven years earlier, at the age of six, he had started to play organized hockey in his hometown of Brantford, Ontario, with boys four years his senior. His first season he scored one goal. The next season he scored 27; the year after that 104; the year after that 196. The season after that, at age ten, standing four feet four inches tall, he scored 378 goals, winning the league scoring race by 238 goals. It was more than an unprecedented number of goals for anyone of any age to score, it was *insane*; it attracted

enough attention in the cozy confines of Brantford that, when the young Wayne was offered an opportunity to move to Toronto to play three years later, he jumped at the chance to escape the glare of the limelight.

Playing in his first Junior B game in Toronto – he was fourteen now – against grown men five and six years older than himself, he scored two goals. Two years later he was playing Junior A for Peterborough. The year after that – the winter I found myself traveling to watch him – he was in Sault Ste. Marie, on his way to breaking the OHA scoring record. A scant sixty days before I made my visit, when he was still sixteen, he had been the top scorer at the World Junior Championship in Quebec City. It was this accomplishment that had brought reporters from the *New York Times* and *Sports Illustrated* to Sault Ste. Marie the week before I'd arrived, the media south of the border having finally woken up to the numbers that those of us north of it had been squinting at for half a decade. And woken up, too, to what those numbers signified: as of that Saturday in 1978, Wayne Gretzky was the most eagerly anticipated hockey prodigy in modern history – more so even than Bobby Orr.

But here was another important number: my own age at the time, twenty-nine. Being twenty-nine in 1978 meant more than just that I was a fledgling sportswriter; it meant that I was a veteran of the last generation of hockey fans, the one that had grown up during the 1960s, before the watershed of expansion. Hockey for us was compact and sacrosanct – a six-team league populated by 120 helmetless men, with discernible features and styles, occasional receding hairlines, and even the odd toupee. The NHL was an adult Cadillac of a league in the 1960s, and the magic numbers that anchored our fan's souls (50 goals in a season, *two* playoff rounds a year) were immutable. By contrast, hockey in the post-expansion 1970s, with numbers going crazy and a teenaged phenomenon surfacing every week, seemed unreal. I'd heard friends dismiss Phil Esposito's 76 goals in 1970-71, even Bobby Orr's 139 points, as just two more examples of the New Era "inflation." But nothing symbolized the inflation of hockey more to us than this skinny blond wraith of a

Wayne Gretzky

BRANTFORD NADROFSKY STEELERS OMHA "AAA" NOVICE ALL-STARS

1971 · 1972

SEASON'S SCHEDULE

Player	TOTALS
W. GRETZKY	378
L. HACHBORN	111
B. CROLEY	46
D. WHITING	32
P. EMMERTON	18
D. DUCKWORTH	8
T. ALLAN	22
S. BODNAR	15
J. VERBURG	2
J. BURTON	5
A. SELINGER	2
C. ANDERSON	5
S. JOHNSON	2

TEAM HONOURS

WON	LOST	TIED
76	8	1

• NOVICE "AAA" ONTARIO SECTIONAL CHAMPIONS
• HUB LEAGUE CHAMPIONS
• HESPELER MINOR OLYMPIC TOURNAMENT CHAMPIONS
• BROOKLIN - WHITBY MINOR NOVICE CHAMPIONS
• KINGSTON YOUNG NATIONAL NOVICE CHAMPIONS

FINAL SCORING STATISTICS

Player	G	A	PTS
WAYNE GRETZKY	378	139	517
LEN HACHBORN	111	80	191
BRIAN CROLEY	46	59	105
DARRELL WHITING	32	49	81
STEVE BODNAR	15	44	59
PAUL EMMERTON	18	37	55
TIM ALLAN	22	30	52
JIM BURTON	5	47	52
AL SELINGER	2	35	37
JIM VERBURG	2	33	35
CHRIS ANDERSON	5	21	26
DAVE DUCKWORTH	8	8	16
SHAWN JOHNSON	2	11	13

GOALIES: GREG STEFAN, GEORGE HOTSON   COACH: BOB HOCKIN   MANAGER: BRIAN HOCKIN   ASS'T COACH: FRANK STEFAN

WAYNE'S INDIVIDUAL HONORS

	GAMES	G.	A.	PTS.
HUB LEAGUE SCORING CHAMPION	14	63	21	84
HESPELER MINOR OLYMPIC SCORING CHAMP	9	50	16	66
M.V.P. BURLINGTON GOLDEN HORSESHOE TOURNAMENT				
OUTSTANDING PLAYER - BROOKVILLE 1000 ISLAND NOVICE TOURNAMENT				
M.V.P. KINGSTON YOUNG NATIONAL NOVICE TOURNAMENT				
M.V.P. NADROFSKY STEELERS				

---

prospect, packing an unlikely name and the most outlandish numbers of all. From the vantage point of the generation I belonged to, there was no way Wayne Gretzky could be anything but a fluke. He could not be for real.

Hence the doubt.

In my notes, taken at the lunch I ate with Wayne Gretzky that afternoon in Ricardo's Restaurant, there are two starred entries: the first his response to my suggestion that, considering his growing celebrity, he might have to say "no" to a reporter one day ("Do you think so? I don't think I'd ever say no to a reporter"); the second his use of the words "aston-

Wayne Gretzky scored 378 goals in 1971 with the Brantford Nadrofsky Steelers, a team that also included future NHLers Len Hachborn and goaltender Greg Stefan.

ished" and "dread" in the same sentence. For some reason that impressed me. Other than that, my memory of the conversation is murky at best.

But memory of that night's game is as vivid as any I've ever seen. My starred notes are too numerous to list, so I'll settle for one of them. It's about something simple, something that happened in the first thirty seconds of the game and remains fixed in my mind like a miniature movie. The seventeen-year-old Gretzky won the opening faceoff, then immediately churned into the Sudbury end. As his own defense-man dumped the puck in, he looped behind the net with a sudden, almost jerky, centrifugal swerve, picked the puck clean out of a tangle of players, then swung out to the far edge of the circle. Apparently leaning *away* from the net, head craned back at it, he threaded a *flat* pass between the legs of one defenseman, behind the heel of another's stick, and onto his own left winger's stick about three feet from the open side of the net – which the winger promptly hit with the puck. Thirty-five seconds, 1–0. I had never seen anything like it. "Looks slow motion," I put down in my notebook, "like everyone else thinks the whistle's gone. All that open ice around him. Where *is* everybody?"

During the course of the rest of the game – I noted this dutifully too – Wayne Gretzky gained clear possession of the puck fourteen times. Of those possessions, six resulted in Sault goals – he scored two and assisted on four. Two more possessions led to shots that required spectacular saves by the opposition goalie, and four more were dangerous passes, misplayed by his linemates. Sitting in the stands, trying to be dispassionate, I knew that what I was witnessing wasn't exactly hockey, but something different, something like basketball in its shooting percentages, baseball in its refutation of chance, and hockey mainly, *critically*, in its artful sudden-ness. I was watching the dawn of something revolu-tionary. (*There was all that open ice. Where was everybody?*)

I was still skeptical.

The doubt was easy to hang onto over the next couple of years, criminally easy actually. In 1978, as history now knows, Wayne (he was becoming Wayne now), maybe not wanting to tarnish his record for leapfrogging age groups, jumped to the pro ranks with the WHA, playing first eight games for Nelson Skalbania's infamous Indianapolis Racers (3 goals, 3 assists), then the rest of the season for the Edmon-ton Oilers. He did accumulate 110 points in his rookie season – in only sixty games – but that was just the WHA, which had tried blue pucks.

And then, in 1979-80, Edmonton was admitted to the NHL.

It was the season my eldest daughter was born. Ordinarily this wouldn't be worthy of mention, but it had an historic and personal connotation that I realized only much later. The fact was that thirty-three years earlier, in 1947, my *father* had had his first child, and that same season another hockey player played his first NHL season – Gordie Howe. My father had mentioned this to me more than once, because he felt that Gordie Howe had been the not-totally-welcome star of his adult years, who came to supplant the childhood heroes who had held him in thrall, the Conachers and the Primeaus and the Jacksons. Because of this, my father said, he had never been totally comfortable with the *idea* of Gordie Howe. In the same way, it occurred to me eventually, Wayne Gretzky, who was fated to be the star of my generation's adulthood, was unavoidably heir to the same kind of discomfort – not just the skepticism directed at a possible fluke, but the suspicion aimed at a young usurper.

At least that was one explanation.

Wayne scored 137 points as an NHL rookie, tying Marcel Dionne for the scoring lead in the process and winning the Hart Trophy as the league's most valuable player. But he must have been doing it with mirrors. He had to be, we knew, because the more we watched him play the more we realized one basic truth: he was the least physically dominating – and so the most physically perplexing – star in modern sport. He was quick enough, but not terrifically fast, his shot was ordinary (he wound up ridiculously high on his slapshot), his style could best be described as herky-jerky, or maybe spiky (of all great contempo-rary athletes, only Magic Johnson has a style as idiosyncratic or unlikely), and half the time he looked half-exhausted. Worse than exhausted, with his sweater hiked over the right side of his pants – a superstitious holdover from the day his father had tucked in a six-year-old Wayne's sweater so it wouldn't impede his shot – he looked like the per-petual over-cool cocky sloppy kid, playing with the big boys, the kid everyone else had *conspired to let succeed*. ("Let him have the puck; he's just a kid.")

There was no other way to explain it, the way he was always a fraction of a second ahead of the play.

It was as though everyone had agreed to start the game a semi-instant after he did, so that the two games – Wayne's and the rest of the world's – superimposed on each other, yielded the fuzzy outline of a double exposure. And how else could anyone account for that weird Gretzky tautology, that to succeed, Gretzky had to succeed? A Bobby Hull rush could be thrilling even if it was aborted. The same with a Frank Mahovlich charge down the wing or a tight Bobby Orr spin at the point or a Guy Lafleur behind-the-back pass. But on the few occasions when Wayne's inventiveness didn't create a clean scoring chance, he was clumsy in failure, usually stumbling or falling, rising forlornly to backcheck with that crazy hunched-over style. To see something mystical when Frank Mahovlich was on the ice, all you had to do was watch Frank; to see magic with Gretzky you had to watch the puck, at least how the puck and Wayne came together – and most critically, you had to see a *result*. Wayne himself, we argued, was not sufficient.

And so the doubt flourished, and Wayne flourished more, and we had an answer for everything. When he won the scoring championship outright in 1980-81 and broke Phil Esposito's points record and Bobby Orr's assist record for a single season (164 points, 109 assists for a twenty-year-old), we said Stanley Cups are won by teams like the Canadiens, not by setting records. And when the Oilers swept the mighty Canadiens in the first round of the playoffs, with Wayne setting a single-playoff-game record for assists with five in the first game in the Forum, (reducing goaltender Richard Sevigny – who had said Guy Lafleur would put Wayne "into his back pocket" – to a state of nervous catatonia by the end of the game), we said, "Wait till they play the Islanders." And when the Oilers extended the Islanders, who were working on their second consecutive Stanley Cup, to six games before losing, with Wayne playing tough, unprecedentedly grim hockey, even though he failed to register a goal, we said "See?" and "Wait till he plays against the Russians." And when Wayne in fact did stink the joint out against the Soviets the following September during the Canada Cup, giving the puck away like a wan midget in the infamous 8–1 championship-game

The Great One breaks Phil Esposito's eleven-year NHL record by firing his 77th goal of the 1981-82 season past Don Edwards on February 24, 1982.

loss that drove a stake through the heart of every fan who *really* admitted which games mattered, we said, "There, you really see now, he has skates of clay, he has a quixotic fragile talent, he is not for real, when we need him most, he will fail us."

But all the time something else was happening. Even after his deepest nadirs, he kept producing the numbers with a stubborn valiance: the season that began with his Canada Cup humiliation, he scored an extraterrestrial *92* goals (50 in 39 games), breaking Phil Esposito's Bob Beamon-like record of 76 by 16 goals and setting another points record of 212 in the process. But it wasn't just numbers; it was *images* too. Slowly, and with a relentlessness to match our reluctance, the pictures of our adult hockey years were becoming Gretzky pictures. Gretzky gliding folded-over to the opening faceoff circle, his stick on his thighs, his pale eyes up and to one side, his gaze positively eerie and foreheadless under his helmet, his sweater, as always, hitched up (by now he was actually using Velcro to make sure it stayed that way). Gretzky veering inside the blue line with that precipitous slant, coming across the slot with the puck, waiting, *waiting*, till not just the opposing goalie but the entire opposing team, you got the feeling, had committed itself (half of them falling down in a mysterious surrender), then pushing a totally ordinary, ice-bound shot into the center of the net. Gretzky setting up behind the net in his "office," head paradoxically down as he looked for

Gretzky and the Oilers led the NHL in goals scored for six straight years. Edmonton is the only NHL club to score 400 goals in a season.

the cutting defenseman, distinguishing between teammates and opponents *by the color of their hockey pants*, so he wouldn't have to waste time looking all the way up (he once complained to a fellow Oiler that he had trouble playing against the Islanders because their pants were the same blue as the Oilers'). Gretzky churning up the wing outside a defenseman, then putting on the brakes in that patented move to let the play catch up; Gretzky faking the huge wind-up on the slapshot, cocking once, cocking twice; Gretzky kneeing the air and punching it like a ramshackle adolescent after a goal; Gretzky hounding an opposing defenseman while killing a penalty, chipping and hacking and taking a ride, because he could do that with the best of them too. Gretzky being Gretzky.

Of course, there were also background photos coming into legendary focus, snapshots from Wayne's childhood becoming as familiar to us as the snaps we took of our own progeny. The backyard rink on Varady Avenue in Brantford; Wayne alone on the ice with his rickety six-year-old legs; Wayne with his arm around his father. The relationship he had with his father was part of the legend too: the arcane list of "Wally's rules" he followed devoutly, with its quixotic first commandment, "Go where the puck's going, not where it's been."

Where was everybody?

In 1983 my second child was born, and the following spring Gretzky and the rest of the young Oilers finally solved the Islanders, with Wayne scoring two goals in the final Stanley Cup victory and putting a large dent in the rumor that he couldn't produce in the "big games." The next year the team repeated as champions, overcoming the media hysteria surrounding alleged drug use. And while the numbers and the pictures were becoming ingrained on our minds – while our children were growing up and Wayne was going on to lead the league in scoring a record eight seasons in a row – setting the single-season assist record and breaking his own scoring record in 1985-86 with 215 points, playing on four Stanley Cup Oiler teams in a five-year span – something *else* was happening, too. Our doubt was changing. It wasn't fading so much as mutating, becoming more intimate.

Why is hockey the greatest game, to watch at least as much as to play? Because, I think, it's the most kinetically empathic game, because even if a person hasn't played, he or she can feel the swift moves and slants of the players in his or her own body more acutely than in any other sport. And with Wayne, the longer he played, the easier it became for us to convince ourselves that we were feeling what he was feeling. (It might have been impossible to *see* the game he was seeing, but it seemed like a breeze to *feel* it.) It was more than his being physically unimposing, it was the *effort* he was obviously expending, it was the tenuousness of his hold on genius, the incredibly tiny margin between terrific success and acute failure that he flirted with every night. If Gretzky was ahead of everyone else, we were starting to know, it was by the slimmest of time-units; he was like a quarterback perpetually getting a pass off the nano-second before he gets hit. The longer Wayne Gretzky played, the more he seemed like an ordinary person who was getting away with something – but *with our best wishes* now. As the 1980s rose and fell, it was no longer a case of us fearing he would succeed but secretly hoping he would fail so we could have our nostalgia vindicated; we *wanted* him to succeed now, but feared he wouldn't, mainly because he was too much like us, and God knows we were fallible.

And then came the play when everything came together.

It was the final game of the 1987 Canada Cup, being played in Hamilton's Copps Coliseum: Team Canada against the Soviet Union in the third and deciding contest of a series that to this point had represented probably the most thrilling, brilliant, continuous display of hockey ever seen. In his nine seasons of pro hockey up to this series, Wayne Gretzky had stubbornly laid to rest every bogeyman that had come to haunt him – the NHL, the Canadiens, the New York Islanders, the charge that he choked in the big games. But the Russians had been the sore exception, the last question mark. In the first two games, both heart-stopping 6–5 affairs, he'd played excellent hockey, driving himself to even greater exhaustion than usual on a "dream" line with Mario Lemieux, amassing five assists in the second game, and leading one Russian journalist to describe the Gretzky–Lemieux combination as an "invisible artillery piece." ("Gretzky comes out of nowhere to load the gun, and Lemieux pulls the trigger.")

Now, in this final game, the Canadians somehow fight back from a 3–0 deficit without Gretzky's help, finding themselves tied 5–5 with two minutes left, and a faceoff in their own zone. And the inexplicable starts to happen. First Team Canada coach Mike Keenan sends Dale Hawerchuk out to take the faceoff, while Gretzky moves to the wing; then Soviet coach Victor Tikhonov leaves a rookie defenseman named Igor Kravchuk out on Gretzky's side. The inexplicable melds with the incredible: the puck is dropped, Hawerchuk wins the draw, Lemieux bangs it up the boards past a pinching Soviet rearguard, and Gretzky gathers it in past center, a three-on-one with Larry Murphy on one side and Lemieux hanging back on the other. Gretzky appears to do nothing but hold the puck, but suddenly Kravchuk, the last Soviet, is sliding on his back following Wayne's fake toward the boards, and the puck has been left more than passed back to Lemieux, who skates in unmolested and calmly fires a wrist shot high into the left side of the Russian net. And even as Wayne leaps into Mario's arms, and they fall on the ice and are mobbed by their teammates, and we enjoy an elation just a bit better than anything we've ever known, the little question tweaks the back of our minds, that tenacious fleck of disbelief: How did he do it? Where was Kravchuk going anyway? Who did he think he was checking? A ghost? A reputation? Janet Jones? *Where was everybody?*

You would think that would be enough, that that goal alone, as celebrated now as any goal ever scored, would lay the doubt to rest. But of course doubt is a fan's only constant, and the Gretzky soap opera had one more episode to play – the episode (including the scene "Marriage to the Starlet") not-so-hyper-

Gretzky addresses the media after being traded to the Kings in August of 1988, conducting press conferences first in Edmonton, and later in Los Angeles.

bolically labeled the "Trade of the Century." In August of 1988 Peter Pocklington sent Wayne Gretzky to the Los Angeles Kings in a deal that involved four other players, three draft choices, a reported $15 million, and the eternal chagrin of a nation. Maybe it was the incongruity of it – Wayne in *Los Angeles*? – but what could have been a dénouement flared into one final question of legitimacy: How would Wayne operate in the hockey boondocks, without the Kurris and the Messiers or even the occasional Mario to pass the puck to? Could the Assist Machine fly solo? Would we now finally see Gretzky disrobed for what he truly was?

And of course we did. On his first shot in a Kings' uniform, Wayne Gretzky scored a goal. By the season's end, he had finished second in scoring to Mario Lemieux, won his ninth Hart Trophy, and led Los Angeles to an astonishing, poetically justified seven-game upset of the Edmonton Oilers in the opening playoff series. The next year he won the scoring title and broke Gordie Howe's all-time points-scored record of 1,850 in – where else? – Edmonton. Point number 1,851 came on a goal that tied the score with a minute left in the third period. Number 1,852 came on a Gretzky goal in overtime that won the game. In both cases, naturally, no one was within shouting range of number 99.

The last time I saw Wayne Gretzky play was in the winter of 1990, in the Montreal Forum. The Kings were fighting for first place overall in the NHL, but it had seemed to me, watching on television in the first few months of the season, that Gretzky had changed his game, that he was carrying the puck less and looking exhausted more, that he had become nothing more than a transition specialist. I was worried in a way that only Gretzky could make people worry. In the Forum that night, in a city that had seen riots when Rocket Richard had been suspended, the Gretzky sweaters outnumbered the Canadien sweaters in the crowd four to one.

On his first shift, Gretzky took the puck hard up the right wing, stopped harder, and fell down. The crowd jeered, but not, it seemed to me, wholeheartedly. On his second shift, coasting on defense at the Montreal blue line, he suddenly moved forward, intercepted that classic between-defensemen ritual

pass, picking it out of the air a foot off the ice and passing it immediately back to his winger, Tomas Sandstrom, who scored. On his fifth shift, he assisted on another Sandstrom goal, anchoring the middle of a pretty three-way passing play. And forechecking again on his first shift in the second period, he anticipated a Montreal behind-the-net clearing pass, intercepted it, and sent an apparently

The mentor and the record-breaker, Gordie Howe and Wayne Gretzky, after Gretzky became the NHL's all-time leading scorer on October 15, 1989.

blind backhand relay into the slot, directly onto the stick of Sandstrom again, who buried it without hesitating.

But it was a play he made that resulted in no goal at all, in the third period when Los Angeles was up

4–1 and the game was essentially over, that stays with me. Marty McSorley, a Kings defenseman, had dumped the puck into the Montreal corner, and suddenly, for no reason it seemed – especially considering how much of the game he'd spent floating at center – Gretzky was churning after the puck, head down. It looked like pure wasted effort; there

The uniform is different, but the play is the same. Wayne Gretzky continues to establish new records as a member of the Los Angeles Kings, winning the Art Ross Trophy in 1990 and 1991, and recording his 2,000th point on October 26, 1990.

was a Canadiens' defenseman back, and the Canadiens' goalie, Patrick Roy, was already moving out of his net, bound to reach the puck first and simply clear it off the boards past the oncoming Gretzky. But just as Roy was dipping his head to do exactly that, Gretzky peeled off towards the boards, blue line high, at exactly the place Roy's clearing pass would ricochet. It was an almost-perfect ruse, failing only because, when the puck ticked the top of Gretzky's stick instead of the center of it, it skipped out of the Montreal zone. If it had hit squarely, he would have had an open net to shoot at. Watching, I thought I truly understood Walter Gretzky's Rule Number 1 for the first time. *"Go where the puck's going, not where it's been."*

I understood not just the hockey sense of it, but the apparent flaw in its tenses too. If you wait a split second too long, the present becomes the past. It had been thirteen years since I'd first watched a teenaged Wayne Gretzky play on a rink in Sault Ste. Marie. In the interim, he'd spent eleven seasons in the NHL, scoring more points than anyone had in the history of hockey and assisting on more goals. He had won the scoring title nine times and been voted the league's most valuable player nine times. He had broken or tied fifty-three official NHL individual records and endured more pressure and publicity than any athlete of his era. Through it all, he responded with uniform grace and dignity. He had assisted on arguably the most famous goal ever scored. He had changed the face of the game he played forever. He had left home for good when he was fourteen. He had married a movie star. He had fathered two children.

He was twenty-nine years old.

It was time to start believing.

A six-foot, four-inch center who scored 282 points in one season of junior hockey was the star of the 1984 entry draft. Mario Lemieux's 133 goals and 149 assists for Laval in the Quebec Major Junior Hockey League made him an obvious choice for the Pittsburgh Penguins, who drafted him first overall. Lemieux would go on to a 100-point rookie campaign with the Penguins and would win the Calder Trophy.

At the third Canada Cup tournament in September of 1984, Team U.S.A. finished a surprising second in the round-robin portion of the tournament. American-born players had become increasingly prominent in the NHL by the mid-1980s, and players on Team U.S.A.'s roster, which included Neal Broten, Chris Chelios, Phil Housley, and Joe Mullen, would be NHL team leaders for much of the decade. The Soviet Union, playing without retired superstar goaltender Vladislav Tretiak, was undefeated in round-robin play. Sweden finished third, and Team Canada finished a disappointing fourth, barely qualifying for the tournament's playoffs. Sweden, which had lost to the

Mario Lemieux, who was awarded the Calder Trophy in 1984-85, joined Dale Hawerchuk and Peter Stastny as the third player to score 100-or-more points in his first NHL season.

United States 7–1 in the round-robin opener, won its semi-final match-up 9–2. Team Canada, playing its best game of the tournament in the other semi-final, defeated the Soviet Union 3–2 in overtime when Mike Bossy deflected Paul Coffey's shot past goaltender Vladimir Myshkin. Coffey had sprawled to break up a Soviet two-on-one rush in Team Canada's end before lugging the puck back to the Soviet zone to set up the winning goal. In the best-of-three final, Canada swept the Swedes by scores of 6–2 and 6–5. John Tonelli was named tournament MVP and demonstrated that a hard-working role-player could complement a superstar line-up.

Shortly after the start of the NHL regular season, Guy Lafleur announced his retirement from the Canadiens. Lafleur, who had never returned to his 50-goal form after injuring his knee late in the 1979-80 season, had just two goals in the first five weeks of 1984-85. In announcing his decision to quit, "The Flower" said that the game had ceased to be fun. Without him, Montreal, now coached by Jacques Lemaire, was led offensively by Mats Naslund, a free-skating Swedish left winger who scored 42 goals in his third season with the Canadiens. The Habs rebuilt their defense, giving regular ice time to three rookies, Chris Chelios, Petr Svoboda, and Tom Kurvers. Svoboda, who defected from Czechoslovakia just before the 1984 entry draft, had been a surprise fifth-overall selection by Montreal. While no longer overpowering, the Habs were a club on the upswing and finished with 94 points to edge Buffalo and Quebec for first place in the competitive Adams Division. Boston was fourth with 82 points. Buffalo's Scotty Bowman established a new mark for coaching wins in his eighteenth season, surpassing Dick Irvin's total of 690. Bowman's coaching career had begun with expansion in 1967 and had taken him to St. Louis, Montreal, and the Sabres. Irvin had coached in Chicago, Toronto, and Montreal, from 1930 to 1956.

Scotty Bowman, who won his sixth Stanley Cup ring with the Pittsburgh Penguins in 1991, holds the NHL record for most wins by a coach, recording 739 victories in 1,276 games behind the bench.

In the Patrick, the Flyers and Islanders swapped places in the standings. Philadelphia revamped its front office, hiring Bobby Clarke as general manager and Mike Keenan as coach. Led by 54 goals from Tim Kerr, the Flyers finished with 113 points and the league's best record. Keenan emphasized defense, and the Flyers responded, allowing 49 fewer goals-against than in 1983-84. Pelle Lindbergh was the club's number-one goaltender and would earn the Vezina Trophy behind a defense led by Mark Howe, Brad McCrimmon, and Brad Marsh. Two 1983 draft selections – Peter Zezel and Rick Tocchet – played regularly for the Flyers in 1984-85. Washington remained one of the best defensive clubs in the NHL, again finishing second with 101 points. With 50 and 53 goals, Mike Gartner and Bob Carpenter were the Caps' top scorers, Carpenter becoming the first U.S.-born player to reach the 50-goal mark. The third-place Islanders got 100-point seasons from Mike Bossy, Brent Sutter, and John Tonelli. Bryan Trottier scored his 1,000th career point in a 4–4 tie against Minnesota in January.

In the Norris Division, Bernie Federko's 107 points and Joe Mullen's 40 goals led St. Louis to a first-place finish under new coach Jacques Demers. Denis Savard of Chicago and John Ogrodnick of Detroit each had 105 points for the division's second- and third-place finishers.

The Smythe was the NHL's strongest division in 1984-85, as Edmonton, Winnipeg, and Calgary finished among the league's top five teams. Three Smythe clubs also contributed the league's top five scorers: Gretzky and Kurri, followed by Hawerchuk, Dionne, and Coffey. Gretzky recorded his third 200-point season with 73 goals and 135 assists to again win the Art Ross and Hart trophies. In January, he became the eighteenth NHL player to record 1,000 points, reaching this milestone in just 424 games. Guy Lafleur, who was the quickest to 1,000 before Gretzky, needed 720 games to get there. Little wonder that, by 1984-85, his sixth NHL season, Gretzky was widely referred to as "The Great One." Second-place Winnipeg improved 23 points in the standings to finish with a franchise-high 96. In addition to Hawerchuk's 53 goals and 130 points, Paul MacLean scored 41 goals and finished with 101 points. Thomas Steen, Laurie Boschman, Brian Mullen, and Doug Smail had 30-goal seasons for the Jets.

Jari Kurri's 71 goals in 1984-85 placed him in a select group with Phil Esposito and Gretzky as the only NHL players to score 70 or more goals in a season. Marcel Dionne of the Kings also reached a scoring milestone in 1984-85, surpassing Stan Mikita to become the NHL's third-highest all-time point-scorer, as the Kings finished fourth to qualify for the playoffs for the first time in three seasons.

The Islanders made an early exit from post-season play for the first time since 1979. In the Patrick Division semi-finals, they withstood two overtime losses to the Washington Capitals before coming back to win three straight, but against the Flyers in the division final, they were shut out twice and lost in five games. Quebec and Montreal each won a five-game series in the

Bernie Federko was the first NHL player to register at least 50 assists in ten consecutive seasons. Federko, who was traded to Detroit in 1989, is the Blues' all-time leader in five offensive categories.

Adams to set the stage for a second consecutive "Battle of Quebec," won this time by the Nordiques in seven games. Quebec won three overtime games in this series, clinching the division championship on Peter Stastny's winning goal 2:22 into extra time. In the Wales Conference finals, the Flyers defeated Quebec in six games, holding the Nordiques to 12 goals for the series.

In the Norris Division, fourth-place Minnesota swept St. Louis, before losing twice in overtime in a six-game loss to Chicago. Darryl Sutter got both overtime winners for the Black Hawks. The Oilers and Jets both advanced in the Smythe, but Jets' star Dale Hawerchuk suffered cracked ribs in Winnipeg's semi-final win over Calgary, leaving the Jets undermanned against the powerful Oilers. Edmonton swept Winnipeg to win the Smythe Division championship, leaving the Jets winless in ten playoff games against the Oilers.

The Campbell Conference finals between the Oilers and Hawks set an NHL record for goals in a playoff series with 69. Jari Kurri scored 12 goals and Gretzky had 18 assists, as at least ten goals were scored in five of the six games. The Oilers advanced to the finals for the third consecutive season.

After losing game one to the Flyers in the Spectrum, the Oilers reeled off four straight wins to capture their second Stanley Cup. Edmonton had too much speed and too much strength for the talented Flyers, mounting a comeback from a 3–1 deficit to win game four, before clinching the Cup with a convincing 8–3 triumph in game five. Gretzky, who won the Conn Smythe Trophy, had 47 points to break his own playoff scoring record.

The speed and passing precision of the Oilers' five-goal-a-game offense contributed to the NHL Rules Committee's decision to allow substitutions in the event of coincidental minor penalties for 1985-86. This new rule, which

Perhaps the finest "money" goalie in the NHL through the second half of the 1980s, Grant Fuhr led the Oilers to their first Stanley Cup in 1984 and is one of only three netminders to win sixteen post-season games in a single playoff year.

almost entirely eliminated situations in which each team had only four skaters on the ice, negated any possibility that players might deliberately draw opponents into incurring coincidental minors to create a less-crowded ice surface that favored the team with superior skaters.

This modification didn't deter the Oilers, who upped their offensive production by 25 goals to 426 for the year. Edmonton finished with 119 points, topping the Smythe Division standings for the fifth consecutive season. The Oilers also became the first winner of the new Presidents' Trophy, awarded to the league's top team in regular-season play. The new award was accompanied by $200,000, to be split evenly between the winning club and its players. The Flyers finished second overall and first in the Patrick Division with 110 points. Wayne Gretzky broke his own NHL single-season records for assists with 163 and points with 215. He also further extended his string of Art Ross and Hart trophies. Gretzky's assist total would in itself have provided him with enough points to win the scoring championship.

Other Oilers continued to produce as well. Jari Kurri scored 68 goals, while Paul Coffey's 48 bettered Bobby Orr's eleven-year-old goal-scoring record for defensemen. Coffey added 90 assists to finish third in league scoring with 138 points. Glenn Anderson added 54 goals and Mark Messier 35 in 63 games, leaving little doubt about why the Oilers were so successful: their offense was the best in the NHL – and they had Gretzky.

The long shadow cast by the Oilers over the Smythe Division forced its clubs to modify their rosters in an attempt to stop the defending Cup champions. For 1985-86, the Calgary Flames added defenseman Gary Suter and left winger Joel Otto. Both were big U.S.-born college players who had been "discovered" by the Flames as a result of diligent scouting. Suter, who would win the Calder Trophy, played for the University of Wisconsin and was the 180th player drafted in 1984. Otto was not drafted, signing instead as a free agent after four years with Bemidji State, a Division II college team in Minnesota. Late in the season, the Flames also traded for two talented veterans, adding Joe Mullen and John Tonelli to the club. The Flames finished in second place in the Smythe Division with 89 points. Vancouver, led by top scorers Petri Skriko and Tony Tanti, finished third, 30 points behind the Flames. The Jets and the Los Angeles Kings were unable to consolidate their gains of 1984-85, both plummeting to the bottom of the standings, the Kings missing the playoffs.

In the Patrick Division, Philadelphia rallied to overcome the tragic death of goaltender Pelle Lindbergh, who was killed in an auto accident in November. Bob Froese and Darren Jensen took over in net, sharing the Jennings Trophy for fewest goals-against. Tim Kerr scored 58 goals, including a league-leading 34 on the power-play. Washington once again finished second, with a franchise-high 107 points, the third-highest total in the league. The Islanders and Rangers finished third and fourth. Mike Bossy scored his 500th goal and 1,000th point, finishing with 61 goals and 62 assists on the year. A nine-year veteran, Bossy had never scored fewer than 50 goals in a season.

Mario Lemieux became the NHL's second-leading scorer in his second season, with 48 goals and 141 points for the fifth-place Penguins. Though still excluded from the playoffs in the Patrick, Pittsburgh enjoyed a 23-point improvement in 1985-86. The New Jersey Devils, in sixth place, won five more games than in 1984-85. Greg Adams was the club's top scorer with 35 goals.

The tightest divisional race was in the Adams, where only 12 points separated first from fifth. Quebec edged Montreal to win its first division title with 92 points, as Michel Goulet scored 50 or more goals for the fourth consecutive season. Peter Stastny remained one of the league's most consistent point producers, finishing with 41 goals and 122 points. The Canadiens were led by Mats Naslund, whose 43 goals and 67 assists placed him eighth in league scoring and made him the first Canadien to finish in the top ten since Lafleur finished third in 1979-80. The Habs salted their 1985-86 line-up with rookies who had contributed to an AHL championship with the Sherbrooke (Quebec) Canadiens in 1984-85. Mike Lalor, Stéphane Richer, Patrick Roy, and Brian Skrudland were all promoted in 1985-86. Feisty right winger Claude Lemieux, the MVP of the Quebec junior playoffs in 1985, was called up late in the season.

Elsewhere in the Adams Division, Boston, under rookie coach Butch Goring, finished third with 86 points. The Hartford Whalers were greatly improved by the addition of goaltender Mike Liut from St. Louis during the off-season and by the mid-season acquisition of John Anderson and Wayne Babych from Quebec, Dave Babych from Winnipeg, and checking specialist Doug Jarvis from Washington. The club finished fourth with 84 points, while

Hartford's Kevin Dineen, seen here escaping from the grasp of Buffalo defender Phil Housley, has appeared in two All-Star Games for the Whalers and is one of the league's finest two-way forwards.

Wendel Clark was the first player selected in the 1985 Entry Draft and made an immediate impact in the NHL, bruising opponents with solid body-checks and, with 34 goals in his freshman campaign, setting a Leaf record for rookies.

Buffalo, with 80, finished fifth and failed to make the playoffs.

Chicago captured first place in the Norris Division with 86 points. Three Black Hawks finished with at least 40 goals: Denis Savard had 47, Troy Murray had 45, and Al Secord had 40. Minnesota got 45 goals from Dino Ciccarelli and 43 from Scott Bjugstad, finishing a close second to Chicago with 85 points. St. Louis, with 83 points, completed a three-team knot at the top of the Norris. Mark Hunter was the Blues' leading scorer with 43 goals. The top three clubs were well clear of the Leafs, who finished fourth with just 57 points. Toronto had used the first-overall selection at the 1985 entry draft to obtain Wendel Clark, a hard-rock left wing who had played defense in junior with the Saskatoon Blades of the Western Hockey League. Clark had an impressive rookie season with the Leafs, and demonstrated that he was a throwback to the rugged days of the six-team league; he had a splendid wrist shot and rapidly established a reputation as one of the toughest players in the NHL.

The Detroit Red Wings paid large bonuses to sign five undrafted U.S. college free agents before the start of the 1985-86 season. General managers around the NHL watched Detroit's experiment with concern, fearing a bidding war for unsigned players if the Wings' additions demonstrated that they could play in the NHL. This didn't happen; only one of the five – Adam Oates – became an NHL star, and his breakthrough didn't occur until his fifth NHL season. The Wings' most promising rookie in 1985-86 was Czech Petr Klima, who donned sweater number 85 to commemorate the year of his defection to the West. Detroit finished the season with 17 wins, 40 points, and 415 goals-against, a mark second only to Washington's 446 in 1974-75.

In the first round of the 1986 playoffs, three of four division winners were upset by fourth-place teams. Hartford eliminated Quebec, and Toronto sidelined Chicago in three-game sweeps, while the Rangers needed five games to defeat Philadelphia. John Vanbiesbrouck, the 1985-86 Vezina Trophy winner and First All-Star Team goaltender, was a standout performer for the Rangers. Of these three upset winners, only New York would win its division final, stopping the Capitals in six games. Washington had qualified for the Patrick final by sweeping the Islanders. The Whalers and Leafs both came up short in their respective seven-game series with Montreal and St. Louis. The seventh game in each series was decided by a 2–1 score, Hartford being eliminated in overtime on a goal by Canadiens' rookie Claude Lemieux.

The Smythe Division playoffs featured a third round of the "Battle of Alberta," as both the Oilers and the Flames advanced by sweeping their first-round opponents. The Oilers, who were lopsided winners of the regular-season series between the two clubs, were heavily favored, but the Flames got great goaltending from Mike Vernon and timely goal-scoring from Joe Mullen and Lanny McDonald. The series was decided on a fluke goal. With game seven tied 2–2, rookie Edmonton defenseman Steve Smith attempted a diagonal clearing pass from behind the net to the left of goaltender Grant Fuhr. The pass hit the heel of Fuhr's skate and bounced into the Edmonton net. Final score: 3–2, Calgary – Smythe Division champs.

For the first time since the NHL had gone to four rounds of playoffs in 1974-75, none of the final four teams in contention was a regular-season division champion; all five teams that had finished with 90 or more points had been eliminated. In the Wales Conference championship, Patrick Roy gave the Canadiens superb goaltending, and the Habs' combination of veterans and rookies eliminated the Rangers in five games. In the Campbell, Doug Wickenheiser's overtime goal in game six brought the Blues back to tie their series with Calgary at three games apiece. In the finale of what was a second

Montreal Canadiens' president Ronald Corey gets a champagne shower following the Habs' Stanley Cup victory in 1986. The Canadiens, behind the goaltending heroics of Patrick Roy, defeated the Calgary Flames in five games to win their twenty-third championship, the most by any professional sports franchise.

consecutive seven-game series for both teams, Al MacInnis and Colin Patterson scored for Calgary as the Flames won 2–1 and advanced to the final for the first time in franchise history.

The Calgary–Montreal match-up was the NHL's first all-Canadian final since the Leafs' last Stanley Cup in 1967. The teams split the first two games of the series, with Montreal winning game two, which ended when Brian Skrudland set a new league record for the fastest goal from the start of overtime, scoring after just nine seconds. The Canadiens won game three in Montreal, and took control of the series two nights later when Claude Lemieux's third-period goal gave the Canadiens a 1–0 win and a three-games-to-one lead in the series after game four. The Canadiens returned to Calgary to win the series and the Cup with a 4–3 win in the Olympic Saddledome in game five. First-year Montreal coach Jean Perron used ten different rookies during the playoffs, getting ten goals from Claude Lemieux and a Conn Smythe Trophy-winning performance from goaltender Patrick Roy. Roy allowed fewer than two goals-against per game in 20 playoff contests. Brett Hull, who recorded 84 points in 42 games for the University of Minnesota–Duluth Bulldogs in 1985-86, made his NHL debut, playing two games for Calgary in the finals. Strangely, the top scorers in the 1986 post-season were Bernie Federko and Doug Gilmour of St. Louis – two players whose team had been eliminated in the third round of the playoffs.

For 1986-87, the NHL's delayed-offside rule was modified to reduce stoppages in play. A delayed offside would no longer be in effect if players of the offending team vacated their opponents' defensive zone.

The division semi-finals were extended from best-of-five to best-of seven games in an attempt to reduce the likelihood of upsets in the first round of the playoffs. In addition, the best-of-seven format also guaranteed at least two home dates for every post-season qualifier. It also increased to 28 the maximum number of playoff games that could be played by any one club. If all 15 series went seven games, 16 teams would participate in a combined 105 post-season contests. The playoffs would now run from early April to late May.

The NHL staged its first supplemental draft in May of 1986. This new draft enabled clubs to select collegiate free agents who were too old to be eligible for the entry draft. It prevented a recurrence of the unrestricted bidding that surrounded the signings of overage free agents in 1985. Players selected in this first supplemental draft included Dave Snuggerud (Buffalo) and Shawn Chambers (Minnesota).

The 1986 entry draft was held in June. Detroit made Michigan State center Joe Murphy the first player chosen. Also drafted were Jimmy Carson (selected second by Los Angeles), Zarley Zalapski (fourth, Pittsburgh), Vince Damphousse (sixth, Toronto), Pat Elynuik (eighth, Winnipeg), Brian

First-round draft choices Craig Janney (left) and Brian Leetch, photographed at the 1986 Entry Draft, were teammates at Boston College and on the U.S. Olympic Team. Leetch, one of the NHL's impressive stock of young, mobile defensemen, won the Calder Trophy in 1989.

Leetch (ninth, New York Rangers), and Craig Janney (thirteenth, Boston).

Numerous changes in coaching and management took place in 1986-87. Before the season began, the Islanders appointed successful junior coach Terry Simpson to replace Al Arbour, who became the club's vice-president of player development after thirteen seasons behind the bench. Phil Esposito became general manager of the Rangers, quickly earning the nickname "Trader Phil." He changed his coach nineteen games into the season, replacing Ted Sator with Tom Webster, a successful minor-pro coach and former player. However, an inner-ear ailment that made air travel impossible forced Webster to give up the position. Esposito finished the season as both coach and general manager and would complete nineteen trades in his first season on the job.

In November, Boston replaced coach Butch Goring with popular former-Bruin Terry O'Reilly. In Buffalo, Gerry Meehan replaced Scotty Bowman as general manager. Meehan employed assistant coach Craig Ramsay as interim head coach before appointing Ted Sator to the position just before Christmas.

Four of the five teams in the Norris Division made coaching changes. In Minnesota, former Islander Lorne Henning was replaced by Glen Sonmor, who had coached the North Stars in the early 1980s. The Red Wings hired Jacques Demers after the popular coach had failed to come to terms on a new contract with the St. Louis Blues. Demers' skills as a motivator and Detroit's emphasis on defense would result in a 38-point improvement for the Wings. The club jumped from fifth to second in the Norris, and trimmed 141 goals from the previous season's record goals-against total.

Jacques Martin, who had coached the Ontario Hockey League champion Guelph Platers in 1985-86, replaced Demers in St. Louis. In Toronto, the Leafs failed to sign Dan Maloney, who left the club to take the head coaching job in Winnipeg. To replace Maloney, the Leafs hired veteran minor-league player and coach John Brophy.

Chicago, the only Norris Division club not to change coaches, changed its team name from the "Black Hawks" to the "Blackhawks." Though the name had always been written as two words, club president Bill Wirtz discovered that the franchise's original NHL charter wrote it as one, and changed the name to conform to the charter.

Midway through the season, the Los Angeles Kings were forced to change coaches, when Pat Quinn was expelled by league president John Ziegler for having signed a contract with and accepted money from the Vancouver Canucks to become president and general manager of the Canucks, beginning in 1987-88. Kings' assistant coach Mike Murphy replaced Quinn behind the bench. Quinn's expulsion was changed to a coaching suspension, and he was fully reinstated several years later.

Two young players from the Quebec Major Junior Hockey League traveled different routes to star as rookies with the Los Angeles Kings. Michigan-born

Luc Robitaille, shown in action during his Calder Trophy-winning rookie campaign in 1986-87, has emerged as the NHL's top left winger, earning four consecutive berths on the First All-Star Team.

Jimmy Carson had scored 70 goals for the Verdun Junior Canadiens during the season just past, and was the Kings' first pick in 1986. Luc Robitaille had been selected 171st overall in the ninth round of the 1984 entry draft after a 32-goal season with the Hull Olympiques. Remaining in junior, he developed his scoring touch, and was named 1986 Canadian Major Junior Player of the Year with 191 points. For the Kings, Carson potted 37 goals, and Robitaille, with 45, won the Calder Trophy. Both had become protégés of Marcel Dionne, but the Kings' superstar was destined to finish the season with another club, moving to the Rangers as part of a multi-player deal in March.

Buffalo's Gilbert Perreault, the NHL's first draft choice in 1970, retired in November. The big centerman was the Sabres' all-time offensive leader, ending his career with 512 goals and 814 assists, for 1,191 points in seventeen seasons with Buffalo.

Regular-season play revealed emerging parity and an increased emphasis on defense in the NHL. Forty-two points separated the league's top and bottom clubs; 79 points had spanned this gap in 1985-86. Edmonton was first overall with 106, the lowest total for the league's top finisher since 1969-70, and only three clubs finished 1986-87 with less than 70 points. By comparison, one season earlier, six teams had finished with less than 60. The league's 21 clubs scored a total of 502 fewer goals in 1986-87 than in the previous season.

The Norris was the NHL's most competitive division in 1986-87, with just nine points separating the first-place St. Louis Blues from last-place Minnesota. The Blues were led by Doug Gilmour, who registered 42 goals and 105 points. Second-place Detroit was a point back of St. Louis and led Chicago by six. Fourth place remained in doubt until the second-last day of the season, when the combination of a Toronto win and a Minnesota loss clinched a berth in the playoffs for the Leafs.

In the Smythe Division, Edmonton finished in first place for the sixth consecutive season, 11 points ahead of the Flames. Gretzky, Kurri, and Messier were first, second, and fourth in league scoring. Gretzky's total of 62 goals and 121 assists was his first sub-200 point season since 1982-83. The Winnipeg Jets gained an additional 40 points and 14 wins over their 1985-86 results. New coach Dan Maloney employed rookie goaltenders Eldon "Pokey" Reddick and Daniel Berthiaume to reduce the Jets' goals-against total to 271, the fourth-best mark in the league. Los Angeles finished four points ahead of Vancouver for the final playoff spot in the Smythe.

Hartford, led by Ron Francis, Kevin Dineen, and John Anderson, finished on top in the Adams Division for the first time in franchise history. Hartford's first-place result meant that four different clubs had finished first in the Adams in as many seasons. The Canadiens, who were the NHL's top defensive club, finished in second place, one point behind the Whalers. Montreal goaltenders Patrick Roy and Brian Hayward shared the Jennings Trophy for fewest goal-against. While Montreal had the best team defense, Boston's Ray

Rod Langway collars a Soviet forward during the first of two games between the NHL All-Stars and the Soviet National Team at Rendez-Vous 87.

Bourque was the NHL's best defenseman and winner of the Norris Trophy. Bourque's 95 points ranked him tenth in league scoring and contributed to his eighth consecutive selection to the NHL All-Star Team. Cam Neely, a big right winger acquired by the Bruins in an off-season deal with Vancouver, was the team's second-highest scorer with 36 goals.

Bourque was a member of the NHL all-star squad that played the Soviet national team in Rendez-Vous 87, a two-game exhibition series that replaced the league's mid-season all-star contest. The event was the brainchild of Nordiques' club president Marcel Aubut and was held in Quebec in the midst of the city's famous Winter Carnival. Dave Poulin of the Flyers scored late in the third period of the first game to give the NHL a 4–3 win. In the second game, young Soviet winger Valeri Kamensky scored two goals and assisted on another as the Soviets won 5–3.

A sidelight to the two games played in Quebec was a well-attended exhibition of artifacts from the collection of the Hockey Hall of Fame. Former NHL referee-in-chief Ian "Scotty" Morrison had been appointed president of the Hockey Hall of Fame prior to Rendez-Vous 87.

In the Patrick Division, Philadelphia once again parlayed its grinding, persistent hockey to a first-place finish and 100 points. The Flyers promoted goaltender Ron Hextall from the AHL's Hershey Bears, and the big rookie proved himself ready for the NHL, appearing in 66 games for a league-leading 37 wins and earning the Vezina Trophy. With 106 penalty minutes, Hextall was also the league's most-penalized netminder, due largely to his habit of

Ron Francis, the career-leader in every offensive category for the Hartford Whalers, recorded a franchise-high six assists in a 10–2 win over the Boston Bruins on March 5, 1987.

wielding his stick to force opposing forwards to vacate his crease. Washington finished second in the Patrick for the fourth consecutive season and was led in scoring by defenseman Larry Murphy, who had 23 goals and 58 assists for 81 points. The Islanders were third, led by Pat LaFontaine and Mike Bossy, who topped the team with 38 goals each. Bossy, who had scored 50-or-more goals in each of his nine previous NHL seasons, was hampered by a painful lower-back ailment, and though he would sit out the 1987-88 season in an attempt to recover, his career as an NHL player was over. In ten spectacular years, Bossy had scored 573 goals and recorded 553 assists for 1,126 points. Though his accomplishments were overshadowed by Wayne Gretzky's record-setting seasons in the early 1980s, Bossy will be remembered as one of the NHL's leading snipers and most prolific goal-scorers.

The Rangers finished fourth in the Patrick with 76 points, leaving Pittsburgh and New Jersey out of the playoffs. Walt Poddubny and Tomas Sandstrom had 40-goal seasons for the Rangers. Mario Lemieux battled knee pain for much of the year and finished with 54 goals in 63 games with the Penguins. The Devils used five goaltenders – Craig Billington, Alain Chevrier, Karl Freisen, Kirk McLean, and Chris Terreri – and allowed 368 goals-against, the most in the NHL.

In the Smythe Divison playoffs, the Oilers needed nine games to eliminate Los Angeles and Winnipeg. The Jets had reached the second round by eliminating Calgary in six. In the Norris, Toronto and Detroit advanced to the division final, which was won by Detroit in seven games. The Wings won the last three games of this series, shutting out Toronto in games five and seven. Detroit added another win in the first game of the Campbell Conference finals with the Oilers, but was overmatched against the best defensive team Glen Sather had ever assembled. The Oilers held the Red Wings to eight goals in the next four games to advance to the Cup finals.

In the Wales Conference, Quebec eliminated Hartford in six games, and the Canadiens swept Boston to set up an all-Quebec Adams Division final. This series proved to be a mirror image of the last time these two clubs met in the post-season. As in 1985, the series went seven games, but this time it was the Canadiens who were victorious. Game five and, perhaps, the series swung on a disallowed goal by Quebec. With the game and the series tied 2–2, the Nordiques scored what appeared to be the winning goal late in the third period, but offsetting minor penalties, whistled just as the puck entered the net, resulted in the goal being nullified. The Canadiens' Ryan Walter scored 14 seconds after the resumption of play to win the game and give the Habs the series lead three games to two. The Nordiques won game six 3–2 on Normand Rochefort's game-winner. But in game seven, a five-goal second period by Montreal sealed the series win for the Canadiens.

In the Patrick, Philadelphia required six games and two shutouts from Ron Hextall to eliminate the Rangers. The series between the Islanders and the Capitals went seven games plus four periods, as the Islanders, who had rallied from a three-games-to-one deficit, added to the Capitals' playoff frustration by eliminating Washington after a marathon 68 minutes of overtime in game seven. The series-winning goal was a screened shot from the right point by Pat LaFontaine. Goaltenders Kelly Hrudey of the Islanders and Bob Mason of the Capitals faced a combined total of 132 shots and were brilliant through the six-and-a-half-hour deciding contest, which began Saturday evening and ended at two o'clock Sunday morning. The game was the fifth-longest in Stanley Cup history.

In the Patrick Division finals, the Islanders again fell behind three games to one before battling back to force a seventh game against the Flyers. In game seven, two short-handed goals by Philadelphia ended the Islanders' hopes of advancing to the Wales Conference finals, which brought together the Flyers, the Canadiens, and the league's two best defenses. The Canadiens held the early edge in most games, and scored at least three goals in every match, but the Flyers capitalized on their opportunities and were the better third-period club, engineering a six-game series win.

The 1987 Stanley Cup finals between the Oilers and Flyers seemed destined to be a short series after Jari Kurri's overtime goal gave the hometown Oilers the lead in the series, two games to none. Returning to Philadelphia for games three and four, the Oilers managed a split to lead the series three games to one. But the Flyers rallied to play superbly in games five and six, winning 4–3 in the Northlands Coliseum and 3–2 in the Spectrum to force a seventh game for the first time in the Stanley Cup finals since Montreal defeated Chicago in 1971.

In game seven, the teams played from their strengths, the Oilers upping the pace and the Flyers playing coach Mike Keenan's rock-solid defensive system in front of Ron Hextall. Philadelphia scored first on a power-play, but the Oilers dominated play and took the lead in the second period on a goal by Jari Kurri. The Flyers, respecting the Oilers' scoring punch, didn't abandon

Ron Hextall, who made his NHL debut as the Flyers' first-string goaltender in 1986-87, won the Vezina Trophy and was selected as a First Team All-Star in his rookie campaign. An excellent puck handler, who often strays from the net to corral the puck for his defensemen, Hextall is the only goalie in the history of the NHL to shoot and score a goal, a feat he has accomplished twice.

their game plan in pursuit of the tying goal and pressed the Oilers until Glenn Anderson put the game out of reach, slipping a long shot past Hextall for a 3–1 lead. Challenged in the finals as never before, the Oilers had won their third Stanley Cup.

With a champion's grace, Gretzky hoisted the Cup and thrust it into the hands of Steve Smith, the young defenseman whose clearing pass had deflected into his own net, eliminating Edmonton in 1986. The Oilers had become one of hockey's great dynasty teams.

Ron Hextall was awarded the Conn Smythe Trophy, joining former Flyer Reggie Leach and goaltenders Glenn Hall and Roger Crozier as the only players to win this award as members of teams that did not win the Cup.

The finest players from the world's leading hockey nations – Canada, Czecho-slovakia, Finland, the Soviet Union, Sweden, and the United States – gathered for the fourth Canada Cup, beginning in late August, 1987. The round-robin portion of the tournament featured Sweden's 5–3 upset of the Soviets and a sizzling 3–2 win by Canada over a determined Team U.S.A. Over the course of the event, Team Canada coach Mike Keenan would make increasing use of his team's not-very-secret weapon, the simultaneous deployment of Wayne Gretzky and Mario Lemieux. With Gretzky dishing him the puck, it was at this tournament that Lemieux established himself as the premier goal-scorer in the game.

Canada Cup chairman Alan Eagleson got his dream match-up of Team Canada and the Soviet Union for the tournament's three-game final series.

Mario Lemieux takes aim and prepares to fire the puck over the glove of Soviet goal-tender Sergei Mylnikov to give Canada a last-minute victory in the 1987 Canada Cup. Lemieux's goal brought one of the most exciting tournaments ever played to an electrifying climax.

All three contests ended in 6–5 scores. The Soviets won game one on a goal by Alexander Semak after five minutes of overtime. In game two, Team Canada faced elimination for thirty minutes of extra time before Lemieux redirected the second of two sharp-angle shots by Gretzky past Soviet goaltender Evgeny Belosheikin for the win. Lemieux and Gretzky hooked up again in Team Canada's comeback win in game three. With less than two minutes to play in the third period, Gretzky broke down the left wing, faked a Soviet defender, and slid a pass back to Lemieux, who snapped a wrist shot into the top of the net. Dale Hawerchuk, who won the face-off that sprung Wayne and Mario, played superb two-way hockey and had a goal and an assist, earning player-of-the-game honors for Team Canada.

In the midst of the Canada Cup final, the Maple Leafs and the Blackhawks completed a five-player deal that sent Steve Thomas, Bob McGill, and three-time 50-goal scorer Rick Vaive to Chicago for Ed Olczyk and Al Secord.

In late November, Edmonton general manager Glen Sather made the first trade involving a key member of the Oilers' Stanley Cup-winning teams when he dealt Paul Coffey to Pittsburgh. Sather and his high-scoring defenseman had been involved in a prolonged salary dispute that had led Coffey to demand a trade. Coffey didn't play in the first two months of the season, as Sather sought the best possible deal. The transaction with Pittsburgh involved seven players: Coffey, Dave Hunter, and Wayne Van Dorp went to the Penguins for Craig Simpson, Dave Hannan, Moe Mantha, and Chris Joseph.

Late in the regular season, Calgary traded wingers Brett Hull and Steve Bozek to St. Louis for defenseman Rob Ramage and goaltender Rick Wamsley. With Calgary, Hull had 26 goals in 52 games, but was considered expendable by the Flames, who had the league's most potent offense in 1987-88.

In the Norris Division, general manager Jim Devellano and coach Jacques Demers of Detroit continued to improve their club, gaining a further 15 points in the standings to finish first. The Wings, who had climbed from 40 to 93 points in two seasons, were led by team captain Steve Yzerman, who had registered 50 goals and 52 assists, despite a knee injury late in the season. Petr Klima scored 37 goals, and big left winger Bob Probert scored 29, along with 398 minutes in penalties. The second-place Blues got a 40-goal performance from Tony McKegney.

The Vaive–Olczyk deal paid dividends for both the Leafs and the Blackhawks in 1987-88. Vaive had 43 goals in Chicago and Olczyk 42 for the Leafs. Toronto played much of the season without Wendel Clark, whose back problems would cause him to miss more than 100 games during the next two seasons. The Minnesota North Stars, under newly appointed general manager Jack Ferreira and new coach Pierre Pagé, would miss the playoffs for the second straight season, despite 41 goals from Dino Ciccarelli and 40 from Brian Bellows. Ferreira had served as director of player development

Paul Coffey, who is the league's most talented offensive defenseman since Bobby Orr, established a new goal-scoring record for defensemen with 48 in 1985-86, while he was with Edmonton. He was traded to the Penguins in 1987.

Steve Yzerman's first 50-goal and 100-point season saw the Red Wings top the Norris Division with 93 points in 1987-88.

for the New York Rangers. Pagé had been an assistant coach in Calgary. Lou Nanne, who had been general manager of the North Stars since 1977-78, was appointed club president.

By far the closest division was the Patrick, where only seven points separated the first- and sixth-place teams. The New York Islanders, riding a 47-goal season from Pat LaFontaine and strong goaltending by Kelly Hrudey and Billy Smith, topped the Patrick with 88 points. Washington finished second in the division for the fifth straight season, employing a goaltending tandem of Clint Malarchuk and Pete Peeters, who together posted the league's second-best goals-against average. Philadelphia's top scorer, Tim Kerr, missed all but eight games with a severe shoulder injury, but the Flyers were still good enough to finish tied with the Capitals at 85 points. In a December game against the Bruins, the Flyers' Ron Hextall became the first netminder to shoot the puck the length of the ice to score a goal in an NHL game. Hextall's historic marker was scored into an empty net. Billy Smith of the New York Islanders had been credited with a goal in 1979-80, but had not shot the puck himself. Smith was the last Islander to touch the puck before an opposing player's pass back to the blue line went the length of the ice and into the empty net.

New Jersey's season was the best in the history of the franchise – 82 points, a fourth-place finish, and the club's first playoff appearance since

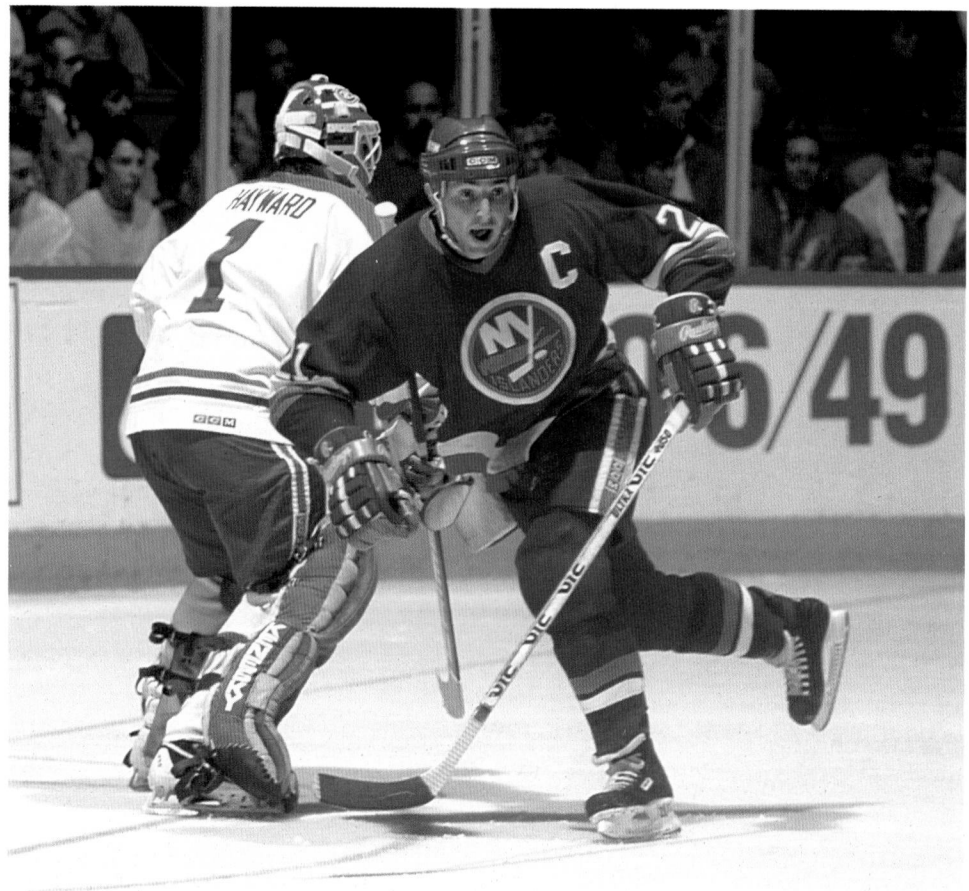

Brent Sutter, one of six brothers from Viking, Alberta, who made hard work and solid effort their game plan every time they came to the rink, runs some subtle interference on Montreal's Brian Hayward. The only Sutter brother to record a 100-point season, Brent was appointed captain of the New York Islanders in 1987.

moving from Colorado. Former Canadian Olympic goaltender Sean Burke joined the Devils after the 1988 Games in Calgary, posting an impressive 3.05 goals-against average in 13 NHL games. The Devils had seven wins and a tie in their last eight games and needed an overtime goal by John MacLean against Chicago on the last night of the season to earn a berth in the playoffs. Pat Verbeek was the Devils' top goal-scorer with 46, and team captain Kirk Muller led the club in points with 94. The Rangers, now coached by Michel Bergeron, formerly of the Nordiques, equaled New Jersey's 82 points, but missed the playoffs by virtue of having two fewer wins.

The most intriguing team in the Patrick was the Pittsburgh Penguins. Mario Lemieux's pre-season tune-up in the Canada Cup primed him to become the NHL's fourth 70-goal scorer. Coupled with 98 assists, Lemieux's 70 goals gave him 168 points and broke Gretzky's seven-year hold on the Art Ross Trophy and eight-year monopoly on the Hart. An additional 40 goals from Dan Quinn and 35 from Randy Cunneyworth gave Pittsburgh the most productive offense in the Patrick. With the arrival of Paul Coffey, the team played to sellout crowds in every NHL city. Despite finishing with a respectable 81 points, the Penguins ended the season in sixth place, out of the playoffs in the tightly bunched Patrick Division.

Lemieux's Hart Trophy-winning season represented a coming of age for the big center, who many felt had come to rival Gretzky as the league's greatest player. Lemieux dominated many games and had become the best one-on-one player in the league. His superior size and strength – he was six-foot four and 210 pounds – combined with his soft touch with the puck made him difficult to check, despite frequent efforts by opponents to shadow him closely. Lemieux, whose work ethic had been questioned in the past, credited playing with Gretzky in the Canada Cup as the spark for his improved performance. His unique uniform number, 66, had come to be identified with Lemieux just as closely as 99 was identified with Gretzky.

The Canadiens finished atop the Adams, breaking 100 points for the first time since 1981-82. The Habs repeated as the league's top defensive team, effectively combining three stay-at-home defensemen (Rick Green, Mike Lalor, and Craig Ludwig) with three who lugged the puck (Chris Chelios, Petr Svoboda, and Larry Robinson). Stéphane Richer became the first Montreal player to score 50 goals since Guy Lafleur in 1979-80. Boston finished second with 94 points, and Ray Bourque won his second Norris Trophy. Cam Neely scored 42 goals, while rookies Glen Wesley, Bob Sweeney, and Bill O'Dwyer played regularly for a Boston club that was supplemented by the late-season addition of Craig Janney and Bob Joyce, members of the U.S. and Canadian teams at the 1988 Winter Olympics. Buffalo showed a 21-point improvement in its first full season under coach Ted Sator to finish third with 85 points. Rookie right winger Ray Sheppard scored 38 goals and was a Calder Trophy finalist. Hartford was solid defensively, finishing fourth, without a 30-goal scorer. Quebec missed the

Ray Bourque, winner of the Norris Trophy as the league's best defenseman in 1987-88, continued his career-long string of consecutive All-Star Team berths, earning his ninth selection in as many NHL seasons.

playoffs, despite an 111-point season from team captain Peter Stastny.

In the Smythe, Calgary finished in first place for the first time since the franchise joined the league as the Atlanta Flames in 1972-73. The Flames promoted coach Terry Crisp from their top farm club, assigning him the task of getting more production from a talented team. Four Flames scored 40 or more goals: Joe Nieuwendyk (51), Hakan Loob (50), Mike Bullard (48), and Joe Mullen (40). Gary Suter and Al MacInnis were the NHL's top-scoring defensemen. Joe Nieuwendyk won the Calder Trophy and became the second first-year player to score 50 goals. He finished two goals shy of Mike Bossy's 53-goal rookie record, set ten seasons before in 1977-78.

The Oilers finished out of first place for the first time since 1980-81. Gretzky tallied 149 points to finish second to Lemieux in scoring. Mark Messier scored 37 goals and finished with 111 points. Craig Simpson, acquired in the deal for Paul Coffey, scored 43 goals for the Oilers, which, combined with the 13 he scored in Pittsburgh, gave him 56 on the season. Without Coffey, the Oilers' defense was led by Charlie Huddy, Kevin Lowe, and Steve Smith. Grant Fuhr proved to be hockey's iron man in 1987-88, appearing in nine games in the Canada Cup and 75 in the regular season to surpass Bernie Parent's mark of 73 with the Flyers in 1973-74.

Winnipeg slipped below .500 but remained in third place, receiving strong showings from Dale Hawerchuk with 44 goals and Paul MacLean with 40. The Kings, playing their first season in 12 without Marcel Dionne, finished fourth. Young snipers Luc Robitaille and Jimmy Carson had 50-goal seasons, and veteran center Bernie Nicholls had 78 points. In March 1988, club president and co-owner Bruce McNall became the Kings' sole owner, buying out Jerry Buss. Vancouver again missed the playoffs, despite 40 goals from Tony Tanti and a fine performance by goaltender Kirk McLean, who appeared in 41 games.

It was the tightly competitive Patrick Division that promised the most intriguing match-ups in the first round of the 1988 Stanley Cup playoffs. The Devils, enjoying a franchise-first series win, sidelined the Islanders in six games, two of which were decided in overtime. Washington, eliminated in quadruple-overtime in 1987, found itself again playing extra time in game seven against the Flyers, this time prevailing on Dale Hunter's goal at 5:57. The Capitals had trailed three games to one in this series. The Patrick Division finals between New Jersey and Washington also went seven, Devils' right winger John MacLean scoring the series-clinching goal. Patrik Sundstrom, acquired by the Devils from Vancouver before the 1987-88 season, set an NHL record for most points in a playoff game with eight, scoring three goals and adding five assists as the Devils defeated the Caps 10–4 in the second game of the series.

In the Adams Division, Montreal and Boston advanced with six-game wins over the Whalers and the Sabres. In the division finals, the Bruins defeated the Canadiens in five games, and ended a 45-year span of 18 consecutive

New Jersey captain Kirk Muller, shown here being checked by Dave Ellett of the Winnipeg Jets, contributed 12 points in the Devils' impressive playoff performance in 1988. The club was eliminated by Boston in the seventh game of the Wales Conference finals.

series losses to the Habs. The Canadiens did not play with their customary discipline in this series, and were particularly ineffective on the power-play.

In the Norris, Detroit's Bob Probert – who would go on to set a club record for most points in one playoff year with 21 – led the Red Wings to series wins over the Leafs and the Blues. Detroit coach Jacques Demers, who was named coach of the year for the second consecutive season, won his first post-season encounter with the St. Louis Blues, whom he had coached from 1983-84 to 1985-86.

The Smythe Division finals were a fourth renewal of the "Battle of

Alberta," as both the Flames and Oilers advanced with five-game wins in the first round. A long series was anticipated, but the Oilers combined sound defense and goaltending with a balanced attack to sweep the Flames in four straight games. A short-handed overtime goal by Wayne Gretzky won game two in Calgary, boosting Edmonton into control of the series. In the Campbell Conference finals, the Oilers eliminated the Red Wings in five games, winning game four on Jari Kurri's overtime goal.

In the Wales Conference finals between the Bruins and the Devils, Boston outscored New Jersey, but the Devils' ability to win low-scoring games – including an overtime victory in game two – kept the series close. After Boston won game three by a score of 6–1 to take the series lead, New Jersey coach Jim Schoenfeld accosted referee Don Koharski and was subsequently suspended for one game by the NHL. The Devils obtained a temporary injunction in a New Jersey court, preventing the imposition of the suspension. When the referee and linesmen scheduled for game four learned that Schoenfeld was going to coach, they refused to take the ice. The start of the game was delayed until substitute officials could be found. The substitutes worked the game with the help of NHL director of officiating John McCauley, who stationed himself in the penalty box for the duration of the match, which was eventually won 3–1 by the Devils.

Between games four and five the NHL held a hearing on the Schoenfeld charges that resulted in Schoenfeld being suspended for game five. The Bruins won and went on to eliminate New Jersey in seven games.

In the Stanley Cup finals, the Oilers defeated the Bruins in four straight games to capture their fourth Stanley Cup in five seasons. Game four in the series was suspended when a power failure left Boston Garden in darkness late in the second period with the score tied 3–3. League by-laws stipulated that this game would be replayed in its entirety at the end of the series, if required to determine a champion. A replay would prove to be unnecessary, but individual statistics from the portion of the game that had been played were included in all tabulations.

With the Oilers leading three games to none, the series returned to Edmonton, where the Oilers clinched the Cup with a 6–3 win in front of their home crowd. Gretzky, Messier, Kurri, and Esa Tikkanen were the leading scorers in post-season play. Gretzky won his second Conn Smythe Trophy and set a new NHL record with 31 assists in one playoff year. With Gretzky and Messier just past their twenty-seventh birthdays, and Kurri turning twenty-eight in May, the Oilers were at the peak of their power.

In June, the Hockey Hall of Fame announced plans to relocate to larger premises in a restored nineteenth-century bank building, located at the corner of Front and Yonge streets in downtown Toronto.

On August 9, 1988, the Edmonton Oilers and Los Angeles Kings completed a trade that sent Wayne Gretzky, Mike Krushelnyski, and Marty McSorley to

Los Angeles for Jimmy Carson, Martin Gélinas, and the Kings' first-round draft picks in 1989, 1991, and 1993. The Oilers also received a reported $15 million.

The trading of Gretzky – clearly the league's greatest player – had no parallel in sports. Analysts of the trade struggled to compare it with any existing deal, and finally settled on the hypothetical trading of baseball's Babe Ruth at the peak of his powers. But even this comparison fell short: Gretzky had dominated the game of hockey, becoming the NHL's all-time assist leader and third-leading point-scorer in just nine seasons. In Los Angeles, the acquisition of Gretzky meant a new glitter and respectability for the Kings. Hockey suddenly became big news in Southern California. In Edmonton, where Gretzky was a hero, disconsolate fans had to content themselves with the hope that their club had acquired players and draft choices that would ensure strong Oiler teams for seasons to come.

When the 1988-89 season began, most of the attention was focused on the Smythe Division, where the Gretzky-less Oilers would be battling the Flames and Kings for the division crown. The Calgary Flames won a league-high 54 games, finishing with 117 points, the best mark in the NHL. The Flames were led by Joe Mullen, who racked up 110 points and hit the 50-goal mark for the first time in his career. Calgary also received solid seasons from Joe Nieuwendyk, who reached the 50-goal plateau for the second consecutive season, and from rearguard Al MacInnis, whose 74 points ranked him third among NHL defensemen. Forward Sergei Priakin became the first player to receive permission from the Soviet Ice Hockey Federation to join an NHL club, and he played in the Flames' last two regular-season contests.

The Los Angles Kings improved by 23 points and finished in second place in the division, their best showing since 1981. The Kings also placed three scorers in the top ten for the second time in franchise history. Wayne Gretzky's 54 goals and 114 assists earned him his ninth Hart Trophy, and Bernie Nicholls, who became only the fifth man in NHL history to reach the 70-goal mark, ranked fourth in scoring with 150 points. Luc Robitaille was the third King to crack the top ten, firing 46 goals and adding 52 assists. Steve Duchesne was the second-highest-scoring defenseman in the NHL, establishing career-high marks with 25 goals and 50 assists.

Meanwhile, the Edmonton Oilers fell to third place, scoring only 325 goals, their lowest total since their first NHL season. Although it was clear that the team was rebuilding, both Jari Kurri and Jimmy Carson had fine campaigns. Kurri connected for 44 goals and 58 assists, while Carson added 49 goals and 51 assists, reaching triple figures in points for the second straight season.

The Vancouver Canucks lassoed the final playoff berth in the Smythe, finishing 10 points ahead of the Winnipeg Jets. The Canucks set a team record by allowing only 253 goals-against, the third-lowest total in the NHL. Rookie Trevor Linden had an impressive freshman season with the Canucks,

Trevor Linden, the second player chosen in the 1988 Entry Draft, was selected to the NHL's All-Rookie Team in 1989, after a 59-point season with the Canucks.

scoring 30 goals and adding 29 assists. The Jets allowed a league-high 355 goals-against and finished out of the playoffs for the first time in seven seasons.

The Detroit Red Wings won the Norris Division crown and were the only team in the division to reach the .500 mark. The Wings' talented young centerman, Steve Yzerman, proved himself to be the NHL's third-best player behind Gretzky and Lemieux, setting three team records with 65 goals, 90 assists, and 155 points. The St. Louis Blues, who finished two points back of the Wings, discovered a potential superstar in Brett Hull. He scored 41 goals and added 43 assists to lead the team in scoring.

Third place in the Norris went to Minnesota. The North Stars, who improved upon their 1987-88 results by 19 points, took part in a major trade with the Washington Capitals. The Stars received Mike Gartner, holder of six Washington team records, in exchange for Dino Ciccarelli, Minnesota's career leader in goals.

The Chicago Blackhawks, now coached by Mike Keenan, finished fourth, needing an overtime marker by Troy Murray in the final game of the season to capture the division's last playoff berth over the Toronto Maple Leafs.

The Patrick Division, which had featured a six-team battle for first place in 1988, was a two-horse race in 1989. The Washington Capitals won their first division crown, winning 41 games and totaling 92 points. The Caps featured a well-balanced attack, led by 42 goals from Geoff Courtnall and 41 from Mike Ridley. Pete Peeters authored four shutouts, the second-highest total in the league. The second-place Pittsburgh Penguins led the NHL in

Perhaps no player possesses a wider range of offensive skills than Mario Lemieux, the only man since 1981 to loosen Wayne Gretzky's grip on the Art Ross Trophy as NHL scoring champion. Lemieux is the only player in NHL history to score five goals in a game in five different ways: even strength, short-handed, powerplay, breakaway, and penalty shot.

Tony Granato, a graduate of the University of Wisconsin and the U.S. Olympic Team, earned a spot on the NHL's All-Rookie Team in 1989 with a 36-goal effort for the New York Rangers.

offense and boasted three of the top six scorers in the league. Mario Lemieux defended his scoring title with 85 goals and 199 points. He also became the second player to score 50 goals in less than 50 games and the second player to score 80 goals in a season. After a mediocre freshman campaign, Rob Brown finished in fifth spot on the scoring ladder with 49 goals and 66 assists. Paul Coffey, returning to the form he displayed as an Edmonton Oiler player, finished sixth in scoring with the fourth 100-point season of his career.

The New York Rangers had two of the league's outstanding rookies in Brian Leetch and Tony Granato, who finished first and second in rookie scoring. New York's young players also benefited from the experience of playing with veteran superstar Guy Lafleur, who had been elected to the Hockey Hall of Fame in August, but who had come out of retirement when Phil Esposito offered him a tryout with the Rangers. Lafleur had a respectable 18 goals and 45 points in his comeback season, including a warmly received two-goal performance against his former teammates in the Montreal Forum and a hat trick against the Los Angeles Kings. The Rangers finished third in the Patrick, but conflict between coach Michel Bergeron and general manager Phil Esposito resulted in Bergeron being fired with two games left in the regular season. Esposito again took over as coach, but he would have little success, losing both remaining games.

The final playoff spot in the Patrick belonged to the Philadelphia Flyers. The Flyers, who had replaced coach Mike Keenan with former player Paul

After more than three years on the sidelines, Hall of Fame member Guy Lafleur made a successful comeback to the NHL, reporting to training camp and winning a spot on the roster of the New York Rangers for 1988-89.

Patrick Roy, whose 2.47 goals-against average was the league's best regular-season mark in 1988-89, also led the NHL in post-season competition, allowing just 2.09 goals-against per game in the 1989 playoffs.

Holmgren, finished with 36 wins and 80 points. The team received ample offense from 48-goal scorer Tim Kerr and steady two-way play from Rick Tocchet, who enjoyed his finest NHL season with 45 goals and 81 points. After reaching the Wales Conference finals in 1988, the New Jersey Devils slumped to fifth place, a result that cost coach Jim Schoenfeld his job. However, the Devils' demise wasn't as dramatic as the fall of the New York Islanders, who went from first place in the Patrick Division in 1987-88 to twentieth overall in the NHL in 1988-89.

In the Adams, the Montreal Canadiens continued to progress. Pat Burns, a former policeman who replaced Jean Perron as coach of the Habs, was named coach of the year after the Canadiens finished with 53 victories and

115 points, their highest point-total of the decade. Chris Chelios won the Norris Trophy, accumulating 73 points on 15 goals and 58 assists. Patrick Roy was the league's finest goaltender, adding the Vezina Trophy to the Jennings Trophy that he shared with back-up Brian Hayward. Roy was the first netminder to win both goaltending trophies in the same season. Montreal also made a key mid-season trade, sending John Kordic to the Leafs in exchange for speedy centerman Russ Courtnall. The Boston Bruins, second-place finishers under coach Terry O'Reilly, received good seasons from Cam Neely and rookie Craig Janney. Neely's 75 points represented a career best, and Janney's 16 goals and 46 assists placed him fourth among rookie scorers.

Pierre Turgeon of the Buffalo Sabres doubled his point production from the previous season, leading the Sabres to third place in the Adams. Buffalo got some much-needed firepower in December, when the club acquired Rick Vaive from Chicago in exchange for Adam Creighton. The tandem of Ron Francis and Kevin Dineen continued to pay dividends for the Hartford Whalers, who captured the division's final playoff spot. Dineen had a "career" year, connecting for 45 goals and setting up 44 others. The Quebec Nordiques dropped to last place and missed post-season play for the second consecutive season.

When the playoffs opened, all eyes were focused on the Smythe Division, in which the Los Angeles Kings and the Edmonton Oilers met in a first-round match-up. Gretzky's Kings surprised the experts by rallying from a three-games-to-one deficit to defeat the defending Cup champions. The other Smythe semi-final was just as exciting, as the Calgary Flames needed a goal by Joel Otto at 19:21 of overtime in game seven to defeat the persistent Vancouver Canucks. Both goaltenders – Calgary's Mike Vernon and Vancouver's Kirk McLean – were standouts in this series. In the division finals, Calgary swept the Kings in four straight games.

In the Norris Division, the Chicago Blackhawks upset favored Detroit in five games. The Hawks then eliminated St. Louis – winners in five games over Minnesota – in another five-game series. This set up a Calgary–Chicago match-up to determine a Campbell Conference champion. The Flames won this series in five games to earn their second trip to the Stanley Cup finals.

The Adams Division was dominated by the Montreal Canadiens, who swept Hartford, setting up a return match with the Boston Bruins, who had eliminated Buffalo. The Canadiens then defeated the Bruins in five games. In the Patrick Division, the Rangers – with Phil Esposito behind the bench – were swept by the Penguins. The Washington Capitals lost in six games to the Flyers, in a series that featured a second career goal scored by Ron Hextall. In the Patrick Division finals, Philadelphia earned the right to meet Montreal for the Wales Conference championship with a seven-game marathon victory over the Penguins. In the conference finals, Montreal allowed

Lanny McDonald prepares to enjoy the fruits of his labor after scoring the go-ahead goal for the Calgary Flames in game six of the 1989 finals. McDonald is the only member of the Flames to have his number retired.

just eight goals-against, eliminating the Flyers in six games to reach the Stanley Cup finals for the thirty-second time in franchise history.

The Montreal–Calgary final was a rematch of the 1986 Cup showdown, but this time the Flames prevailed in six closely contested matches. In the final game, with the result still very much in the balance, veteran Lanny McDonald, who would announce his retirement in August, scored the goal that clinched the series for the Flames. Al MacInnis, the first defenseman to lead the post-season scoring parade, was awarded the Conn Smythe Trophy.

In 1989-90, the NHL enjoyed its eleventh consecutive season of increased attendance. Fan interest was sparked by the growing parity among the league's twenty-one teams. This season, only one club, the Boston Bruins, reached 100 points, the first time since 1970-71 that fewer than two teams had hit the century plateau. The divisional races were tighter than ever, with the average gap between first and fourth place in each division down to 16 points. Earlier in the decade, this margin had been as high as 35 points.

The pre-season headlines and the early-season focus centered on nine Soviet players who had joined NHL teams – including four of the five members of the Soviet Union's elite "Green Unit" that had led the Soviet national team since the early 1980s. Igor Larionov and Vladimir Krutov signed with Vancouver, Sergei Makarov signed with Calgary, and Viacheslav Fetisov signed with New Jersey. With the exception of Makarov, who would win the Calder Trophy, their play was inconsistent. The Green Unit's fifth member, Alexei Kasatonov, joined New Jersey in mid-season and played well.

On October 15, 1989, Wayne Gretzky became the NHL's all-time scoring

Montreal's Bobby Smith (15) sets up shop behind the Calgary net, closely watched by Flames' defensemen Rob Ramage (55) and Brad McCrimmon (4), during the 1989 Stanley Cup finals. The Flames won the Cup in six games, defeating the Habs 4–2 at the Montreal Forum, marking the only occasion since the club entered the NHL in 1917 that the Canadiens have lost the deciding game in the Stanley Cup finals on home ice.

leader, surpassing his boyhood idol, Gordie Howe, in a game between the Kings and Gretzky's former club, the Oilers, in Edmonton's Northlands Coliseum. Gretzky tied Howe's record of 1,850 early in the game, and broke it with a goal in the last minute, sending the game to overtime, in which Gretzky scored the game winner.

Under new coach Mike Milbury, Boston improved by 13 points from the previous season to finish first in the Adams Division and capture the Presidents' Trophy with 101 points. Cam Neely, now considered one of the league's premier power forwards, scored 55 goals, while Ray Bourque, who would win the Norris Trophy for the third time in four years, added 19 goals and 65 assists. Dave Poulin and Brian Propp, acquired during the season from Philadelphia, added leadership and experience. Goaltenders Réjean Lemelin and Andy Moog cut Boston's goals-against by 24 from 1988-89 and shared the Jennings Trophy, combining for five shutouts. Buffalo, sparked by Pierre Turgeon's 106 points, by star defenseman Phil Housley, and by the goaltending of Daren Puppa, challenged the Bruins all year, finishing in second, just two points behind Boston. The Canadiens were led by goal-

Wayne Gretzky tucks the puck in the top corner, over the outstretched glove of Edmonton goalie Bill Ranford, to become the NHL's all-time leading scorer, surpassing Gordie Howe's old point mark of 1,850. In typical Gretzky fashion, the record goal was scored in the last minute of the game with the Kings' net empty, and forced overtime. Gretzky later scored the game winner.

An all-time all-star Boston Bruins team, created by artist Mike Gardner. From left to right: Lionel Hitchman, Eddie Shore, Art Ross, Tiny Thompson, Cooney Weiland, Dit Clapper, Bobby Bauer, Bill Cowley, Milt Schmidt, Woody Dumart, Frank Brimsek, Fern Flaman, Leo Boivin, Don McKenney, Johnny Bucyk, Phil Esposito, Gerry Cheevers, Harry Sinden, Bobby Orr, Terry O'Reilly, Rick Middleton, Raymond Bourque, Cam Neely. Seated in the distinctive yellow seats of Boston Garden: Charles F. Adams, Walter Brown, Weston Adams, Sr.

tender Patrick Roy, who posted a 2.53 average and won his second consecutive Vezina Trophy. The Habs finished third in the division. Stéphane Richer potted 51 goals, his second 50-goal campaign in three seasons. Ron Francis reached the 100-point plateau for the first time in his career, helping Hartford corral the last playoff spot in the Adams.

In Quebec, the Nordiques rehired coach Michel Bergeron and signed Guy Lafleur, who would score 12 goals and 22 assists in 39 games in the city where he had starred as a junior. The club faltered in the standings, winning just 12 games and collecting only 31 points, the lowest total by an NHL team since the Washington Capitals in 1974-75. But Joe Sakic was a bright spot, scoring 39 goals and 102 points in his second NHL season, as the Nordiques continued to sign talented youngsters.

In the Patrick, each team in the division spent time in first place. The scramble for playoff spots was resolved only on the last weekend of the season, but it was the Rangers, following the tight-checking, defensive strategy of new coach Roger Neilson, who finished on top to capture their first division championship since 1941-42. Neil Smith, a former director of scouting with the Detroit Red Wings, replaced Phil Esposito as the Rangers' general manager. Smith orchestrated the late-season addition of top scorers Bernie Nicholls from Los Angeles and Mike Gartner from Minnesota, who gave New York extra scoring punch to go with John Ogrodnick and rookie Darren Turcotte. The Rangers' defense, led by James Patrick and Brian Leetch, and by goaltenders John Vanbiesbrouck and Mike Richter, cut goals-against by 40.

The most improved team in the division, New Jersey, bettered its previous season's performance by 17 points, finishing just two behind the Rangers.

John MacLean notched 41 goals for the Devils, who received spectacular goaltending from Chris Terreri late in the season. The Washington Capitals, known to stress tight defensive hockey, loosened up in an attempt to keep pace with the stronger offenses of division rivals, but dropped seven points in the standings to finish third. Dino Ciccarelli continued to be one of the league's top snipers with 41 goals. The Islanders, getting another big season from Pat LaFontaine (54 goals and 104 points), experienced a roller-coaster year and squeaked into the playoffs on the final night, when Pittsburgh lost in overtime. The Penguins, strong for most of the season, slipped to fifth when Mario Lemieux missed 21 games because of injury. Philadelphia, only two points behind the Islanders, finished last, missing the playoffs for the first time since 1971-72. Injuries – particularly to goaltender Ron Hextall, who was out most of the season – contributed to the Flyers' plunge.

In the Norris Division, every team improved its record. Chicago, playing coach Mike Keenan's tightly disciplined style, jumped from fourth to first place and improved 22 points. With a balanced offense (Steve Thomas, Steve Larmer, Denis Savard, Adam Creighton, and exciting rookie Jeremy Roenick) and a solid defense (Doug Wilson, Dave Manson, Keith Brown, and Steve Konroyd), Keenan could afford to experiment with his goaltenders, who often played below his expectations. In St. Louis, the Blues' Brett Hull emerged as the league's top goal-scorer with 72, the most ever by an NHL right winger. The Blues finished five points behind Chicago. Toronto, third-best in league scoring, third-worst in league defense, finished in third place, three points behind St. Louis. The Leafs, whose 80 points were the most recorded by the team in a decade, were paced by Gary Leeman's 51 goals.

Joe Sakic, a 160-point scorer in junior hockey, broke the 100-point barrier in the NHL in his second season with the Nordiques.

By the end of the 1980s, Brett Hull had developed into the NHL's most feared sniper, and one of the league's most accurate shooters. Hull, who scored 50 goals for Moncton in the AHL in 1987, led the NHL with 72 goals in 1989-90.

The Minnesota North Stars, the subject of relocation rumors, mirrored the Islanders' season, with a good start and a good finish bracketing a poor mid-season. They finished in fourth place, six points better than in 1988-89. Brian Bellows was the North Stars' scoring leader with 55 goals, and goaltender Jon Casey emerged as one of the NHL's best. Detroit demonstrated how tightly competitive the Norris Division had become. By winning just six fewer games than a year earlier, the Red Wings dropped from first to last place. Center Steve Yzerman's total of 62 goals was second to Hull's 72. Gerard Gallant added another 36. But the Wings were an unsettled team. Bob Probert and Petr Klima, who was later traded to Edmonton, had off-ice problems, and Adam Oates was traded to St. Louis. At the season's end, both manager Jim Devellano and coach Jacques Demers lost their jobs.

The emotional and spiritual leader of the Edmonton Oilers both on and off the ice, Mark Messier was the popular choice as league MVP in 1990, winning his first Hart Trophy and leading the Oilers back into the Stanley Cup winners' circle.

Calgary, the defending Cup champs, again finished atop the Smythe Division, two points behind Boston for first place overall, but recorded 18 fewer points than in 1988-89 and allowed 61 more goals-against. Joe Nieuwendyk had 45 goals, and little Theoren Fleury, who had played well in the previous season's playoffs, scored 31. Sergei Makarov added 24 goals and 62 assists.

Edmonton finished nine points behind the Flames and became better adjusted to life without Gretzky. Led by Mark Messier, who had 45 goals and 84 assists, the Oilers were rejuvenated by an influx of young forwards, including a "Kid Line" made up of Adam Graves, Joe Murphy, and rookie Martin Gélinas, who had been part of the package that came from Los Angeles in the Gretzky trade. Third-place Winnipeg's improvement of 21 points earned the Jack Adams Award for coach Bob Murdoch. Team speed and strong defense, led by Dave Ellett and Fredrik Olausson, characterized the Jets' play. In Los Angeles, defense was a liability, despite the signing of veteran free agent Larry Robinson. Gretzky's 40 goals and 142 points led the league, and Luc Robitaille had 52 goals, but the Kings' goals-against average ranked eighteenth in the NHL. Vancouver skidded to 64 points and finished fifth in the Smythe, a drop attributable in part to the disappointing debut of the Canucks' Soviet players.

In the Smythe Division playoffs, Calgary faced the Gretzky-less Kings in the first two games of the opening round, but could only gain a split. The defending champs' defensive woes proved fatal, as they were outscored 29–24 on the series by the Kings, who scored 12 goals in game four alone on hat tricks by Tomas Sandstrom, Tony Granato, and Dave Taylor. The Flames' bid to repeat as Cup champion ended in game six after an apparent Flames' goal was disallowed in overtime. The series ended when Mike Krushelnyski's fluttering chip-shot eluded the glove of Calgary goaltender Mike Vernon. In the other division semi-final, Edmonton rallied from a three-games-to-one deficit to defeat the much-improved Winnipeg Jets in seven games. The Edmonton comeback featured superb goaltending by Bill Ranford and timely play by the Oilers' veterans. Buoyed by that win, Edmonton rode Ranford's continued fine play past Los Angeles, winning the Smythe Division finals with surprising ease in four straight.

In the Norris, St. Louis eliminated the Leafs, who were unable to stop the Blues' offense. Minnesota extended the inconsistent Blackhawks to seven games. Throughout this series and in the next round, Chicago coach Mike Keenan became known as "Captain Hook" for his willingness to yank the Hawks' starting goaltender in an effort to fire up the team. The division finals between the Hawks and Blues went seven games, Chicago winning the final contest 8–2 in the only one-sided game of this hard-fought series. Brett Hull was the top performer for St. Louis, scoring 13 goals in 12 playoff games.

In the Adams, Hartford had the Bruins on the ropes in game five and could have taken a series lead of three games to one with a victory. But Dave

Vancouver and Los Angeles Own Planes

The Vancouver Canucks and Los Angeles Kings are the only two teams in NHL history that have owned airplanes. The Kings purchased their plane during the 1989-90 season; the Canucks, who have since sold their plane, operated theirs during the mid-1980s.

The first hockey club to own a plane was Tulsa of the North American Hockey League. Tulsa owner Sam Avery purchased a twenty-one-seat DC-3 during the 1949-50 season so his players could avoid overcrowded trains.

Poulin sparked a comeback to win the game and tie the series at two, and Boston went on to win in seven games. In the division's other semi-final, Montreal dumped the Sabres in six games in a battle of the league's top goalies, Patrick Roy and Daren Puppa. In the Adams Division finals, the Bruins took advantage of Montreal injuries and a sub-par performance from Patrick Roy to win in five games.

In the Patrick Division's latest "Battle of New York," the Islanders could not match the Rangers' offense, although three of the five games that the Rangers needed to eliminate their rivals were decided by one goal. Washington rebounded, after trailing New Jersey two games to one, to win three straight. Five of the six very physical games were decided by one goal. The Caps' lost Dino Ciccarelli for the Patrick finals against the Rangers, but the newly discovered scoring touch of John Druce and hard-nosed physical play gave Washington the series in five games. It was the first division championshp in franchise history for the Caps.

In the Conference finals, Boston swept the Capitals in four straight to win the Prince of Wales Trophy. Neely, Bourque, Moog, and center Craig Janney were standouts for Boston, while Druce was the Caps' playoff hero, scoring 14 goals in 15 games. In the Campbell Conference, Edmonton bounced back after falling behind two games to one and eliminated the Blackhawks in six games. Ranford maintained his superiority in goal, and Messier, thought to be injured, played with great courage and leadership. Despite the series loss, Chicago fans cheered the emergence of rookie Jeremy Roenick, who scored 11 goals in 20 playoff games.

In the Stanley Cup finals, the Oilers triumphed over the Bruins in five games, thanks to contributions from every part of their roster – veterans such as Messier, Kurri, Anderson, and Lowe, young players such as Graves, Murphy, and Gélinas. The Oilers played tight defense, which shut down the

Edmonton's "Kid Line" (left to right, Joe Murphy, Adam Graves, and Martin Gélinas) poses with the Stanley Cup following the Oilers' fifth championship in 1990. Graves and Murphy arrived in Edmonton from Detroit on November 2, 1989, in one of Glen Sather's wisest trades. Together with Gélinas, the trio played a major role in the Edmonton win. Another young forward, center Mark Lamb, also added to the Oilers' balanced attack in the playoffs.

Boston attack, and employed an exceptional transition game, taking advantage of their superior team speed. Simpson led Edmonton with 16 goals and 15 assists, followed by Messier's nine goals and 22 assists. The Conn Smythe Trophy went to Bill Ranford, who posted a 2.53 goals-against average and a .912 save percentage in 22 games. Coach John Muckler became the thirteenth first-year head coach to win the Stanley Cup. Two years after the trade of hockey's greatest player, Oilers' president and general manager Glen Sather had rebuilt a champion, his fifth in seven seasons.

Prior to the end of the 1990 playoffs, the league announced that it would return to the San Francisco Bay area by granting a new franchise to begin play in 1991-92 in San Jose, California. The owners of the new franchise – later named the San Jose Sharks – were George and Gordon Gund, who had previously owned the Minnesota North Stars. The awarding of the franchise stemmed from the Gunds' earlier announcement of their intention to move the North Stars to the Bay area because of continuing financial losses in Minnesota.

The NHL's governors, who had previously announced plans to expand in the 1990s, maintained their opposition to franchise relocation. When investors came forward to purchase the North Stars and keep them in Minnesota, the Gunds were granted a new franchise in San Jose. An agreement between the two ownership groups established a "cross-pollination" draft that would enable the Sharks to secure the rights to a number of players in the North Stars' organization after the conclusion of the 1991 playoffs. Having lost players in the cross-pollination draft, the North Stars would participate with the Sharks in an expansion draft in which each NHL franchise would lose one player.

The North Stars' management team departed when the franchise was sold. General manager Jack Ferreira went to San Jose, and coach Pierre Pagé and assistant Dave Chambers joined Quebec as general manager and coach respectively.

The new North Stars' organization was headed by owners Howard Baldwin (a former managing partner with the Hartford Whalers) and Morris Belzberg. Shortly after the deal was completed with the Gunds, Norman Green, who had been a part-owner of the Calgary Flames, became a partner in the North Stars. The revamped club assembled a hockey department headed by general manager Bob Clarke, who had left his career-long home with Philadelphia, and former Montreal captain Bob Gainey, who was installed as coach. Prior to the start of the season, Green offered his shares in the Flames for sale and bought out Baldwin and Belzberg to become the sole owner of the club.

The off-season saw a great deal of activity, with numerous intriguing trades, hirings, and firings. Detroit replaced general manager Jim Devellano and coach Jacques Demers with former Washington coach Bryan Murray.

The revamped North Stars reacquired one of the franchise's brightest former stars, signing veteran center Bobby Smith before the start of the 1990-91 season.

Clarke was replaced in Philadelphia with Russ Farwell, a highly successful junior hockey executive. Pittsburgh's Craig Patrick hired former Calgary coach Bob Johnson to run the Penguins' bench. Terry Crisp, who had replaced Johnson in Calgary and won the Cup in 1989, was replaced by Doug Risebrough, who had been the Flames' assistant general manager.

Buffalo and Winnipeg swapped franchise players in Phil Housley and Dale Hawerchuk. Minnesota acquired former Flyers Brian Propp and Ilkka Sinisalo and reacquired Bobby Smith, who had begun his career as a North Star, from Montreal. Brad McCrimmon went from Calgary to Detroit. Joe Mullen went from Calgary to Pittsburgh. The Penguins also signed former Islander superstar Bryan Trottier, who had become a free agent. Edmonton's Jari Kurri left the NHL, signing with the Milan Devils, a club in the top division of Italian hockey.

The St. Louis Blues completed two significant free-agent signings, retaining Brett Hull, who had played out his option, and acquiring Washington's star defenseman Scott Stevens in a move that required heavy compensation in top draft choices to the Caps. Hull and Stevens both received multi-million-dollar contracts, signaling an upward trend in salaries. The Red Wings created their own share of headlines when they signed Sergei Fedorov, one of the top young players in the Soviet Union, after he left the Soviet team during the Goodwill Games in Seattle to defect to the United States.

Detroit's Sergei Fedorov adjusted quickly to NHL hockey, and finished as the league's top-scoring rookie, with 79 points in 1990-91.

The most active team in the off-season was Montreal. In addition to losing Bobby Smith, the Canadiens swapped defenseman Chris Chelios to Chicago for center Denis Savard, and also moved Claude Lemieux, Craig Ludwig, and Brian Hayward. In addition, Mats Naslund retired from the NHL, causing the Habs line-up to look strikingly different from the team that had won the Cup in 1986 and had gone to the finals in 1989. The Canadiens also joined the North Stars in the second pre-season Friendship Tour of the Soviet Union. (The Washington Capitals and Calgary Flames had played exhibition games and held training camps in the Soviet Union before the start of the previous season.)

Another training-camp highlight came from Florida, where the Kings and Penguins played an exhibition game before a record crowd of 25,037 fans in the Florida Sun Coast Dome. A headline of a different sort came a few weeks later when NHL president John Ziegler issued a one-year suspension to Edmonton's star goaltender Grant Fuhr for admitted substance abuse.

Two nights into the regular season, when Detroit played Washington, brothers coached against each other for only the fourth time in NHL history. Bryan and Terry Murray joined Frank and Lester Patrick (Boston and the Rangers, 1934), Lynn and Muzz Patrick (Boston and the Rangers, 1954), and Johnny and Larry Wilson (Colorado and Detroit, 1977).

On October 26, Wayne Gretzky became the first player in NHL history to record 2,000 points, when he assisted on Tomas Sandstrom's goal against Winnipeg goaltender Bob Essensa. On November 24, the Islanders' Al Arbour coached his 1,300th game, becoming only the second coach in league history to reach this milestone. (Dick Irvin heads the list with 1,437 games.)

In December of 1990, the NHL's board of governors granted two additional franchises to begin play in the 1992-93 season. The Tampa Bay Lightning, headed by Hall-of-Famer Phil Esposito, would be the league's first Florida entry and southernmost franchise, while the Ottawa Senators, headed by Bruce Firestone, would restore NHL hockey to a city that had been home to ten Stanley Cup champions, four of which were earned by the old Senators in the first ten years of the NHL.

The 1990-91 regular season featured a five-team race for first place in the overall standings, with four of the contending teams playing in the Campbell Conference. The Norris Division battle for top honors between Chicago and St. Louis saw the Blackhawks capture both the Norris title and the Presidents' Trophy with 106 points. The Blackhawks received superb goaltending from rookie Ed Belfour, who would capture the Calder, Jennings, and Vezina trophies, and from forwards Steve Larmer and Jeremy Roenick. The St. Louis Blues finished just one point behind Chicago. Brett Hull, who won the Hart Trophy, scored 86 goals to record the NHL's third-highest single-season goal-scoring mark, and had 50 goals in his first 49 games, to become only the fifth player in NHL history to score "50-in-50." Adam Oates, who played alongside Hull, notched 90 assists and 115 points in just 61 games.

Goaltender Ed Belfour's first full NHL season saw the Calder and Vezina trophy-winner appear in seventy-four of the Blackhawks' eighty games.

An inconsistent Detroit team finished third in the Norris, despite another strong season from Steve Yzerman and the emergence of Sergei Fedorov as the league's top-scoring rookie. Minnesota began the season poorly and was 13–28–8 at the All-Star break, but went 14–9–6 down the stretch to finish fourth. The North Stars' improvement resulted from strong goaltending by Jon Casey and improved team defense. The Toronto Maple Leafs also started poorly, replaced coach Doug Carpenter with Tom Watt, and made a dozen trades by the March 5 trading deadline. Despite this drastic revamping, the Leafs fell behind the improving North Stars and finished out of the playoffs.

Two other contenders for the Presidents' Trophy came from the Smythe Division. Los Angeles set team records for wins (46) and points (102) in finishing atop its division for the first time in franchise history. Wayne Gretzky led the Kings and the NHL with 163 points, earning his ninth Art Ross Trophy. The club reduced its goals-against by 83 from the previous season. In Calgary, the Flames were led by center Theoren Fleury with 51 goals and defenseman Al MacInnis, who had 103 points to record the third 100-point season of his career. Petr Klima scored 40 goals for the Oilers, but the loss of Jari Kurri, combined with injuries to Mark Messier, resulted in a general decline in offense, as the defending Cup champions finished with 80 points, their lowest total in ten seasons.

Los Angeles's Larry Robinson, one of the NHL's tallest players, works against Calgary's Theoren Fleury, one of the league's shortest. Fleury enjoyed his most productive NHL season in 1990-91, scoring 51 goals for the Flames.

After a dismal mid-season slump, which cost coach Bob McCammon his job, Vancouver was jolted by a late-season deal with St. Louis which brought Cliff Ronning, Geoff Courtnall, Sergio Momesso, and Robert Dirk to the Canucks and enabled the team to capture the final Smythe Division playoff spot by finishing two points ahead of Winnipeg. The Jets, who were an 85-point team in 1989-90, dropped 22 points in the standings in 1990-91. Despite a heroic performance by goaltender Bob Essensa, the Jets finished fifth, costing coach Bob Murdoch his job.

In the Adams Division, Boston was the Wales Conference's sole contender for the Presidents' Trophy. The Bruins were again led by Ray Bourque and Cam Neely and overcame numerous injuries to win their second straight division title. Montreal's young defense corps fared well, but injuries to goaltender Patrick Roy and other key players short-circuited any momentum the team could muster. The Habs finished second, 11 points behind the Bruins' 100. A late-season spurt by the Sabres pushed Buffalo into third spot as both Dale Hawerchuk and Uwe Krupp had solid seasons.

After a slow start, Hartford negotiated two major trades with Pittsburgh, acquiring scorers Rob Brown and John Cullen and defenseman Zarley Zalapski from the Penguins. The Whalers, who also received a 43-goal performance from Pat Verbeek, finished fourth, but registered their lowest point total since the club began its run of six straight playoff appearances in 1986. This decline would cost coach Rick Ley his job. The play of Joe Sakic and Mats Sundin, plus the first overall selection in the 1991 Entry Draft were positive developments to come out of Quebec's fourth consecutive fifth-place finish in the Adams. Hall-of-Famer Guy Lafleur, playing in his final NHL season, received tributes throughout the league, including a rocking chair from the Canucks on his last visit to the Pacific Coliseum.

In the Patrick Division, Pittsburgh began the season without superstar Mario Lemieux, who would miss 54 games because of back surgery and subsequent complications. By the time he returned to the line-up, the Penguins had developed a balanced attack led by Mark Recchi, Kevin Stevens, and Paul Coffey. Lemieux's return, coupled with a trade that brought Ulf Samuelsson and Ron Francis from Hartford, sparked the Penguins to their first division title in franchise history.

The remaining playoff spots in the Patrick were not finalized until the last few games of the season. The Rangers started strongly and remained in first place for much of the regular season, largely due to excellent goaltending by Mike Richter and the scoring of Mike Gartner, but injuries caught up with the club, and they faded late in the season to finish second. Washington found its long-sought-after number-one goaltender in Don Beaupre, and Kevin Hatcher emerged as a dominant defenseman, but the Caps' offense sputtered and the club finished third. Chris Terreri's goaltending and John MacLean's goal-scoring helped New Jersey tie down the division's final playoff berth. Philadelphia scored just 252 goals, the club's lowest total since

All-Star Cam Neely validated his credentials as one of the toughest and most talented players in the NHL, scoring 50-plus goals for the second consecutive season in 1990-91.

1971-72, despite Rick Tocchet's 40, and finished fifth and out of the playoffs for the second straight season. The Islanders got another strong performance from Pat LaFontaine and heroic goaltending from Glenn Healy, but struggled to their second last-place finish in three seasons.

As the playoffs began, Larry Robinson of the Los Angeles Kings extended two career playoff records. He held the record for most playoff games played (and would extend it to 225 in 1991) and for most consecutive years in the playoffs (19). The 1991 playoffs would also see the Kings' Wayne Gretzky become the league's all-time playoff goal-scoring leader with 93, breaking the mark of 92 held by his former Edmonton linemate Jari Kurri.

In their Smythe Division semi-final round, the Kings overcame a 2–1 deficit in games to eliminate Vancouver in six. The other Smythe Division semi-final series proved to be one of the finest playoff match-ups in years, with Edmonton and Calgary playing seven fast, physical games, of which the last two were decided in overtime, before the Oilers prevailed. In the Smythe finals, for the second consecutive year Edmonton ousted Los Angeles, this time needing six games, of which four went into overtime and two of these into double overtime. In winning the Smythe Division's playoff championship, the Oilers played five consecutive overtime games.

Chicago became the first regular-season championship team in twenty years to be eliminated in the first round of the playoffs, when Minnesota, propelled by a record-tying 15 power-play goals, upset the Blackhawks in six games to win their Norris Division semi-final series. In the other Norris semi-final, the Red Wings took a three-games-to-one lead on the Blues as another upset appeared likely. But the Blues rallied to win three in a row and take the series. The Norris Division finals proved to be another showcase for the North Stars' unlikely heroics, as Minnesota shut down the Blues' big scorers and eliminated St. Louis in six games.

The Adams Division semi-final match-ups echoed those of the previous season, with similar results. Boston and Hartford again split their first four games, but this time the Bruins won the next two to take the series. Wild bounces and scrambled play marked the Montreal–Buffalo series, but with the series tied at two, an overtime goal by Russ Courtnall in game five turned the tide in favor of the Canadiens, who went on to win in six games. Andy Moog's brilliant goaltending was the difference in the seven-game Boston–Montreal Adams Division final series, as the Bruins advanced to the Wales Conference finals for the second consecutive season.

New Jersey and Pittsburgh played a closely-contested Patrick Division semi-final series. An opening-game Devils' victory was followed by an overtime contest in game two that ended when rookie Jaromir Jagr scored a superb, swooping goal that tied the series. The Devils won two of the next three games and had a chance to eliminate the Penguins on home ice in a game in which Tom Barrasso, the Penguins' regular goaltender, was sidelined by an injury. But back-up goaltender Frank Pietrangelo played

strongly, as the Penguins won game six 4–3 and then polished off the Devils 4–0 to take the series.

In the Patrick Division's other semi-final, the Rangers and Capitals split their first four games. Dino Ciccarelli's overtime marker won game five for the Caps, who cruised to a series win in game six. In the Patrick Division finals, Barrasso's sharp play backstopped the Penguins' battered defense (Paul Coffey had broken his jaw), while forwards Mario Lemieux, Kevin Stevens, and Mark Recchi proved too potent for Washington. The Caps won the first game of the series, but were eliminated in five.

In the Campbell Conference finals, Minnesota continued its Cinderella playoff year, capitalizing on power-play opportunities, playing solid team defense, and getting sharp goaltending from Jon Casey. The North Stars, who had played in front of exceedingly small crowds early in the season, were now selling out every game. Against an Oilers' line-up hampered by injuries, Minnesota needed only five games to advance to the club's first Stanley Cup final-series appearance since 1981. The Penguins, who had never played in a Wales Conference final series, fell behind Boston two games to none, losing the second contest in overtime. But the Penguins' stronger forwards and physical defensemen enabled Pittsburgh to sweep

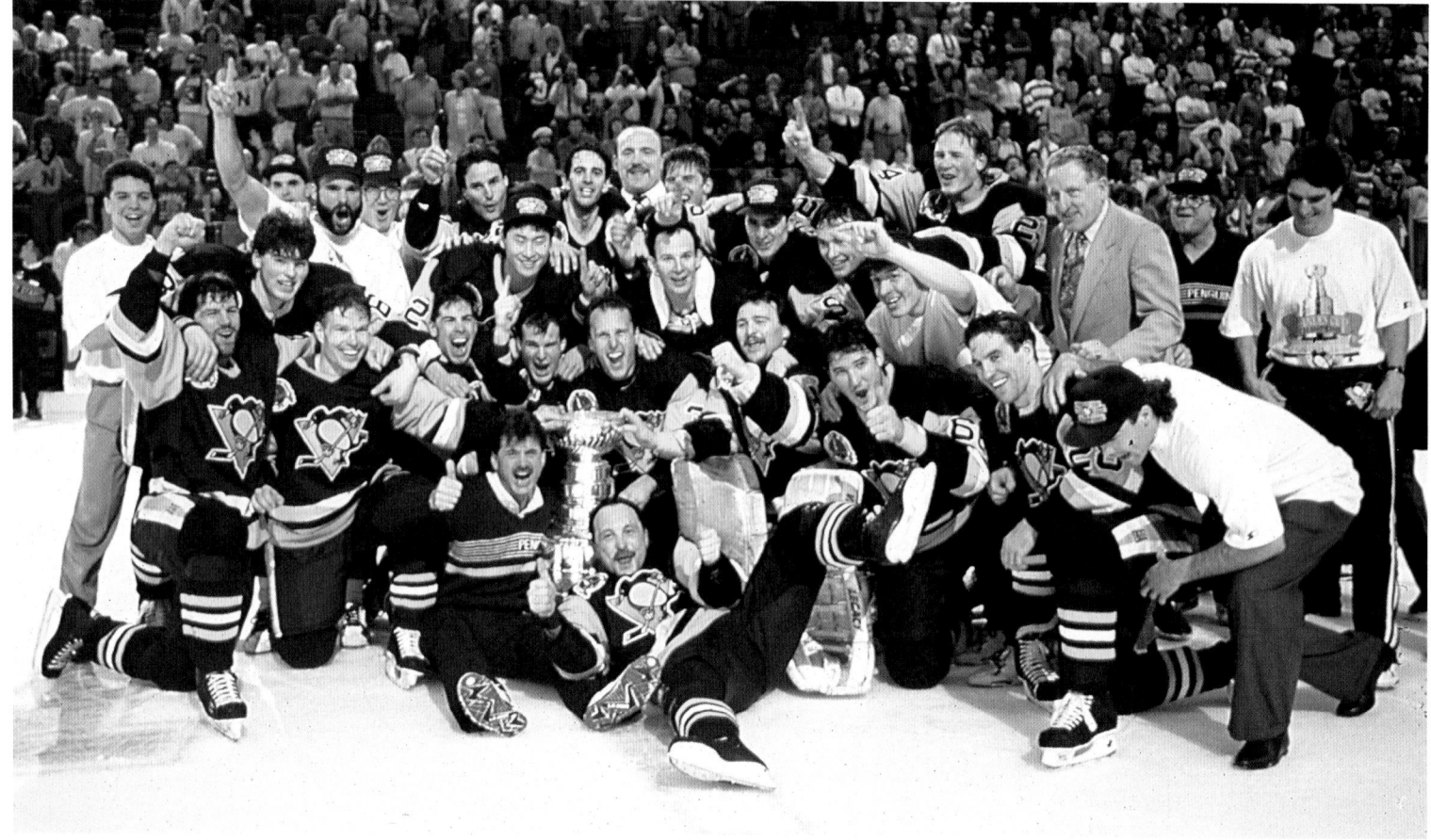

No player appeared to enjoy the Penguins' 1991 Stanley Cup championship as much as the club's most experienced playoff performer. Bryan Trottier (number 19, front row, to the right of the Cup) was a member of four consecutive championship teams with the New York Islanders in the 1980s.

the next four games and earn the club a place in the Stanley Cup finals for the first time in franchise history.

The Pittsburgh–Minnesota match-up for the Stanley Cup represented the first time since Chicago played Detroit in 1934 that neither of the finalists had previously won the Cup. After splitting games one and two, Minnesota took the lead in the series by winning game three, in which Mario Lemieux was a last-minute scratch from Pittsburgh's line-up due to back spasms sustained while unlacing his skates after the pre-game skate. Lemieux returned to action in game four and, in each of the next three games, the Penguins opened up large early leads. The North Stars, forced into the unfamiliar position of playing from behind, had to abandon the defensive style that had served them well through three rounds of the playoffs. Their comeback attempts fell just short in games four and five, but in the sixth and final game, the Penguins' firepower proved overwhelming, resulting in an 8–0 shutout win. This was the largest margin of victory ever recorded in a deciding Stanley Cup final game.

Goaltending and defense contributed to the Penguins' Stanley Cup championship, but what set the club apart was its depth and talent on the forward line with the likes of Kevin Stevens, Mark Recchi, Bryan Trottier, Ron Francis, Jaromir Jagr, Joe Mullen, Bob Errey, Phil Bourque, and, most significantly, Mario Lemieux, who was the leading scorer in the playoffs and

a near-unanimous choice for the Conn Smythe Trophy.

Despite playing at less than top condition, Lemieux was the dominant player in the finals, playing a regular shift and on special teams, scoring spectacular and timely goals, killing penalties, and displaying an intensity that critics thought he had always lacked. By leading his team to a Stanley Cup championship in his seventh NHL season, Lemieux emerged from the shadow of Wayne Gretzky's accomplishments. When it mattered most, Lemieux brought his game and the hockey world's appreciation of his skills and character to a new level.

Heading into the NHL's seventy-fifth anniversary season, the game continues to grow and change. Long-time Flames' executive Cliff Fletcher has left Calgary to become the president and general manager of the Toronto Maple Leafs. Jari Kurri has signed a contract to return to the NHL to play for the Los Angeles Kings. Junior sensation Eric Lindros was selected first overall by the Quebec Nordiques in the 1991 entry draft, while the San Jose Sharks, stocked with newly-drafted players, are poised to begin play in the Smythe Division as the NHL's twenty-second franchise.

Since the formation of the NHL in 1917, and throughout the game's history, thrilling moments have been a part of league and Stanley Cup play. There have been countless comebacks and upsets, five-goal games and shutouts, dynasty clubs and one-season wonders. And though it would seem that everything that could happen in hockey has already taken place, for those of us who care about the sport, every game contains at least one nugget of something we've never seen before: a little move, a deft pass, a quick glove-save. For us, the game always changes and remains fresh. For us, something as simple as a listing of players' names has the power to sweep us through three-quarters of a century.

The National Hockey League: Malone, Shore, Richard, Howe, Hull, Orr, Lafleur, Bossy, Gretzky, Lemieux, and . . .

Junior superstar Eric Lindros, shown here in the uniform of the Ontario Hockey League All-Stars, was selected first overall by the Quebec Nordiques in the 1991 Entry Draft.

Pat Falloon (center) was the first player drafted by the NHL's newest franchise, the San Jose Sharks. Shaking Falloon's hand is San Jose general manager Jack Ferreira, while director of player personnel, Chuck Grillo, looks on. Assigned to the Smythe Division, the team's first NHL season (1991-92) coincides with the NHL's seventy-fifth.

Photo Credits

Notes on Essayists

Jean Béliveau is a member of the Hockey Hall of Fame. A 507-goal scorer with the Canadiens, he played on ten Stanley Cup winners and won the Hart, Art Ross, and Conn Smythe trophies. He is the Canadiens' senior vice-president of corporate affairs.

Red Fisher is a member of the Hockey Hall of Fame's Player Selection Committee and a recipient of the Elmer Ferguson Memorial Award for jounalistic achievement. He is a veteran hockey reporter, covering the Canadiens for the Montreal *Gazette*.

Trent Frayne's column in Toronto's *Globe and Mail* contained some of Canada's most informed sports opinions. He is the author of numerous books, including *The Best of Times: Fifty Years of Canadian Sports*.

Jay Greenberg covered the Flyers for fourteen seasons, three with the Philadelphia *Bulletin* and eleven with the *Daily News*. He is currently a staff writer for *Sports Illustrated*.

Stu Hackel is a life-long hockey fan who is the NHL's director of broadcasting, publishing, and video. He is a former editor of *Goal Magazine*.

John Halligan is a long-time hockey communications executive with both the NHL and the New York Rangers. He is currently the director of communications for the NHL's anniversary celebrations.

Dick Irvin is well-known for his pioneering color commentary on "Hockey Night in Canada." He is the author of two recent books about the sport: *Now Back to You Dick* and *The Habs*.

Brian McFarlane has worked as a host and commentator for "Hockey Night in Canada," NBC, and CBS. He has written more than thirty books about hockey, including *100 Years of Hockey*.

Brian O'Neill is the NHL's executive vice-president. He began his association with the league at the time of the 1967 expansion, and worked closely with NHL president Clarence Campbell

Frank Orr is a recipient of the Hockey Hall of Fame's Elmer Ferguson Memorial Award for journalistic achievement. He writes a regular sports column for the *Toronto Star*.

Paul Quarrington won the Governor-General's award for literature for his novel *Whale Music*. The character Percival Leary first appeared in Quarrington's novel *King Leary*.

Francis Rosa is another recipient of the Hockey Hall of Fame's Elmer Ferguson Memorial Award. A former sports editor of the *Boston Globe*, he covered the Bruins full time, beginning in 1970.

Jay Teitel is the winner of numerous National Magazine Awards in Canada. A journalist and screenwriter, he is also the author of *The Argo Bounce*, a book about the Canadian Football League's Toronto franchise.

Bob Verdi has written a column for the *Hockey News*, has contributed to numerous hockey publications, and covers the Blackhawks for the Chicago *Tribune*.

Charles Wilkins is the author of five books. He is also the co-author of the adventure story *Paddle to the Amazon* and of a collection of essays about stars of the NHL's six-team era, titled *After the Applause*.

NHL Member Clubs

listed in order of first season of play

Montreal Canadiens

First NHL Season: 1917-18

Franchise Record in NHL:
2391w – 1415L – 706T, .608

Best Season: 1943-44,
38w – 5L – 7T, .830

Playoff Record in NHL:
351w – 214L – 8T, .620

Stanley Cup Wins: 23 (1916*, 1924, 1930, 1931, 1944, 1946, 1953, 1956, 1957, 1958, 1959, 1960, 1965, 1966, 1968, 1969, 1971, 1973, 1976, 1977, 1978, 1979, 1986)

Key Personnel: Jean Béliveau, Toe Blake, Yvan Cournoyer, Ken Dryden, Bill Durnan, Bob Gainey, Bernie Geoffrion, George Hainsworth, Doug Harvey, Aurel Joliat, Elmer Lach, Guy Lafleur, Newsy Lalonde, Jacques Laperrière, Jacques Lemaire, Frank Mahovlich, Joe Malone, Howie Morenz, Jacques Plante, Henri and Maurice Richard, Larry Robinson, Patrick Roy, Georges Vezina, Gump Worsley

Montreal Wanderers

Only NHL Season: 1917-18

Franchise Record in NHL:
1w – 5L, .167

No NHL playoff record.

Stanley Cup Wins: 4 (1906*, 1907*, 1908*, 1910*)

Key Personnel: Odie and Sprague Cleghorn (pre-NHL), Harry Hyland (pre-NHL and NHL), Ernie Johnson (pre-NHL), Jack Marshall (pre-NHL), Art Ross (pre-NHL and NHL), Ernie Russell (pre-NHL)

Ottawa Senators

First NHL Season: 1917-18

Last NHL Season: 1933-34

Franchise Record in NHL:
258w – 221L – 63T, .534

Best Season: 1919-20,
19w – 5L, .792

Playoff Record in NHL:
18w – 17L – 6T, .512

Stanley Cup Wins: 10 (1903*, 1904*, 1905*, 1906*, 1909*, 1911*, 1920, 1921, 1923, 1927)

Key Personnel: Clint Benedict (pre-NHL and NHL), George Boucher (pre-NHL and NHL), Punch Broadbent (pre-NHL and NHL), King Clancy, Jack Darragh (pre-NHL and NHL), Cy Denneny (pre-NHL and NHL), Eddie Gerard (pre-NHL and NHL), Percy LeSueur (pre-NHL), Frank Nighbor (pre-NHL and NHL), Art Ross (pre-NHL)

Toronto Arenas/ Toronto St. Patricks

First NHL Season: 1917-18

Last NHL Season: 1925-26

Franchise Record in NHL:
120w – 129L – 9T, .483

Best Season: 1924-25,
19w – 11L, .633

Playoff Record: 8w – 7L – 3T, .528

Stanley Cup Wins: 2 (1918, 1922)

Key Personnel: Jack Adams, Harry Cameron (pre-NHL and NHL), Hap Day, Corbett Denneny (pre-NHL and NHL), Babe Dye, Frank Foyston (pre-NHL), Hap Holmes (pre-NHL and NHL), Jack Marshall (pre-NHL), Reg Noble (pre-NHL and NHL), John Ross Roach

Quebec Bulldogs

Only NHL Season: 1919-20

Franchise Record in NHL:
4w – 20L, .167

No NHL playoff record.

Stanley Cup Wins: 2 (1912*, 1913*)

Key Personnel: Rusty Crawford (pre-NHL), Joe Hall (pre-NHL), Joe Malone (pre-NHL and NHL), Paddy Moran (pre-NHL), Tommy Smith (pre-NHL), Hod Stuart (pre-NHL)

Hamilton Tigers

First NHL Season: 1920-21

Last NHL Season: 1924-25

Franchise Record:
47w – 78L – 1T, .377

Best Season: 1924-25,
19w – 10L – 1T, .650

No playoff record.

Key Personnel: Billy Burch, Jake Forbes, Joe Malone, Goldie Prodgers, Mickey Roach

Boston Bruins

First NHL Season: 1924-25

Franchise Record:
2084w – 1617L – 651T, .554

Best Season: 1929-30,
38w – 5L – 1T, .875

Playoff Record: 212w – 216L – 6T, .495

Stanley Cup Wins: 5 (1929, 1939, 1941, 1970, 1972)

Key Personnel: Ray Bourque, Frank Brimsek, John Bucyk, Gerry Cheevers, Dit Clapper, Bill Cowley, Phil Esposito, Rick Middleton, Cam Neely, Bobby Orr, Brad Park, Bill Quackenbush, Jean Ratelle, Milt Schmidt, Eddie Shore, Nels Stewart, Tiny Thompson, Cooney Weiland

Montreal Maroons

First NHL Season: 1924-25

Last NHL Season: 1937-38

Franchise Record:
271w – 260L – 91T, .509

Best Season: 1925-26,
20w – 11L – 5T, .625

Playoff Record: 20w – 21L – 9T, .490

Stanley Cup Wins: 2 (1926, 1935)

Key Personnel: Clint Benedict, Toe Blake, Punch Broadbent, Lionel Conacher, Alex Connell, Red Dutton, Baldy Northcott, Babe Siebert, Nels Stewart

*pre-NHL

NEW YORK AMERICANS/ BROOKLYN AMERICANS

First NHL Season: 1925-26

Last NHL Season: 1941-42

Franchise Record:
255w – 402L – 127T, .406

Best Season: 1928-29,
19w – 13L – 12T, .568

Playoff Record: 6w – 11L – 1T, .361
Stanley Cup semi-finalists in 1936 and 1938.

Key Personnel: Billy Burch, Lorne Carr, Red Dutton, Chuck Rayner, Sweeney Schriner, Bullet Joe Simpson, Nels Stewart, Roy Worters

PITTSBURGH PIRATES

First NHL Season: 1925-26

Last NHL Season: 1929-30

Franchise Record:
67w – 122L – 23T, .370

Best Season: 1925-26,
19w – 16L – 1T, .542

Playoff Record: 1w – 2L – 1T, .375
Both playoff series' defeats were to eventual Stanley Cup winners.

Key Personnel: Odie Cleghorn (player-coach), Lionel Conacher, Baldy Cotton, Frank Fredrickson (player-coach), Roy Worters

CHICAGO BLACKHAWKS

First NHL Season: 1926-27

Franchise Record:
1745w – 1876L – 665T, .485

Best Season:
1970-71, 49w – 20L – 9T, .686
1971-72, 46w – 17L – 15T, .686

Playoff Record:
156w – 185L – 5T, .458

Stanley Cup Wins: 3 (1934, 1938, 1961)

Key Personnel: Doug Bentley, Max Bentley, Tony Esposito, Bill Gadsby, Charlie Gardiner, Glenn Hall, Bill Hay, Bobby Hull, Dennis Hull, Dick Irvin, Steve Larmer, Stan Mikita, Pierre Pilote, Jeremy Roenick, Denis Savard, Doug Wilson, Ken Wharram

DETROIT COUGARS/ DETROIT FALCONS

First NHL Season: 1926-27

Last NHL Season: 1931-32

Franchise Record:
98w – 128L – 42T, .444

Best Season: 1928-29,
19w – 16L – 9T, .534

Playoff Record: 0w – 3L – 1T, .125
Played in two series, losing them both.

Key Personnel: Larry Aurie, Carson Cooper, Frank Foyston, Ebbie Goodfellow, George Hay, Hap Holmes, Duke Keats, Herbie Lewis, Reg Noble, Jack Walker

NEW YORK RANGERS

First NHL Season: 1926-27

Franchise Record:
1779w – 1817L – 690T, .496

Best Seasons:
1970-71, 49w – 18L – 11T, .699
1971-72, 48w – 17L – 13T, .699

Playoff Record: 143w – 163L – 8T, .468

Stanley Cup Wins: 3 (1928, 1933, 1940)

Key Personnel: Andy Bathgate, Frank Boucher, Johnny Bower, Bill Cook, Bun Cook, Phil Esposito, Bill Gadsby, Bernie Geoffrion, Ed Giacomin, Rod Gilbert, Vic Hadfield, Doug Harvey, Bryan Hextall, Sr., Harry Howell, Ching Johnson, Brian Leetch, Brad Park, Lynn Patrick, Jacques Plante, Jean Ratelle, John Vanbiesbrouck, Gump Worsley

TORONTO MAPLE LEAFS

First NHL Season: 1926-27

Franchise Record:
1927w – 1921L – 664T, .501*

Best Season: 1950-51,
41w – 16L – 13T, .679

Playoff Record:
177w – 194L – 3T, .477*

Stanley Cup Wins: 11 (1932, 1942, 1945, 1947, 1948, 1949, 1951, 1962, 1963, 1964, 1967)

Key Personnel: Syl Apps, George Armstrong, Ace Bailey, Johnny Bower, Turk Broda, King Clancy, Wendel Clark, Charlie Conacher, Hap Day, Paul Henderson, Tim Horton, Busher Jackson, Red Kelly, Ted Kennedy, Dave Keon, Gary Leeman, Harry Lumley, Frank Mahovlich, Lanny McDonald, Joe Primeau, Borje Salming, Darryl Sittler, Rick Vaive

*Includes totals of the Toronto Arenas/Toronto St. Patricks

PHILADELPHIA QUAKERS

Only NHL Season: 1930-31

Franchise Record:
4w – 36L – 4T, .136

No playoff record.

Key Personnel: Wilf Cude, Jake Forbes, Syd Howe, Hib Milks. Managed and coached by Hall of Famer Cooper Smeaton.

DETROIT RED WINGS

First NHL Season: 1932-33

Franchise Record:
1759w – 1842L – 685T, .490*

Best Season: 1950-51,
44w – 13L – 13T, .721

Playoff Record:
158w – 167L – 1T, .486*

Stanley Cup Wins: 7 (1936, 1937, 1943, 1950, 1952, 1954, 1955)

Key Personnel: Sid Abel, Larry Aurie, Roger Crozier, Alex Delvecchio, Marcel Dionne, Bill Gadsby, Glenn Hall, Syd Howe, Gordie Howe, Red Kelly, Herbie Lewis, Ted Lindsay, Frank Mahovlich, Marcel Pronovost, Bill Quackenbush, Mickey Redmond, Terry Sawchuk, Norm Ullman, Steve Yzerman

*Includes totals of the Detroit Cougars/Detroit Falcons

St. Louis Eagles

Only NHL Season: 1934-35

Franchise Record:
11w – 31l – 6t, .292

No playoff record.

Key Personnel: Bill Beveridge, Bill Cowley, Frank Finnigan, Syd Howe, Carl Voss. Managed and coached by Eddie Gerard, who was later replaced by George Boucher.

Los Angeles Kings

First NHL Season: 1967-68

Franchise Record:
744w – 878l – 276t, .465

Best Season: 1974-75,
42w – 17l – 21t, .656

Playoff Record: 40w – 72l, .357
Upset defending Stanley Cup champions during playoffs in 1989 and 1990.

Key Personnel: Marcel Dionne, Butch Goring, Wayne Gretzky, Kelly Hrudey, Larry Robinson, Luc Robitaille, Terry Sawchuk, Charlie Simmer, Dave Taylor, Rogie Vachon

Minnesota North Stars

First NHL Season: 1967-68

Franchise Record:
690w – 890l – 318t, .447

Best Season: 1982-83,
40w – 24l – 16t, .600

Playoff Record: 77w – 82l, .484
Stanley Cup finalists in 1981 and 1991.

Key Personnel: Brian Bellows, Neal Broten, Jon Casey, Dino Ciccarelli, Bill Goldsworthy, Danny Grant, Craig Hartsburg, Cesare Maniago, Gilles Meloche, Lou Nanne, J. P. Parise, Bobby Smith, Gump Worsley

Oakland Seals/ California Seals/ California Golden Seals

First NHL Season: 1967-68

Last NHL Season: 1975-76

Franchise Record:
182w – 401l – 115t, .343

Best Season: 1968-69,
29w – 36l – 11t, .454

Playoff Record: 3w – 8l, .273
Played in two playoff series, losing both.

Key Personnel: Bob Baun, Ivan Boldirev, Ted Hampson, Bill Hicke, Charlie Hodge, Harry Howell, Reggie Leach, Al MacAdam, Dennis Maruk, Walt McKechnie, Gilles Meloche, Craig Patrick, Charlie Simmer, Carol Vadnais

Philadelphia Flyers

First NHL Season: 1967-68

Franchise Record:
953w – 641l – 304t, .582

Best Season: 1979-80,
48w – 12l – 20t, .725

Playoff Record: 116w – 107l, .520

Stanley Cup Wins: 2 (1974, 1975)

Key Personnel: Bill Barber, Bobby Clarke, Gary Dornhoefer, Ron Hextall, Mark Howe, Tim Kerr, Reggie Leach, Rick MacLeish, Bernie Parent, Brian Propp, Rick Tocchet, Jim and Joe Watson

Pittsburgh Penguins

First NHL Season: 1967-68

Franchise Record:
709w – 921l – 268t, .444

Best Season: 1974-75,
37w – 28l – 15t, .556

Playoff Record: 44w – 42l, .512

Stanley Cup Wins: 1 (1991)

Key Personnel: Syl Apps, Jr., Tom Barrasso, Les Binkley, Randy Carlyle, Paul Coffey, John Cullen, Rick Kehoe, Pierre Larouche, Mario Lemieux, Jean Pronovost, Mark Recchi, Kevin Stevens

St. Louis Blues

First NHL Season: 1967-68

Franchise Record:
780w – 825l – 293t, .488

Best Season: 1980-81,
45w – 18l – 17t, .669

Playoff Record: 84w – 105l, .444
Stanley Cup finalists in 1968, 1969, 1970.

Key Personnel: Red Berenson, Bernie Federko, Doug Gilmour, Glenn Hall, Brett Hull, Mike Liut, Joe Mullen, Adam Oates, Barclay Plager, Jacques Plante, Rob Ramage, Brian Sutter, Garry Unger

Buffalo Sabres

First NHL Season: 1970-71

Franchise Record:
797w – 601l – 274t, .559

Best Season: 1974-75,
49w – 16l – 15t, .706

Playoff Record: 51w – 65l, .440
Stanley Cup finalists in 1975.

Key Personnel: Dave Andreychuk, Tom Barrasso, Roger Crozier, Danny Gare, Dale Hawerchuk, Tim Horton, Phil Housley, Rick Martin, Gil Perreault, René Robert, Jim Schoenfeld, Pierre Turgeon

Vancouver Canucks

First NHL Season: 1970-71

Franchise Record:
566w – 855l – 251t, .414

Best Season: 1974-75,
38w – 32l – 10t, .538

Playoff Record: 21w – 37l, .362
Stanley Cup finalists in 1982.

Key Personnel: André Boudrias, Richard Brodeur, Thomas Gradin, Orland Kurtenbach, Don Lever, Trevor Linden, Stan Smyl, Harold Snepsts, Tony Tanti, Dale Tallon

ATLANTA FLAMES

First NHL Season: 1972-73

Last NHL Season: 1979-80

Franchise Record:
268w – 260L – 108T, .506

Best Season: 1978-79,
41w – 31L – 8T, .563

Playoff Record:
2w – 15L, .118
Played in six series, losing them all.

Key Personnel: Dan Bouchard, Bill Clement, Guy Chouinard, Tom Lysiak, Phil Myre, Willi Plett, Pat Quinn, Eric Vail

NEW YORK ISLANDERS

First NHL Season: 1972-73

Franchise Record:
722w – 571L – 223T, .550

Best Season: 1981-82,
54w – 16L – 10T, .738

Playoff Record: 119w – 77L, .607

Stanley Cup Wins: 4 (1980, 1981, 1982, 1983)

Key Personnel: Mike Bossy, Clark Gillies, Butch Goring, Kelly Hrudey, Pat LaFontaine, Denis Potvin, Chico Resch, Billy Smith, Brent Sutter, John Tonelli, Bryan Trottier

KANSAS CITY SCOUTS

First NHL Season: 1974-75

Last NHL Season: 1975-76

Franchise Record:
27w – 110L – 23T, .241

Best Season: 15w – 54L – 11T, .256

No playoff record.

Key Personnel: Gary Bergman, Guy Charron, Nick Libett, Simon Nolet, Wilf Paiment, Craig Patrick

WASHINGTON CAPITALS

First NHL Season: 1974-75

Franchise Record:
536w – 643L – 181T, .461

Best Season: 1985-86,
50w – 23L – 7T, .669

Playoff Record: 37w – 42L, .468
Stanley Cup semi-finalists in 1990.

Key Personnel: Dave Christian, Dino Ciccarelli, Mike Gartner, Kevin Hatcher, Dale Hunter, Doug Jarvis, Rod Langway, Larry Murphy, Pete Peeters, Scott Stevens, Ryan Walter

CLEVELAND BARONS

First NHL Season: 1976-77

Last NHL Season: 1977-78

Franchise Record:
47w – 87L – 26T, .375

Best Season: 1976-77,
25w – 42L – 13T, .394

No playoff record.

Key Personnel: Al MacAdam, Dennis Maruk, Walt McKechnie, Gilles Meloche, Jim Neilson, Jim Pappin, J. P. Parise, Charlie Simmer

COLORADO ROCKIES

First NHL Season: 1976-77

Last NHL Season: 1981-82

Franchise Record:
113w – 281L – 86T, .325

Best Season: 1977-78,
19w – 40L – 21T, .369

Playoff Record: 0w – 2L, .000

Key Personnel: Brent Ashton, Barry Beck, Doug Favell, Lanny McDonald, Simon Nolet, Wilf Paiment, Rob Ramage, Chico Resch, René Robert

EDMONTON OILERS

First NHL Season: 1979-80

Franchise Record:
521w – 315L – 124T, .607

Best Season: 1983-84,
57w – 18L – 5T, .744

Playoff Record: 112w – 52L, .683

Stanley Cup Wins: 5 (1984, 1985, 1987, 1988, 1990)

Key Personnel: Glenn Anderson, Paul Coffey, Grant Fuhr, Randy Gregg, Wayne Gretzky, Charlie Huddy, Jari Kurri, Kevin Lowe, Mark Messier, Andy Moog, Bill Ranford, Esa Tikkanen

HARTFORD WHALERS

First NHL Season: 1979-80

Franchise Record:
370w – 466L – 124T, .450

Best Season: 1986-87,
43w – 30L – 7T, .581

Playoff Record: 15w – 27L, .357
Lost deciding game of 1986 division final in overtime to eventual Stanley Cup winner.

Key Personnel: John Cullen, Kevin Dineen, Ron Francis, Gordie Howe, Mark Howe, Dave Keon, Mike Liut, Mike Rogers, Pat Verbeek

QUEBEC NORDIQUES

First NHL Season: 1979-80

Franchise Record:
366w – 469L – 125T, .446

Best Season: 1983-84,
42w – 28L – 10T, .588

Playoff Record: 31w – 37L, .456
Stanley Cup semi-finalists in 1982 and 1985.

Key Personnel: Dan Bouchard, Michel Goulet, Dale Hunter, Guy Lafleur, Joe Sakic, Anton and Peter Stastny, Mats Sundin, Marc Tardif

WINNIPEG JETS

First NHL Season: 1979-80

Franchise Record:
357w – 475L – 128T, .439

Best Season: 1984-85,
43w – 27L – 10T, .600

Playoff Record: 12w – 31L, .279
Lost playoff series to eventual Stanley Cup champions in 1984, 1985, 1987, 1988, 1990.

Key Personnel: Dave Babych, Laurie Boschman, Dave Ellett, Dale Hawerchuk, Phil Housley, Bobby Hull, Morris Lukowich, Serge Savard, Doug Smail, Thomas Steen

CALGARY FLAMES

First NHL Season: 1980-81

Franchise Record:
451w – 305L – 124T, .583

Best Season: 1988-89,
54w – 17L – 9T, .731

Playoff Record: 59w – 56L, .513

Stanley Cup Wins: 1 (1989)

Key Personnel: Theoren Fleury, Reggie Lemelin, Hakan Loob, Al MacInnis, Lanny McDonald, Joe Mullen, Joe Nieuwendyk, Kent Nilsson, Jim Peplinski, Paul Reinhart, Gary Suter, Mike Vernon

NEW JERSEY DEVILS

First NHL Season: 1982-83

Franchise Record:
247w – 392L – 81T, .399

Best Season: 1989-90,
37w – 34L – 9T, .519

Playoff Record: 16w – 17L, .485
Stanley Cup semi-finalists in 1988.

Key Personnel: Mel Bridgman, Sean Burke, Aaron Broten, Viacheslav Fetisov, John MacLean, Kirk Muller, Chico Resch, Brendan Shanahan, Peter Stastny, Pat Verbeek

SAN JOSE SHARKS

First NHL Season: 1991-92

Key Personnel: Pat Falloon, Brian Hayward, Tony Hrkac, Kelly Kisio, Brian Mullen, Neil Wilkinson, Rob Zetter

Year-By-Year Final Standings

*Stanley Cup winner.

1917-18

Team	GP	W	L	T	GF	GA	PTS
Montreal	22	13	9	0	115	84	26
*Toronto	22	13	9	0	108	109	26
Ottawa	22	9	13	0	102	114	18
**Mtl. Wanderers	6	1	5	0	17	35	2

**Montreal Arena burned down and Wanderers forced to withdraw from League. Canadiens and Toronto each counted a win for defaulted games with Wanderers.

1918-19

Team	GP	W	L	T	GF	GA	PTS
Ottawa	18	12	6	0	71	53	24
Montreal	18	10	8	0	88	78	20
Toronto	18	5	13	0	64	92	10

1919-20

Team	GP	W	L	T	GF	GA	PTS
*Ottawa	24	19	5	0	121	64	38
Montreal	24	13	11	0	129	113	26
Toronto	24	12	12	0	119	106	24
Quebec	24	4	20	0	91	177	8

1920-21

Team	GP	W	L	T	GF	GA	PTS
Toronto	24	15	9	0	105	100	30
*Ottawa	24	14	10	0	97	75	28
Montreal	24	13	11	0	112	99	26
Hamilton	24	6	18	0	92	132	12

1921-22

Team	GP	W	L	T	GF	GA	PTS
Ottawa	24	14	8	2	106	84	30
*Toronto	24	13	10	1	98	97	27
Montreal	24	12	11	1	88	94	25
Hamilton	24	7	17	0	88	105	14

1922-23

Team	GP	W	L	T	GF	GA	PTS
*Ottawa	24	14	9	1	77	54	29
Montreal	24	13	9	2	73	61	28
Toronto	24	13	10	1	82	88	27
Hamilton	24	6	18	0	81	110	12

1923-24

Team	GP	W	L	T	GF	GA	PTS
Ottawa	24	16	8	0	74	54	32
*Montreal	24	13	11	0	59	48	26
Toronto	24	10	14	0	59	85	20
Hamilton	24	9	15	0	63	68	18

1924-25

Team	GP	W	L	T	GF	GA	PTS
Hamilton	30	19	10	1	90	60	39
Toronto	30	19	11	0	90	84	38
Montreal	30	17	11	2	93	56	36
Ottawa	30	17	12	1	83	66	35
Mtl. Maroons	30	9	19	2	45	65	20
Boston	30	6	24	0	49	119	12

1925-26

Team	GP	W	L	T	GF	GA	PTS
Ottawa	36	24	8	4	77	42	52
*Mtl. Maroons	36	20	11	5	91	73	45
Pittsburgh	36	19	16	1	82	70	39
Boston	36	17	15	4	92	85	38
NY Americans	36	12	20	4	68	89	28
Toronto	36	12	21	3	92	114	27
Montreal	36	11	24	1	79	108	23

1926-27
Canadian Division

Team	GP	W	L	T	GF	GA	PTS
*Ottawa	44	30	10	4	86	69	64
Montreal	44	28	14	2	99	67	58
Mtl. Maroons	44	20	20	4	71	68	44
NY Americans	44	17	25	2	82	91	36
Toronto	44	15	24	5	79	94	35

American Division

Team	GP	W	L	T	GF	GA	PTS
New York	44	25	13	6	95	72	56
Boston	44	21	20	3	97	89	45
Chicago	44	19	22	3	115	116	41
Pittsburgh	44	15	26	3	79	108	33
Detroit	44	12	28	4	76	105	28

1927-28
Canadian Division

Team	GP	W	L	T	GF	GA	PTS
Montreal	44	26	11	7	116	48	59
Mtl. Maroons	44	24	14	6	96	77	54
Ottawa	44	20	14	10	78	57	50
Toronto	44	18	18	8	89	88	44
NY Americans	44	11	27	6	63	128	28

American Division

Team	GP	W	L	T	GF	GA	PTS
Boston	44	20	13	11	77	70	51
*New York	44	19	16	9	94	79	47
Pittsburgh	44	19	17	8	67	76	46
Detroit	44	19	19	6	88	79	44
Chicago	44	7	34	3	68	134	17

1928-29
Canadian Division

Team	GP	W	L	T	GF	GA	PTS
Montreal	44	22	7	15	71	43	59
NY Americans	44	19	13	12	53	53	50
Toronto	44	21	18	5	85	69	47
Ottawa	44	14	17	13	54	67	41
Mtl. Maroons	44	15	20	9	67	65	39

American Division

Team	GP	W	L	T	GF	GA	PTS
*Boston	44	26	13	5	89	52	57
New York	44	21	13	10	72	65	52
Detroit	44	19	16	9	72	63	47
Pittsburgh	44	9	27	8	46	80	26
Chicago	44	7	29	8	33	85	22

1929-30
Canadian Division

Team	GP	W	L	T	GF	GA	PTS
Mtl. Maroons	44	23	16	5	141	114	51
*Montreal	44	21	14	9	142	114	51
Ottawa	44	21	15	8	138	118	50
Toronto	44	17	21	6	116	124	40
NY Americans	44	14	25	5	113	161	33

American Division

Team	GP	W	L	T	GF	GA	PTS
Boston	44	38	5	1	179	98	77
Chicago	44	21	18	5	117	111	47
New York	44	17	17	10	136	143	44
Detroit	44	14	24	6	117	133	34
Pittsburgh	44	5	36	3	102	185	13

1930-31
Canadian Division

Team	GP	W	L	T	GF	GA	PTS
*Montreal	44	26	10	8	129	89	60
Toronto	44	22	13	9	118	99	53
Mtl. Maroons	44	20	18	6	105	106	46
NY Americans	44	18	16	10	76	74	46
Ottawa	44	10	30	4	91	142	24

American Division

Boston	44	28	10	6	143	90	62
Chicago	44	24	17	3	108	78	51
New York	44	19	16	9	106	87	47
Detroit	44	16	21	7	102	105	39
Philadelphia	44	4	36	4	76	184	12

1931-32
Canadian Division

Team	GP	W	L	T	GF	GA	PTS
Montreal	48	25	16	7	128	111	57
*Toronto	48	23	18	7	155	127	53
Mtl. Maroons	48	19	22	7	142	139	45
NY Americans	48	16	24	8	95	142	40

American Division

New York	48	23	17	8	134	112	54
Chicago	48	18	19	11	86	101	47
Detroit	48	18	20	10	95	108	46
Boston	48	15	21	12	122	117	42

1932-33
Canadian Division

Team	GP	W	L	T	GF	GA	PTS
Toronto	48	24	18	6	119	111	54
Mtl. Maroons	48	22	20	6	135	119	50
Montreal	48	18	25	5	92	115	41
NY Americans	48	15	22	11	91	118	41
Ottawa	48	11	27	10	88	131	32

American Division

Boston	48	25	15	8	124	88	58
Detroit	48	25	15	8	111	93	58
*New York	48	23	17	8	135	107	54
Chicago	48	16	20	12	88	101	44

1933-34
Canadian Division

Team	GP	W	L	T	GF	GA	PTS
Toronto	48	26	13	9	174	119	61
Montreal	48	22	20	6	99	101	50
Mtl. Maroons	48	19	18	11	117	122	49
NY Americans	48	15	23	10	104	132	40
Ottawa	48	13	29	6	115	143	32

American Division

Detroit	48	24	14	10	113	98	58
*Chicago	48	20	17	11	88	83	51
New York	48	21	19	8	120	113	50
Boston	48	18	25	5	111	130	41

1934-35
Canadian Division

Team	GP	W	L	T	GF	GA	PTS
Toronto	48	30	14	4	157	111	64
*Mtl. Maroons	48	24	19	5	123	92	53
Montreal	48	19	23	6	110	145	44
NY Americans	48	12	27	9	100	142	33
St. Louis	48	11	31	6	86	144	28

American Division

Boston	48	26	16	6	129	112	58
Chicago	48	26	17	5	118	88	57
New York	48	22	20	6	137	139	50
Detroit	48	19	22	7	127	114	45

1935-36
Canadian Division

Team	GP	W	L	T	GF	GA	PTS
Mtl. Maroons	48	22	16	10	114	106	54
Toronto	48	23	19	6	126	106	52
NY Americans	48	16	25	7	109	122	39
Montreal	48	11	26	11	82	123	33

American Division

*Detroit	48	24	16	8	124	103	56
Boston	48	22	20	6	92	83	50
Chicago	48	21	19	8	93	92	50
New York	48	19	17	12	91	96	50

1936-37
Canadian Division

Team	GP	W	L	T	GF	GA	PTS
Montreal	48	24	18	6	115	111	54
Mtl. Maroons	48	22	17	9	126	110	53
Toronto	48	22	21	5	119	115	49
NY Americans	48	15	29	4	122	161	34

American Division

*Detroit	48	25	14	9	128	102	59
Boston	48	23	18	7	120	110	53
New York	48	19	20	9	117	106	47
Chicago	48	14	27	7	99	131	35

1937-38
Canadian Division

Team	GP	W	L	T	GF	GA	PTS
Toronto	48	24	15	9	151	127	57
NY Americans	48	19	18	11	110	111	49
Montreal	48	18	17	13	123	128	49
Mtl. Maroons	48	12	30	6	101	149	30

American Division

Boston	48	30	11	7	142	89	67
New York	48	27	15	6	149	96	60
*Chicago	48	14	25	9	97	139	37
Detroit	48	12	25	11	99	133	35

1938-39

Team	GP	W	L	T	GF	GA	PTS
*Boston	48	36	10	2	156	76	74
New York	48	26	16	6	149	105	58
Toronto	48	19	20	9	114	107	47
NY Americans	48	17	21	10	119	157	44
Detroit	48	18	24	6	107	128	42
Montreal	48	15	24	9	115	146	39
Chicago	48	12	28	8	91	132	32

1939-40

Team	GP	W	L	T	GF	GA	PTS
Boston	48	31	12	5	170	98	67
*New York	48	27	11	10	136	77	64
Toronto	48	25	17	6	134	110	56
Chicago	48	23	19	6	112	120	52
Detroit	48	16	26	6	91	126	38
NY Americans	48	15	29	4	106	140	34
Montreal	48	10	33	5	90	168	25

1940-41

Team	GP	W	L	T	GF	GA	PTS
*Boston	48	27	8	13	168	102	67
Toronto	48	28	14	6	145	99	62
Detroit	48	21	16	11	112	102	53
New York	48	21	19	8	143	125	50
Chicago	48	16	25	7	112	139	39
Montreal	48	16	26	6	121	147	38
NY Americans	48	8	29	11	99	186	27

1941-42

Team	GP	W	L	T	GF	GA	PTS
New York	48	29	17	2	177	143	60
*Toronto	48	27	18	3	158	136	57
Boston	48	25	17	6	160	118	56
Chicago	48	22	23	3	145	155	47
Detroit	48	19	25	4	140	147	42
Montreal	48	18	27	3	134	173	39
Brooklyn	48	16	29	3	133	175	35

1942-43

Team	GP	W	L	T	GF	GA	PTS
*Detroit	50	25	14	11	169	124	61
Boston	50	24	17	9	195	176	57
Toronto	50	22	19	9	198	159	53
Montreal	50	19	19	12	181	191	50
Chicago	50	17	18	15	179	180	49
New York	50	11	31	8	161	253	30

1943-44

Team	GP	W	L	T	GF	GA	PTS
*Montreal	50	38	5	7	234	109	83
Detroit	50	26	18	6	214	177	58
Toronto	50	23	23	4	214	174	50
Chicago	50	22	23	5	178	187	49
Boston	50	19	26	5	223	268	43
New York	50	6	39	5	162	310	17

1944-45

Team	GP	W	L	T	GF	GA	PTS
Montreal	50	38	8	4	228	121	80
Detroit	50	31	14	5	218	161	67
*Toronto	50	24	22	4	183	161	52
Boston	50	16	30	4	179	219	36
Chicago	50	13	30	7	141	194	33
New York	50	11	29	10	154	247	32

1945-46

Team	GP	W	L	T	GF	GA	PTS
*Montreal	50	28	17	5	172	134	61
Boston	50	24	18	8	167	156	56
Chicago	50	23	20	7	200	178	53
Detroit	50	20	20	10	146	159	50
Toronto	50	19	24	7	174	185	45
New York	50	13	28	9	144	191	35

1946-47

Team	GP	W	L	T	GF	GA	PTS
Montreal	60	34	16	10	189	138	78
*Toronto	60	31	19	10	209	172	72
Boston	60	26	23	11	190	175	63
Detroit	60	22	27	11	190	193	55
New York	60	22	32	6	167	186	50
Chicago	60	19	37	4	193	274	42

1947-48

Team	GP	W	L	T	GF	GA	PTS
*Toronto	60	32	15	13	182	143	77
Detroit	60	30	18	12	187	148	72
Boston	60	23	24	13	167	168	59
New York	60	21	26	13	176	201	55
Montreal	60	20	29	11	147	169	51
Chicago	60	20	34	6	195	225	46

1948-49

Team	GP	W	L	T	GF	GA	PTS
Detroit	60	34	19	7	195	145	75
Boston	60	29	23	8	178	163	66
Montreal	60	28	23	9	152	126	65
*Toronto	60	22	25	13	147	161	57
Chicago	60	21	31	8	173	211	50
New York	60	18	31	11	133	172	47

1949-50

Team	GP	W	L	T	GF	GA	PTS
*Detroit	70	37	19	14	229	164	88
Montreal	70	29	22	19	172	150	77
Toronto	70	31	27	12	176	173	74
New York	70	28	31	11	170	189	67
Boston	70	22	32	16	198	228	60
Chicago	70	22	38	10	203	244	54

1950-51

Team	GP	W	L	T	GF	GA	PTS
Detroit	70	44	13	13	236	139	101
*Toronto	70	41	16	13	212	138	95
Montreal	70	25	30	15	173	184	65
Boston	70	22	30	18	178	197	62
New York	70	20	29	21	169	201	62
Chicago	70	13	47	10	171	280	36

1951-52

Team	GP	W	L	T	GF	GA	PTS
*Detroit	70	44	14	12	215	133	100
Montreal	70	34	26	10	195	164	78
Toronto	70	29	25	16	168	157	74
Boston	70	25	29	16	162	176	66
New York	70	23	34	13	192	219	59
Chicago	70	17	44	9	158	241	43

1952-53

Team	GP	W	L	T	GF	GA	PTS
Detroit	70	36	16	18	222	133	90
*Montreal	70	28	23	19	155	148	75
Boston	70	28	29	13	152	172	69
Chicago	70	27	28	15	169	175	69
Toronto	70	27	30	13	156	167	67
New York	70	17	37	16	152	211	50

1953-54

Team	GP	W	L	T	GF	GA	PTS
*Detroit	70	37	19	14	191	132	88
Montreal	70	35	24	11	195	141	81
Toronto	70	32	24	14	152	131	78
Boston	70	32	28	10	177	181	74
New York	70	29	31	10	161	182	68
Chicago	70	12	51	7	133	242	31

1954-55

Team	GP	W	L	T	GF	GA	PTS
*Detroit	70	42	17	11	204	134	95
Montreal	70	41	18	11	228	157	93
Toronto	70	24	24	22	147	135	70
Boston	70	23	26	21	169	188	67
New York	70	17	35	18	150	210	52
Chicago	70	13	40	17	161	235	43

1955-56

Team	GP	W	L	T	GF	GA	PTS
*Montreal	70	45	15	10	222	131	100
Detroit	70	30	24	16	183	148	76
New York	70	32	28	10	204	203	74
Toronto	70	24	33	13	153	181	61
Boston	70	23	34	13	147	185	59
Chicago	70	19	39	12	155	216	50

1956-57

Team	GP	W	L	T	GF	GA	PTS
Detroit	70	38	20	12	198	157	88
*Montreal	70	35	23	12	210	155	82
Boston	70	34	24	12	195	174	80
New York	70	26	30	14	184	227	66
Toronto	70	21	34	15	174	192	57
Chicago	70	16	39	15	169	225	47

1957-58

Team	GP	W	L	T	GF	GA	PTS
*Montreal	70	43	17	10	250	158	96
New York	70	32	25	13	195	188	77
Detroit	70	29	29	12	176	207	70
Boston	70	27	28	15	199	194	69
Chicago	70	24	39	7	163	202	55
Toronto	70	21	38	11	192	226	53

1958-59

Team	GP	W	L	T	GF	GA	PTS
*Montreal	70	39	18	13	258	158	91
Boston	70	32	29	9	205	215	73
Chicago	70	28	29	13	197	208	69
Toronto	70	27	32	11	189	201	65
New York	70	26	32	12	201	217	64
Detroit	70	25	37	8	167	218	58

1959-60

Team	GP	W	L	T	GF	GA	PTS
*Montreal	70	40	18	12	255	178	92
Toronto	70	35	26	9	199	195	79
Chicago	70	28	29	13	191	180	69
Detroit	70	26	29	15	186	197	67
Boston	70	28	34	8	220	241	64
New York	70	17	38	15	187	247	49

1960-61

Team	GP	W	L	T	GF	GA	PTS
Montreal	70	41	19	10	254	188	92
Toronto	70	39	19	12	234	176	90
*Chicago	70	29	24	17	198	180	75
Detroit	70	25	29	16	195	215	66
New York	70	22	38	10	204	248	54
Boston	70	15	42	13	176	254	43

1961-62

Team	GP	W	L	T	GF	GA	PTS
Montreal	70	42	14	14	259	166	98
*Toronto	70	37	22	11	232	180	85
Chicago	70	31	26	13	217	186	75
New York	70	26	32	12	195	207	64
Detroit	70	23	33	14	184	219	60
Boston	70	15	47	8	177	306	38

1962-63

Team	GP	W	L	T	GF	GA	PTS
*Toronto	70	35	23	12	221	180	82
Chicago	70	32	21	17	194	178	81
Montreal	70	28	19	23	225	183	79
Detroit	70	32	25	13	200	194	77
New York	70	22	36	12	211	233	56
Boston	70	14	39	17	198	281	45

1963-64

Team	GP	W	L	T	GF	GA	PTS
Montreal	70	36	21	13	209	167	85
Chicago	70	36	22	12	218	169	84
*Toronto	70	33	25	12	192	172	78
Detroit	70	30	29	11	191	204	71
New York	70	22	38	10	186	242	54
Boston	70	18	40	12	170	212	48

1964-65

Team	GP	W	L	T	GF	GA	PTS
Detroit	70	40	23	7	224	175	87
*Montreal	70	36	23	11	211	185	83
Chicago	70	34	28	8	224	176	76
Toronto	70	30	26	14	204	173	74
New York	70	20	38	12	179	246	52
Boston	70	21	43	6	166	253	48

1965-66

Team	GP	W	L	T	GF	GA	PTS
*Montreal	70	41	21	8	239	173	90
Chicago	70	37	25	8	240	187	82
Toronto	70	34	25	11	208	187	79
Detroit	70	31	27	12	221	194	74
Boston	70	21	43	6	174	275	48
New York	70	18	41	11	195	261	47

1966-67

Team	GP	W	L	T	GF	GA	PTS
Chicago	70	41	17	12	264	170	94
Montreal	70	32	25	13	202	188	77
*Toronto	70	32	27	11	204	211	75
New York	70	30	28	12	188	189	72
Detroit	70	27	39	4	212	241	58
Boston	70	17	43	10	182	253	44

1967-68

East Division

Team	GP	W	L	T	GF	GA	PTS
*Montreal	74	42	22	10	236	167	94
New York	74	39	23	12	226	183	90
Boston	74	37	27	10	259	216	84
Chicago	74	32	26	16	212	222	80
Toronto	74	33	31	10	209	176	76
Detroit	74	27	35	12	245	257	66

West Division

Team	GP	W	L	T	GF	GA	PTS
Philadelphia	74	31	32	11	173	179	73
Los Angeles	74	31	33	10	200	224	72
St. Louis	74	27	31	16	177	191	70
Minnesota	74	27	32	15	191	226	69
Pittsburgh	74	27	34	13	195	216	67
Oakland	74	15	42	17	153	219	47

1968-69

East Division

Team	GP	W	L	T	GF	GA	PTS
*Montreal	76	46	19	11	271	202	103
Boston	76	42	18	16	303	221	100
New York	76	41	26	9	231	196	91
Toronto	76	35	26	15	234	217	85
Detroit	76	33	31	12	239	221	78
Chicago	76	34	33	9	280	246	77

West Division

Team	GP	W	L	T	GF	GA	PTS
St. Louis	76	37	25	14	204	157	88
Oakland	76	29	36	11	219	251	69
Philadelphia	76	20	35	21	174	225	61
Los Angeles	76	24	42	10	185	260	58
Pittsburgh	76	20	45	11	189	252	51
Minnesota	76	18	43	15	189	270	51

1969-70

East Division

Team	GP	W	L	T	GF	GA	PTS
Chicago	76	45	22	9	250	170	99
*Boston	76	40	17	19	277	216	99
Detroit	76	40	21	15	246	199	95
New York	76	38	22	16	246	189	92
Montreal	76	38	22	16	244	201	92
Toronto	76	29	34	13	222	242	71

West Division

Team	GP	W	L	T	GF	GA	PTS
St. Louis	76	37	27	12	224	179	86
Pittsburgh	76	26	38	12	182	238	64
Minnesota	76	19	35	22	224	257	60
Oakland	76	22	40	14	169	243	58
Philadelphia	76	17	35	24	197	225	58
Los Angeles	76	14	52	10	168	290	38

1970-71

East Division

Team	GP	W	L	T	GF	GA	PTS
Boston	78	57	14	7	399	207	121
New York	78	49	18	11	259	177	109
*Montreal	78	42	23	13	291	216	97
Toronto	78	37	33	8	248	211	82
Buffalo	78	24	39	15	217	291	63
Vancouver	78	24	46	8	229	296	56
Detroit	78	22	45	11	209	308	55

West Division

Team	GP	W	L	T	GF	GA	PTS
Chicago	78	49	20	9	277	184	107
St. Louis	78	34	25	19	223	208	87
Philadelphia	78	28	33	17	207	225	73
Minnesota	78	28	34	16	191	223	72
Los Angeles	78	25	40	13	239	303	63
Pittsburgh	78	21	37	20	221	240	62
California	78	20	53	5	199	320	45

1971-72

East Division

Team	GP	W	L	T	GF	GA	PTS
*Boston	78	54	13	11	330	204	119
New York	78	48	17	13	317	192	109
Montreal	78	46	16	16	307	205	108
Toronto	78	33	31	14	209	208	80
Detroit	78	33	35	10	261	262	76
Buffalo	78	16	43	19	203	289	51
Vancouver	78	20	50	8	203	297	48

West Division

Team	GP	W	L	T	GF	GA	PTS
Chicago	78	46	17	15	256	166	107
Minnesota	78	37	29	12	212	191	86
St. Louis	78	28	39	11	208	247	67
Pittsburgh	78	26	38	14	220	258	66
Philadelphia	78	26	38	14	200	236	66
California	78	21	39	18	216	288	60
Los Angeles	78	20	49	9	206	305	49

1972-73

East Division

Team	GP	W	L	T	GF	GA	PTS
*Montreal	78	52	10	16	329	184	120
Boston	78	51	22	5	330	235	107
NY Rangers	78	47	23	8	297	208	102
Buffalo	78	37	27	14	257	219	88
Detroit	78	37	29	12	265	243	86
Toronto	78	27	41	10	247	279	64
Vancouver	78	22	47	9	233	339	53
NY Islanders	78	12	60	6	170	347	30

West Division

Team	GP	W	L	T	GF	GA	PTS
Chicago	78	42	27	9	284	225	93
Philadelphia	78	37	30	11	296	256	85
Minnesota	78	37	30	11	254	230	85
St. Louis	78	32	34	12	233	251	76
Pittsburgh	78	32	37	9	257	265	73
Los Angeles	78	31	36	11	232	245	73
Atlanta	78	25	38	15	191	239	65
California	78	16	46	16	213	323	48

1973-74

East Division

Team	GP	W	L	T	GF	GA	PTS
Boston	78	52	17	9	349	221	113
Montreal	78	45	24	9	293	240	99
NY Rangers	78	40	24	14	300	251	94
Toronto	78	35	27	16	274	230	86
Buffalo	78	32	34	12	242	250	76
Detroit	78	29	39	10	255	319	68
Vancouver	78	24	43	11	224	296	59
NY Islanders	78	19	41	18	182	247	56

West Division

Team	GP	W	L	T	GF	GA	PTS
*Philadelphia	78	50	16	12	273	164	112
Chicago	78	41	14	23	272	164	105
Los Angeles	78	33	33	12	233	231	78
Atlanta	78	30	34	14	214	238	74
Pittsburgh	78	28	41	9	242	273	65
St. Louis	78	26	40	12	206	248	64
Minnesota	78	23	38	17	235	275	63
California	78	13	55	10	195	342	36

1974-75

PRINCE OF WALES CONFERENCE

Norris Division

Team	GP	W	L	T	GF	GA	PTS
Montreal	80	47	14	19	374	225	113
Los Angeles	80	42	17	21	269	185	105
Pittsburgh	80	37	28	15	326	289	89
Detroit	80	23	45	12	259	335	58
Washington	80	8	67	5	181	446	21

Adams Division

Team	GP	W	L	T	GF	GA	PTS
Buffalo	80	49	16	15	354	240	113
Boston	80	40	26	14	345	245	94
Toronto	80	31	33	16	280	309	78
California	80	19	48	13	212	316	51

CLARENCE CAMPBELL CONFERENCE

Patrick Division

*Philadelphia	80	51	18	11	293	181	113
NY Rangers	80	37	29	14	319	276	88
NY Islanders	80	33	25	22	264	221	88
Atlanta	80	34	31	15	243	233	83

Smythe Division

Vancouver	80	38	32	10	271	254	86
St. Louis	80	35	31	14	269	267	84
Chicago	80	37	35	8	268	241	82
Minnesota	80	23	50	7	221	341	53
Kansas City	80	15	54	11	184	328	41

1975-76

PRINCE OF WALES CONFERENCE

Norris Division

Team	GP	W	L	T	GF	GA	PTS
*Montreal	80	58	11	11	337	174	127
Los Angeles	80	38	33	9	263	265	85
Pittsburgh	80	35	33	12	339	303	82
Detroit	80	26	44	10	226	300	62
Washington	80	11	59	10	224	394	32

Adams Division

Boston	80	48	15	17	313	237	113
Buffalo	80	46	21	13	339	240	105
Toronto	80	34	31	15	294	276	83
California	80	27	42	11	250	278	65

CLARENCE CAMPBELL CONFERENCE

Patrick Division

Philadelphia	80	51	13	16	348	209	118
NY Islanders	80	42	21	17	297	190	101
Atlanta	80	35	33	12	262	237	82
NY Rangers	80	29	42	9	262	333	67

Smythe Division

Chicago	80	32	30	18	254	261	82
Vancouver	80	33	32	15	271	272	81
St. Louis	80	29	37	14	249	290	72
Minnesota	80	20	53	7	195	303	47
Kansas City	80	12	56	12	190	351	36

1976-77

PRINCE OF WALES CONFERENCE

Norris Division

Team	GP	W	L	T	GF	GA	PTS
*Montreal	80	60	8	12	387	171	132
Los Angeles	80	34	31	15	271	241	83
Pittsburgh	80	34	33	13	240	252	81
Washington	80	24	42	14	221	307	62
Detroit	80	16	55	9	183	309	41

Adams Division

Boston	80	49	23	8	312	240	106
Buffalo	80	48	24	8	301	220	104
Toronto	80	33	32	15	301	285	81
Cleveland	80	25	42	13	240	292	63

CLARENCE CAMPBELL CONFERENCE

Patrick Division

Philadelphia	80	48	16	16	323	213	112
NY Islanders	80	47	21	12	288	193	106
Atlanta	80	34	34	12	264	265	80
NY Rangers	88	29	37	14	272	310	72

Smythe Division

St. Louis	80	32	39	9	239	276	73
Minnesota	80	23	39	18	240	310	64
Chicago	80	26	43	11	240	298	63
Vancouver	80	25	42	13	235	294	63
Colorado	80	20	46	14	226	307	54

1977-78

PRINCE OF WALES CONFERENCE

Norris Division

Team	GP	W	L	T	GF	GA	PTS
*Montreal	80	59	10	11	359	183	129
Detroit	80	32	34	14	252	266	78
Los Angeles	80	31	34	15	243	245	77
Pittsburgh	80	25	37	18	254	321	68
Washington	80	17	49	14	195	321	48

Adams Division

Boston	80	51	18	11	333	218	113
Buffalo	80	44	19	17	288	215	105
Toronto	80	41	29	10	271	237	92
Cleveland	80	22	45	13	230	325	57

CLARENCE CAMPBELL CONFERENCE

Patrick Division

NY Islanders	80	48	17	15	334	210	111
Philadelphia	80	45	20	15	296	200	105
Atlanta	80	34	27	19	274	252	87
NY Rangers	80	30	37	13	279	280	73

Smythe Division

Chicago	80	32	29	19	230	220	83
Colorado	80	19	40	21	257	305	59
Vancouver	80	20	43	17	239	320	57
St. Louis	80	20	47	13	195	304	53
Minnesota	80	18	53	9	218	325	45

1978-79

PRINCE OF WALES CONFERENCE

Norris Division

Team	GP	W	L	T	GF	GA	PTS
*Montreal	80	52	17	11	337	204	115
Pittsburgh	80	36	31	13	281	279	85
Los Angeles	80	34	34	12	292	286	80
Washington	80	24	41	15	273	338	63
Detroit	80	23	41	16	252	295	62

Adams Division

Boston	80	43	23	14	316	270	100
Buffalo	80	36	28	16	280	263	88
Toronto	80	34	33	13	267	252	81
Minnesota	80	28	40	12	257	289	68

CLARENCE CAMPBELL CONFERENCE

Patrick Division

NY Islanders	80	51	15	14	358	214	116
Philadelphia	80	40	25	15	281	248	95
NY Rangers	80	40	29	11	316	292	91
Atlanta	80	41	31	8	327	280	90

Smythe Division

Chicago	80	29	36	15	244	277	73
Vancouver	80	25	42	13	217	291	63
St. Louis	80	18	50	12	249	348	48
Colorado	80	15	53	12	210	331	42

1979-80

PRINCE OF WALES CONFERENCE

Norris Division

Team	GP	W	L	T	GF	GA	PTS
Montreal	80	47	20	13	328	240	107
Los Angeles	80	30	36	14	290	313	74
Pittsburgh	80	30	37	13	251	303	73
Hartford	80	27	34	19	303	312	73
Detroit	80	26	43	11	268	306	63

Adams Division

Buffalo	80	47	17	16	318	201	110
Boston	80	46	21	13	310	234	105
Minnesota	80	36	28	16	311	253	88
Toronto	80	35	40	5	304	327	75
Quebec	80	25	44	11	248	313	61

CLARENCE CAMPBELL CONFERENCE

Patrick Division

Philadelphia	80	48	12	20	327	254	116
*NY Islanders	80	39	28	13	281	247	91
NY Rangers	80	38	32	10	308	284	86
Atlanta	80	35	32	13	282	269	83
Washington	80	27	40	13	261	293	67

Smythe Division

Chicago	80	34	27	19	241	250	87
St. Louis	80	34	34	12	266	278	80
Vancouver	80	27	37	16	256	281	70
Edmonton	80	28	39	13	301	322	69
Winnipeg	80	20	49	11	214	314	51
Colorado	80	19	48	13	234	308	51

1980-81

PRINCE OF WALES CONFERENCE

Norris Division

Team	GP	W	L	T	GF	GA	PTS
Montreal	80	45	22	13	332	232	103
Los Angeles	80	43	24	13	337	290	99
Pittsburgh	80	30	37	13	302	345	73
Hartford	80	21	41	18	292	372	60
Detroit	80	19	43	18	252	339	56

Adams Division

Buffalo	80	39	20	21	327	250	99
Boston	80	37	30	13	316	272	87
Minnesota	80	35	28	17	291	263	87
Quebec	80	30	32	18	314	318	78
Toronto	80	28	37	15	322	367	71

CLARENCE CAMPBELL CONFERENCE

Patrick Division

*NY Islanders	80	48	18	14	355	260	110
Philadelphia	80	41	24	15	313	249	97
Calgary	80	39	27	14	329	298	92
NY Rangers	80	30	36	14	312	317	74
Washington	80	26	36	18	286	317	70

Smythe Division

St. Louis	80	45	18	17	352	281	107
Chicago	80	31	33	16	304	315	78
Vancouver	80	28	32	20	289	301	76
Edmonton	80	29	35	16	328	327	74
Colorado	80	22	45	13	258	344	57
Winnipeg	80	9	57	14	246	400	32

1981-82

CLARENCE CAMPBELL CONFERENCE

Norris Division

Team	GP	W	L	T	GF	GA	PTS
Minnesota	80	37	23	20	346	288	94
Winnipeg	80	33	33	14	319	332	80
St. Louis	80	32	40	8	315	349	72
Chicago	80	30	38	12	332	363	72
Toronto	80	20	44	16	298	380	56
Detroit	80	21	47	12	270	351	54

Smythe Division

Edmonton	80	48	17	15	417	295	111
Vancouver	80	30	33	17	290	286	77
Calgary	80	29	34	17	334	345	75
Los Angeles	80	24	41	15	314	369	63
Colorado	80	18	49	13	241	362	49

PRINCE OF WALES CONFERENCE

Adams Division

Montreal	80	46	17	17	360	223	109
Boston	80	43	27	10	323	285	96
Buffalo	80	39	26	15	307	273	93
Quebec	80	33	31	16	356	345	82
Hartford	80	21	41	18	264	351	60

Patrick Division

*NY Islanders	80	54	16	10	385	250	118
NY Rangers	80	39	27	14	316	306	92
Philadelphia	80	38	31	11	325	313	87
Pittsburgh	80	31	36	13	310	337	75
Washington	80	26	41	13	319	338	65

1982-83

CLARENCE CAMPBELL CONFERENCE

Norris Division

Team	GP	W	L	T	GF	GA	PTS
Chicago	80	47	23	10	338	268	104
Minnesota	80	40	24	16	321	290	96
Toronto	80	28	40	12	293	330	68
St. Louis	80	25	40	15	285	316	65
Detroit	80	21	44	15	263	344	57

Smythe Division

Edmonton	80	47	21	12	424	315	106
Calgary	80	32	34	14	321	317	78
Vancouver	80	30	35	15	303	309	75
Winnipeg	80	33	39	8	311	333	74
Los Angeles	80	27	41	12	308	365	66

PRINCE OF WALES CONFERENCE

Adams Division

Boston	80	50	20	10	327	228	110
Montreal	80	42	24	14	350	286	98
Buffalo	80	38	29	13	318	285	89
Quebec	80	34	34	12	343	336	80
Hartford	80	19	54	7	261	403	45

Patrick Division

Philadelphia	80	49	23	8	326	240	106
*NY Islanders	80	42	26	12	302	226	96
Washington	80	39	25	16	306	283	94
NY Rangers	80	35	35	10	306	287	80
New Jersey	80	17	49	14	230	338	48
Pittsburgh	80	18	53	9	257	394	45

1983-84

CLARENCE CAMPBELL CONFERENCE

Norris Division

Team	GP	W	L	T	GF	GA	PTS
Minnesota	80	39	31	10	345	344	88
St. Louis	80	32	41	7	293	316	71
Detroit	80	31	42	7	298	323	69
Chicago	80	30	42	8	277	311	68
Toronto	80	26	45	9	303	387	61

Smythe Division

*Edmonton	80	57	18	5	446	314	119
Calgary	80	34	32	14	311	314	82
Vancouver	80	32	39	9	306	328	73
Winnipeg	80	31	38	11	340	374	73
Los Angeles	80	23	44	13	309	376	59

PRINCE OF WALES CONFERENCE

Adams Division

Boston	80	49	25	6	336	261	104
Buffalo	80	48	25	7	315	257	103
Quebec	80	42	28	10	360	278	94
Montreal	80	35	40	5	286	295	75
Hartford	80	28	42	10	288	320	66

Patrick Division

NY Islanders	80	50	26	4	357	269	104
Washington	80	48	27	5	308	226	101
Philadelphia	80	44	26	10	350	290	98
NY Rangers	80	42	29	9	314	304	93
New Jersey	80	17	56	7	231	350	41
Pittsburgh	80	16	58	6	254	390	38

1984-85

CLARENCE CAMPBELL CONFERENCE

Norris Division

Team	GP	W	L	T	GF	GA	PTS
St. Louis	80	37	31	12	299	288	86
Chicago	80	38	35	7	309	299	83
Detroit	80	27	41	12	313	357	66
Minnesota	80	25	43	12	268	321	62
Toronto	80	20	52	8	253	358	48

Smythe Division

*Edmonton	80	49	20	11	401	298	109
Winnipeg	80	43	27	10	358	332	96
Calgary	80	41	27	12	363	302	94
Los Angeles	80	34	32	14	339	326	82
Vancouver	80	25	46	9	284	401	59

PRINCE OF WALES CONFERENCE

Adams Division

Montreal	80	41	27	12	309	262	94
Quebec	80	41	30	9	323	275	91
Buffalo	80	38	28	14	290	237	90
Boston	80	36	34	10	303	287	82
Hartford	80	30	41	9	268	318	69

Patrick Division

Philadelphia	80	53	20	7	348	241	113
Washington	80	46	25	9	322	240	101
NY Islanders	80	40	34	6	345	312	86
NY Rangers	80	26	44	10	295	345	62
New Jersey	80	22	48	10	264	346	54
Pittsburgh	80	24	51	5	276	385	53

1985-86

CLARENCE CAMPBELL CONFERENCE

Norris Division

Team	GP	W	L	T	GF	GA	PTS
Chicago	80	39	33	8	351	349	86
Minnesota	80	38	33	9	327	305	85
St. Louis	80	37	34	9	302	291	83
Toronto	80	25	48	7	311	386	57
Detroit	80	17	57	6	266	415	40

Smythe Division

Edmonton	80	56	17	7	426	310	119
Calgary	80	40	31	9	354	315	89
Winnipeg	80	26	47	7	295	372	59
Vancouver	80	23	44	13	282	333	59
Los Angeles	80	23	49	8	284	389	54

PRINCE OF WALES CONFERENCE

Adams Division

Quebec	80	43	31	6	330	289	92
*Montreal	80	40	33	7	330	280	87
Boston	80	37	31	12	311	288	86
Hartford	80	40	36	4	332	302	84
Buffalo	80	37	37	6	296	291	80

Patrick Division

Philadelphia	80	53	23	4	335	241	110
Washington	80	50	23	7	315	272	107
NY Islanders	80	39	29	12	327	284	90
NY Rangers	80	36	38	6	280	276	78
Pittsburgh	80	34	38	8	313	305	76
New Jersey	80	28	49	3	300	374	59

1986-87

CLARENCE CAMPBELL CONFERENCE

Norris Division

Team	GP	W	L	T	GF	GA	PTS
St. Louis	80	32	33	15	281	293	79
Detroit	80	34	36	10	260	274	78
Chicago	80	29	37	14	290	310	72
Toronto	80	32	42	6	286	319	70
Minnesota	80	30	40	10	296	314	70

Smythe Division

*Edmonton	80	50	24	6	372	284	106
Calgary	80	46	31	3	318	289	95
Winnipeg	80	40	32	8	279	271	88
Los Angeles	80	31	41	8	318	341	70
Vancouver	80	29	43	8	282	314	66

PRINCE OF WALES CONFERENCE

Adams Division

Hartford	80	43	30	7	287	270	93
Montreal	80	41	29	10	277	241	92
Boston	80	39	34	7	301	276	85
Quebec	80	31	39	10	267	276	72
Buffalo	80	28	44	8	280	308	64

Patrick Division

Philadelphia	80	46	26	8	310	245	100
Washington	80	38	32	10	285	278	86
NY Islanders	80	35	33	12	279	281	82
NY Rangers	80	34	38	8	307	323	76
Pittsburg	80	30	38	12	297	290	72
New Jersey	80	29	45	6	293	368	64

1987-88

CLARENCE CAMPBELL CONFERENCE

Norris Division

Team	GP	W	L	T	GF	GA	PTS
Detroit	80	41	28	11	322	269	93
St. Louis	80	34	38	8	278	294	76
Chicago	80	30	41	9	284	326	69
Toronto	80	21	49	10	273	345	52
Minnesota	80	19	48	13	242	349	51

Smythe Division

Calgary	80	48	23	9	397	305	105
*Edmonton	80	44	25	11	363	288	99
Winnipeg	80	33	36	11	292	310	77
Los Angeles	80	30	42	8	318	359	68
Vancouver	80	25	46	9	272	320	59

PRINCE OF WALES CONFERENCE

Adams Division

Montreal	80	45	22	13	298	238	103
Boston	80	44	30	6	300	251	94
Buffalo	80	37	32	11	283	305	85
Hartford	80	35	38	7	249	267	77
Quebec	80	32	43	5	271	306	69

Patrick Division

NY Islanders	80	39	31	10	308	267	88
Washington	80	38	33	9	281	249	85
Philadelphia	80	38	33	9	292	282	85
New Jersey	80	38	36	6	295	296	82
NY Rangers	80	36	34	10	300	283	82
Pittsburgh	80	36	35	9	319	316	81

1988-89

CLARENCE CAMPBELL CONFERENCE

Norris Division

Team	GP	W	L	T	GF	GA	PTS
Detroit	80	34	34	12	313	316	80
St. Louis	80	33	35	12	275	285	78
Minnesota	80	27	37	16	258	278	70
Chicago	80	27	41	12	297	335	66
Toronto	80	28	46	6	259	342	62

Smythe Division

*Calgary	80	54	17	9	354	226	117
Los Angeles	80	42	31	7	376	335	91
Edmonton	80	38	34	8	325	306	84
Vancouver	80	33	39	8	251	253	74
Winnipeg	80	26	42	12	300	355	64

PRINCE OF WALES CONFERENCE

Adams Division

Montreal	80	53	18	9	315	218	115
Boston	80	37	29	14	289	256	88
Buffalo	80	38	35	7	291	299	83
Hartford	80	37	38	5	299	290	79
Quebec	80	27	46	7	269	342	61

Patrick Division

Washington	80	41	29	10	305	259	92
Pittsburgh	80	40	33	7	347	349	87
NY Rangers	80	37	35	8	310	307	82
Philadelphia	80	36	36	8	307	285	80
New Jersey	80	27	41	12	281	325	66
NY Islanders	80	28	47	5	265	325	61

1989-90

CLARENCE CAMPBELL CONFERENCE

Norris Division

Team	GP	W	L	T	GF	GA	PTS
Chicago	80	41	33	6	316	294	88
St. Louis	80	37	34	9	295	279	83
Toronto	80	38	38	4	337	358	80
Minnesota	80	36	40	4	284	291	76
Detroit	80	28	38	14	288	323	70

Smythe Division

Calgary	80	42	23	15	348	265	99
*Edmonton	80	38	28	14	315	283	90
Winnipeg	80	37	32	11	298	290	85
Los Angeles	80	34	39	7	338	337	75
Vancouver	80	25	41	14	245	306	64

PRINCE OF WALES CONFERENCE

Adams Division

Boston	80	46	25	9	289	232	101
Buffalo	80	45	27	8	286	248	98
Montreal	80	41	28	11	288	234	93
Hartford	80	38	33	9	275	268	85
Quebec	80	12	61	7	240	407	31

Patrick Division

NY Rangers	80	36	31	13	279	267	85
New Jersey	80	37	34	9	295	288	83
Washington	80	36	38	6	284	275	78
NY Islanders	80	31	38	11	281	288	73
Pittsburgh	80	32	40	8	318	359	72
Philadelphia	80	30	39	11	290	297	71

1990-91

CLARENCE CAMPBELL CONFERENCE

Norris Division

Team	GP	W	L	T	GF	GA	PTS
Chicago	80	49	23	8	284	211	106
St. Louis	80	47	22	11	310	250	105
Detroit	80	34	38	8	273	298	76
Minnesota	80	27	39	14	256	266	68
Toronto	80	23	46	11	241	318	57

Smythe Division

Los Angeles	80	46	24	10	340	254	102
Calgary	80	46	26	8	344	263	100
Edmonton	80	37	37	6	272	272	80
Vancouver	80	28	43	9	243	315	65
Winnipeg	80	26	43	11	260	288	63

PRINCE OF WALES CONFERENCE

Adams Division

Boston	80	44	24	12	299	264	100
Montreal	80	39	30	11	273	249	89
Buffalo	80	31	30	19	292	278	81
Hartford	80	31	38	11	238	276	73
Quebec	80	16	50	14	236	354	46

Patrick Division

*Pittsburgh	80	41	33	6	342	305	88
NY Rangers	80	36	31	13	297	265	85
Washington	80	37	36	7	258	258	81
New Jersey	80	32	33	15	272	264	79
Philadelphia	80	33	37	10	252	267	76
NY Islanders	80	25	45	10	223	290	60

Index

*Next page: Veteran defenseman Lionel
Conacher played twelve seasons in the
NHL with the Pirates, Americans,
Maroons, and Black Hawks. A superb
all-round athlete, Conacher was named
Canada's athlete of the
half-century by Canadian Press in
1950. In addition to earning three all-
star selections and playing on two
Stanley Cup winners in the 1930s,
Conacher was a successful wrestler and
boxer and played Triple-A baseball,
professional football, and lacrosse.*